Aho-Girl

\\'ahô͵gərl\\ *Japanese, noun.*
A clueless girl.

9 | Hiroyuki

CHARACTER PROFILES

AHO-GIRL's Cast of Characters

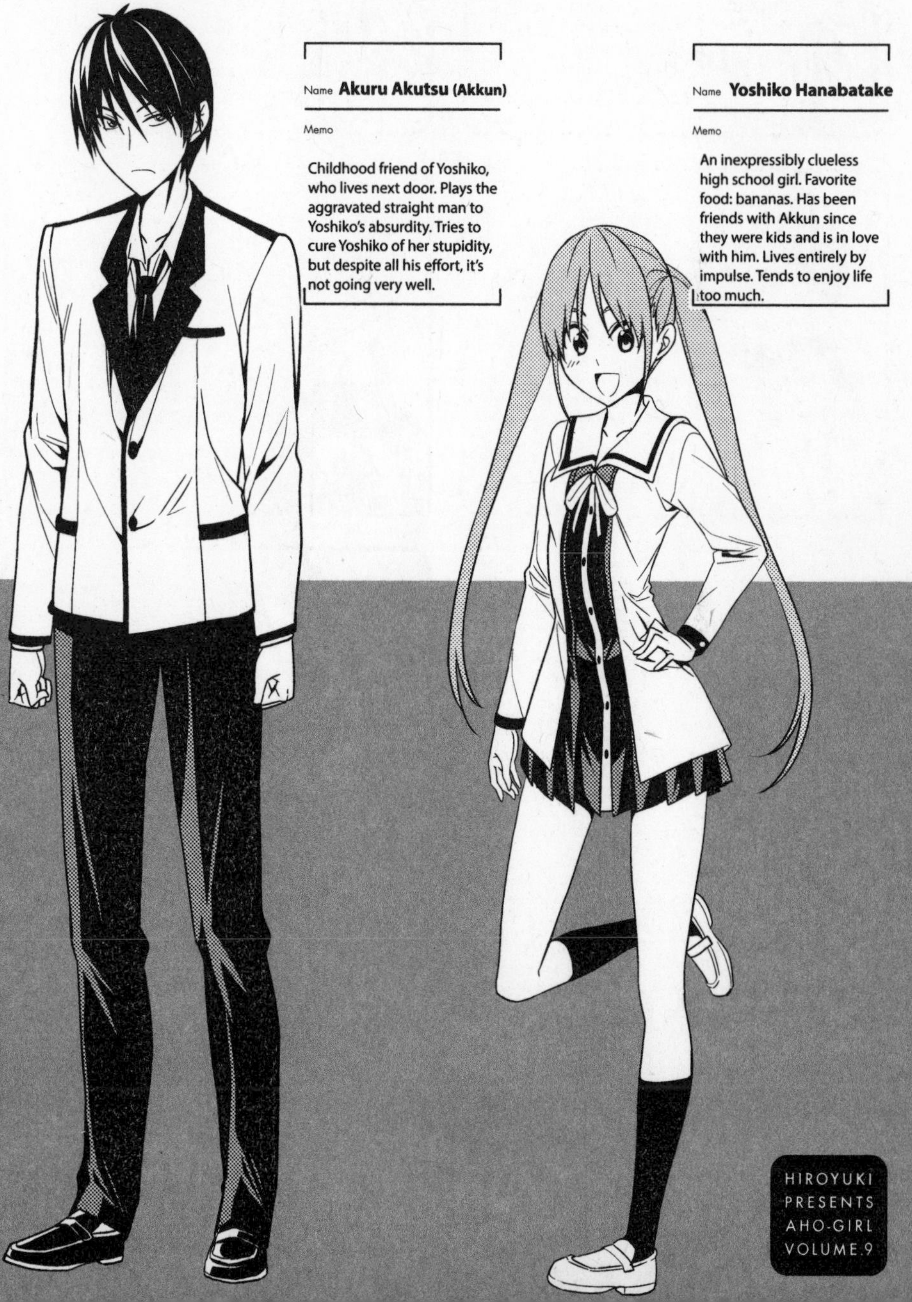

Name **Akuru Akutsu (Akkun)**

Memo

Childhood friend of Yoshiko, who lives next door. Plays the aggravated straight man to Yoshiko's absurdity. Tries to cure Yoshiko of her stupidity, but despite all his effort, it's not going very well.

Name **Yoshiko Hanabatake**

Memo

An inexpressibly clueless high school girl. Favorite food: bananas. Has been friends with Akkun since they were kids and is in love with him. Lives entirely by impulse. Tends to enjoy life too much.

HIROYUKI PRESENTS AHO-GIRL VOLUME.9

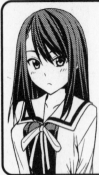

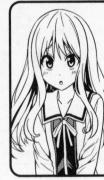

Name **Sayaka Sumino**

Memo

Yoshiko's friend. She's a very kind girl. She knows her kindness lands her in all sorts of trouble, yet she remains kind. Worries about being boring.

Name **Head Monitor**

Memo

An upperclassman at Yoshiko's school. Has fallen head over heels for Akkun and begun to stray from the moral path, but she doesn't realize it. G cup.

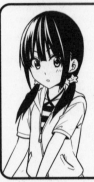

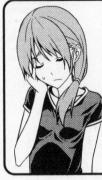

Name **Yoshie Hanabatake**

Memo

Yoshiko's mother. While she does worry about Yoshiko, she's far more worried about her own sunset years. Will use any means necessary to fix Yoshiko up with Akkun.

Name **Ruri Akutsu**

Memo

While her brother Akkun is an overachiever, Ruri's not quite so fortunate. She is constantly dismayed by her terrible grades. Perhaps the day will come when all her hard work pays off. Hates Yoshiko.

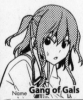

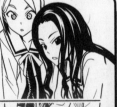

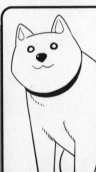

Name **Dog**

Memo

A ridiculously big dog Yoshiko found at the park. Started out vicious, but once vanquished by Yoshiko, has become docile. Is quite clever and tries to stop Yoshiko from her wilder impulses.

Name **Gang of Gals**

Memo

Yoshiko's classmates. Yoshiko's been pushing their buttons ever since she first noticed them. Shiina (right) has a very chaste relationship with her boyfriend.

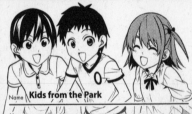

Name **Kids from the Park**

Memo

Yoshiko's play friends. These three kids include two very serious, grown-up boys concerned by Yoshiko's idiocy, and a girl named Nozomi who idolizes her. Can often be found playing at the park.

AHO·GIRL

CONTENTS

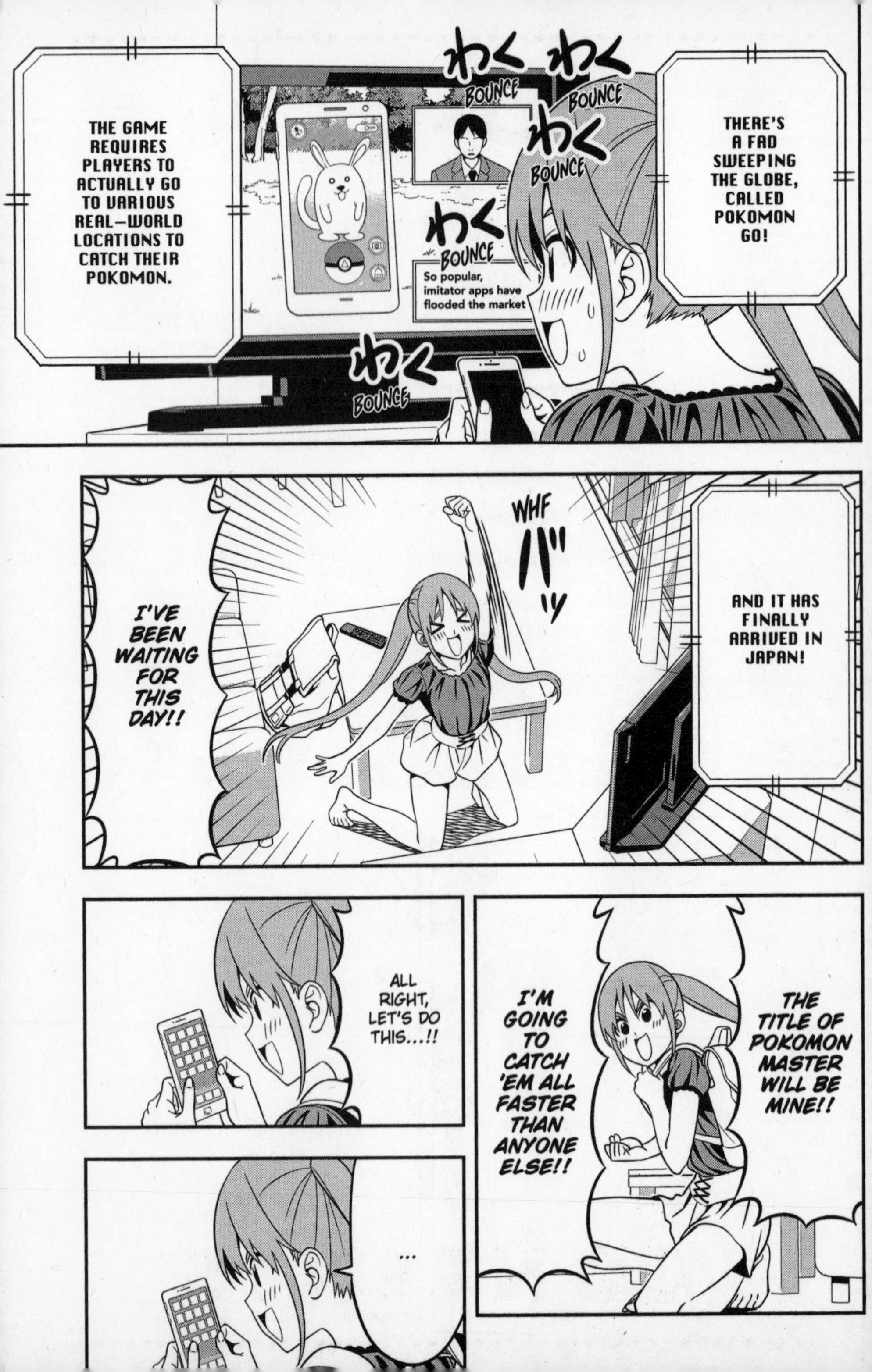
THERE'S A FAD SWEEPING THE GLOBE, CALLED POKOMON GO!
わく BOUNCE
わく BOUNCE
わく BOUNCE
わく BOUNCE
わく BOUNCE
So popular, imitator apps have flooded the market
THE GAME REQUIRES PLAYERS TO ACTUALLY GO TO VARIOUS REAL-WORLD LOCATIONS TO CATCH THEIR POKOMON.
AND IT HAS FINALLY ARRIVED IN JAPAN!
WHF
バッ
I'VE BEEN WAITING FOR THIS DAY!!
THE TITLE OF POKOMON MASTER WILL BE MINE!!
I'M GOING TO CATCH 'EM ALL FASTER THAN ANYONE ELSE!!
ALL RIGHT, LET'S DO THIS...!!
...

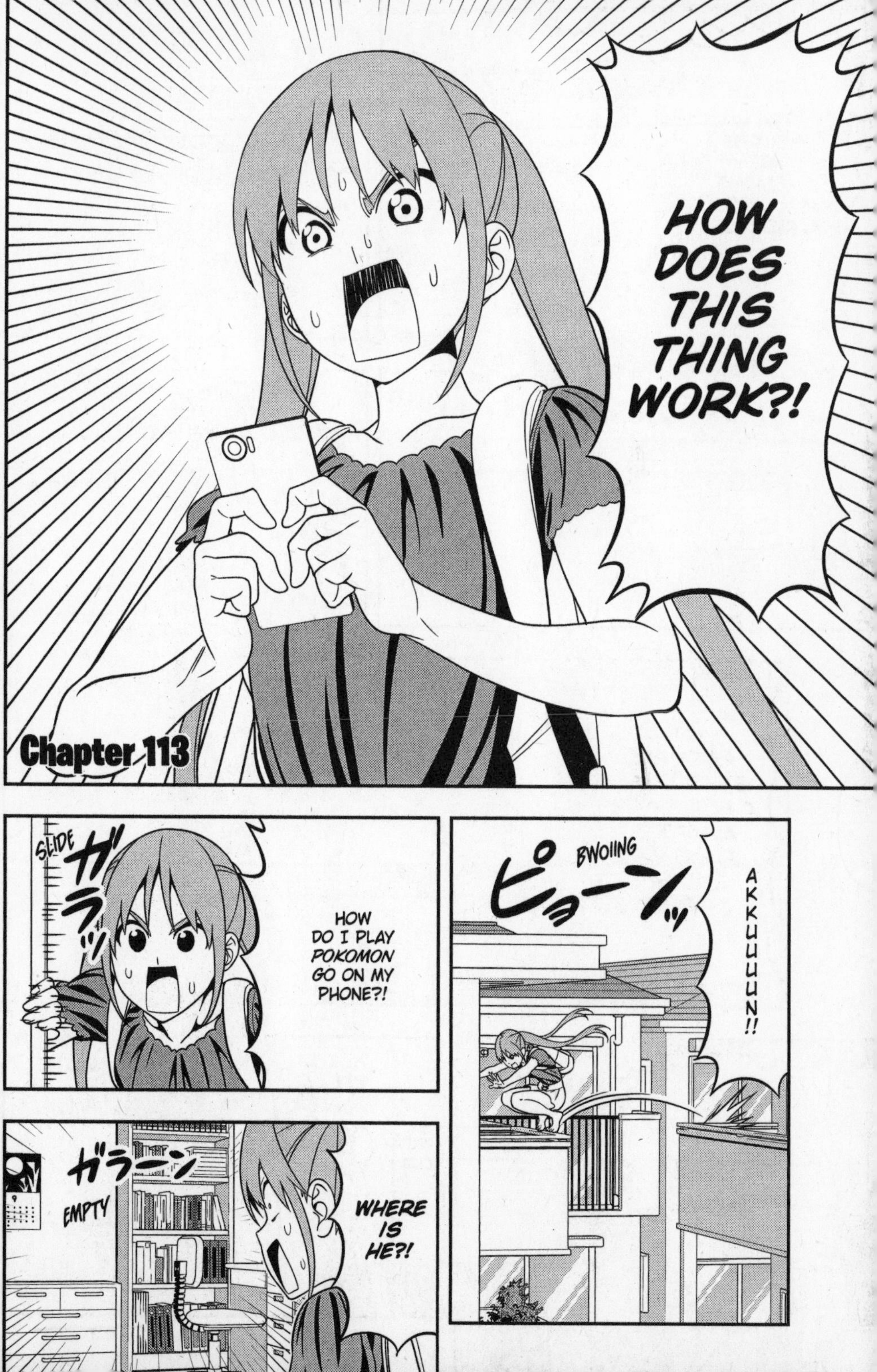
HOW DOES THIS THING WORK?!
Chapter 113
BWOIING
ピョーンッ
AKKUUUUUN!!
SLIDE
ガラッ
HOW DO I PLAY POKOMON GO ON MY PHONE?!
ガラーン
EMPTY
WHERE IS HE?!

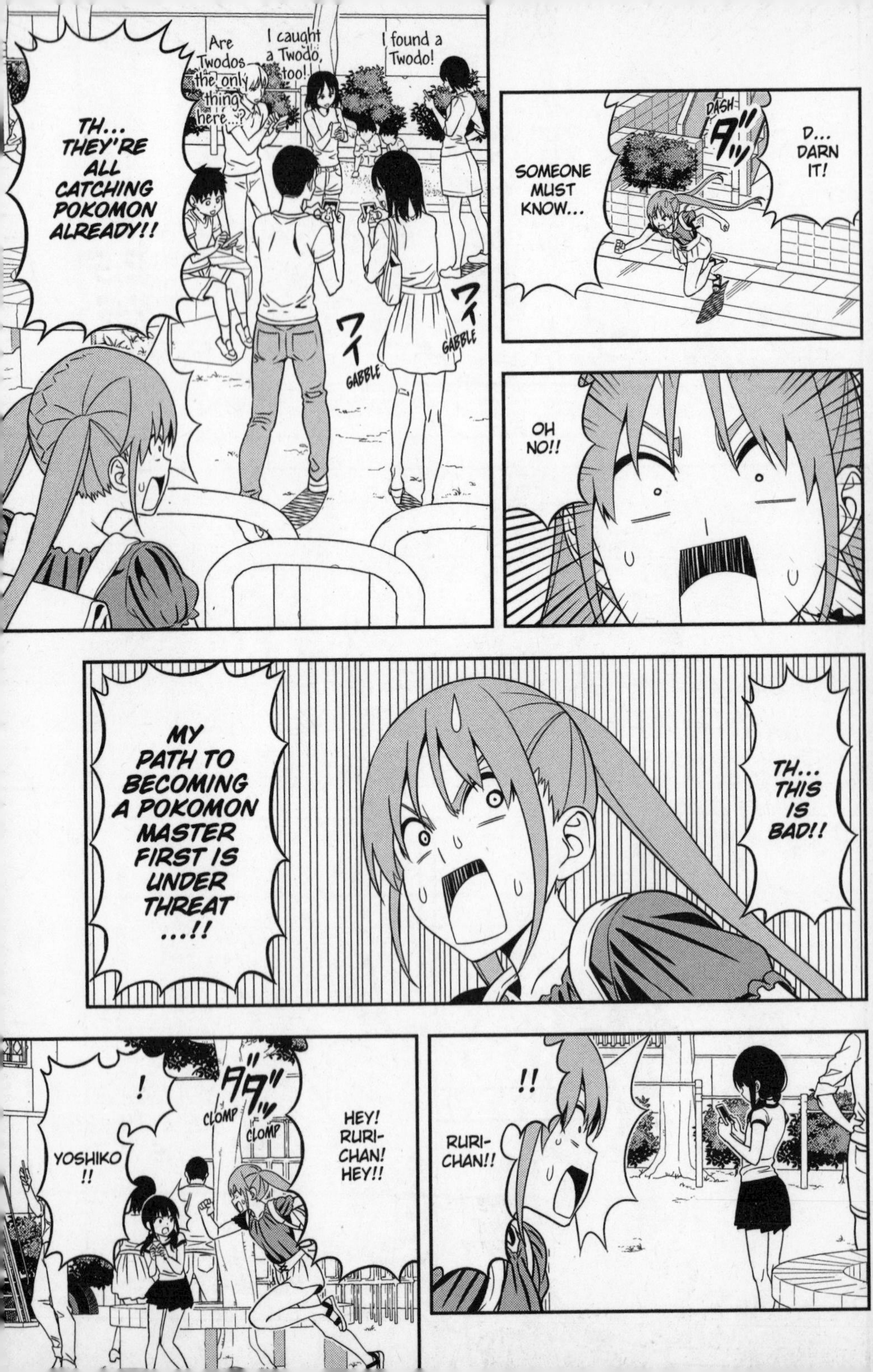
DASH
D... DARN IT!
SOMEONE MUST KNOW...
OH NO!!
I found a Twodo!
I caught a Twodo, too!
Are Twodos the only thing here...?
TH... THEY'RE ALL CATCHING POKOMON ALREADY!!
GABBLE
GABBLE
TH... THIS IS BAD!!
MY PATH TO BECOMING A POKOMON MASTER FIRST IS UNDER THREAT ...!!
!!
RURI-CHAN!!
HEY! RURI-CHAN! HEY!!
CLOMP
CLOMP
!
YOSHIKO!!

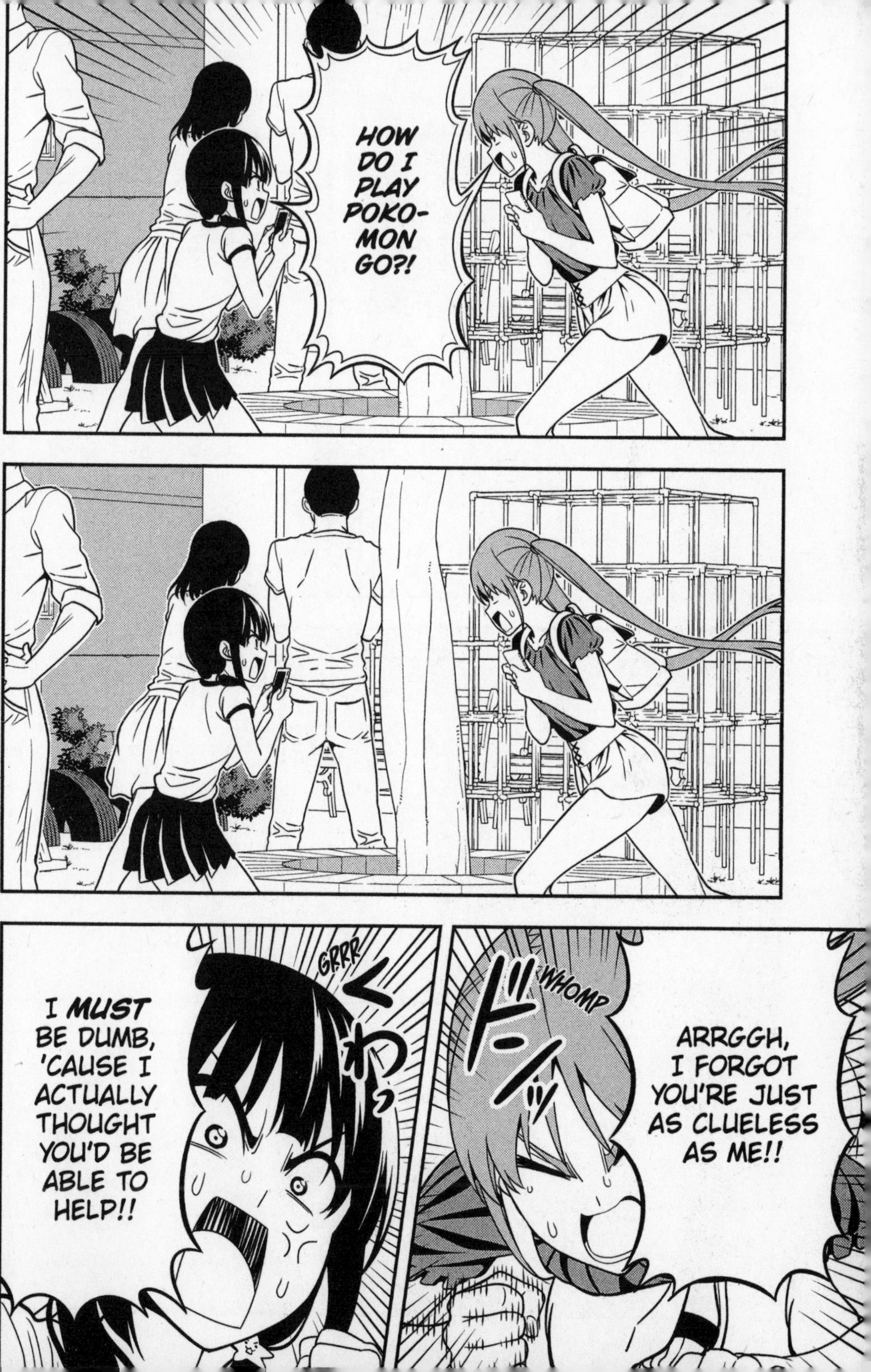
HOW DO I PLAY POKO-MON GO?!
WHOMP
ARRGGH, I FORGOT YOU'RE JUST AS CLUELESS AS ME!!
GRRR
I MUST BE DUMB, 'CAUSE I ACTUALLY THOUGHT YOU'D BE ABLE TO HELP!!

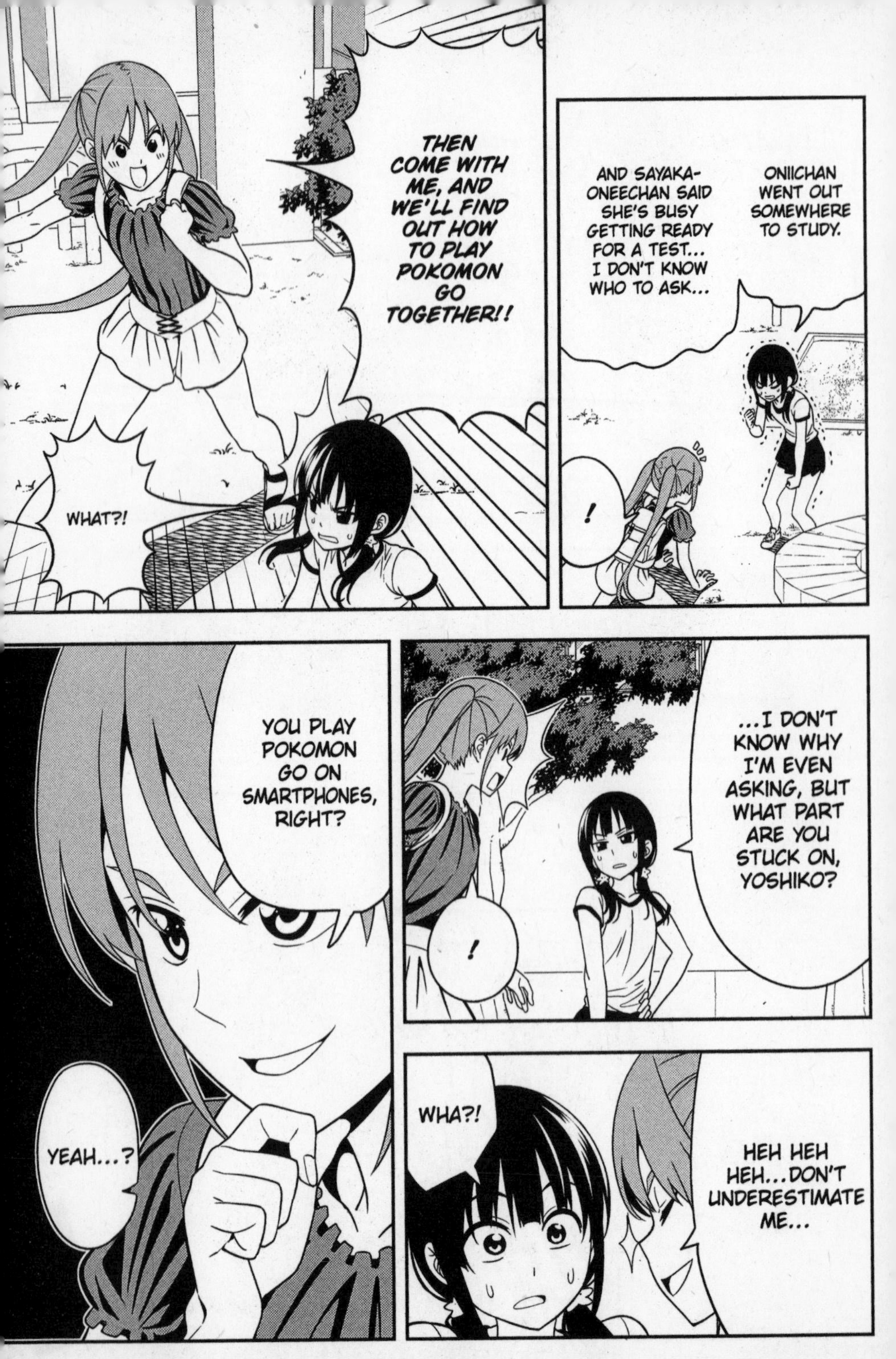
ONIICHAN WENT OUT SOMEWHERE TO STUDY.
AND SAYAKA-ONEECHAN SAID SHE'S BUSY GETTING READY FOR A TEST... I DON'T KNOW WHO TO ASK...
!
THEN COME WITH ME, AND WE'LL FIND OUT HOW TO PLAY POKOMON GO TOGETHER!!
WHAT?!
...I DON'T KNOW WHY I'M EVEN ASKING, BUT WHAT PART ARE YOU STUCK ON, YOSHIKO?
!
HEH HEH HEH...DON'T UNDERESTIMATE ME...
WHA?!
YOU PLAY POKOMON GO ON SMARTPHONES, RIGHT?
YEAH...?

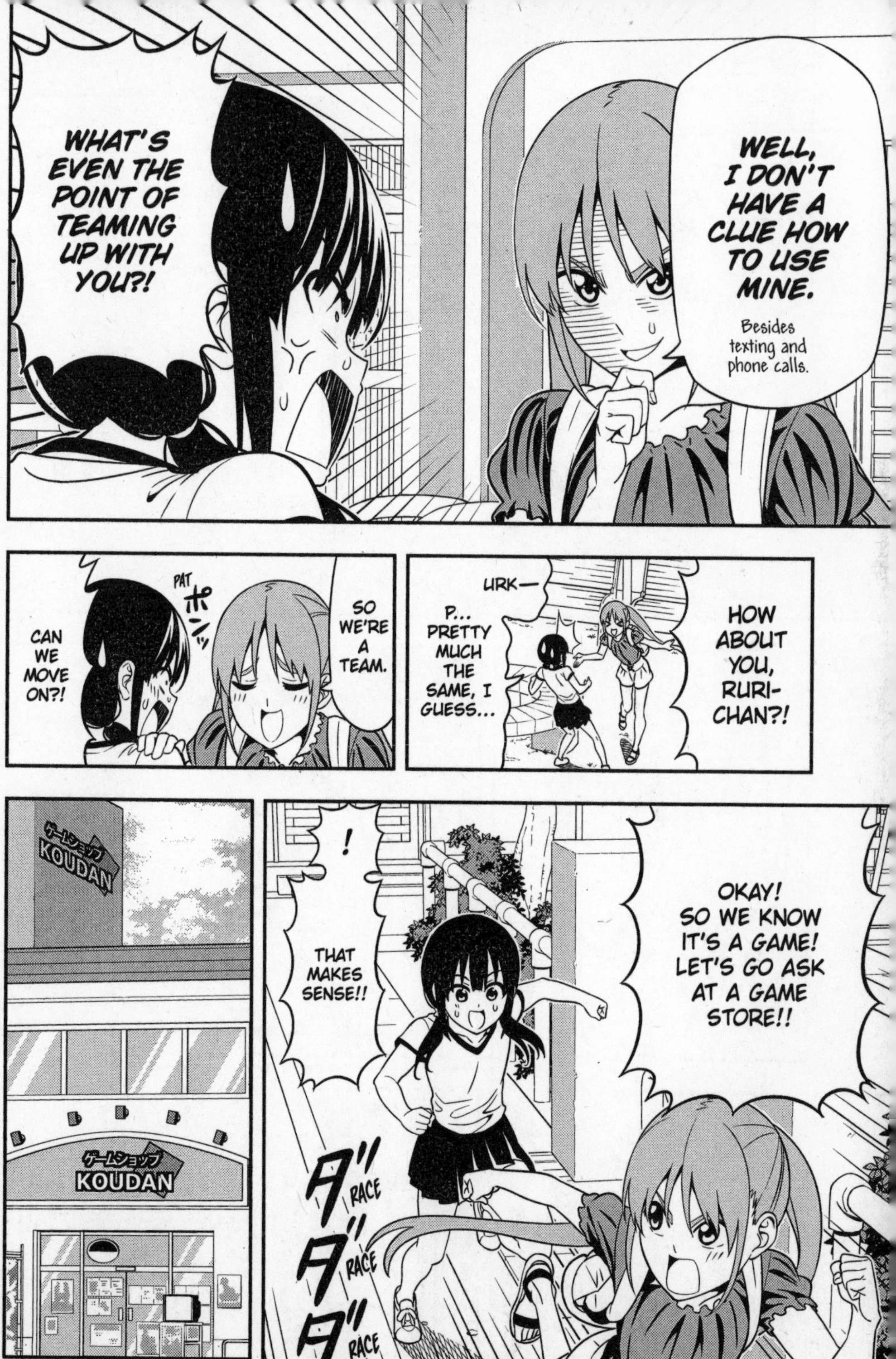
WELL, I DON'T HAVE A CLUE HOW TO USE MINE.
Besides texting and phone calls.
WHAT'S EVEN THE POINT OF TEAMING UP WITH YOU?!
HOW ABOUT YOU, RURI-CHAN?!
URK—
P... PRETTY MUCH THE SAME, I GUESS...
SO WE'RE A TEAM.
PAT ポンッ
CAN WE MOVE ON?!
OKAY! SO WE KNOW IT'S A GAME! LET'S GO ASK AT A GAME STORE!!
!
THAT MAKES SENSE!!
ダ RACE ダ RACE ダ RACE ッ
ゲームショップ KOUDAN
ゲームショップ KOUDAN
SIGNS: GAME SHOP

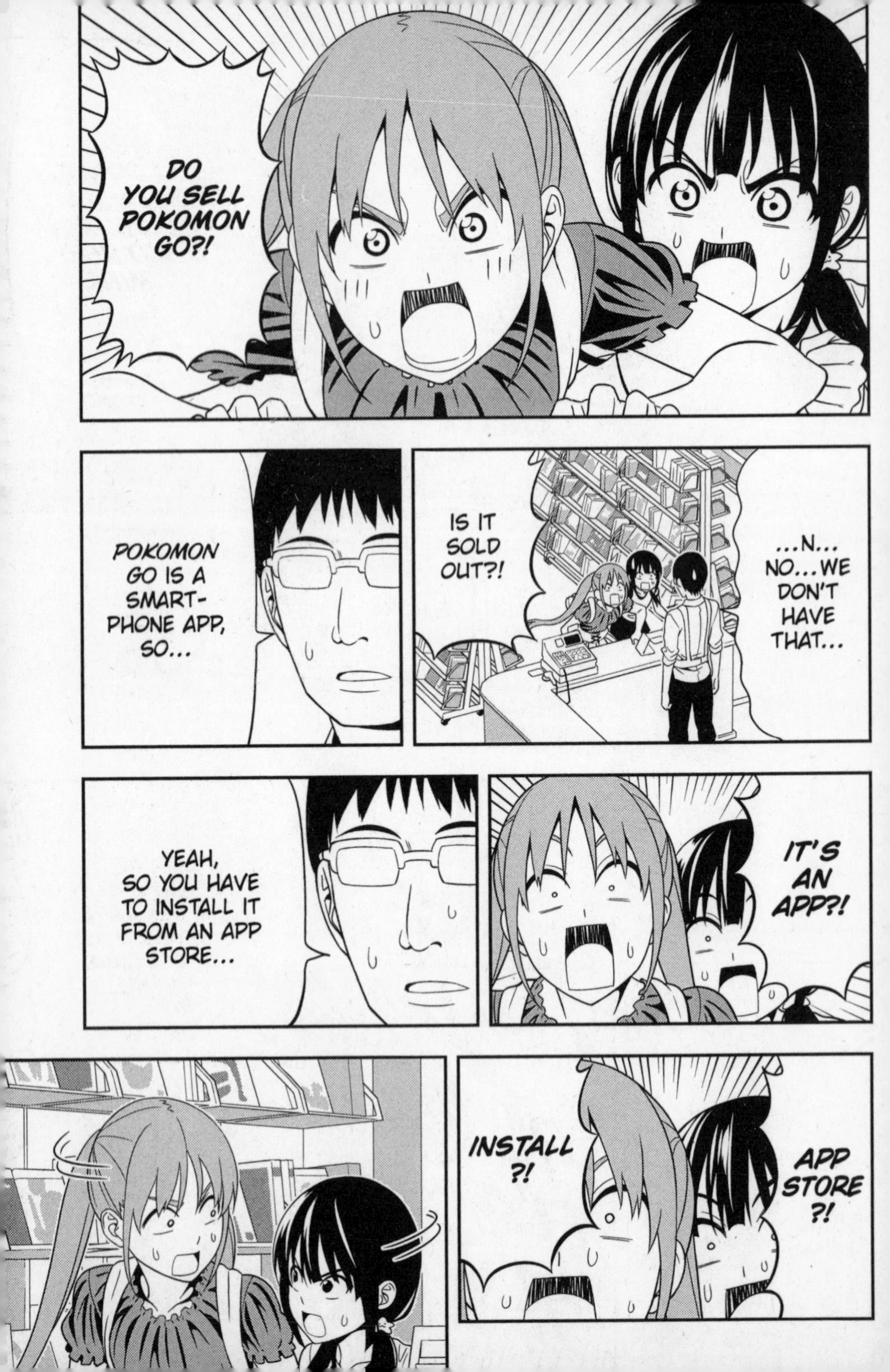
DO YOU SELL POKOMON GO?!
IS IT SOLD OUT?!
...N... NO...WE DON'T HAVE THAT...
POKOMON GO IS A SMART-PHONE APP, SO...
IT'S AN APP?!
YEAH, SO YOU HAVE TO INSTALL IT FROM AN APP STORE...
INSTALL ?!
APP STORE ?!

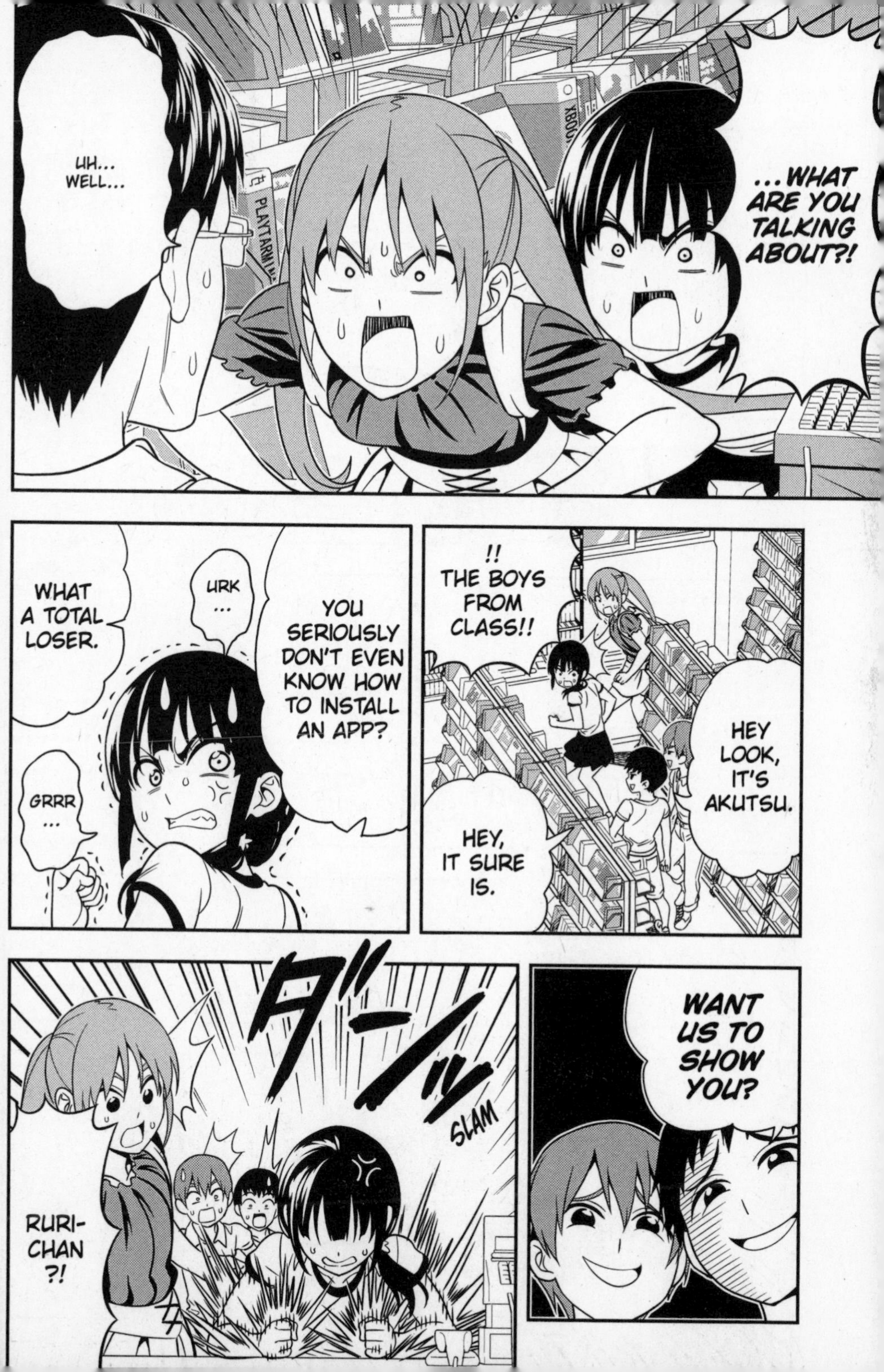

...WHAT ARE YOU TALKING ABOUT?!
UH... WELL...
!! THE BOYS FROM CLASS!!
HEY LOOK, IT'S AKUTSU.
HEY, IT SURE IS.
YOU SERIOUSLY DON'T EVEN KNOW HOW TO INSTALL AN APP?
URK ...
WHAT A TOTAL LOSER.
GRRR ...
WANT US TO SHOW YOU?
ダーンッ
SLAM
RURI-CHAN ?!

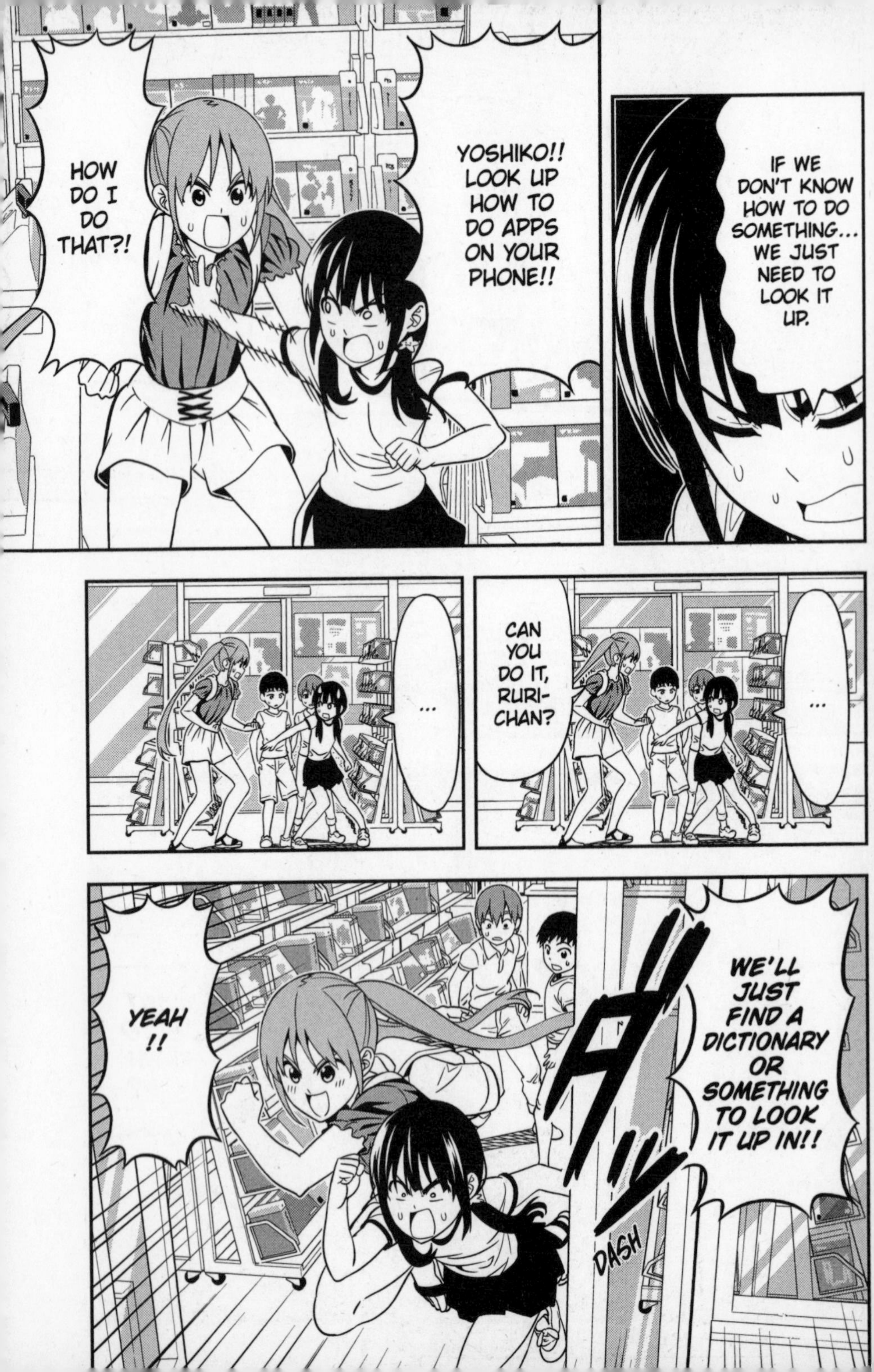
IF WE DON'T KNOW HOW TO DO SOMETHING... WE JUST NEED TO LOOK IT UP.
YOSHIKO!! LOOK UP HOW TO DO APPS ON YOUR PHONE!!
HOW DO I DO THAT?!
...
CAN YOU DO IT, RURI-CHAN?
...
WE'LL JUST FIND A DICTIONARY OR SOMETHING TO LOOK IT UP IN!!
DASH
YEAH!!

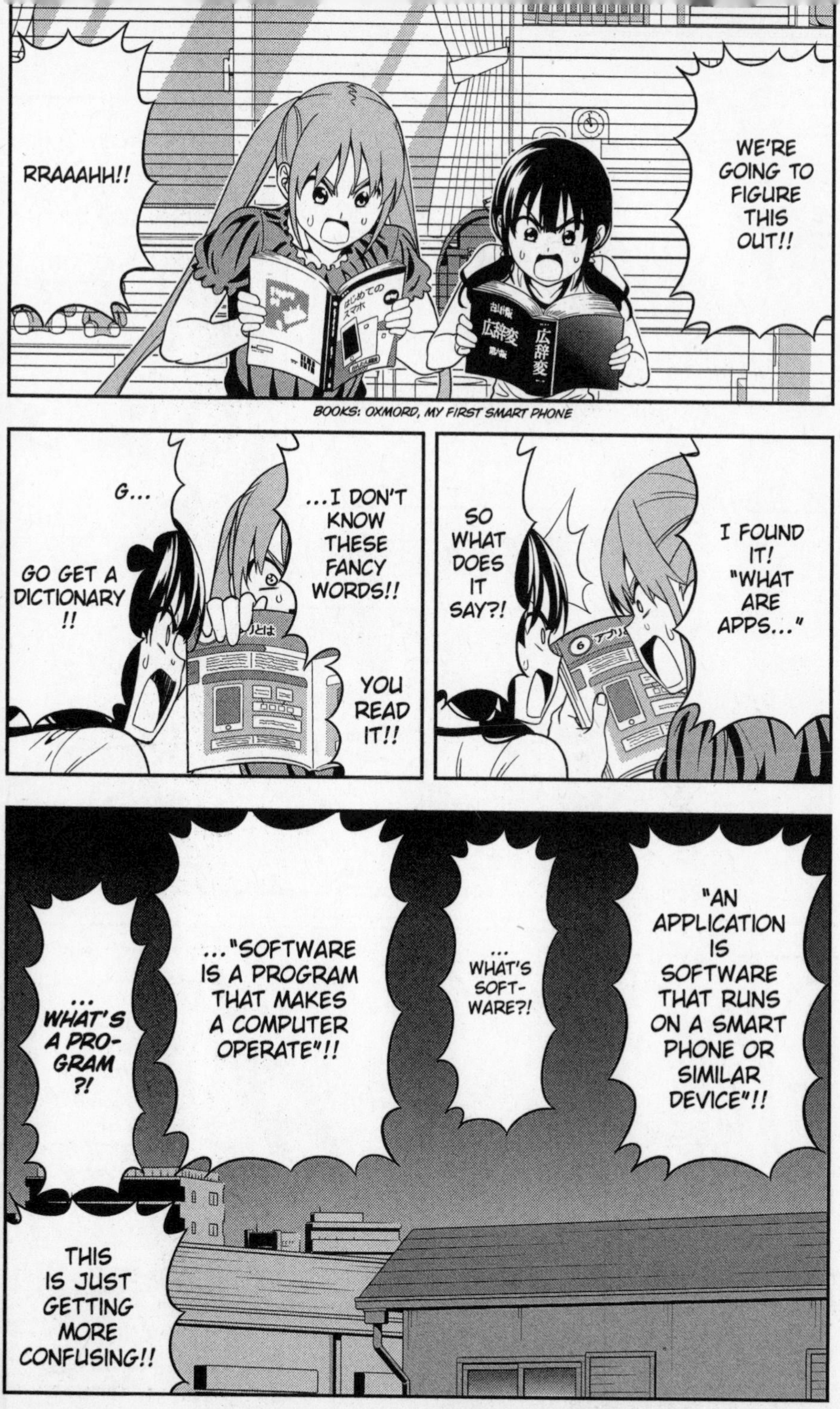
WE'RE GOING TO FIGURE THIS OUT!!
RRAAAHH!!
BOOKS: OXMORD, MY FIRST SMART PHONE
I FOUND IT! "WHAT ARE APPS..."
SO WHAT DOES IT SAY?!
...I DON'T KNOW THESE FANCY WORDS!!
G...
GO GET A DICTIONARY!!
YOU READ IT!!
"AN APPLICATION IS SOFTWARE THAT RUNS ON A SMART PHONE OR SIMILAR DEVICE"!!
... WHAT'S SOFTWARE?!
..."SOFTWARE IS A PROGRAM THAT MAKES A COMPUTER OPERATE"!!
... *WHAT'S A PROGRAM?!*
THIS IS JUST GETTING MORE CONFUSING!!

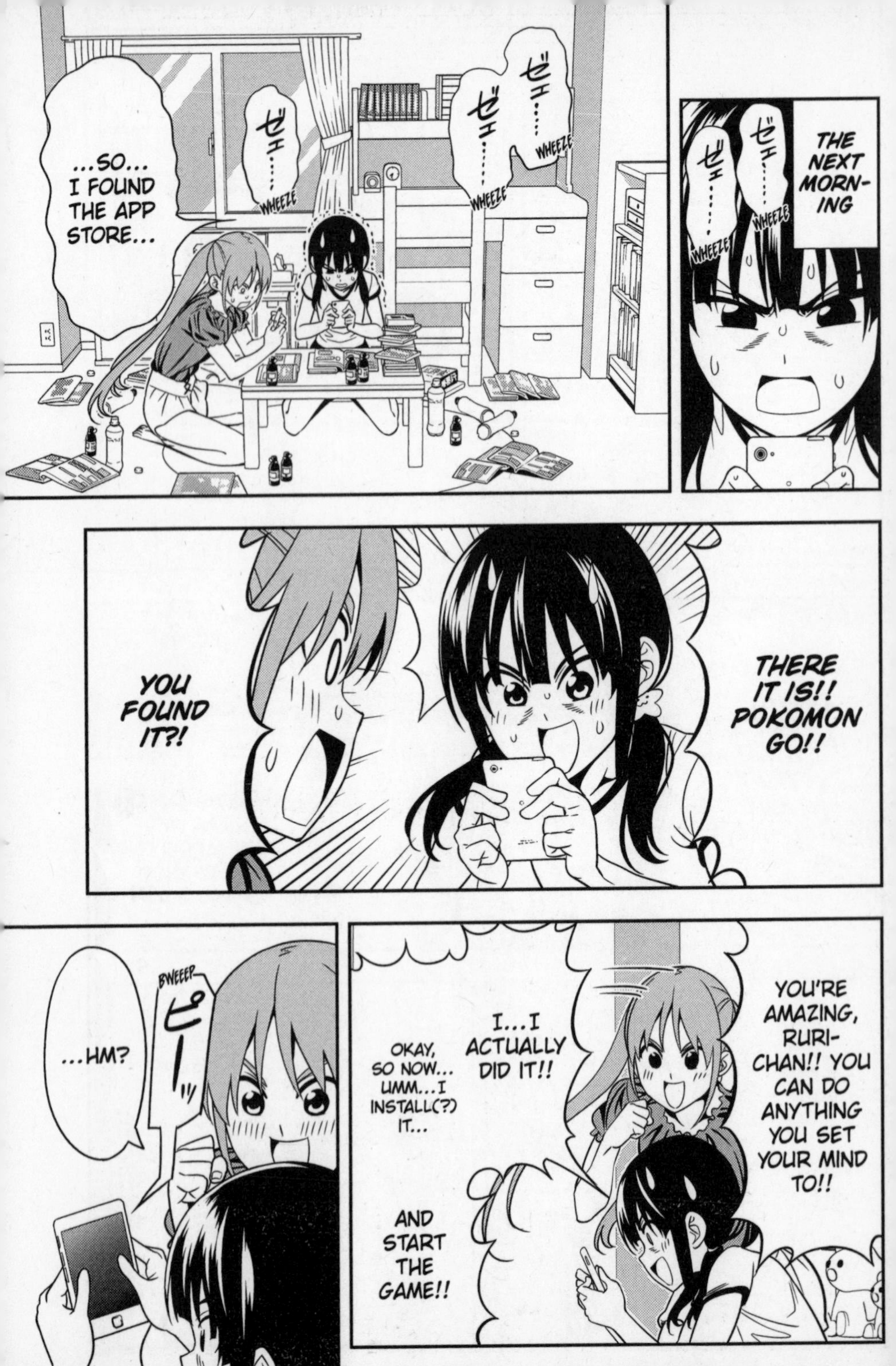
THE NEXT MORNING
ゼェ… WHEEZE
ゼェ… WHEEZE
ゼェ… WHEEZE
ゼェ… WHEEZE
ゼェ… WHEEZE
...SO... I FOUND THE APP STORE...
THERE IT IS!! POKOMON GO!!
YOU FOUND IT?!
YOU'RE AMAZING, RURI-CHAN!! YOU CAN DO ANYTHING YOU SET YOUR MIND TO!!
I...I ACTUALLY DID IT!!
OKAY, SO NOW... UMM...I INSTALL(?) IT...
AND START THE GAME!!
ピー BWEEEP
...HM?

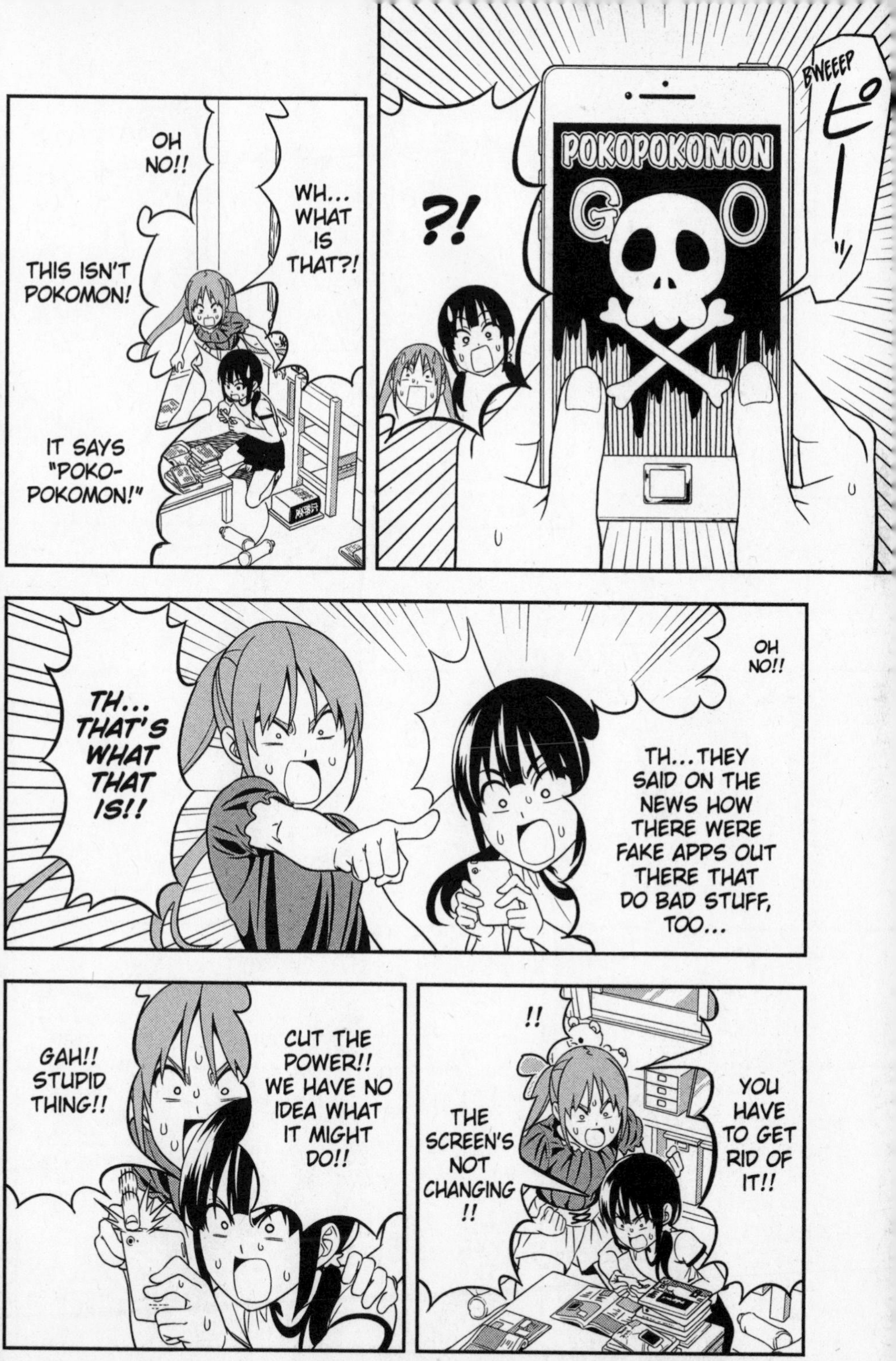
BWEEEP
ピー
POKOPOKOMON
GO
?!
WH... WHAT IS THAT?!
OH NO!!
THIS ISN'T POKOMON!
IT SAYS "POKO-POKOMON!"
OH NO!!
TH...THEY SAID ON THE NEWS HOW THERE WERE FAKE APPS OUT THERE THAT DO BAD STUFF, TOO...
TH... THAT'S WHAT THAT IS!!
YOU HAVE TO GET RID OF IT!!
!!
THE SCREEN'S NOT CHANGING!!
CUT THE POWER!! WE HAVE NO IDEA WHAT IT MIGHT DO!!
GAH!! STUPID THING!!

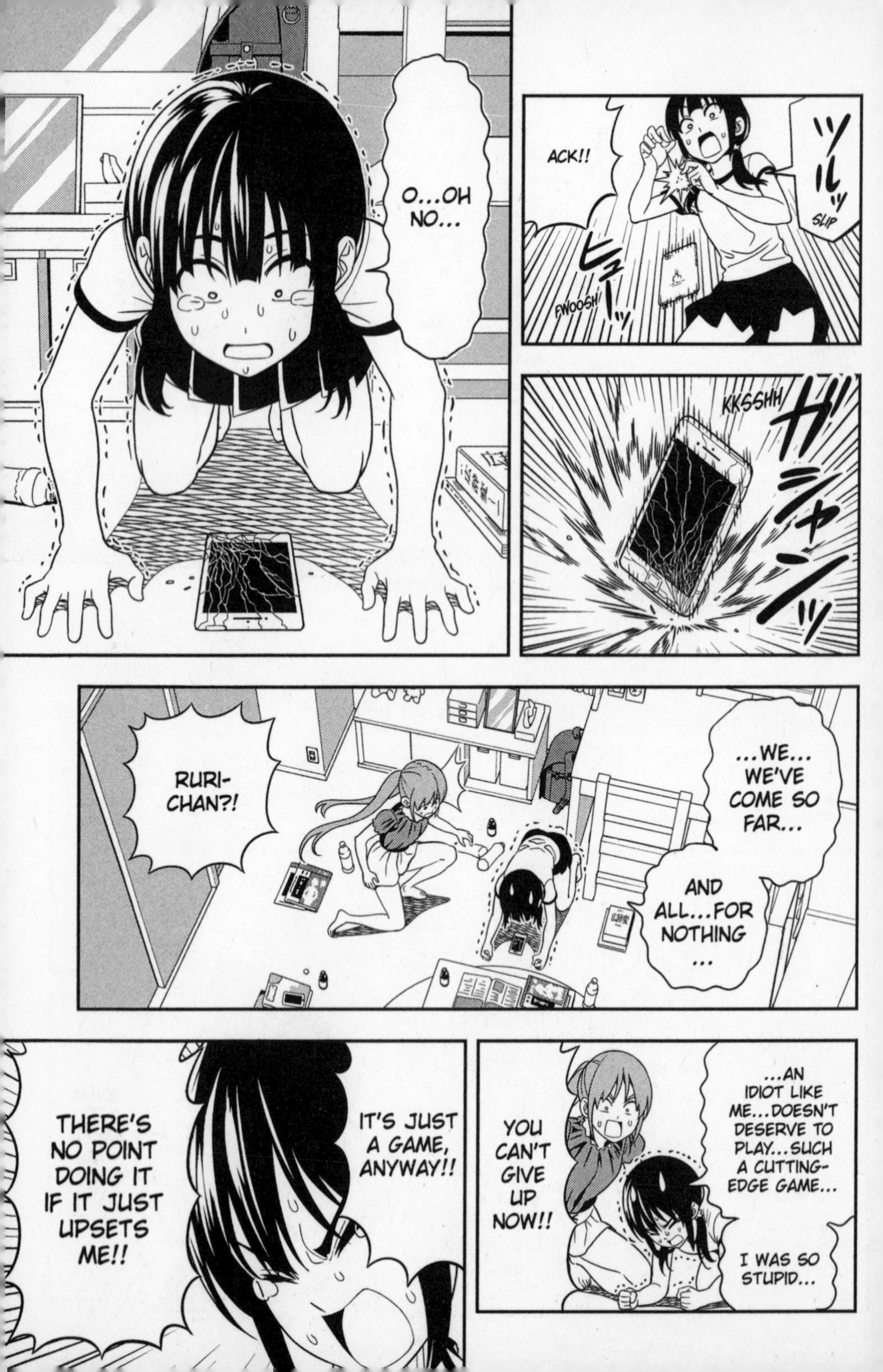
ACK!!
ツルッ
SLIP
ヒューッ
FWOOSH
KKSSHH
ガシャーンッ
O...OH NO...
...WE... WE'VE COME SO FAR...
AND ALL...FOR NOTHING ...
RURI-CHAN?!
...AN IDIOT LIKE ME...DOESN'T DESERVE TO PLAY...SUCH A CUTTING-EDGE GAME...
I WAS SO STUPID...
YOU CAN'T GIVE UP NOW!!
IT'S JUST A GAME, ANYWAY!!
THERE'S NO POINT DOING IT IF IT JUST UPSETS ME!!

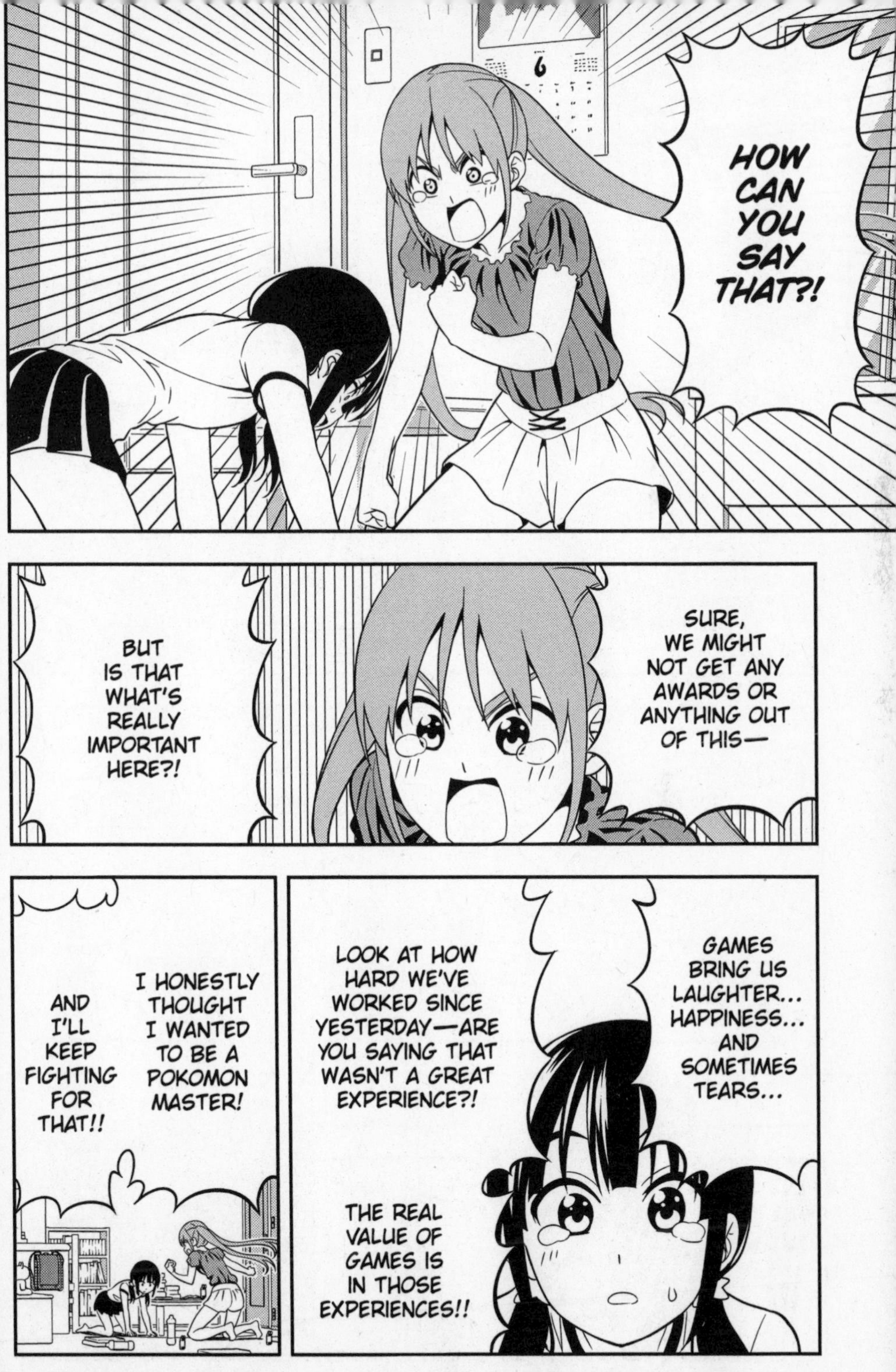
HOW CAN YOU SAY THAT?!
SURE, WE MIGHT NOT GET ANY AWARDS OR ANYTHING OUT OF THIS—
BUT IS THAT WHAT'S REALLY IMPORTANT HERE?!
GAMES BRING US LAUGHTER... HAPPINESS... AND SOMETIMES TEARS...
LOOK AT HOW HARD WE'VE WORKED SINCE YESTERDAY—ARE YOU SAYING THAT WASN'T A GREAT EXPERIENCE?!
THE REAL VALUE OF GAMES IS IN THOSE EXPERIENCES!!
I HONESTLY THOUGHT I WANTED TO BE A POKOMON MASTER!
AND I'LL KEEP FIGHTING FOR THAT!!

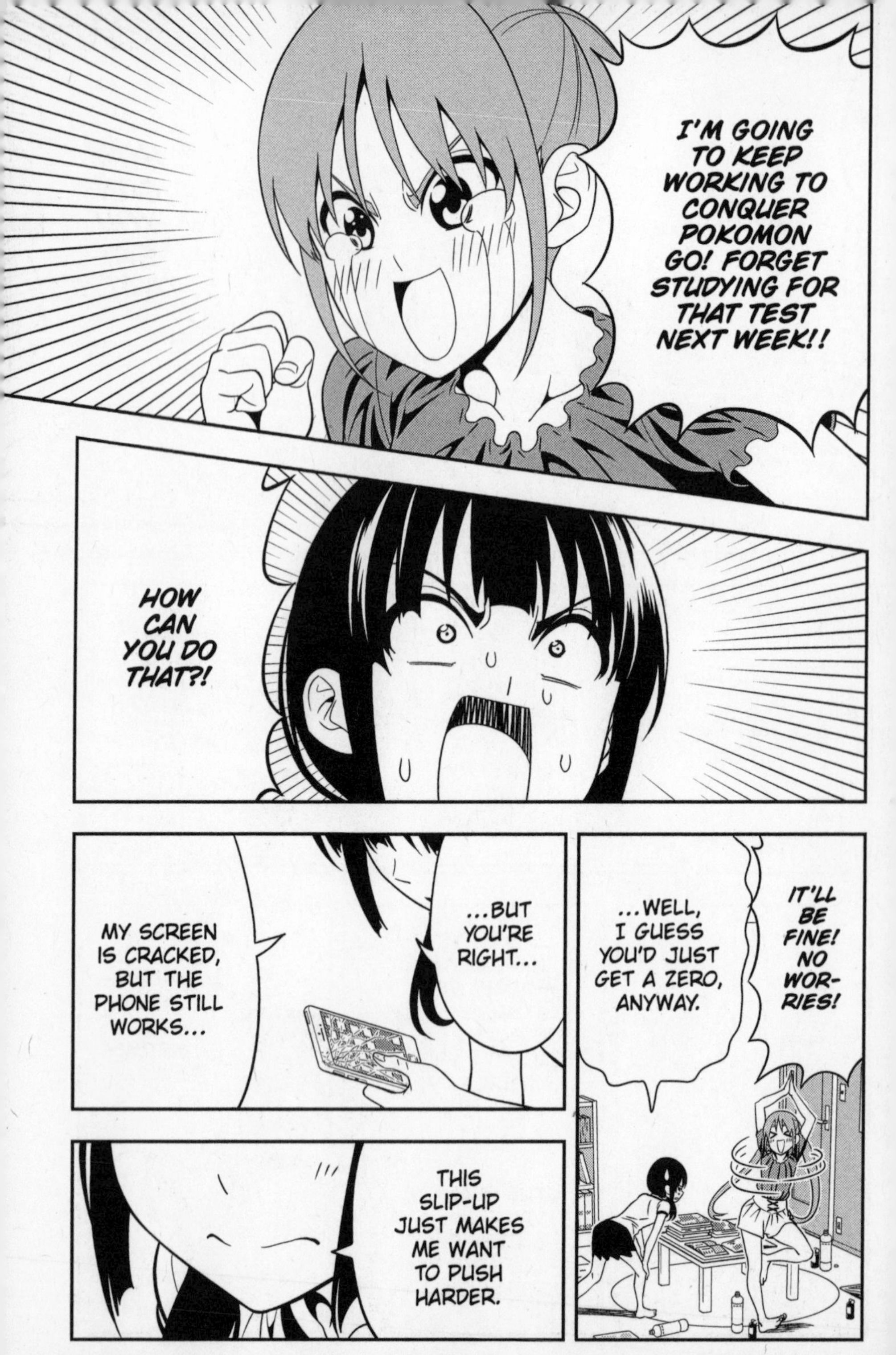
I'M GOING TO KEEP WORKING TO CONQUER POKOMON GO! FORGET STUDYING FOR THAT TEST NEXT WEEK!!
HOW CAN YOU DO THAT?!
IT'LL BE FINE! NO WOR-RIES!
...WELL, I GUESS YOU'D JUST GET A ZERO, ANYWAY.
...BUT YOU'RE RIGHT...
MY SCREEN IS CRACKED, BUT THE PHONE STILL WORKS...
THIS SLIP-UP JUST MAKES ME WANT TO PUSH HARDER.

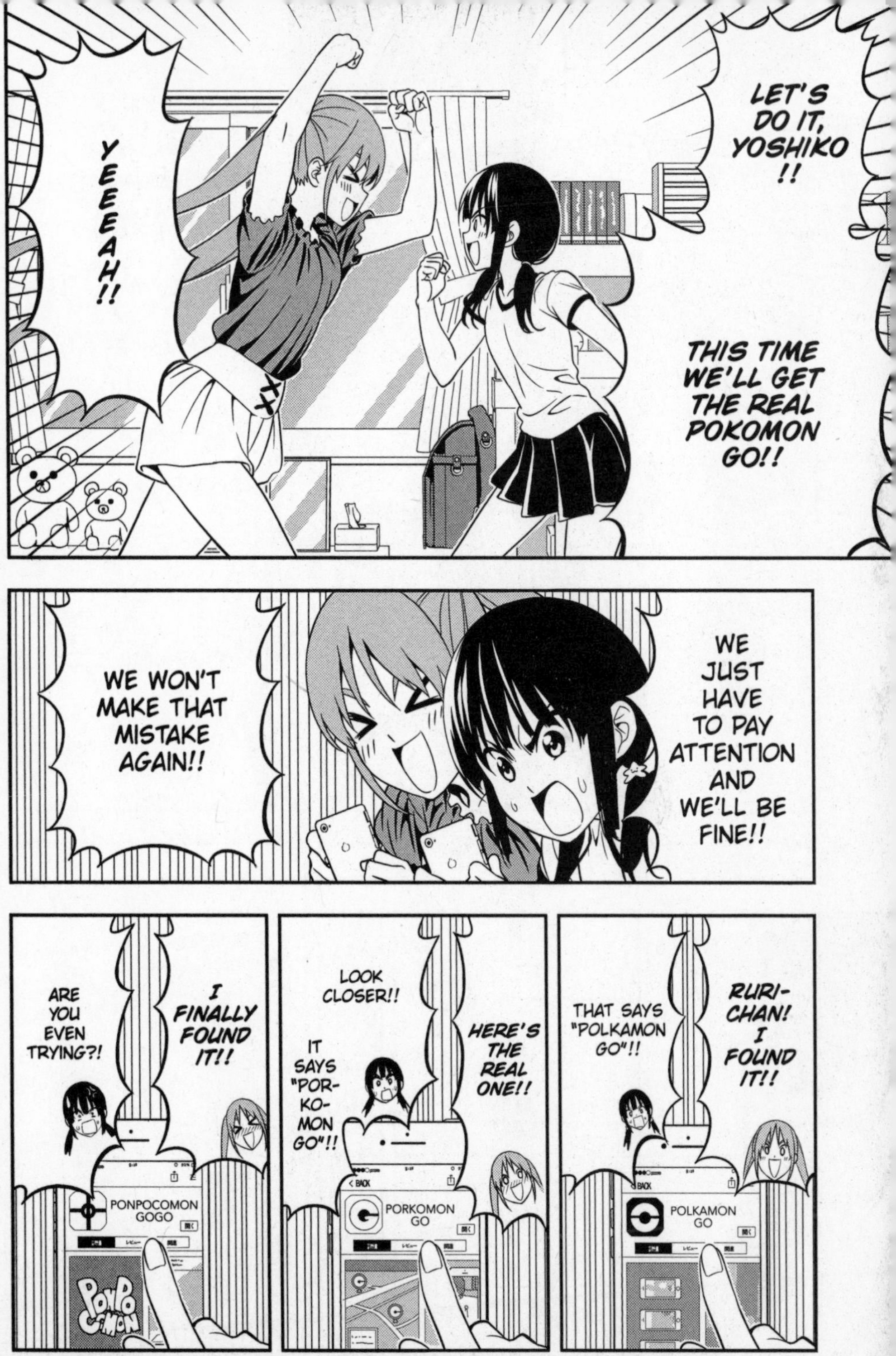
LET'S DO IT, YOSHIKO!!
YEEEAH!!
THIS TIME WE'LL GET THE REAL POKOMON GO!!
WE JUST HAVE TO PAY ATTENTION AND WE'LL BE FINE!!
WE WON'T MAKE THAT MISTAKE AGAIN!!
RURI-CHAN! I FOUND IT!!
THAT SAYS "POLKAMON GO"!!
POLKAMON GO
HERE'S THE REAL ONE!!
LOOK CLOSER!!
IT SAYS "POR-KO-MON GO"!!
BACK
PORKOMON GO
I FINALLY FOUND IT!!
ARE YOU EVEN TRYING?!
PONPOCOMON GOGO
PONPOCOMON

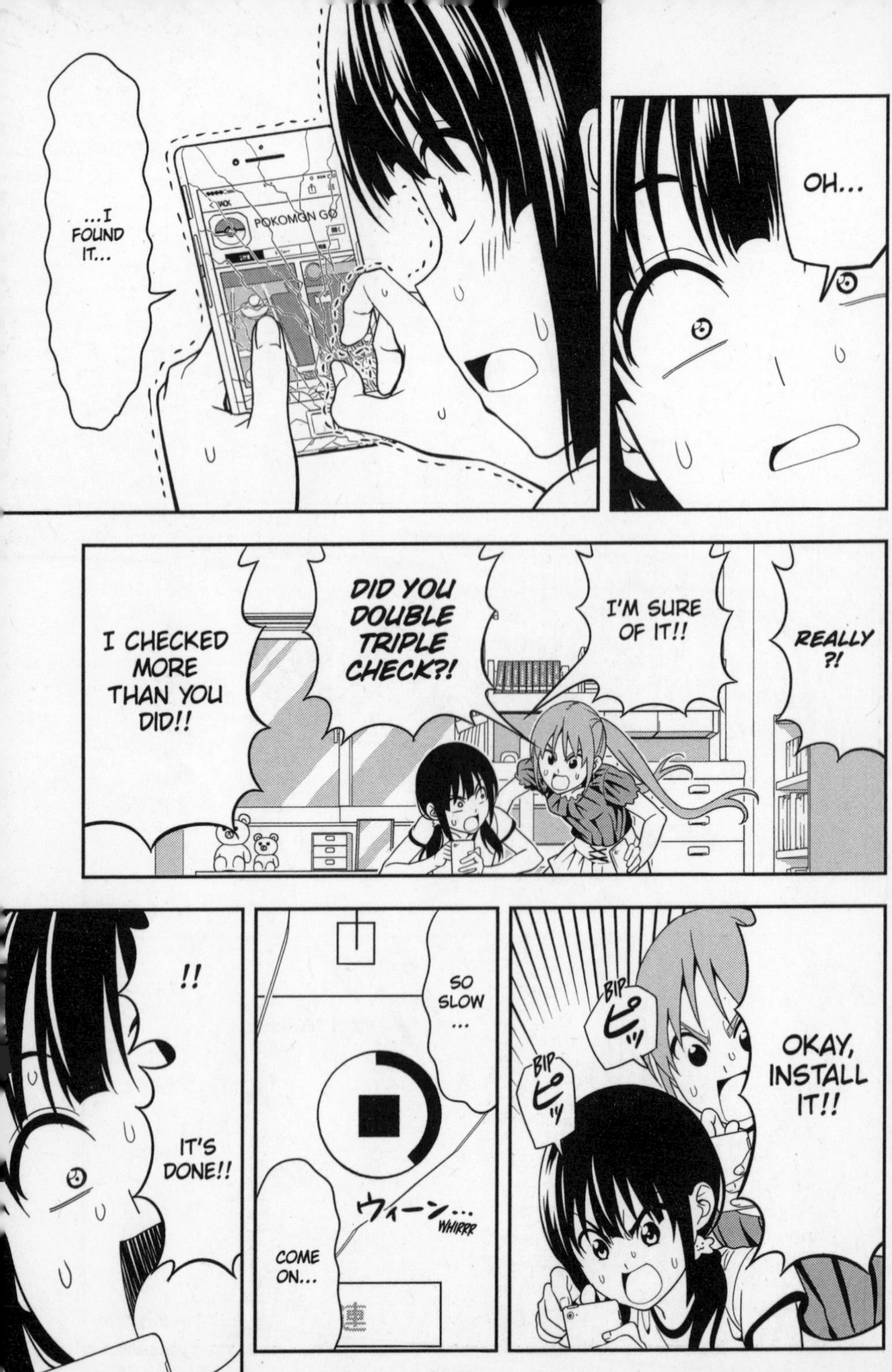
OH...
...I FOUND IT...
POKOMON GO
REALLY?!
I'M SURE OF IT!!
DID YOU DOUBLE TRIPLE CHECK?!
I CHECKED MORE THAN YOU DID!!
OKAY, INSTALL IT!!
ピッ BIP
ピッ BIP
SO SLOW...
ウィーン… WHIRRR
COME ON...
!!
IT'S DONE!!

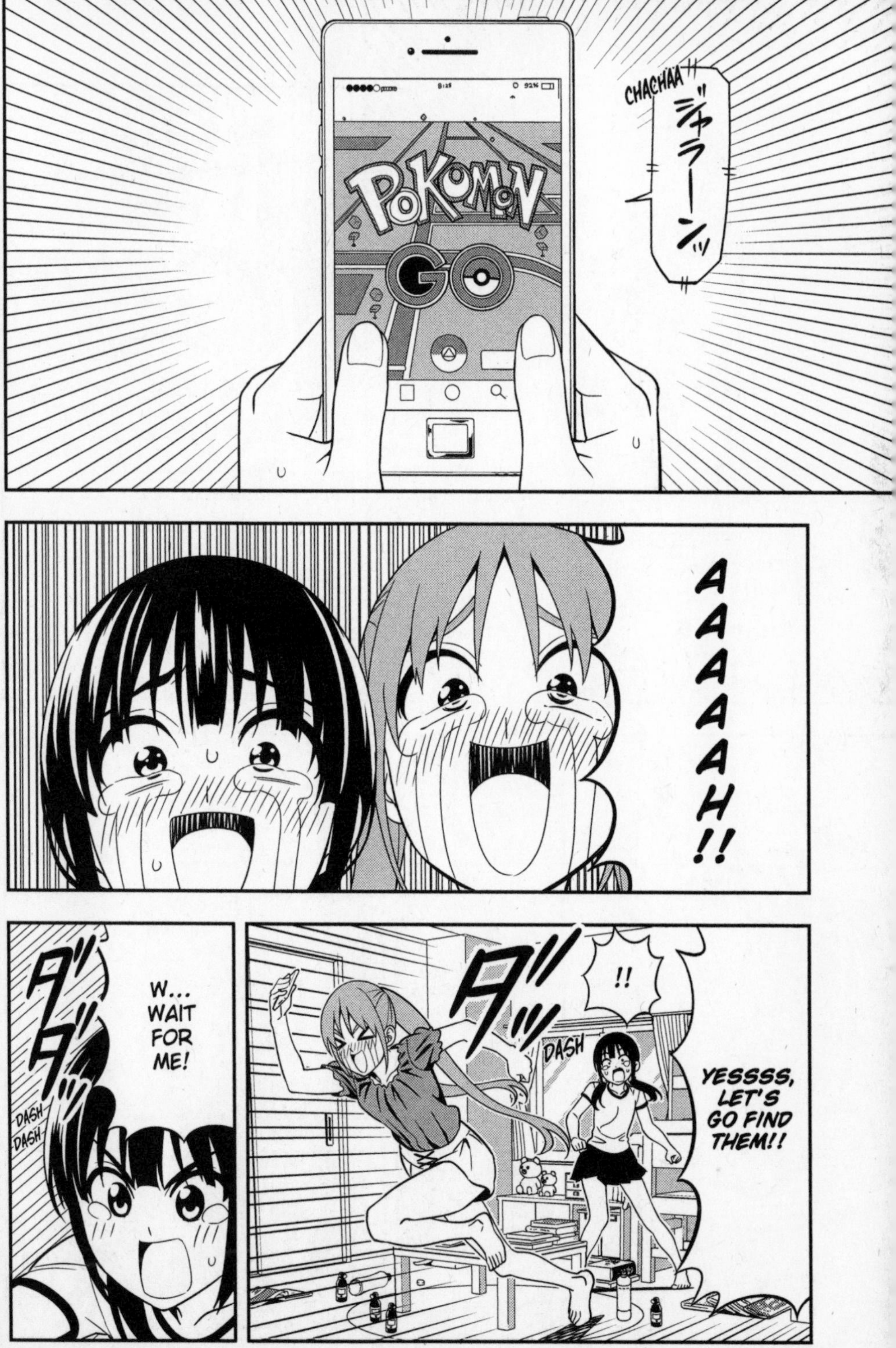
POKOMON
GO
CHACHAA
ジャラーンッ
AAAAAAH!!
!!
YESSSS, LET'S GO FIND THEM!!
ダッ
DASH
ダダダ
DASH
DASH
W... WAIT FOR ME!

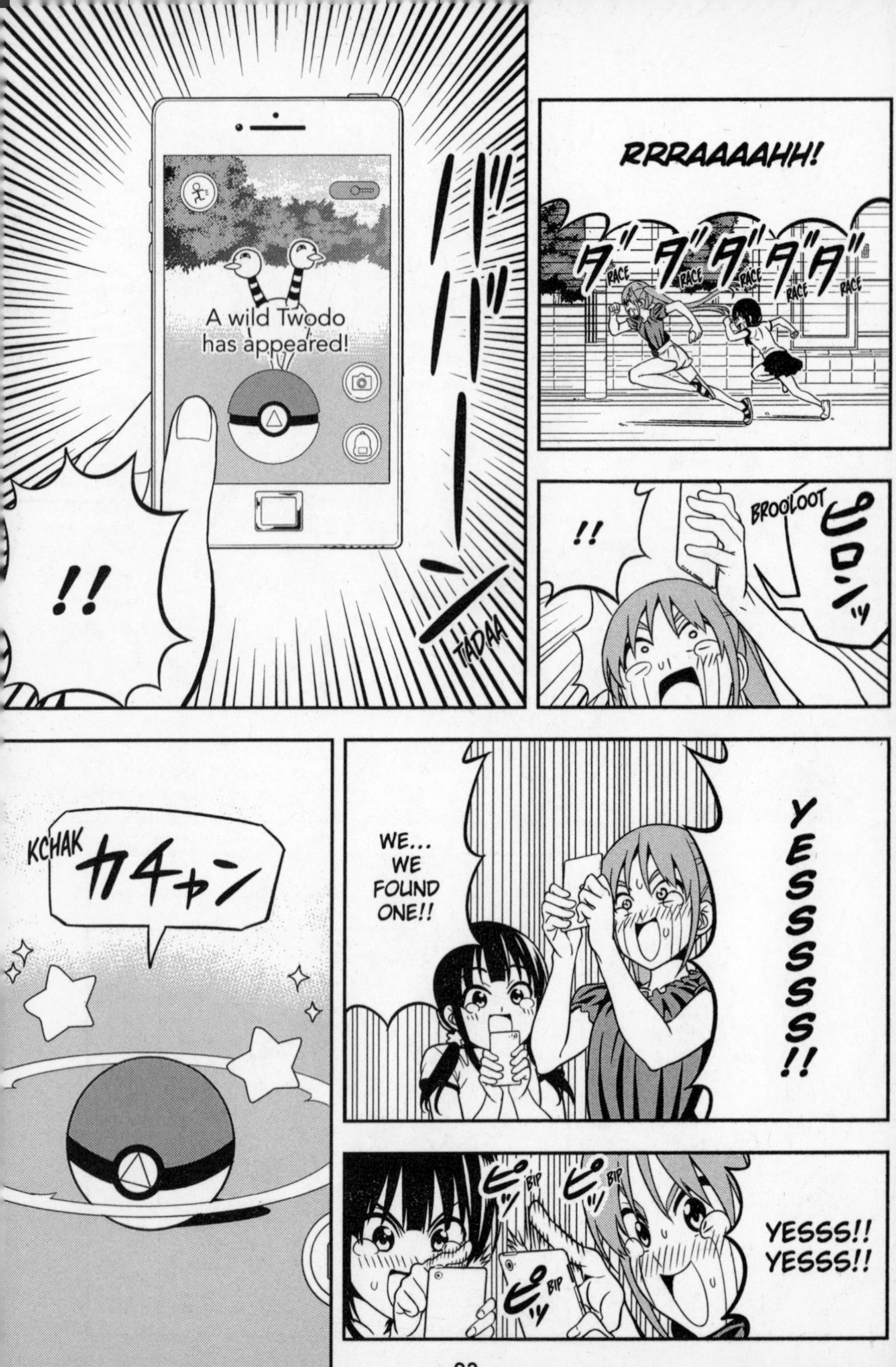
RRRAAAAHH!
ダダダダダ
RACE RACE RACE RACE RACE
!!
BROOLOOT
ピロンッ
A wild Twodo has appeared!
!!
TADAA
YESSSSS!!
WE... WE FOUND ONE!!
ピッ BIP
ピッ BIP
ピッ BIP
YESSS!! YESSS!!
KCHAK
カチャン

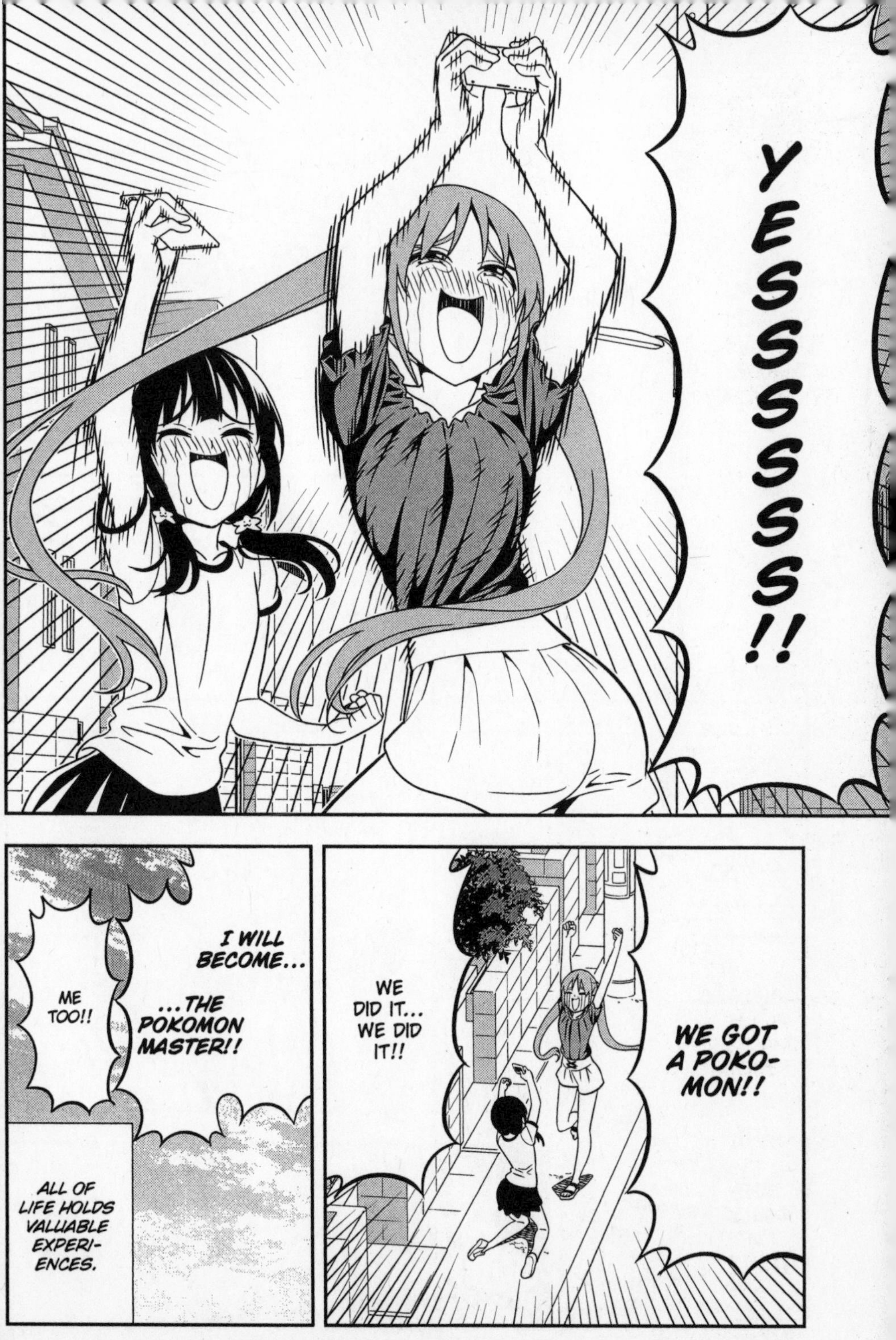
YESSSSSSS!!
WE GOT A POKO-MON!!
WE DID IT... WE DID IT!!
I WILL BECOME...
...THE POKOMON MASTER!!
ME TOO!!
ALL OF LIFE HOLDS VALUABLE EXPERI-ENCES.

Twodo GO

ONE HOUR LATER
TWODOS ARE THE ONLY THING SHOWING UP ANYMORE!!
ME TOO! TWODOS ARE ALL I SEE!!
C'MON, TWODO!!
GIVE IT A REST AL-READY!!

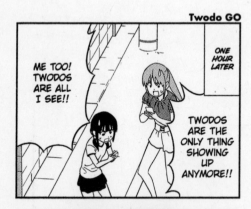

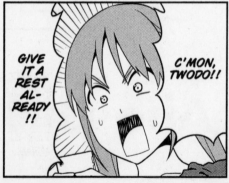

(How far will you walk? How far, how far?)

Aho-Girl

\'ahô,gərl\ *Japanese, noun*.

A clueless girl.

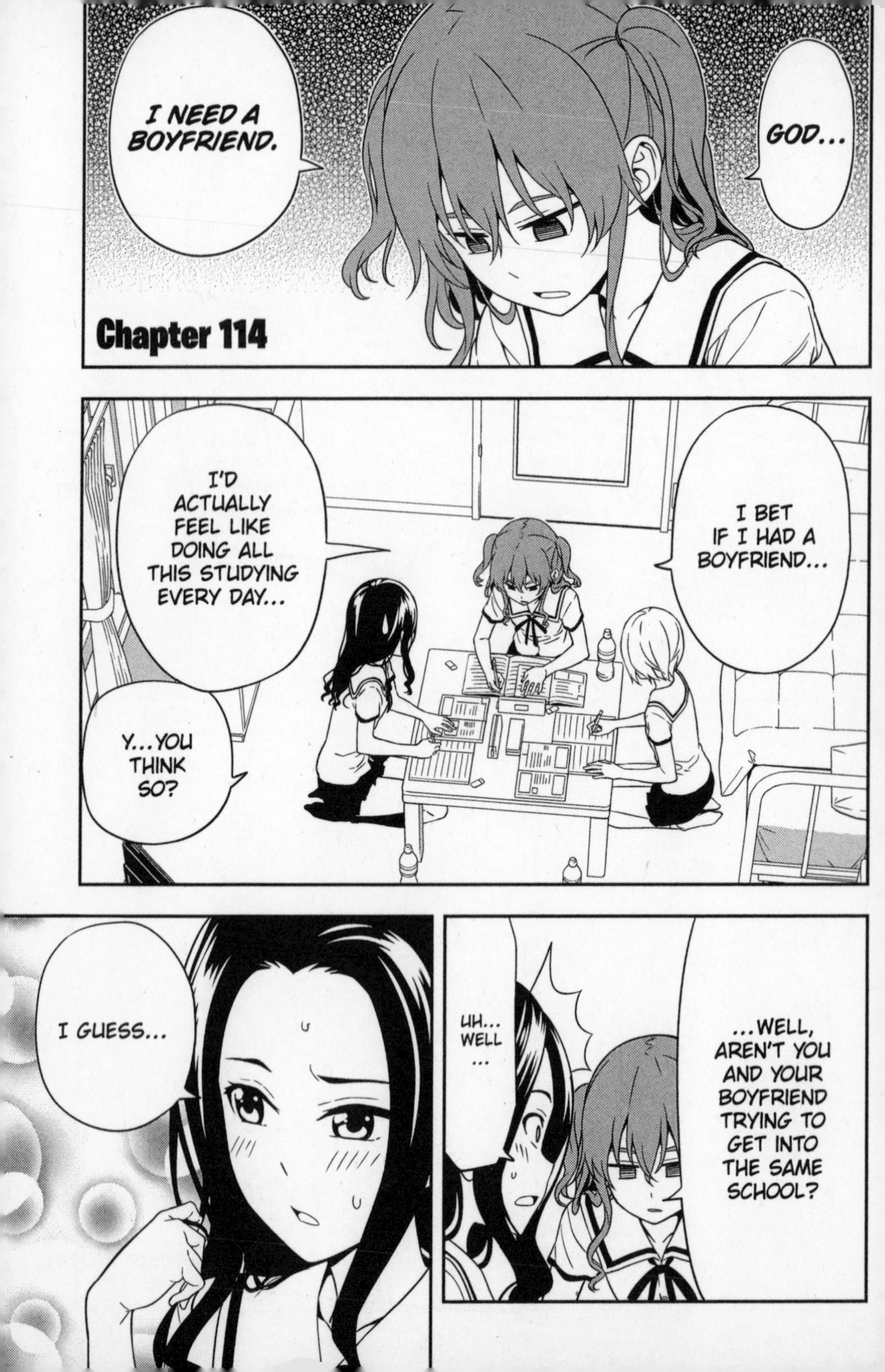
GOD...
I NEED A BOYFRIEND.
Chapter 114
I BET IF I HAD A BOYFRIEND...
I'D ACTUALLY FEEL LIKE DOING ALL THIS STUDYING EVERY DAY...
Y...YOU THINK SO?
...WELL, AREN'T YOU AND YOUR BOYFRIEND TRYING TO GET INTO THE SAME SCHOOL?
UH... WELL ...
I GUESS...

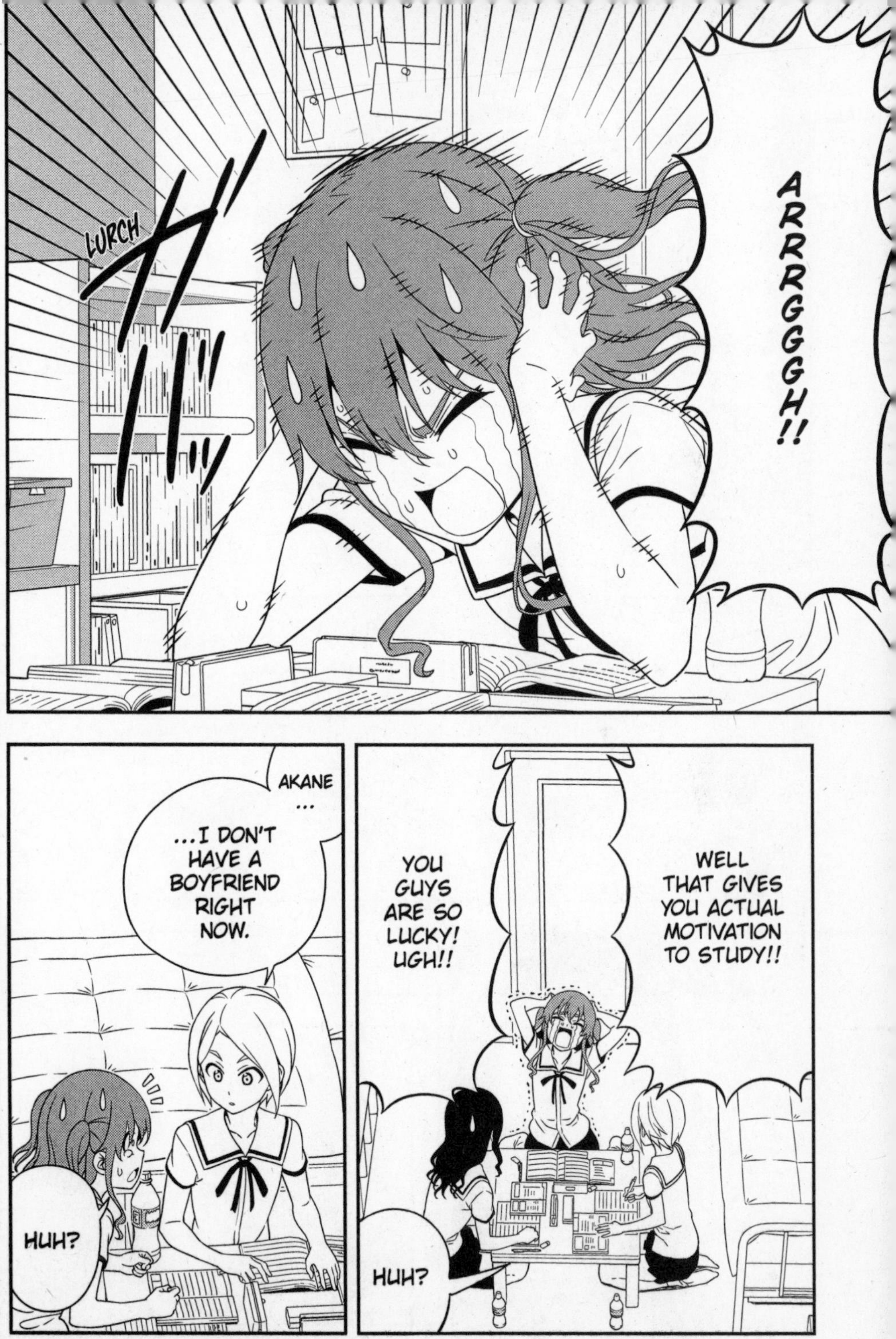
ARRRGGGH!!
LURCH
WELL THAT GIVES YOU ACTUAL MOTIVATION TO STUDY!!
YOU GUYS ARE SO LUCKY! UGH!!
HUH?
AKANE ...
...I DON'T HAVE A BOYFRIEND RIGHT NOW.
HUH?

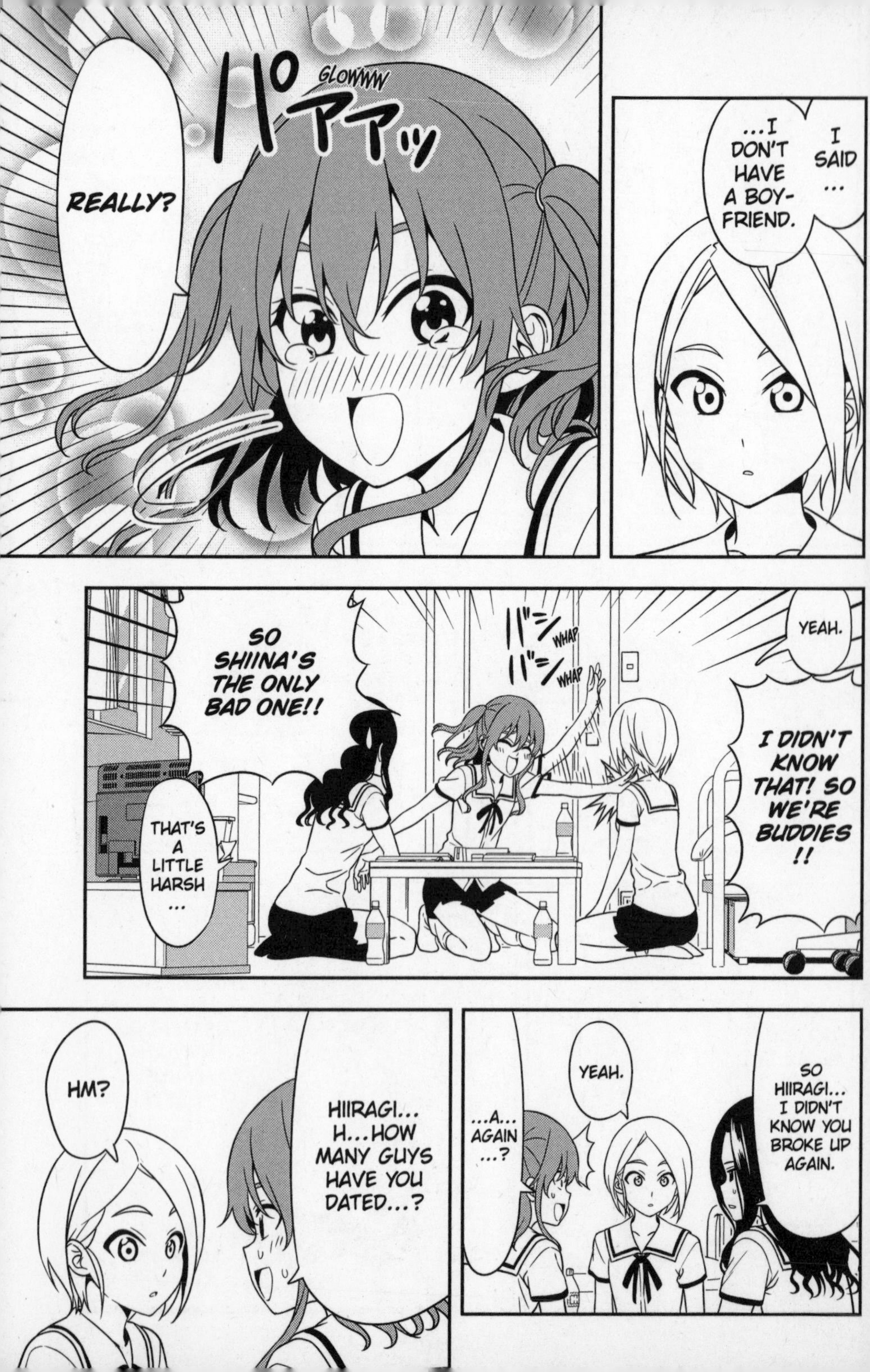
I SAID ...
...I DON'T HAVE A BOY-FRIEND.
パアアッ
GLOWWW
REALLY?
YEAH.
I DIDN'T KNOW THAT! SO WE'RE BUDDIES!!
バシ WHAP
バシ WHAP
SO SHIINA'S THE ONLY BAD ONE!!
THAT'S A LITTLE HARSH...
SO HIIRAGI... I DIDN'T KNOW YOU BROKE UP AGAIN.
YEAH.
...A... AGAIN...?
HIIRAGI... H...HOW MANY GUYS HAVE YOU DATED...?
HM?

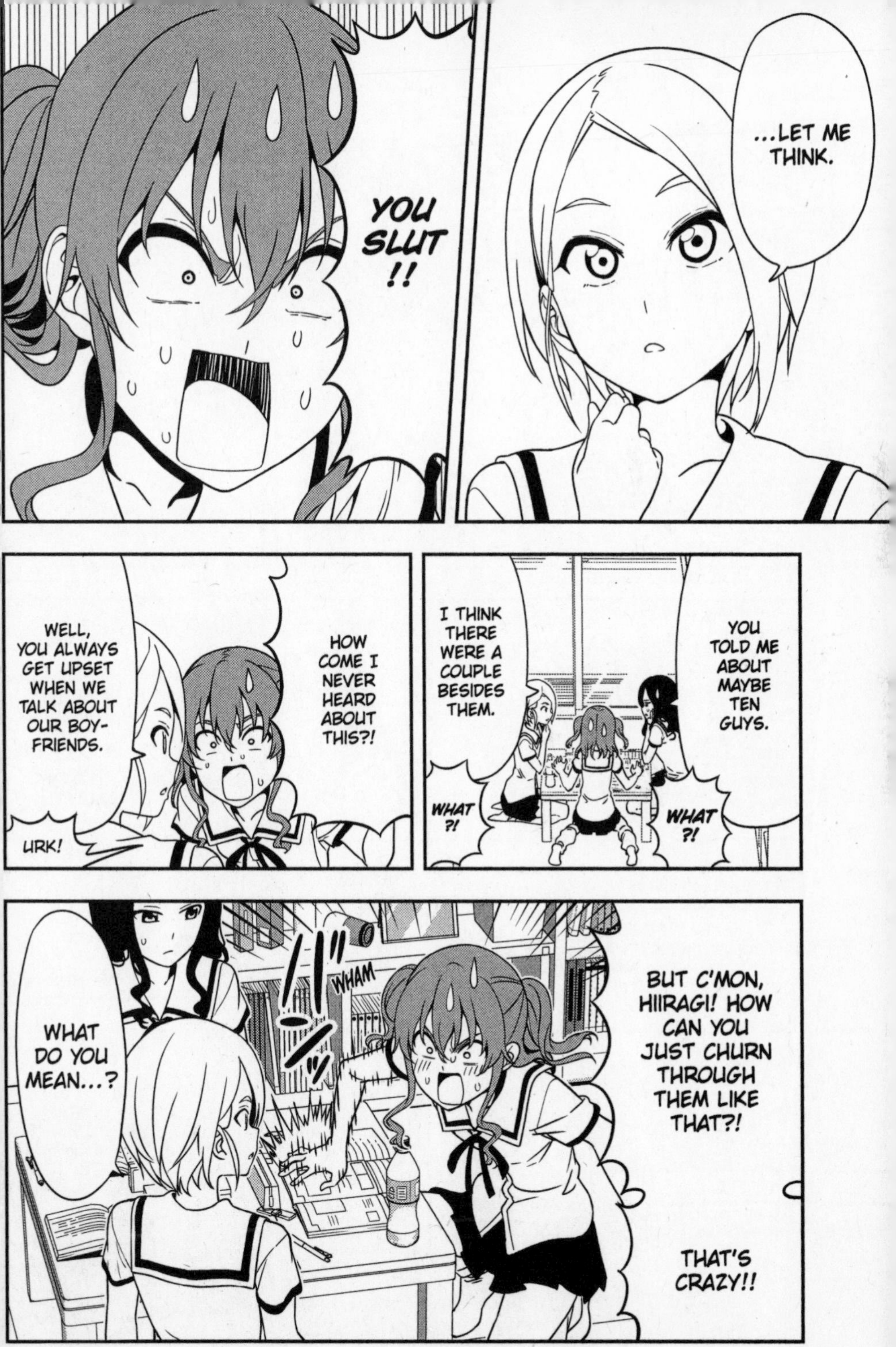
...LET ME THINK.
YOU SLUT !!
YOU TOLD ME ABOUT MAYBE TEN GUYS.
WHAT?!
I THINK THERE WERE A COUPLE BESIDES THEM.
WHAT?!
HOW COME I NEVER HEARD ABOUT THIS?!
WELL, YOU ALWAYS GET UPSET WHEN WE TALK ABOUT OUR BOY-FRIENDS.
URK!
BUT C'MON, HIIRAGI! HOW CAN YOU JUST CHURN THROUGH THEM LIKE THAT?!
THAT'S CRAZY!!
WHAM
WHAT DO YOU MEAN...?

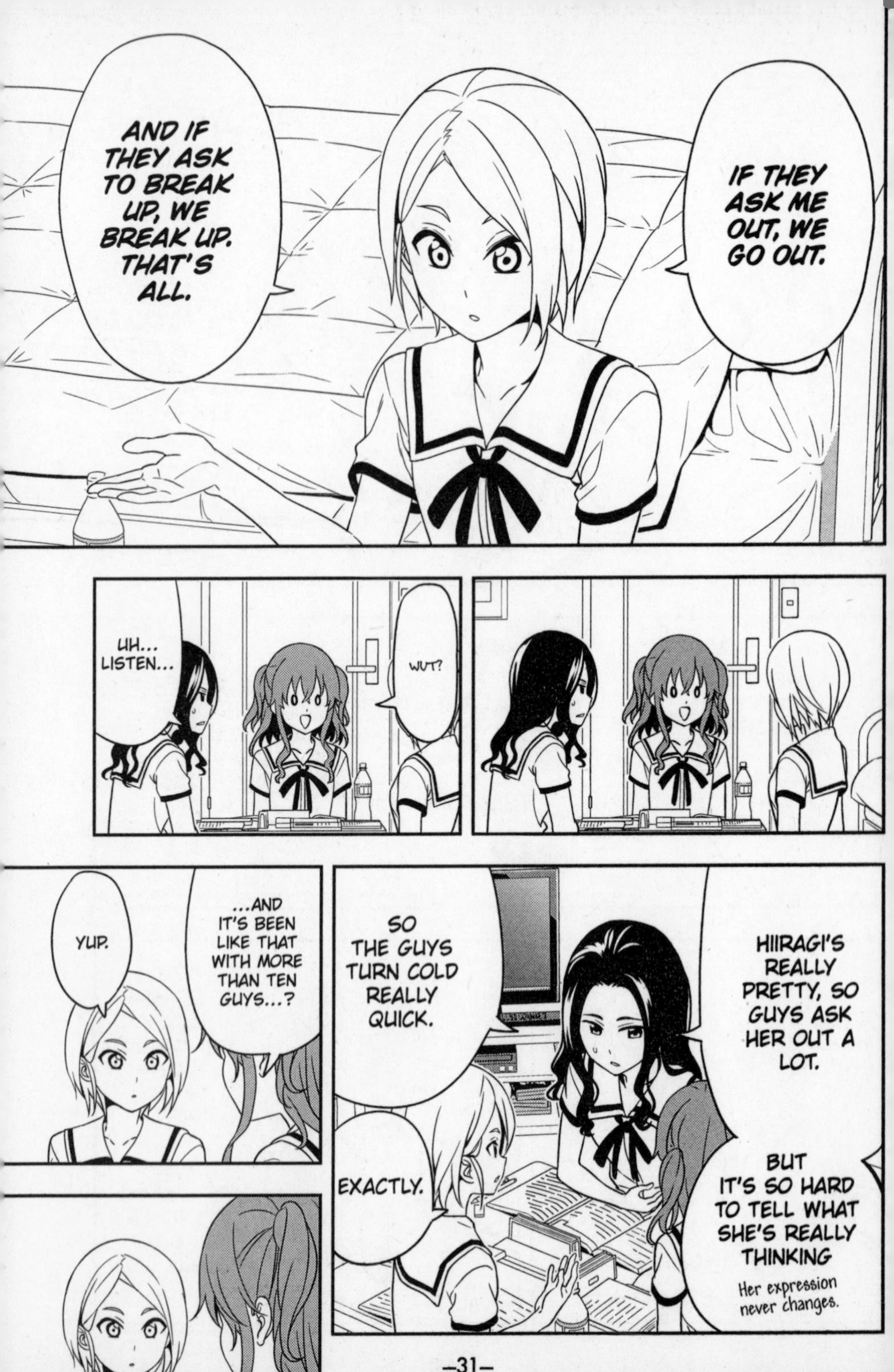
IF THEY ASK ME OUT, WE GO OUT.
AND IF THEY ASK TO BREAK UP, WE BREAK UP. THAT'S ALL.
UH... LISTEN...
WUT?
HIIRAGI'S REALLY PRETTY, SO GUYS ASK HER OUT A LOT.
SO THE GUYS TURN COLD REALLY QUICK.
BUT IT'S SO HARD TO TELL WHAT SHE'S REALLY THINKING
Her expression never changes.
EXACTLY.
...AND IT'S BEEN LIKE THAT WITH MORE THAN TEN GUYS...?
YUP.

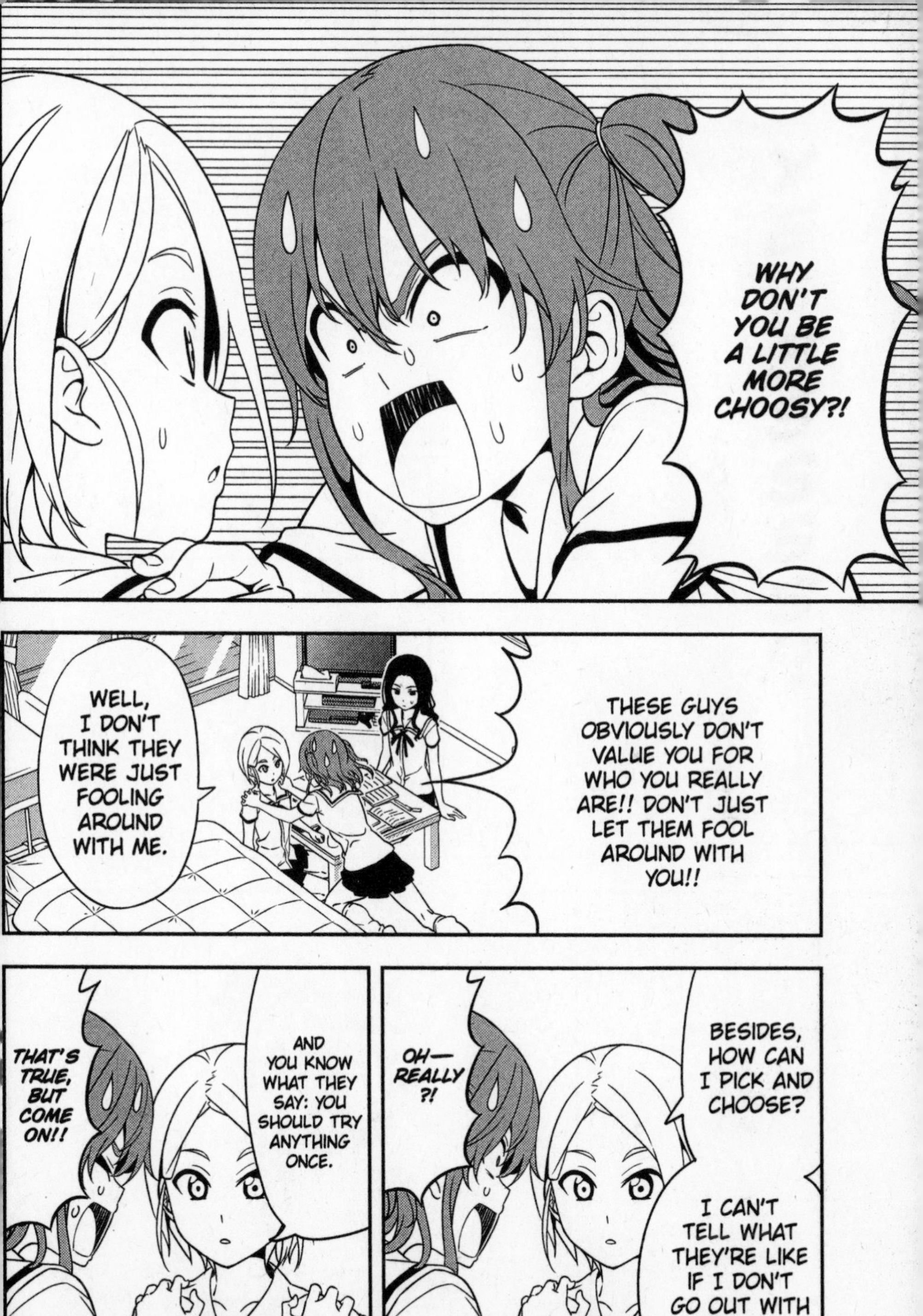
WHY DON'T YOU BE A LITTLE MORE CHOOSY?!
THESE GUYS OBVIOUSLY DON'T VALUE YOU FOR WHO YOU REALLY ARE!! DON'T JUST LET THEM FOOL AROUND WITH YOU!!
WELL, I DON'T THINK THEY WERE JUST FOOLING AROUND WITH ME.
BESIDES, HOW CAN I PICK AND CHOOSE?
I CAN'T TELL WHAT THEY'RE LIKE IF I DON'T GO OUT WITH THEM.
OH—REALLY?!
AND YOU KNOW WHAT THEY SAY: YOU SHOULD TRY ANYTHING ONCE.
THAT'S TRUE, BUT COME ON!!

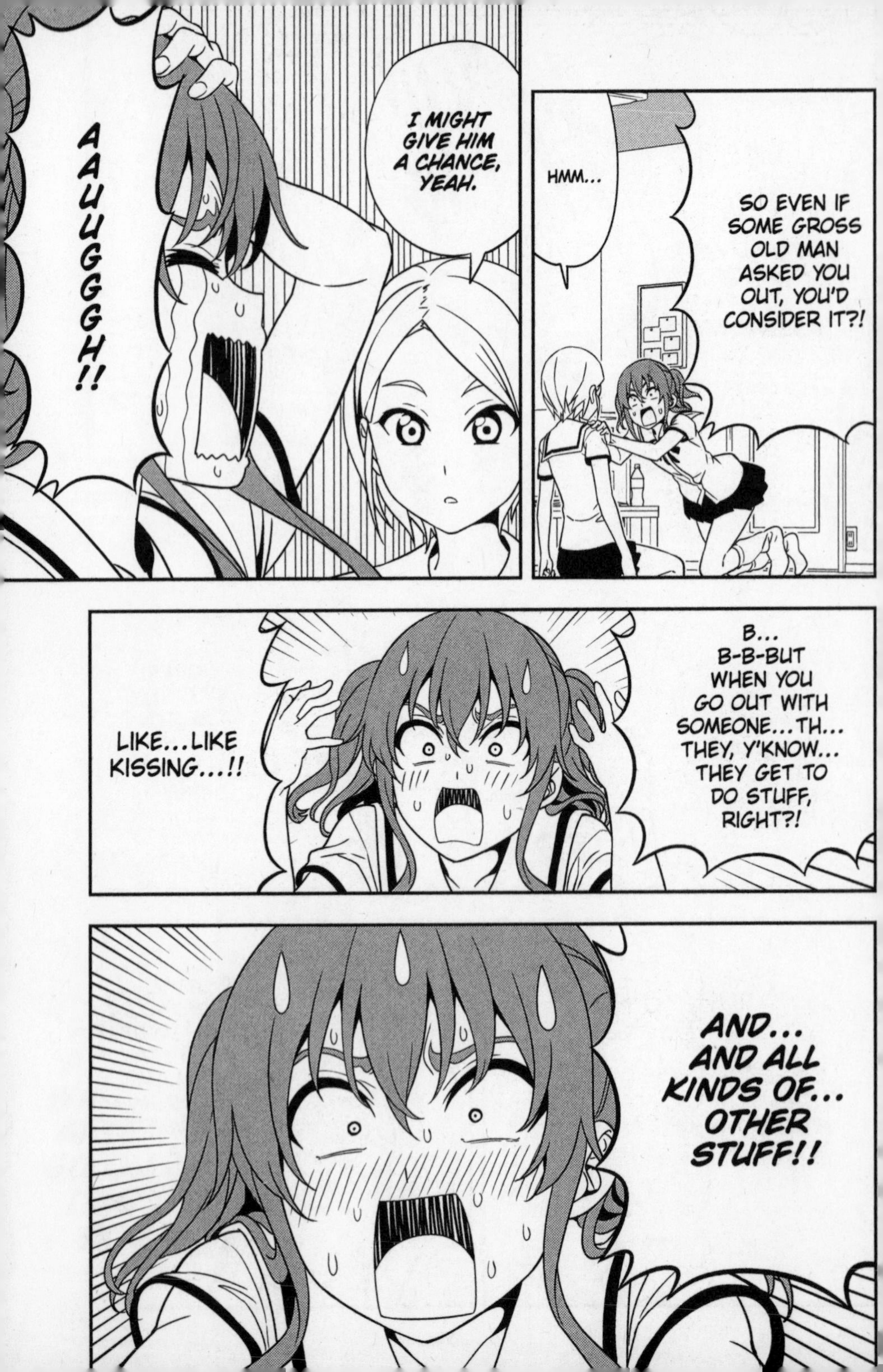
SO EVEN IF SOME GROSS OLD MAN ASKED YOU OUT, YOU'D CONSIDER IT?!
HMM...
I MIGHT GIVE HIM A CHANCE, YEAH.
AAUUGGGH!!
B... B-B-BUT WHEN YOU GO OUT WITH SOMEONE...TH... THEY, Y'KNOW... THEY GET TO DO STUFF, RIGHT?!
LIKE...LIKE KISSING...!!
AND... AND ALL KINDS OF... OTHER STUFF!!

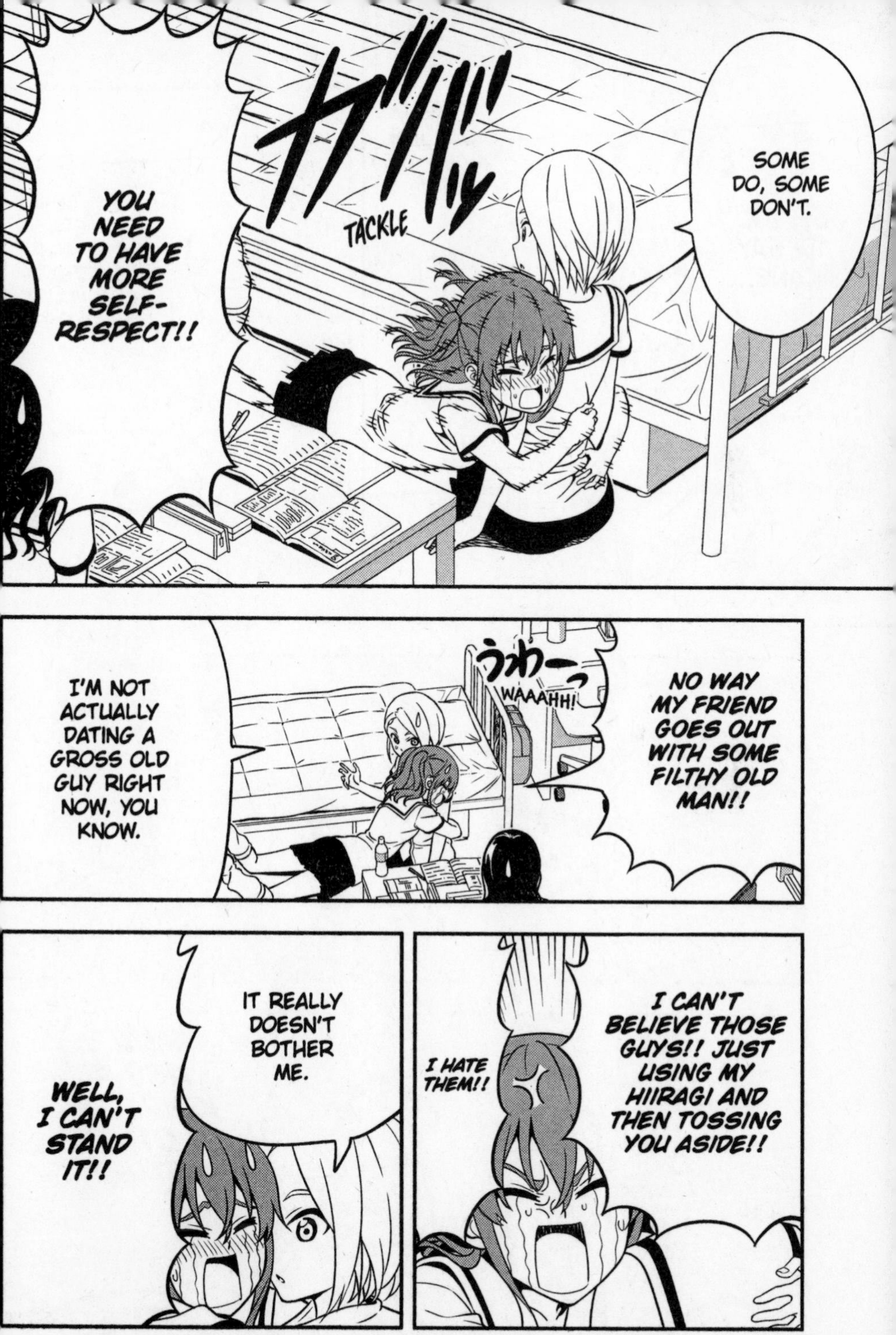
SOME DO, SOME DON'T.
ガバッ
TACKLE
YOU NEED TO HAVE MORE SELF-RESPECT!!
NO WAY MY FRIEND GOES OUT WITH SOME FILTHY OLD MAN!!
うわー
WAAAHH!
I'M NOT ACTUALLY DATING A GROSS OLD GUY RIGHT NOW, YOU KNOW.
I CAN'T BELIEVE THOSE GUYS!! JUST USING MY HIIRAGI AND THEN TOSSING YOU ASIDE!!
I HATE THEM!!
IT REALLY DOESN'T BOTHER ME.
WELL, I CAN'T STAND IT!!

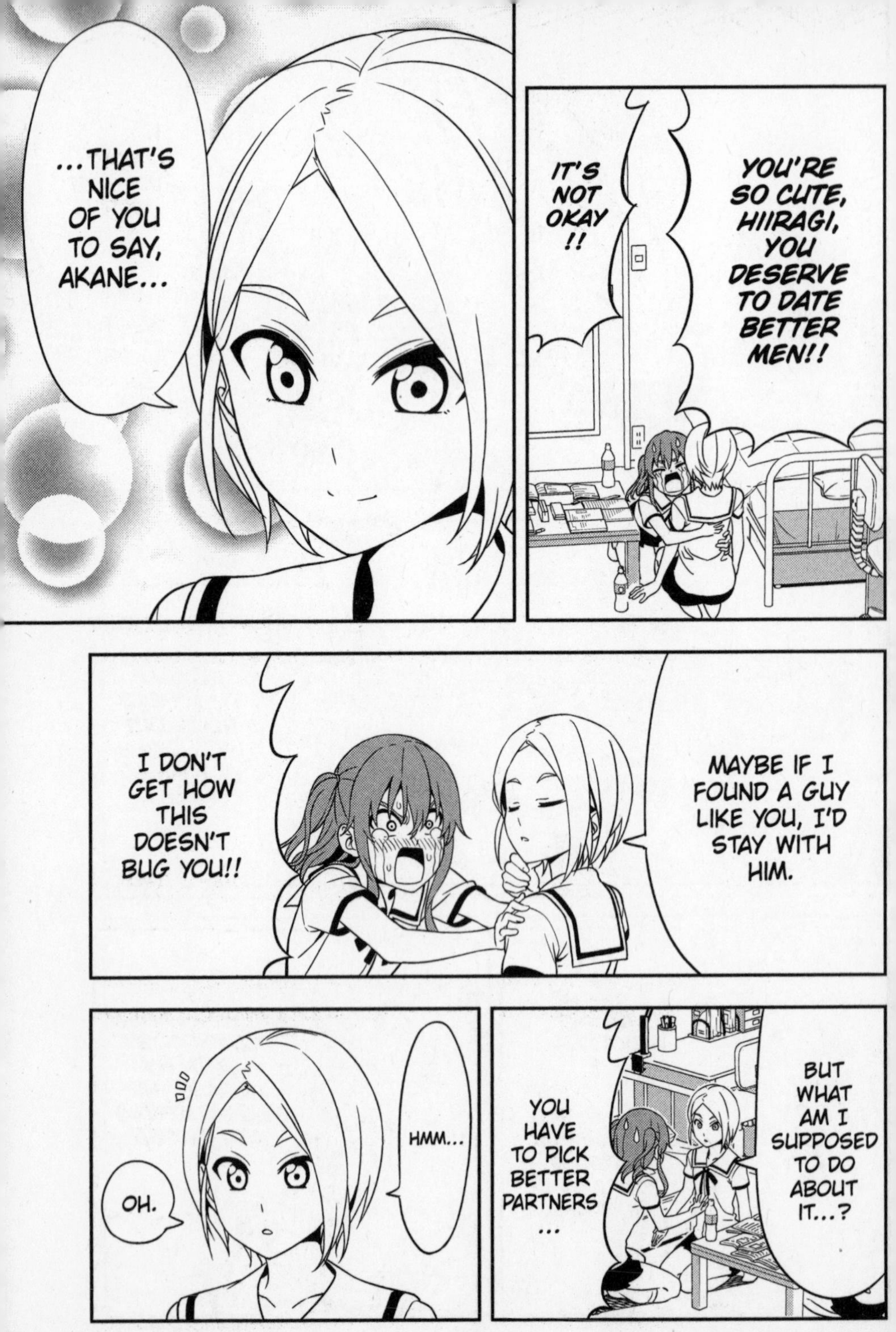
YOU'RE SO CUTE, HIIRAGI, YOU DESERVE TO DATE BETTER MEN!!
IT'S NOT OKAY !!
...THAT'S NICE OF YOU TO SAY, AKANE...
MAYBE IF I FOUND A GUY LIKE YOU, I'D STAY WITH HIM.
I DON'T GET HOW THIS DOESN'T BUG YOU!!
BUT WHAT AM I SUPPOSED TO DO ABOUT IT...?
YOU HAVE TO PICK BETTER PARTNERS ...
HMM...
OH.

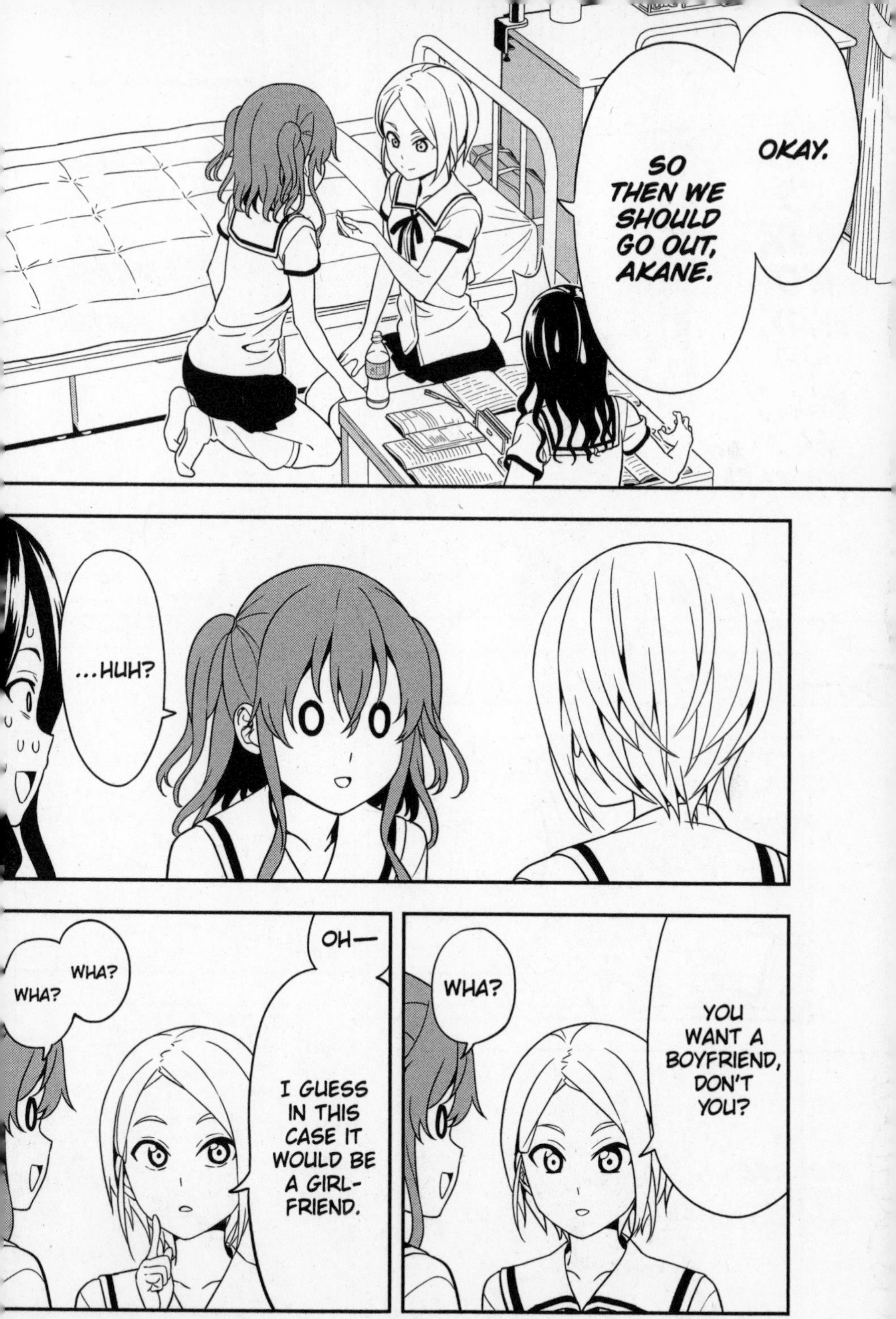
OKAY.
SO THEN WE SHOULD GO OUT, AKANE.
...HUH?
YOU WANT A BOYFRIEND, DON'T YOU?
WHA?
OH— I GUESS IN THIS CASE IT WOULD BE A GIRL-FRIEND.
WHA? WHA?

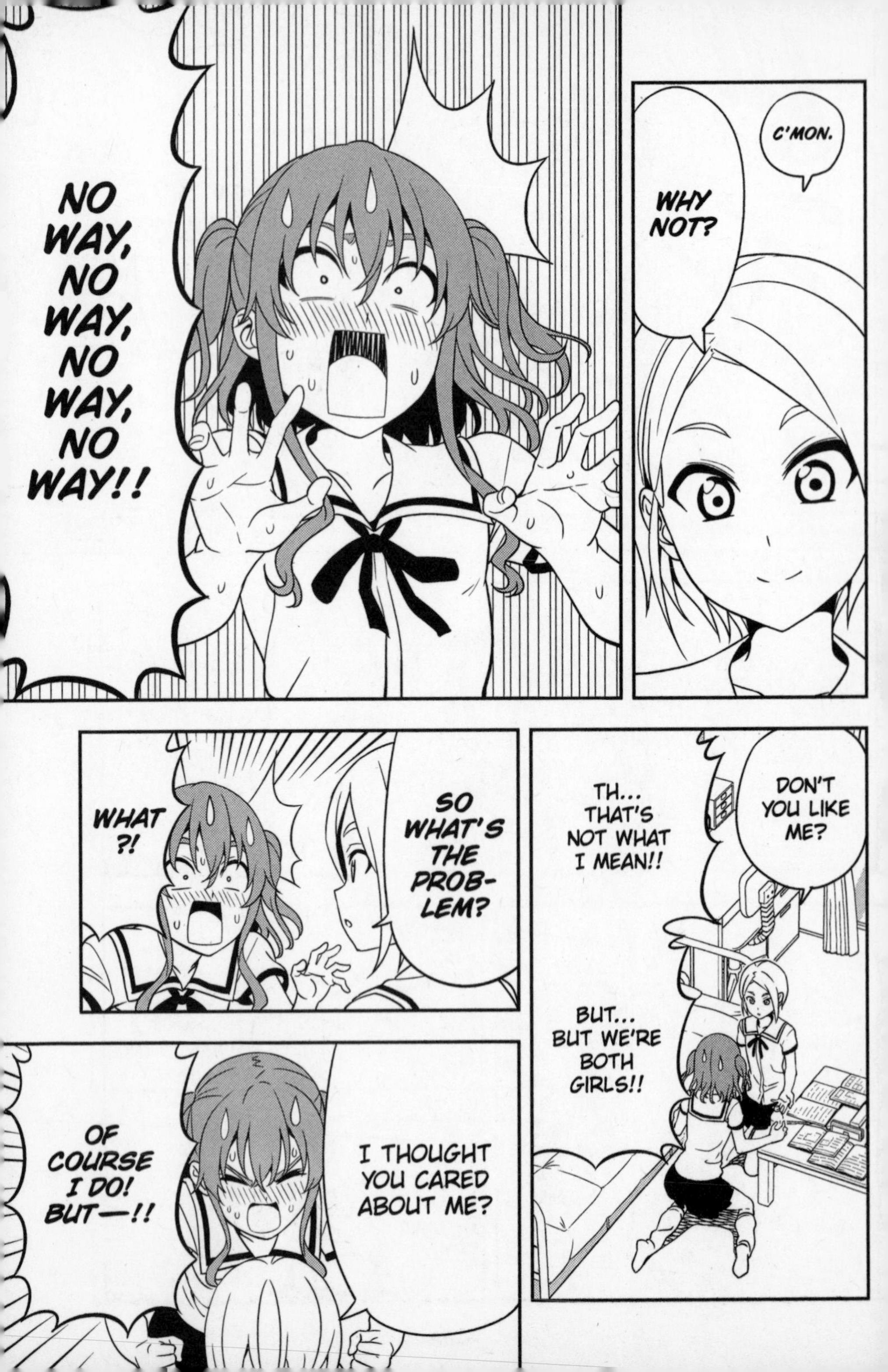
C'MON.
WHY NOT?
NO WAY, NO WAY, NO WAY, NO WAY!!
DON'T YOU LIKE ME?
TH... THAT'S NOT WHAT I MEAN!!
BUT... BUT WE'RE BOTH GIRLS!!
SO WHAT'S THE PROB-LEM?
WHAT?!
I THOUGHT YOU CARED ABOUT ME?
OF COURSE I DO! BUT—!!

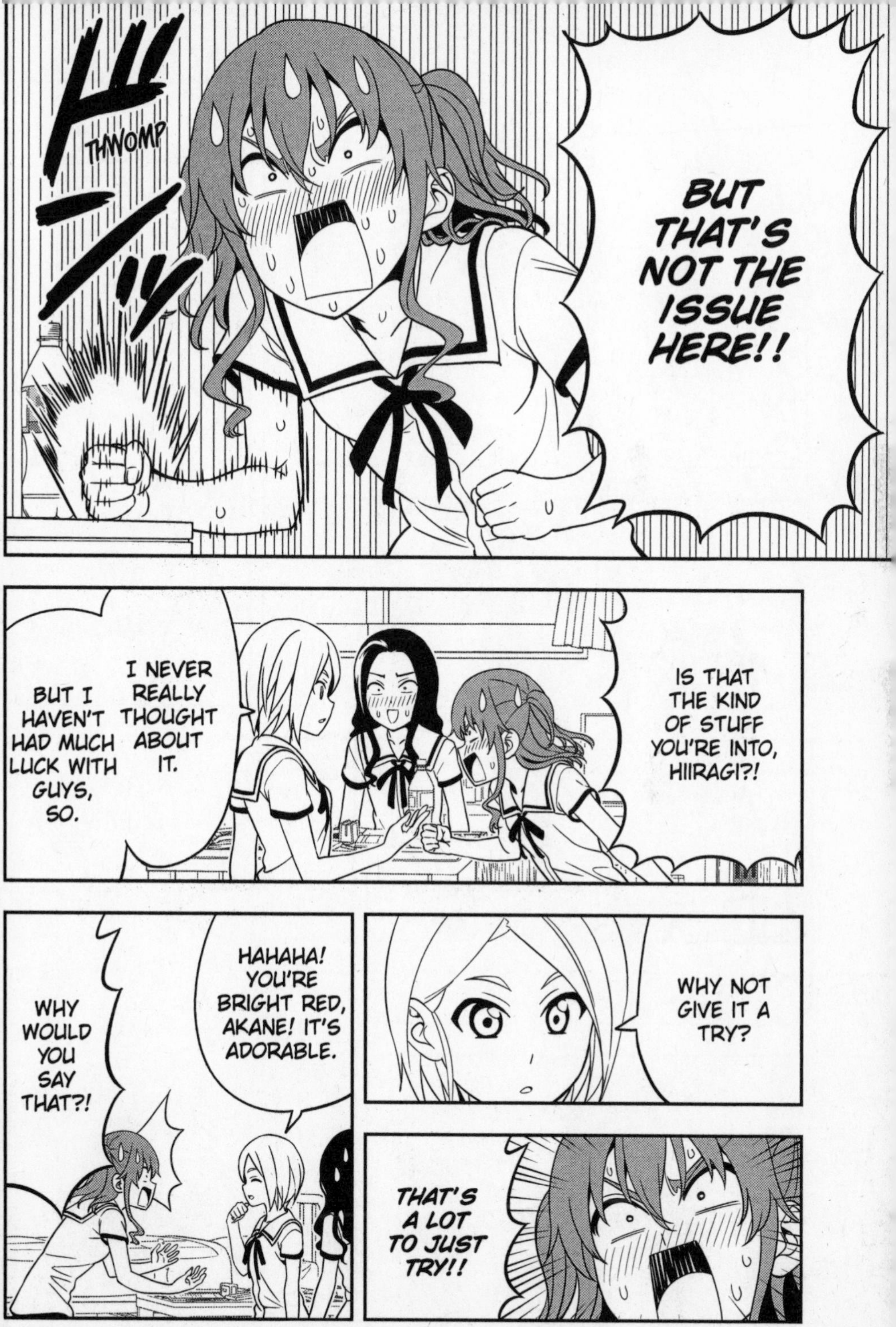

BUT THAT'S NOT THE ISSUE HERE!!
THWOMP
IS THAT THE KIND OF STUFF YOU'RE INTO, HIIRAGI?!
I NEVER REALLY THOUGHT ABOUT IT.
BUT I HAVEN'T HAD MUCH LUCK WITH GUYS, SO.
WHY NOT GIVE IT A TRY?
THAT'S A LOT TO JUST TRY!!
HAHAHA! YOU'RE BRIGHT RED, AKANE! IT'S ADORABLE.
WHY WOULD YOU SAY THAT?!

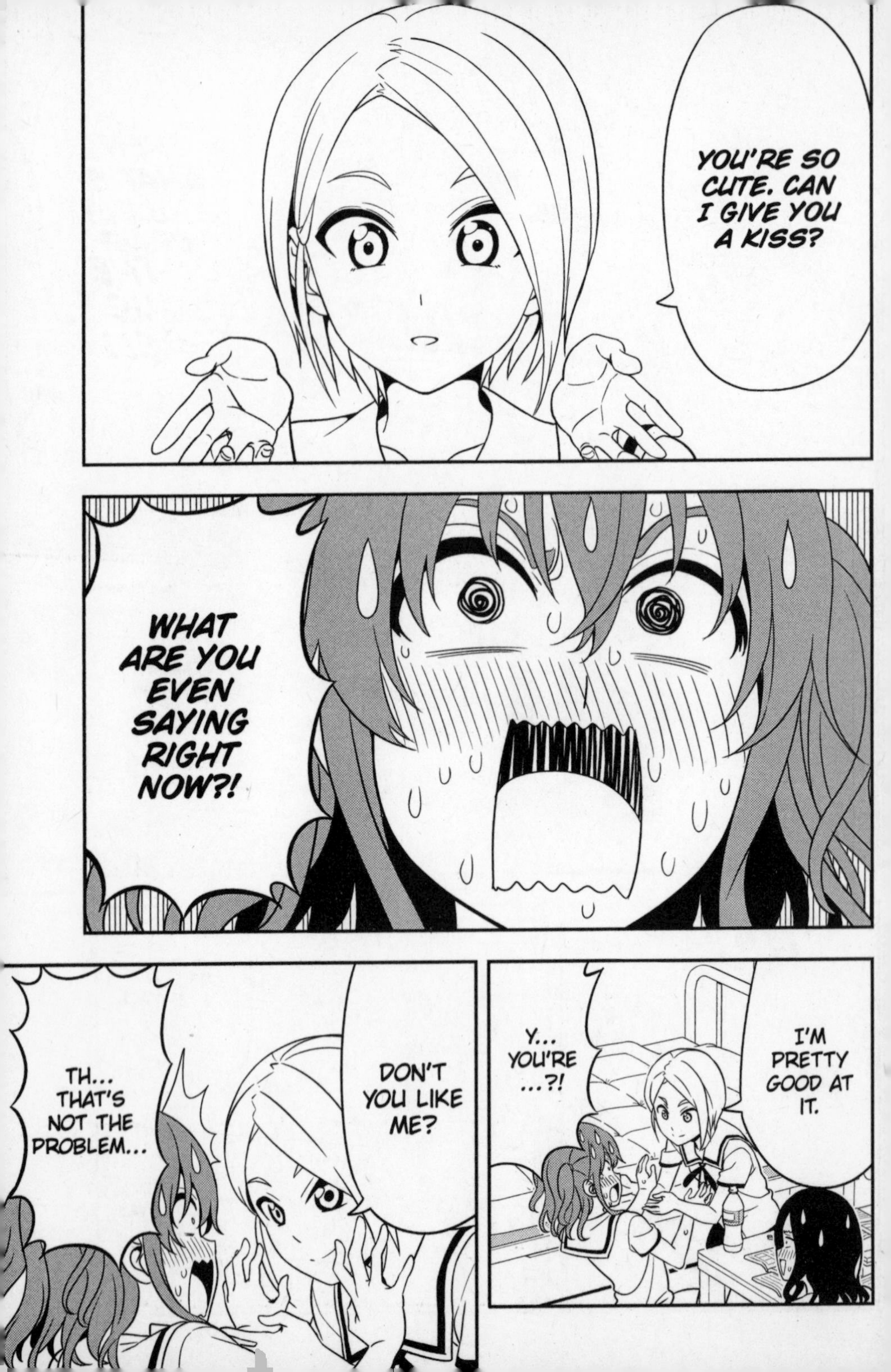
YOU'RE SO CUTE. CAN I GIVE YOU A KISS?
WHAT ARE YOU EVEN SAYING RIGHT NOW?!
I'M PRETTY GOOD AT IT.
Y... YOU'RE ...?!
DON'T YOU LIKE ME?
TH... THAT'S NOT THE PROBLEM...

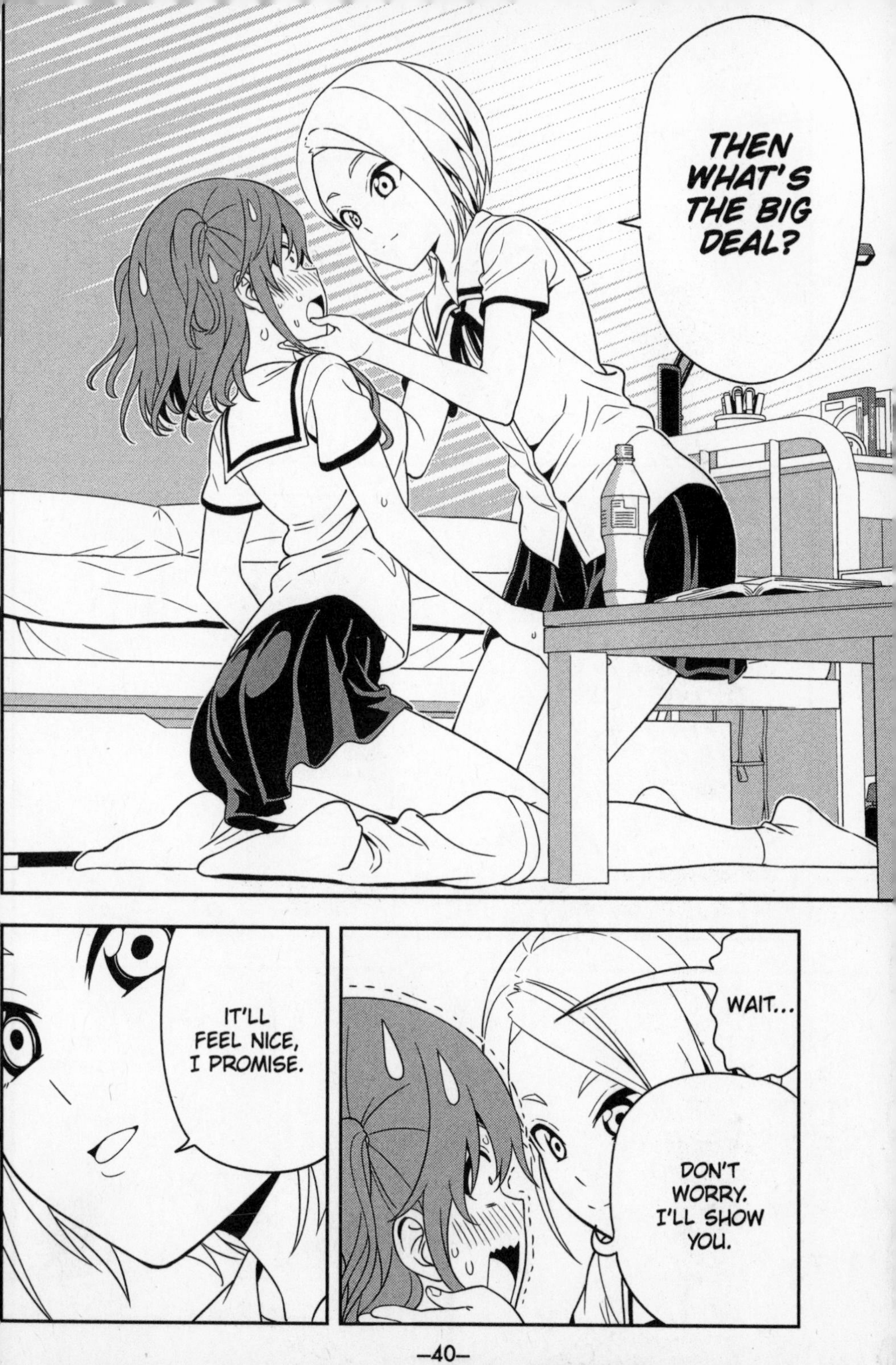
THEN WHAT'S THE BIG DEAL?
WAIT...
DON'T WORRY. I'LL SHOW YOU.
IT'LL FEEL NICE, I PROMISE.

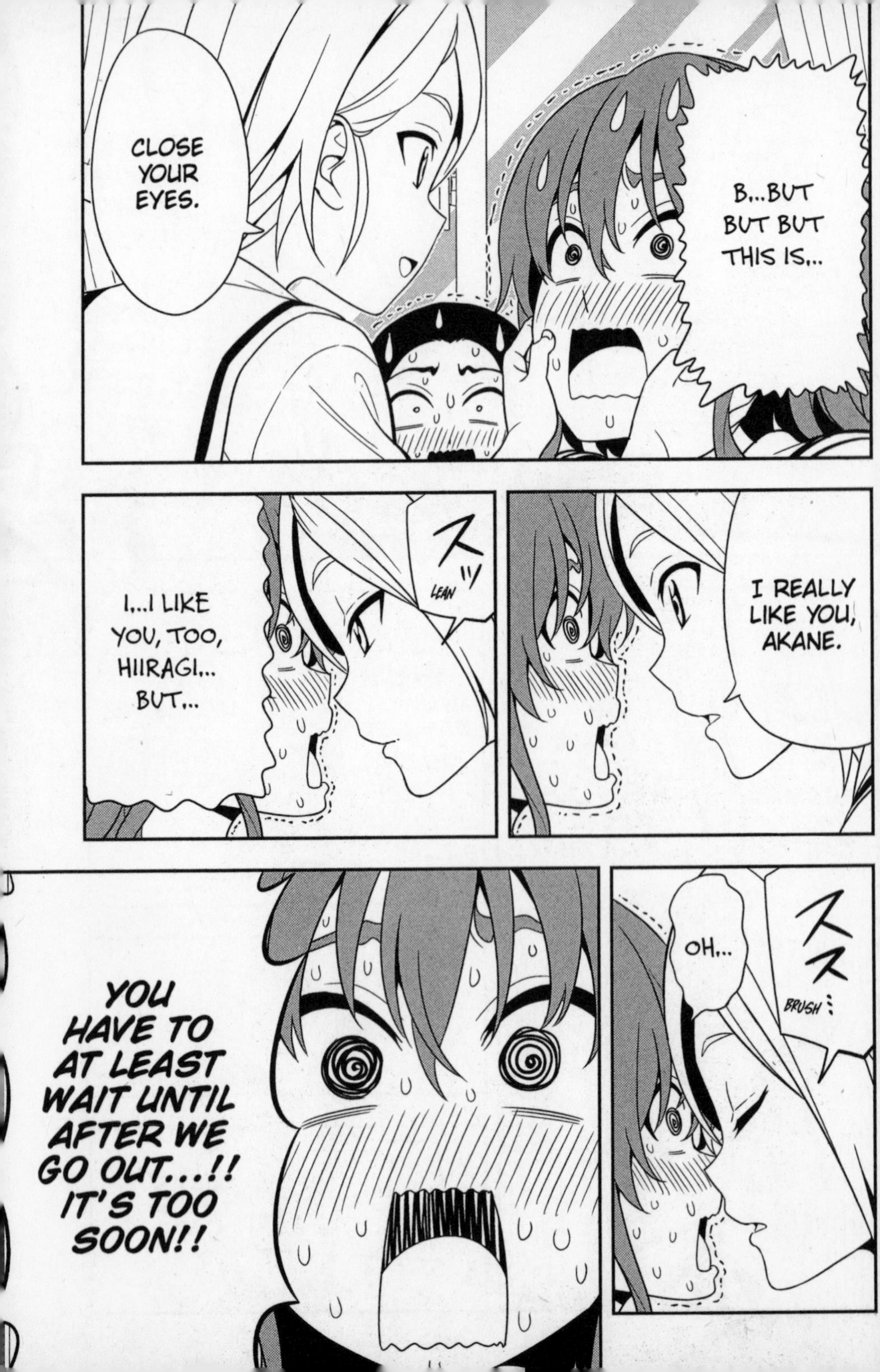
B...BUT BUT BUT THIS IS...
CLOSE YOUR EYES.
I REALLY LIKE YOU, AKANE.
スッ
LEAN
I...I LIKE YOU, TOO, HIIRAGI... BUT...
スス
BRUSH
OH...
YOU HAVE TO AT LEAST WAIT UNTIL AFTER WE GO OUT...!! IT'S TOO SOON!!

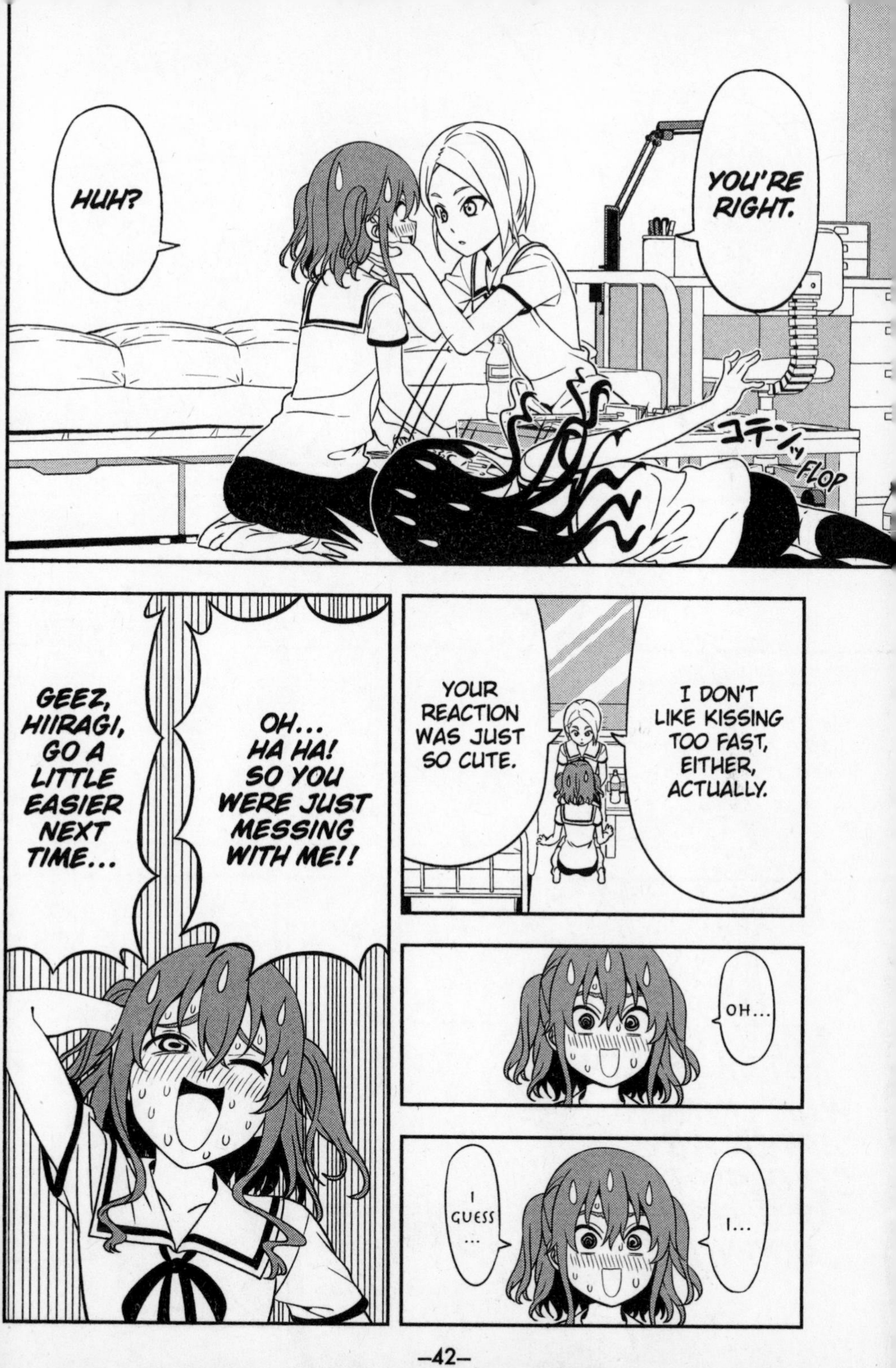
YOU'RE RIGHT.
HUH?
コテンッ
FLOP
I DON'T LIKE KISSING TOO FAST, EITHER, ACTUALLY.
YOUR REACTION WAS JUST SO CUTE.
OH...
I...
I GUESS ...
OH... HA HA! SO YOU WERE JUST MESSING WITH ME!!
GEEZ, HIIRAGI, GO A LITTLE EASIER NEXT TIME...

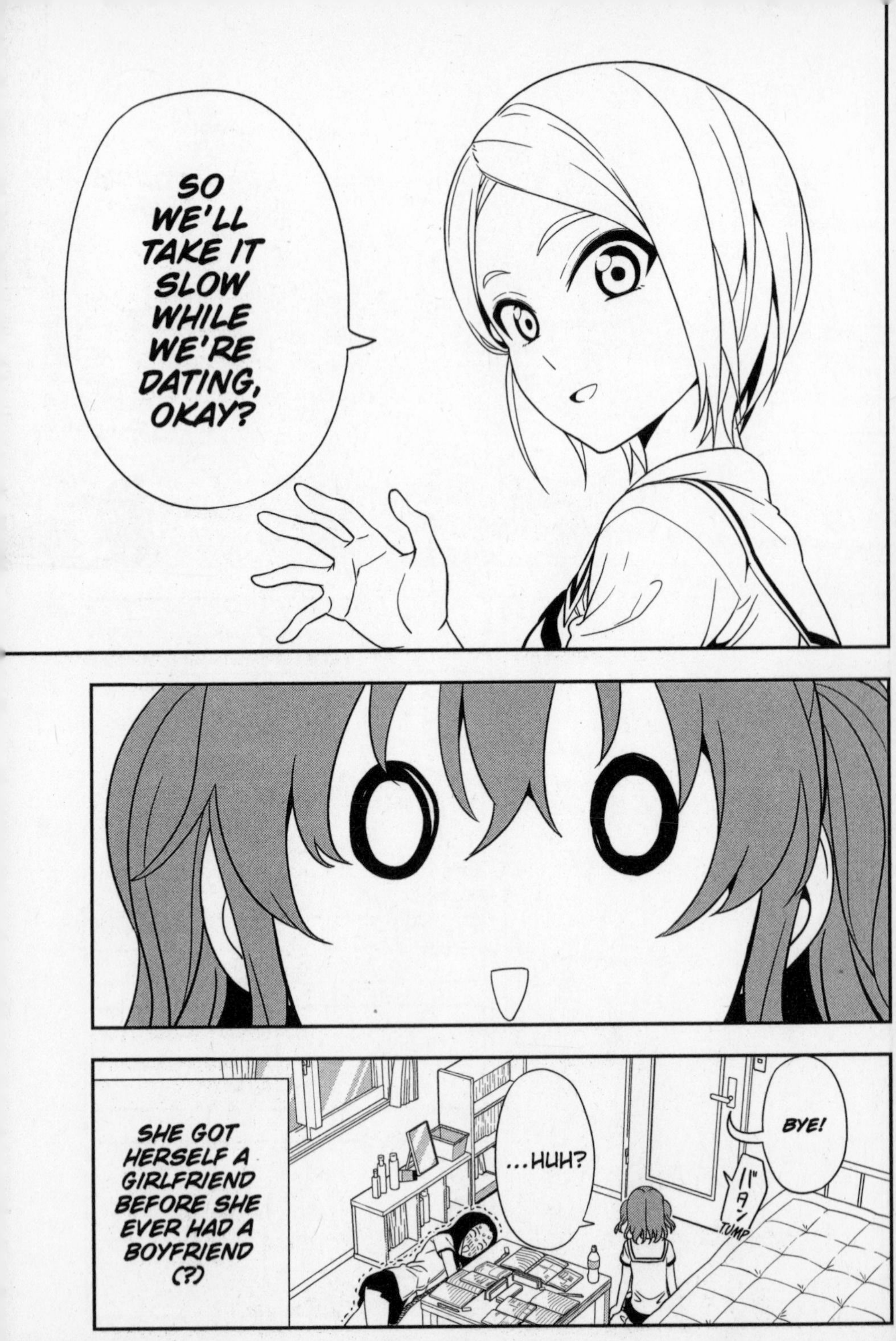
SO WE'LL TAKE IT SLOW WHILE WE'RE DATING, OKAY?
BYE!
バタン
TUMP
...HUH?
SHE GOT HERSELF A GIRLFRIEND BEFORE SHE EVER HAD A BOYFRIEND (?)

I Got No Clue What to Do Next

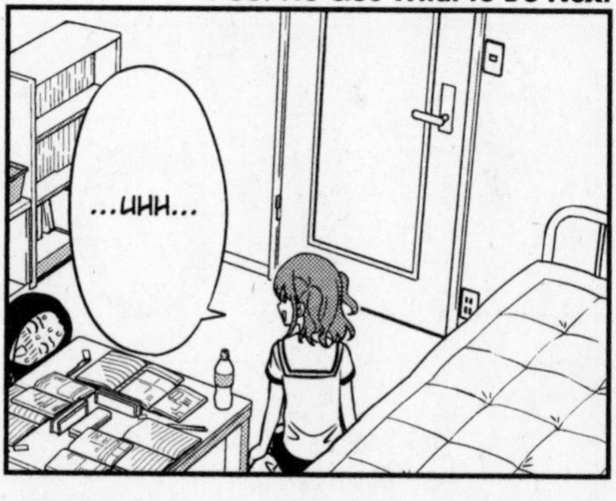
...UHH...

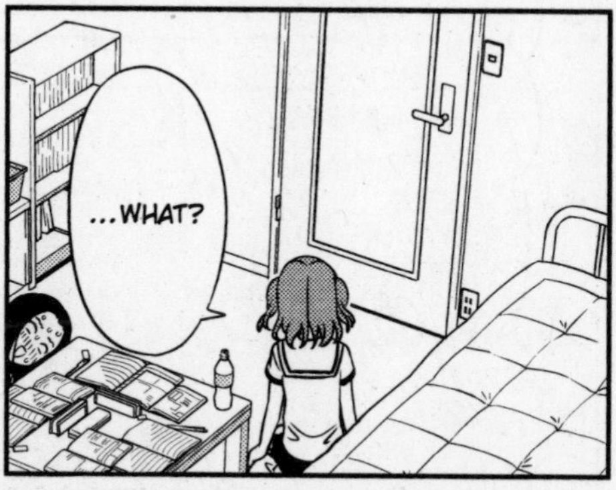
...WHAT?

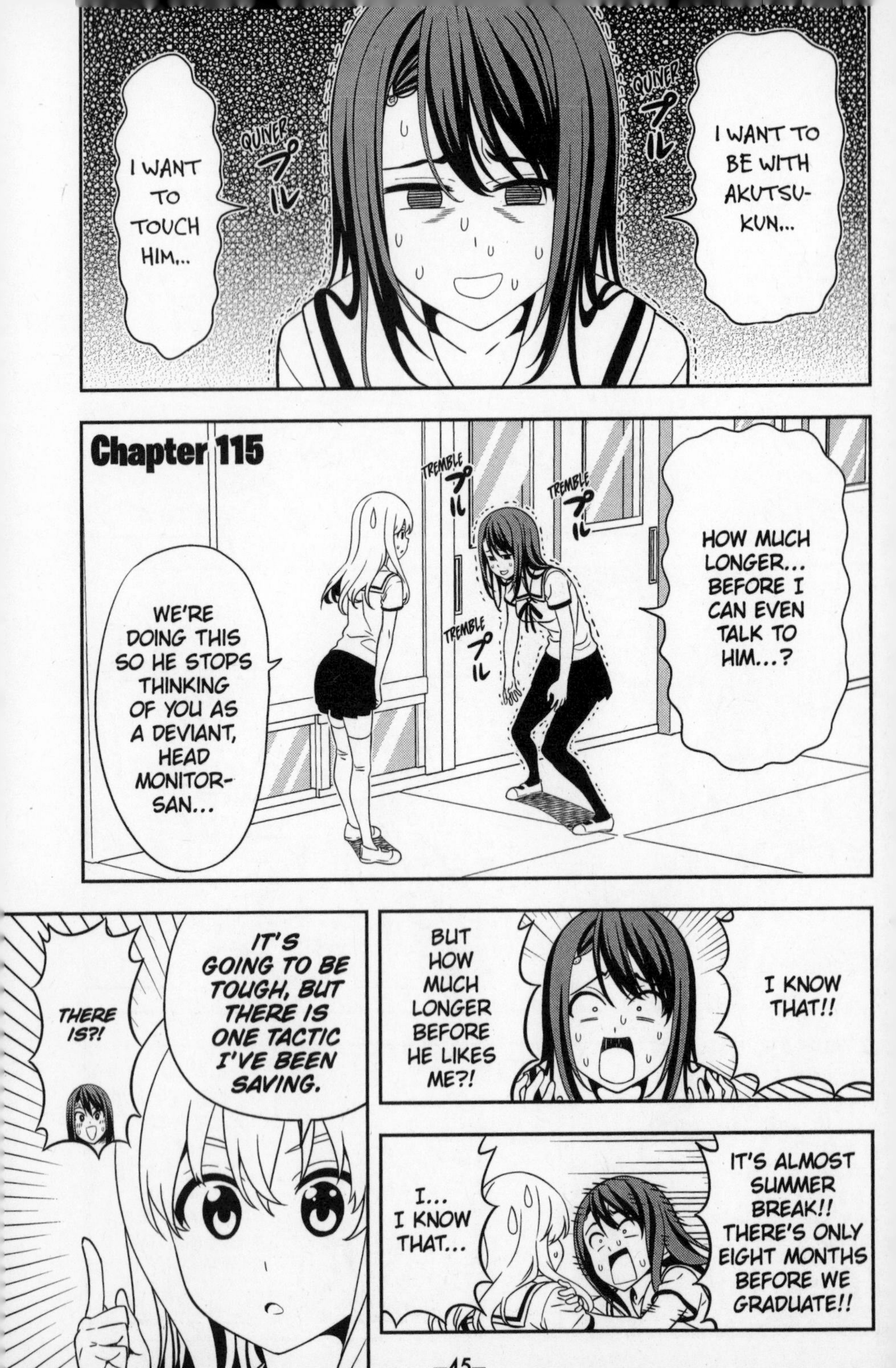
I WANT TO BE WITH AKUTSU-KUN...
QUIVER
プル
QUIVER
プル
I WANT TO TOUCH HIM...
HOW MUCH LONGER... BEFORE I CAN EVEN TALK TO HIM...?
TREMBLE
プル
TREMBLE
プル
TREMBLE
プル
Chapter 115
WE'RE DOING THIS SO HE STOPS THINKING OF YOU AS A DEVIANT, HEAD MONITOR-SAN...
I KNOW THAT!!
BUT HOW MUCH LONGER BEFORE HE LIKES ME?!
IT'S ALMOST SUMMER BREAK!! THERE'S ONLY EIGHT MONTHS BEFORE WE GRADUATE!!
I... I KNOW THAT...
IT'S GOING TO BE TOUGH, BUT THERE IS ONE TACTIC I'VE BEEN SAVING.
THERE IS?!

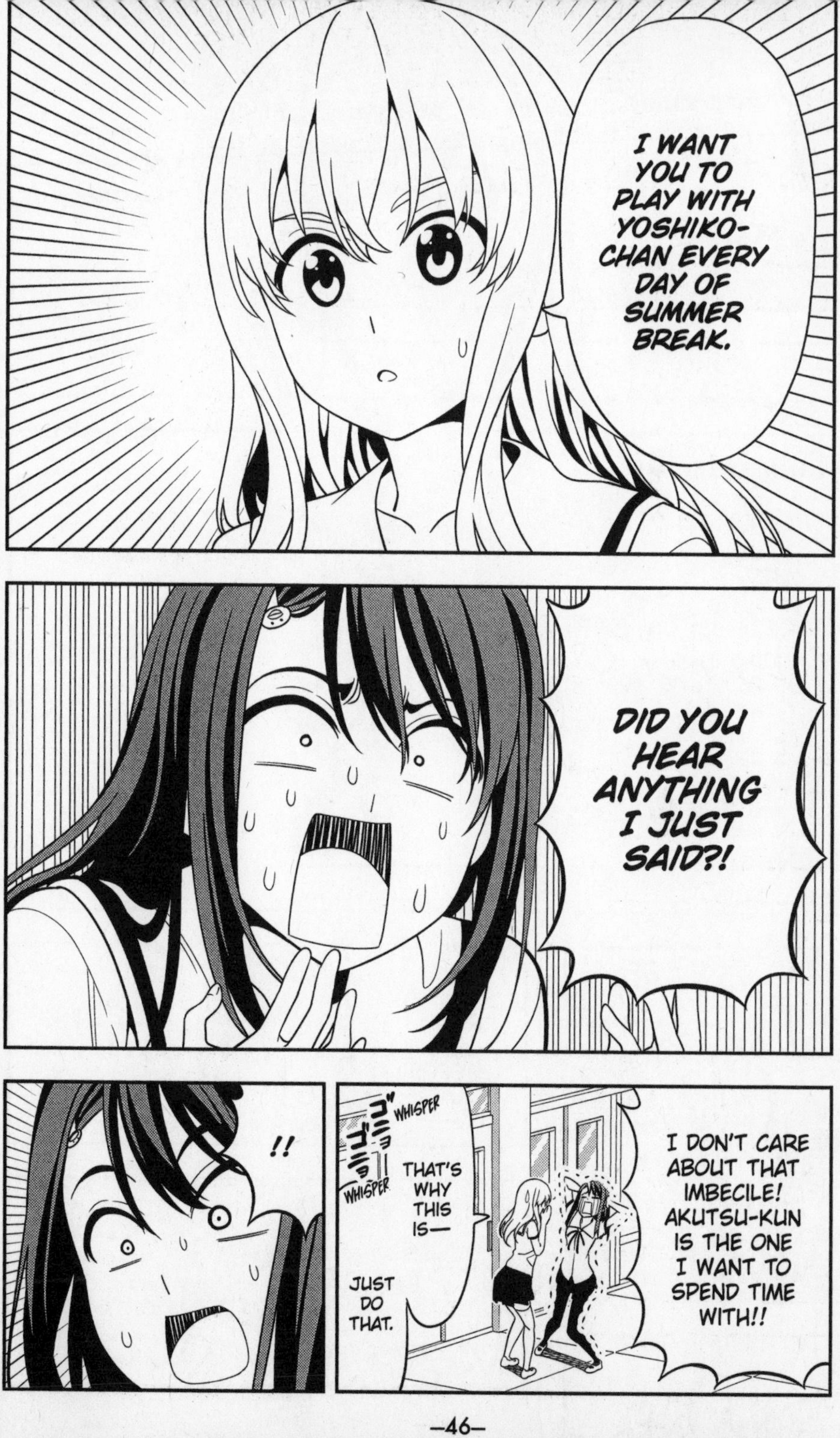
I WANT YOU TO PLAY WITH YOSHIKO-CHAN EVERY DAY OF SUMMER BREAK.
DID YOU HEAR ANYTHING I JUST SAID?!
I DON'T CARE ABOUT THAT IMBECILE! AKUTSU-KUN IS THE ONE I WANT TO SPEND TIME WITH!!
WHISPER
WHISPER
THAT'S WHY THIS IS—
JUST DO THAT.
!!

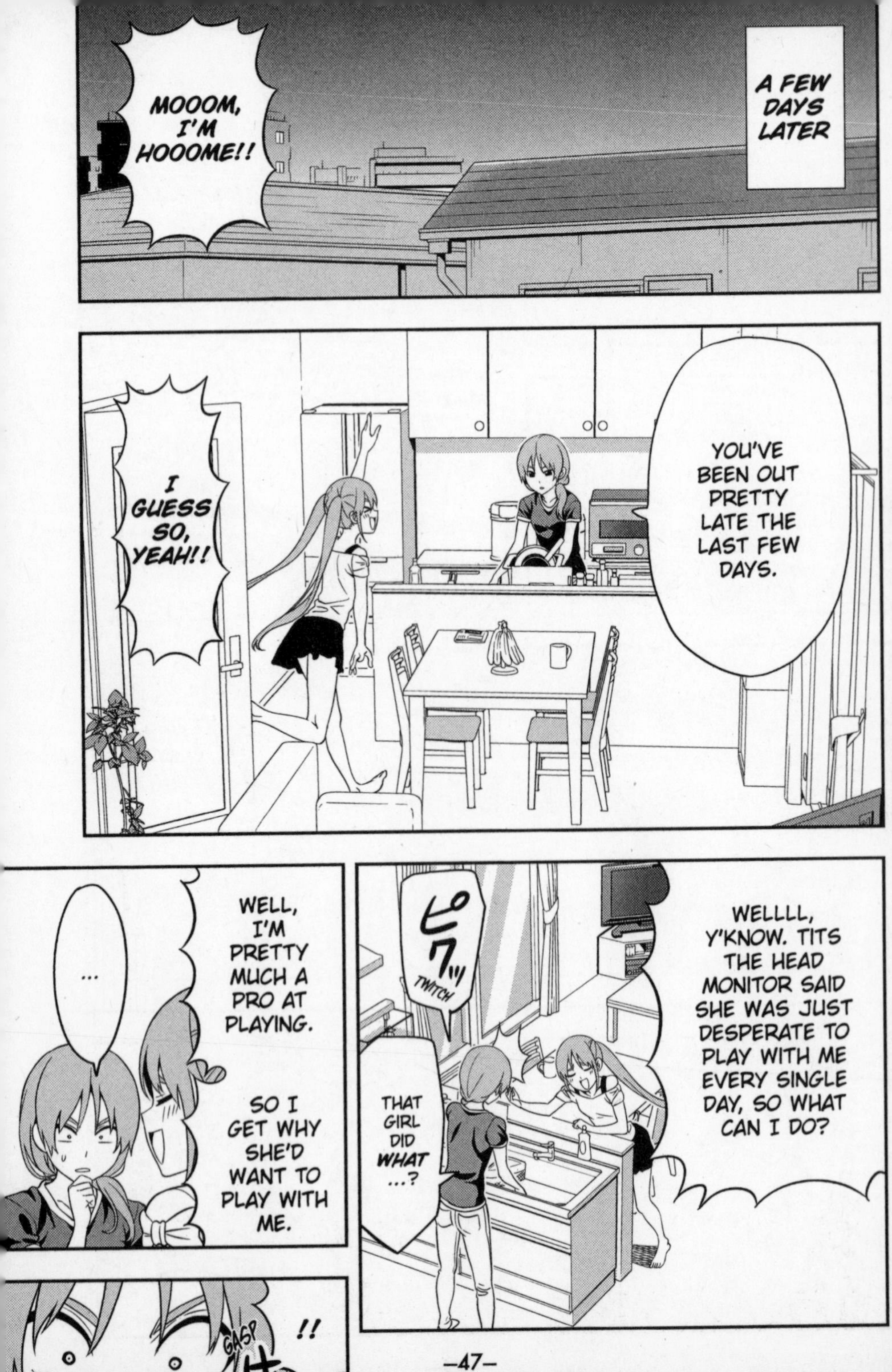
A FEW DAYS LATER
MOOOM, I'M HOOOME!!
YOU'VE BEEN OUT PRETTY LATE THE LAST FEW DAYS.
I GUESS SO, YEAH!!
WELLLL, Y'KNOW. TITS THE HEAD MONITOR SAID SHE WAS JUST DESPERATE TO PLAY WITH ME EVERY SINGLE DAY, SO WHAT CAN I DO?
ピクッ
TWITCH
THAT GIRL DID WHAT ...?
WELL, I'M PRETTY MUCH A PRO AT PLAYING.
SO I GET WHY SHE'D WANT TO PLAY WITH ME.
...
!!
GASP

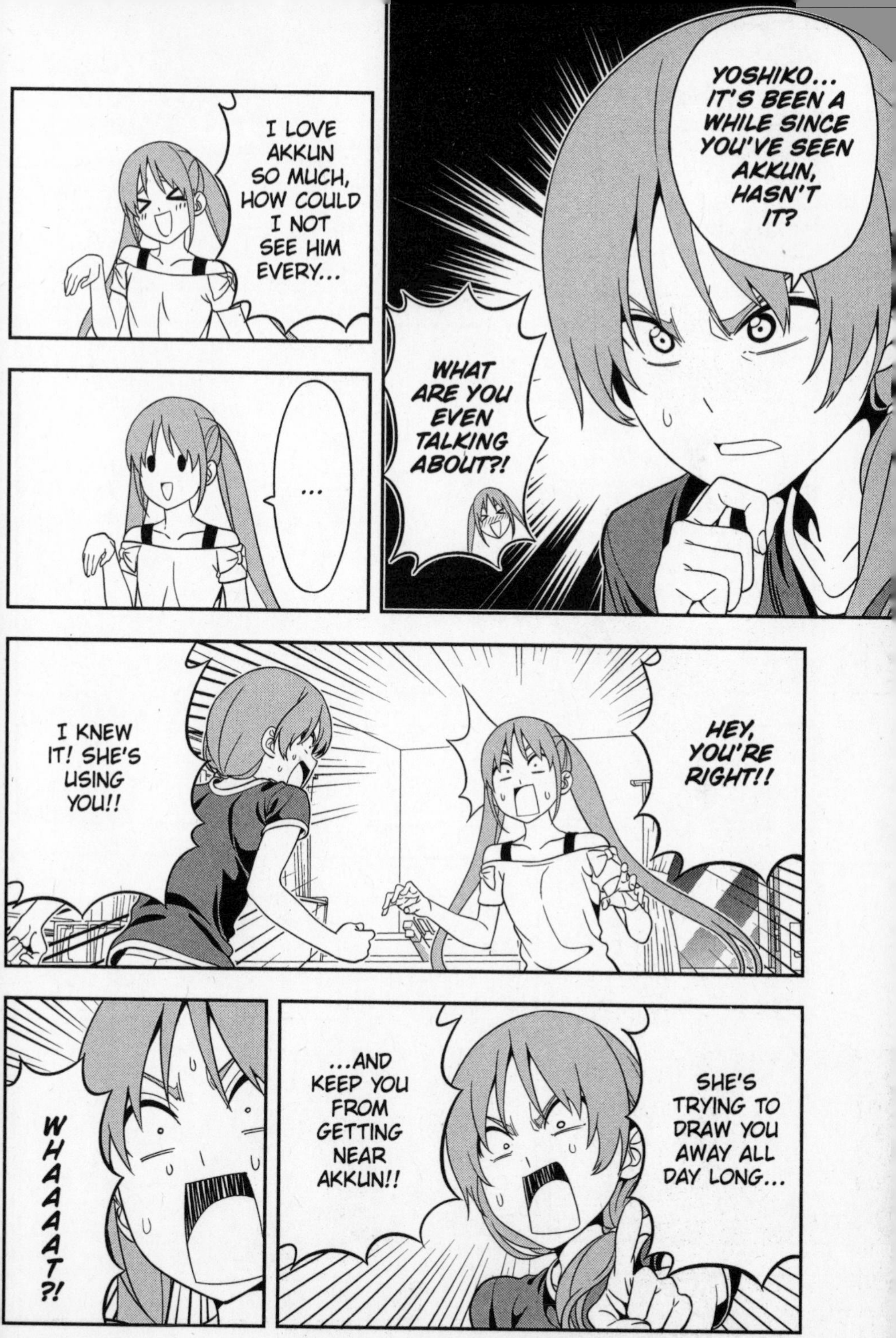
YOSHIKO... IT'S BEEN A WHILE SINCE YOU'VE SEEN AKKUN, HASN'T IT?
WHAT ARE YOU EVEN TALKING ABOUT?!
I LOVE AKKUN SO MUCH, HOW COULD I NOT SEE HIM EVERY...
...
HEY, YOU'RE RIGHT!!
I KNEW IT! SHE'S USING YOU!!
SHE'S TRYING TO DRAW YOU AWAY ALL DAY LONG...
...AND KEEP YOU FROM GETTING NEAR AKKUN!!
WHAAAAAT?!

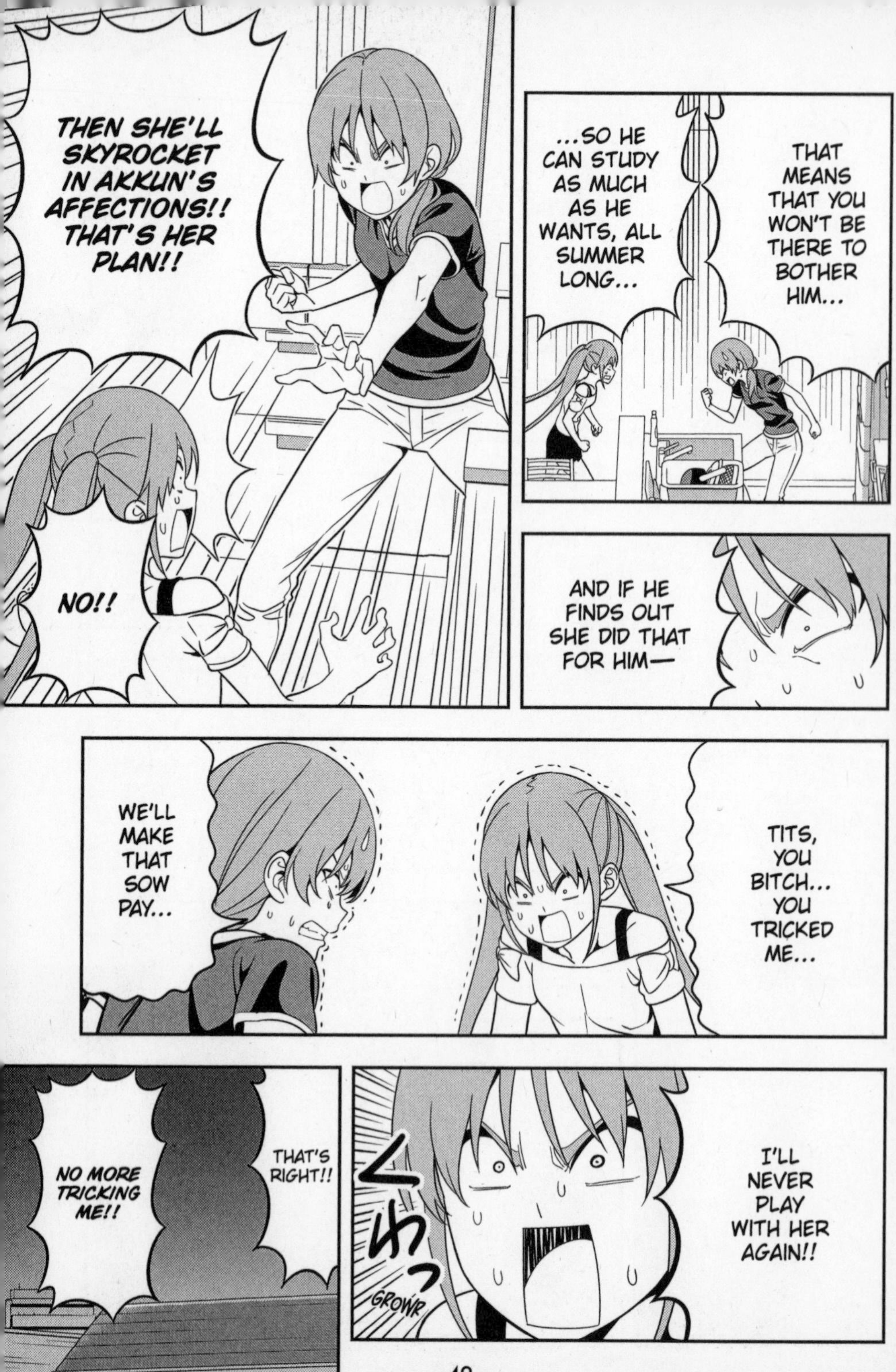
THAT MEANS THAT YOU WON'T BE THERE TO BOTHER HIM...
...SO HE CAN STUDY AS MUCH AS HE WANTS, ALL SUMMER LONG...
AND IF HE FINDS OUT SHE DID THAT FOR HIM—
THEN SHE'LL SKYROCKET IN AKKUN'S AFFECTIONS!! THAT'S HER PLAN!!
NO!!
TITS, YOU BITCH... YOU TRICKED ME...
WE'LL MAKE THAT SOW PAY...
I'LL NEVER PLAY WITH HER AGAIN!!
くわっ
GROWR
THAT'S RIGHT!!
NO MORE TRICKING ME!!

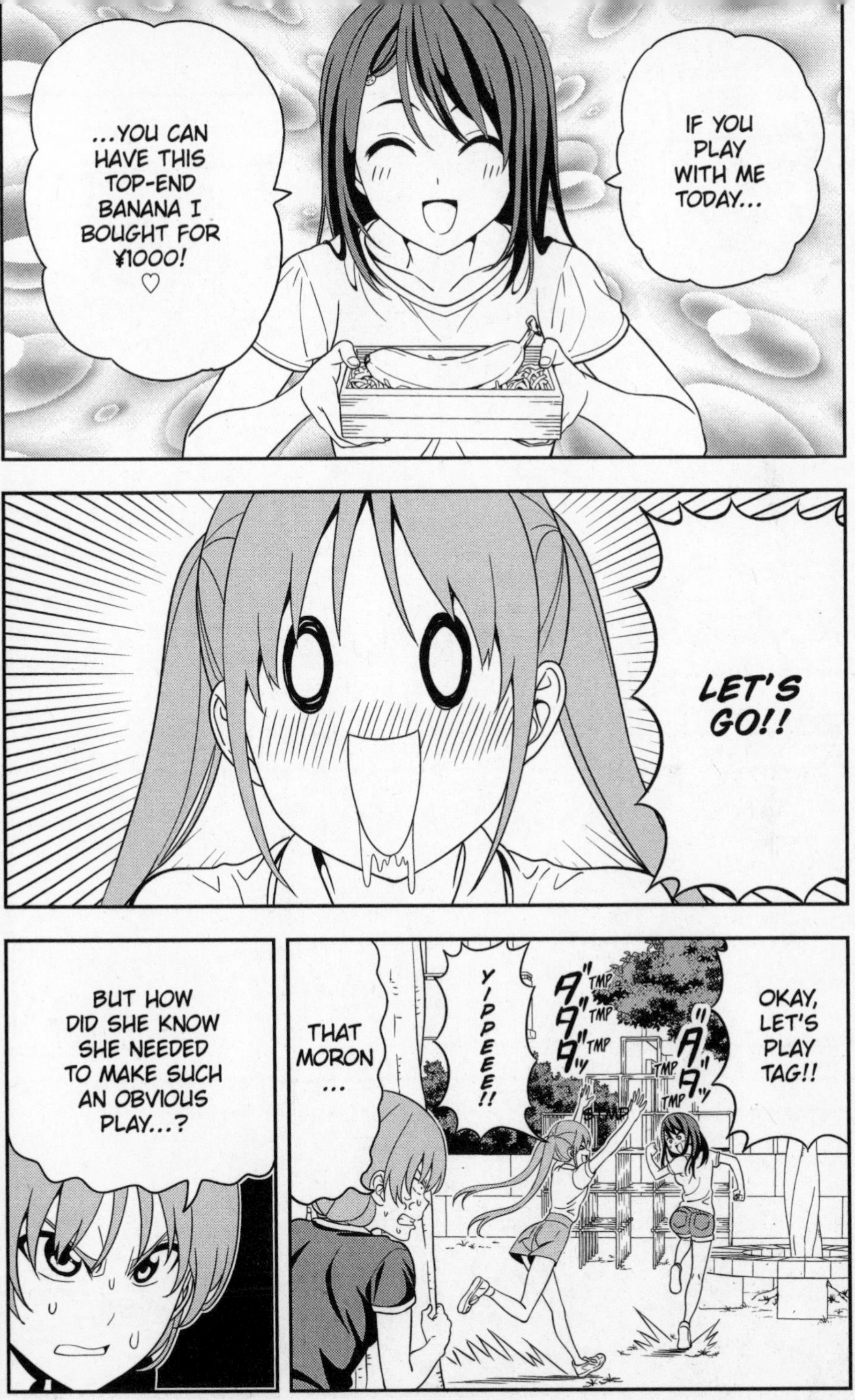
IF YOU PLAY WITH ME TODAY...
...YOU CAN HAVE THIS TOP-END BANANA I BOUGHT FOR ¥1000! ♡
LET'S GO!!
OKAY, LET'S PLAY TAG!!
TMP TMP
TMP TMP TMP
YIPPEEE!!
THAT MORON ...
BUT HOW DID SHE KNOW SHE NEEDED TO MAKE SUCH AN OBVIOUS PLAY...?

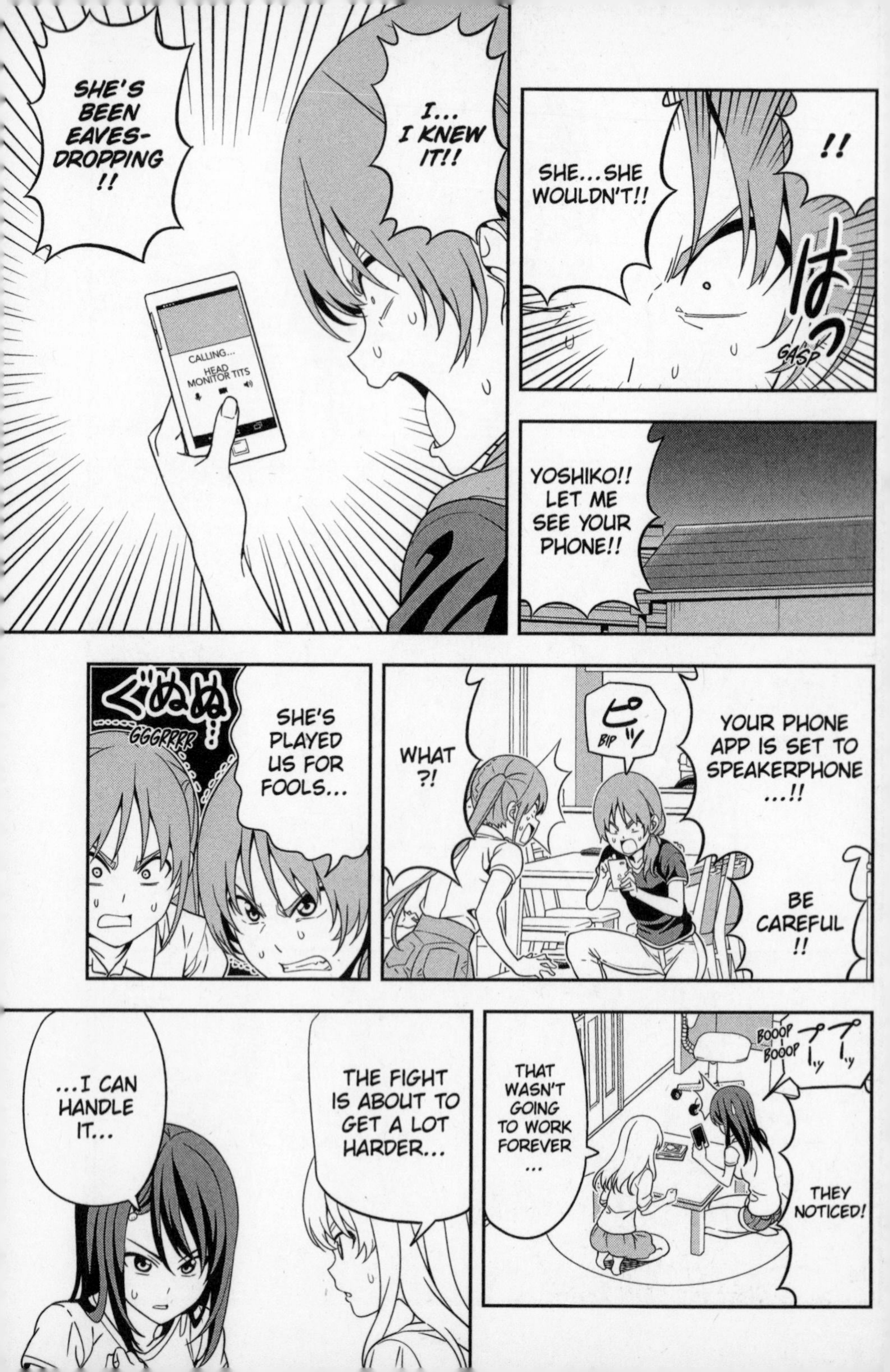
!!
はっ
GASP
SHE...SHE WOULDN'T!!
YOSHIKO!! LET ME SEE YOUR PHONE!!
I... I KNEW IT!!
SHE'S BEEN EAVES-DROPPING!!
CALLING...
HEAD MONITOR TITS
YOUR PHONE APP IS SET TO SPEAKERPHONE ...!!
BE CAREFUL!!
ピッ
BIP
WHAT?!
ぐぬぬ
GGGRRRR
SHE'S PLAYED US FOR FOOLS...
ププッ
BOOOP BOOOP
THEY NOTICED!
THAT WASN'T GOING TO WORK FOREVER...
THE FIGHT IS ABOUT TO GET A LOT HARDER...
...I CAN HANDLE IT...

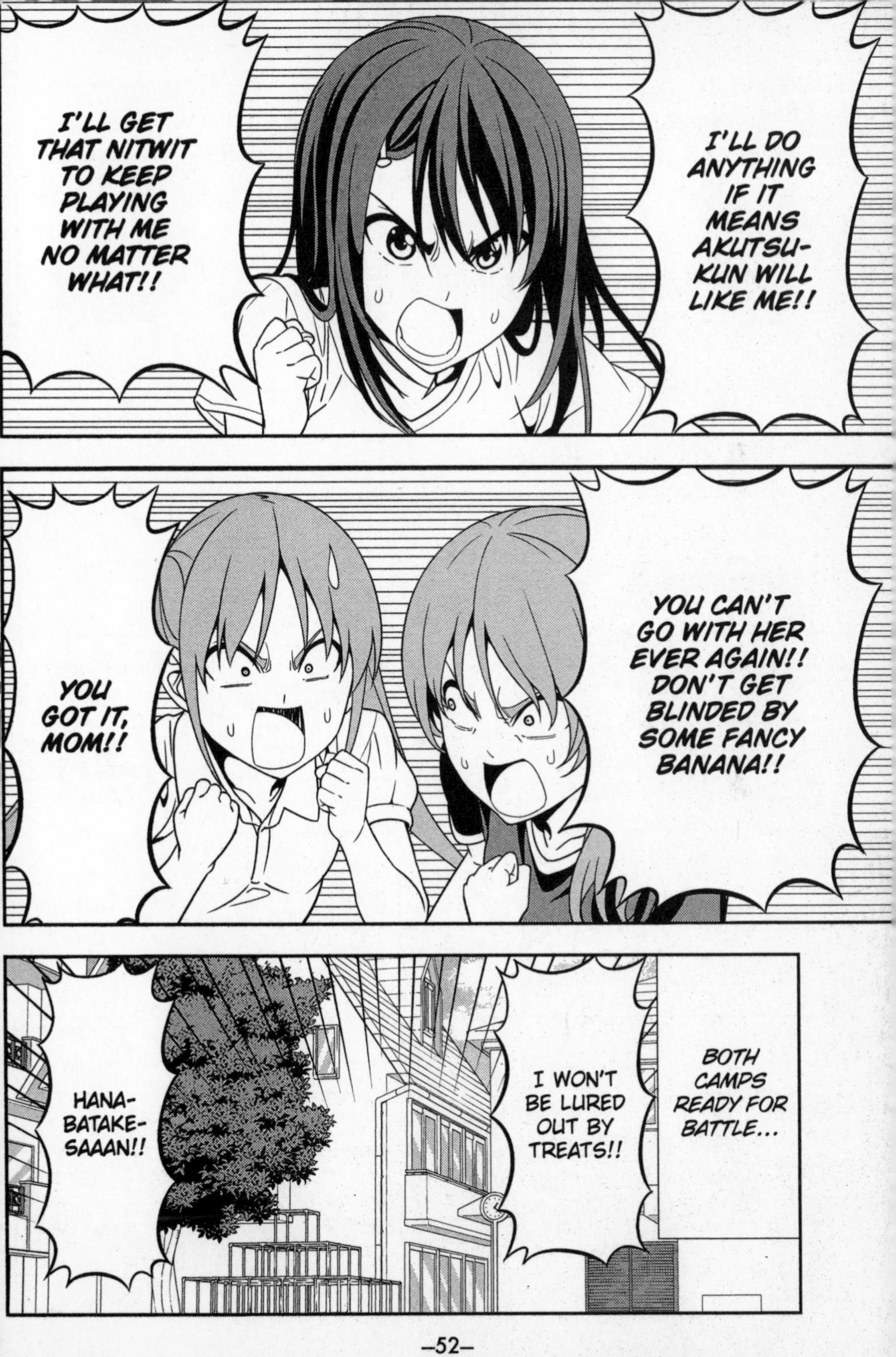
I'LL DO ANYTHING IF IT MEANS AKUTSU-KUN WILL LIKE ME!!
I'LL GET THAT NITWIT TO KEEP PLAYING WITH ME NO MATTER WHAT!!
YOU CAN'T GO WITH HER EVER AGAIN!! DON'T GET BLINDED BY SOME FANCY BANANA!!
YOU GOT IT, MOM!!
BOTH CAMPS READY FOR BATTLE...
I WON'T BE LURED OUT BY TREATS!!
HANA-BATAKE-SAAAN!!

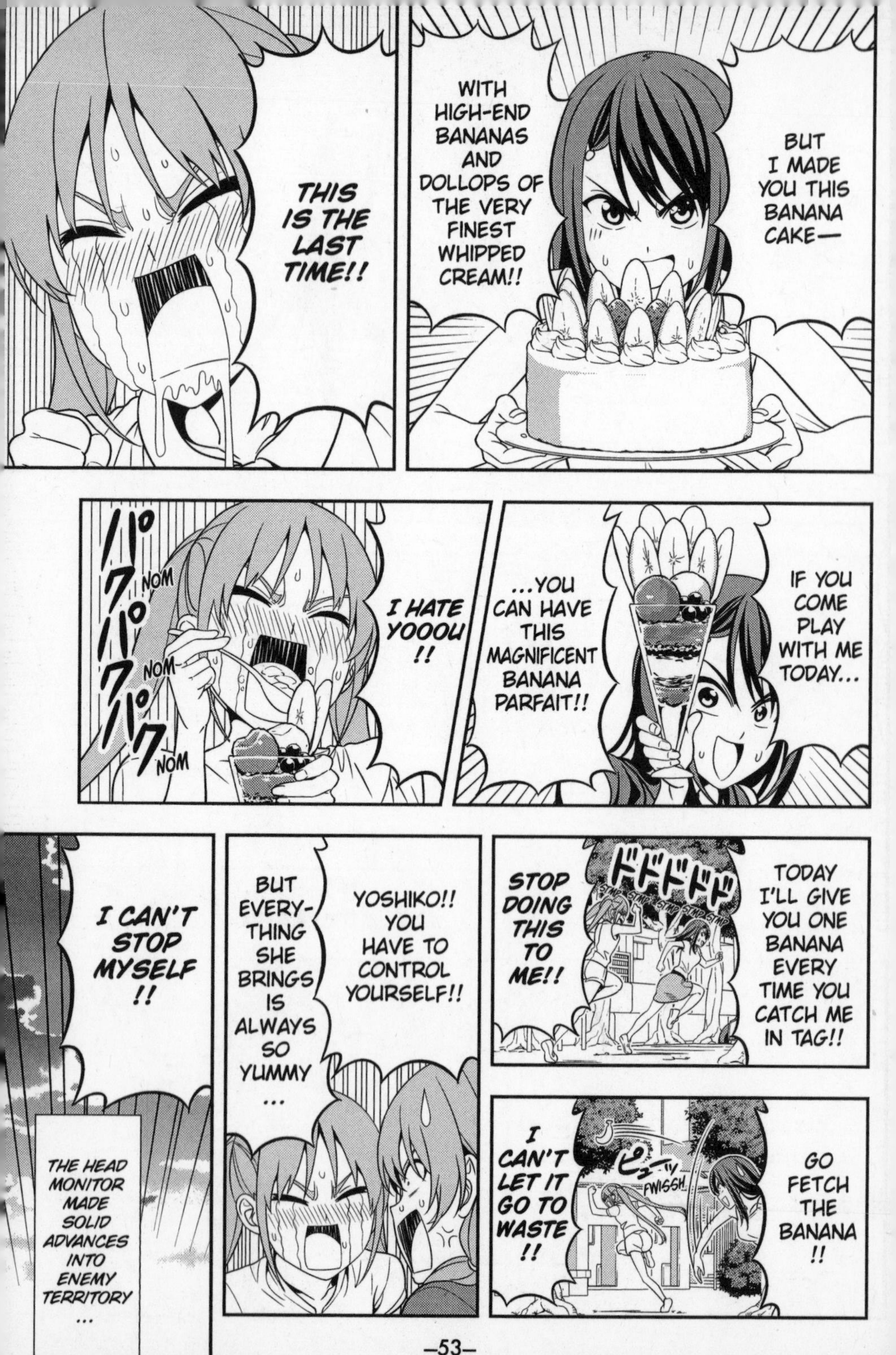
BUT I MADE YOU THIS BANANA CAKE—
WITH HIGH-END BANANAS AND DOLLOPS OF THE VERY FINEST WHIPPED CREAM!!
THIS IS THE LAST TIME!!
IF YOU COME PLAY WITH ME TODAY...
...YOU CAN HAVE THIS MAGNIFICENT BANANA PARFAIT!!
I HATE YOOOU!!
パクパクパク
NOM NOM NOM
TODAY I'LL GIVE YOU ONE BANANA EVERY TIME YOU CATCH ME IN TAG!!
ドドドドド
STMP STMP STMP STMP STMP
STOP DOING THIS TO ME!!
GO FETCH THE BANANA!!
ピューッ
FWISSH
I CAN'T LET IT GO TO WASTE!!
YOSHIKO!! YOU HAVE TO CONTROL YOURSELF!!
BUT EVERYTHING SHE BRINGS IS ALWAYS SO YUMMY...
I CAN'T STOP MYSELF!!
THE HEAD MONITOR MADE SOLID ADVANCES INTO ENEMY TERRITORY...

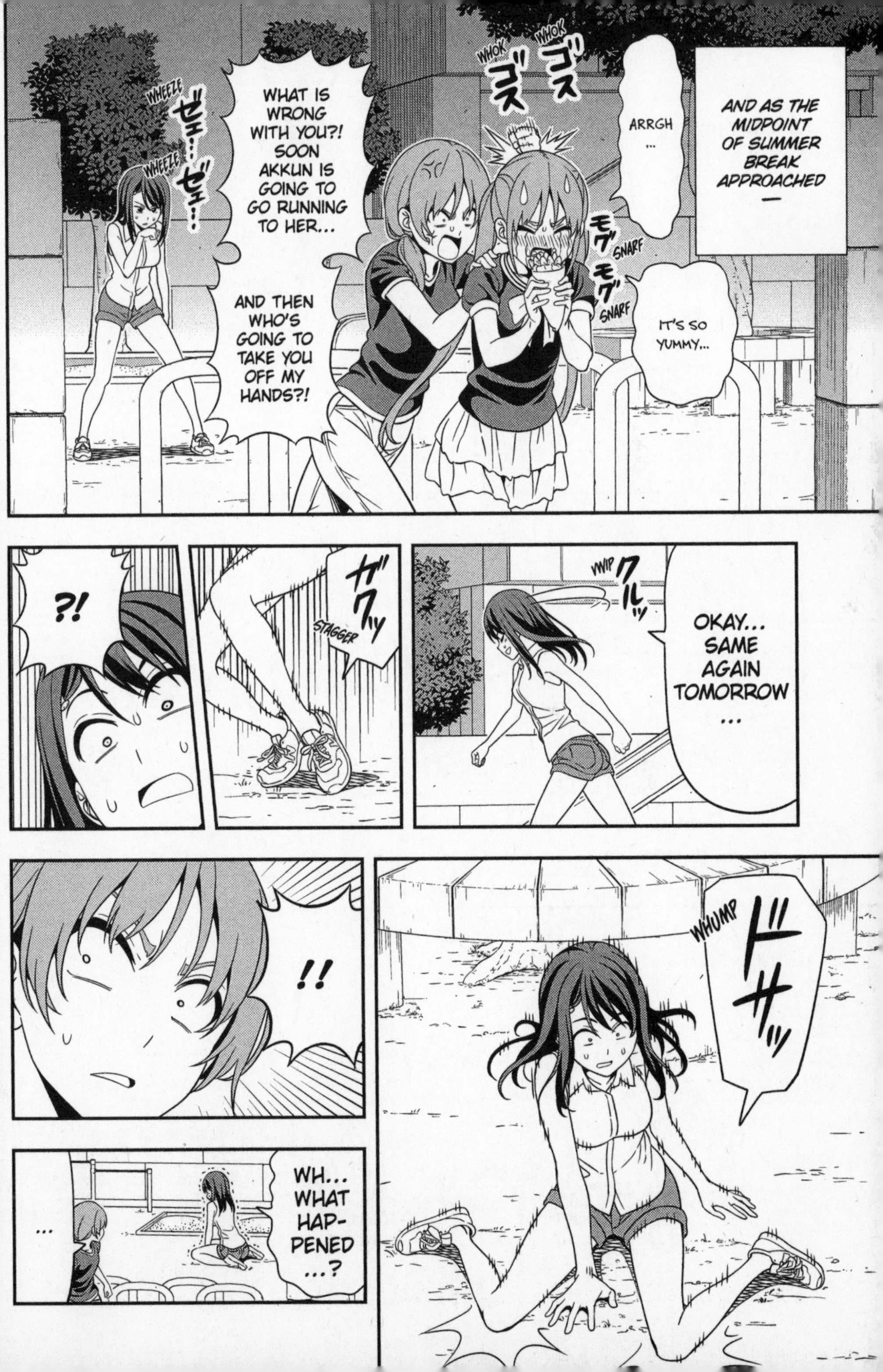
AND AS THE MIDPOINT OF SUMMER BREAK APPROACHED —
ARRGH ...
WHOK ゴス
WHOK ゴス
IT'S SO YUMMY...
SNARF モグ
SNARF モグ
WHAT IS WRONG WITH YOU?! SOON AKKUN IS GOING TO GO RUNNING TO HER...
AND THEN WHO'S GOING TO TAKE YOU OFF MY HANDS?!
WHEEZE ゼェ...
WHEEZE ゼェ...
OKAY... SAME AGAIN TOMORROW ...
VWIP クルッ
STAGGER ガクッ
?!
WHUMP ドサッ
!!
WH... WHAT HAP-PENED ...?
...

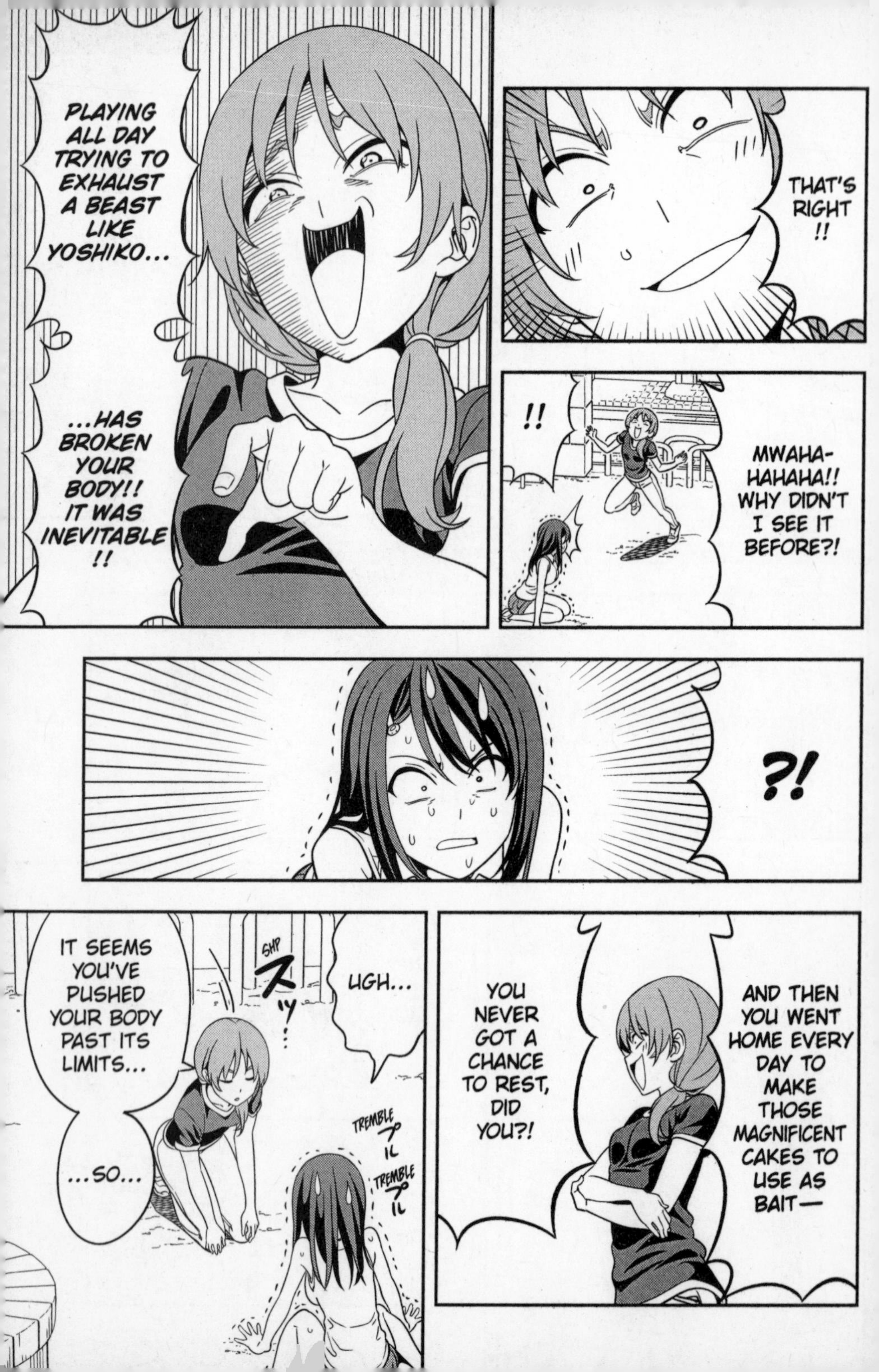
THAT'S RIGHT !!
MWAHA-HAHAHA!! WHY DIDN'T I SEE IT BEFORE?!
!!
PLAYING ALL DAY TRYING TO EXHAUST A BEAST LIKE YOSHIKO...
...HAS BROKEN YOUR BODY!! IT WAS INEVITABLE !!
?!
AND THEN YOU WENT HOME EVERY DAY TO MAKE THOSE MAGNIFICENT CAKES TO USE AS BAIT—
YOU NEVER GOT A CHANCE TO REST, DID YOU?!
UGH...
SHP
IT SEEMS YOU'VE PUSHED YOUR BODY PAST ITS LIMITS...
TREMBLE
TREMBLE
...SO...

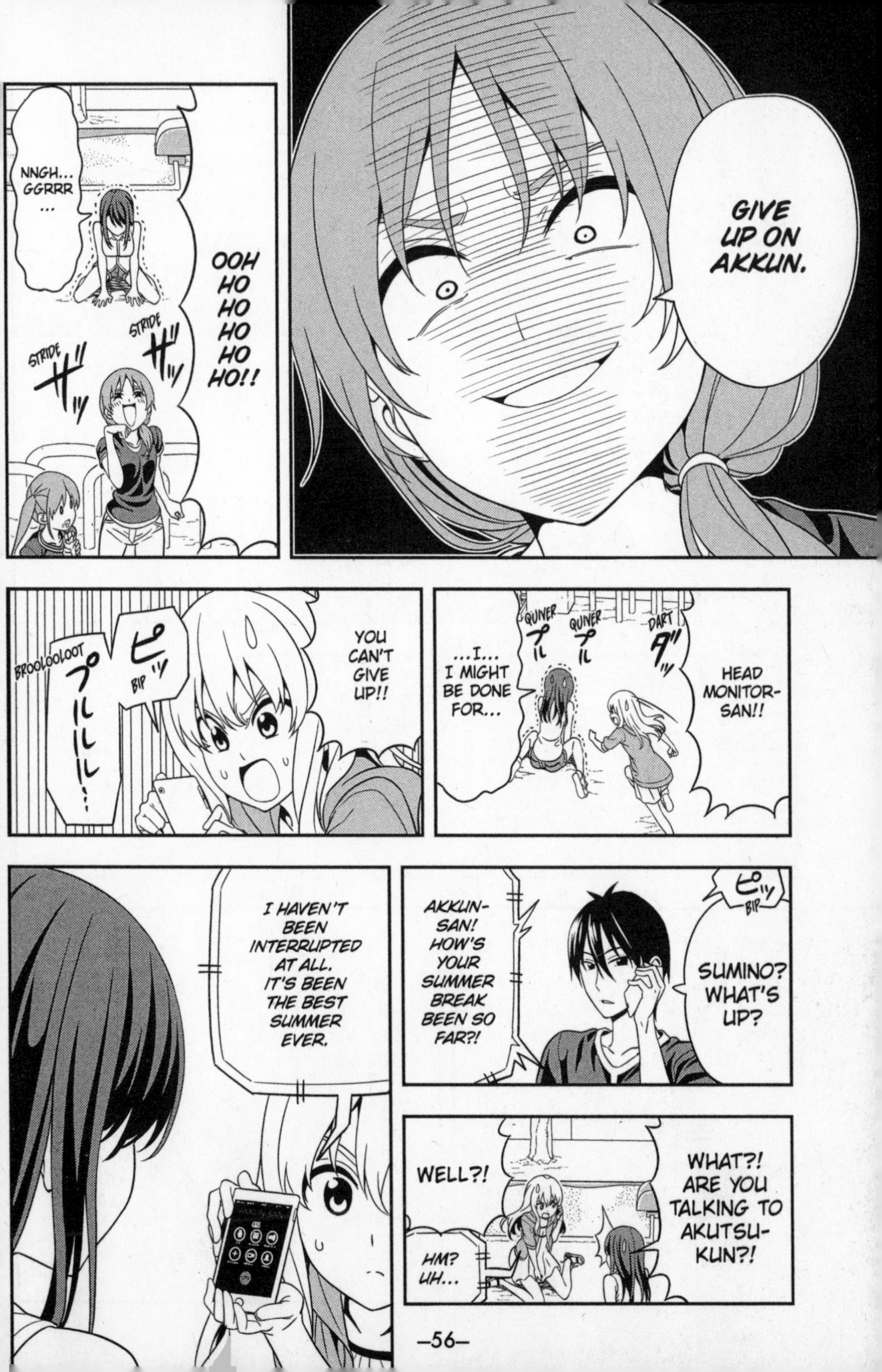
GIVE UP ON AKKUN.
NNGH... GGRRR ...
OOH HO HO HO HO HO HO!!
STRIDE
STRIDE
HEAD MONITOR-SAN!!
DART
QUIVER
QUIVER
...I... I MIGHT BE DONE FOR...
YOU CAN'T GIVE UP!!
BIP
BROOLOOLOOT
BIP
SUMINO? WHAT'S UP?
AKKUN-SAN! HOW'S YOUR SUMMER BREAK BEEN SO FAR?!
WHAT?! ARE YOU TALKING TO AKUTSU-KUN?!
WELL?!
HM? UH...
I HAVEN'T BEEN INTERRUPTED AT ALL. IT'S BEEN THE BEST SUMMER EVER.

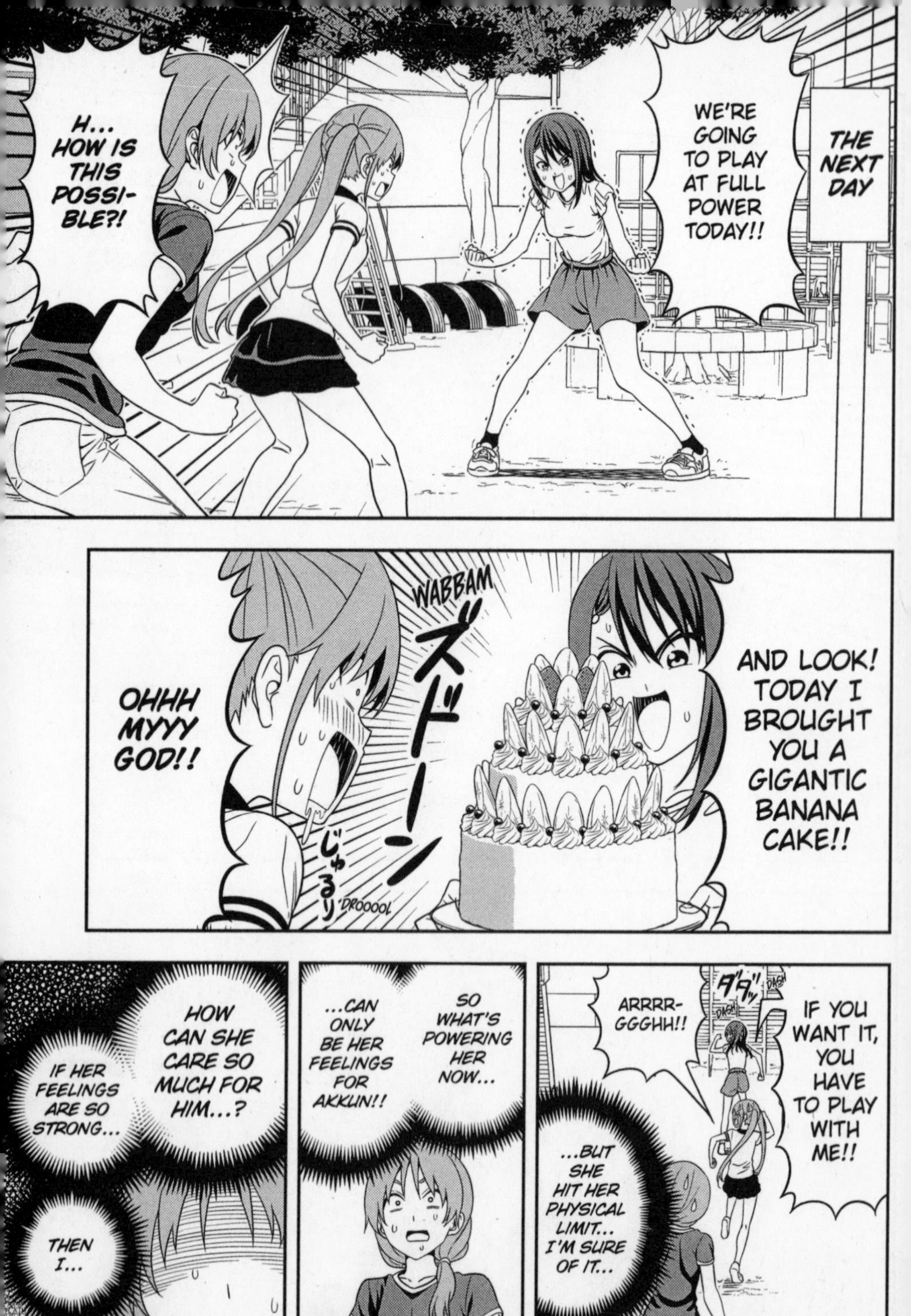
THE NEXT DAY
WE'RE GOING TO PLAY AT FULL POWER TODAY!!
H... HOW IS THIS POSSI-BLE?!
AND LOOK! TODAY I BROUGHT YOU A GIGANTIC BANANA CAKE!!
ズドーン
WABBAM
OHHH MYYY GOD!!
じゅるり
DROOOOL
IF YOU WANT IT, YOU HAVE TO PLAY WITH ME!!
ダダッ
DASH
DASH
ARRRR-GGGHH!!
...BUT SHE HIT HER PHYSICAL LIMIT... I'M SURE OF IT...
SO WHAT'S POWERING HER NOW...
...CAN ONLY BE HER FEELINGS FOR AKKUN!!
HOW CAN SHE CARE SO MUCH FOR HIM...?
IF HER FEELINGS ARE SO STRONG...
THEN I...

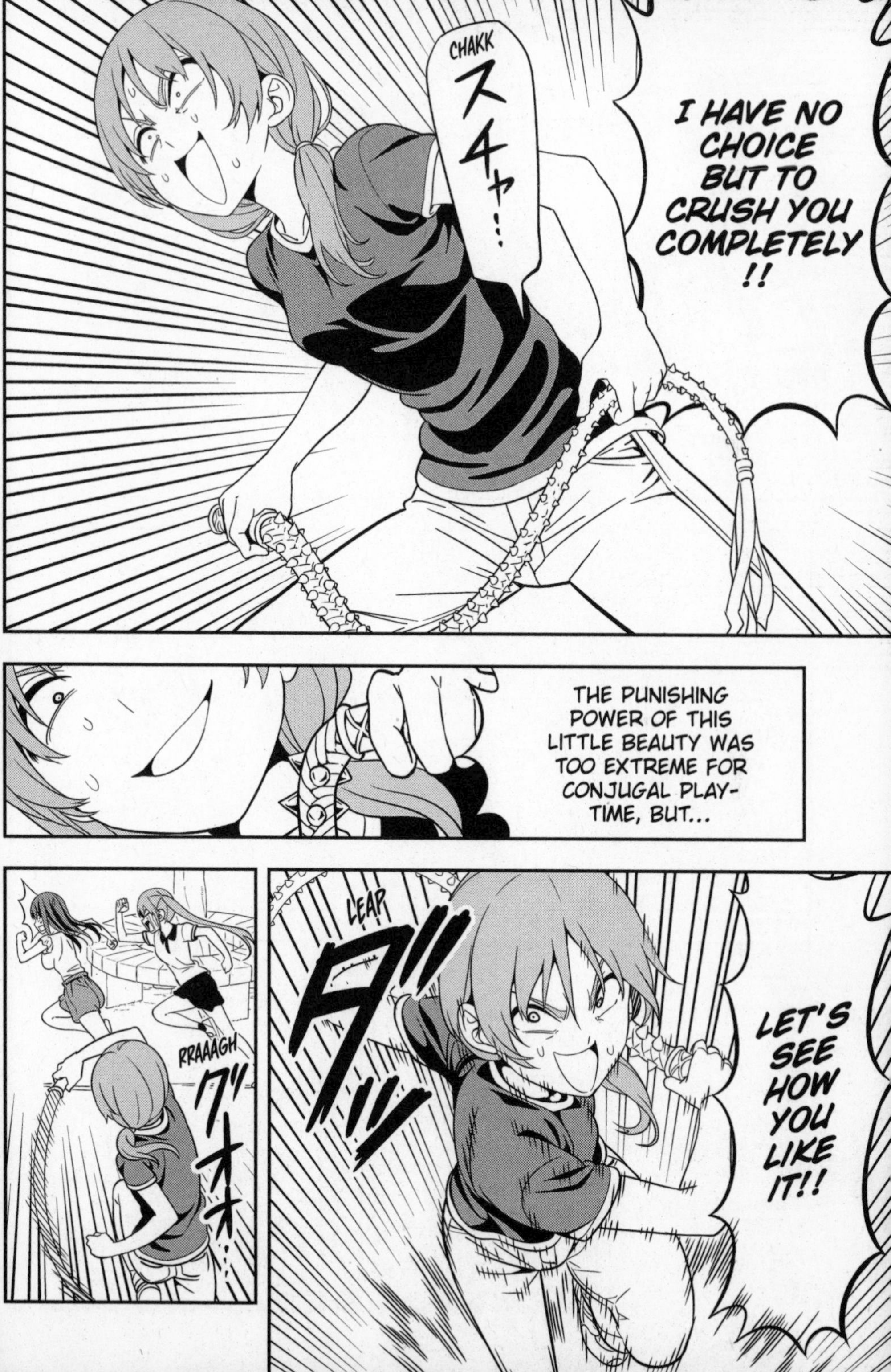
I HAVE NO CHOICE BUT TO CRUSH YOU COMPLETELY!!
CHAKK
スチャ…
THE PUNISHING POWER OF THIS LITTLE BEAUTY WAS TOO EXTREME FOR CONJUGAL PLAY-TIME, BUT...
LET'S SEE HOW YOU LIKE IT!!
LEAP
ダッ
RRAAAGH
グオオ…

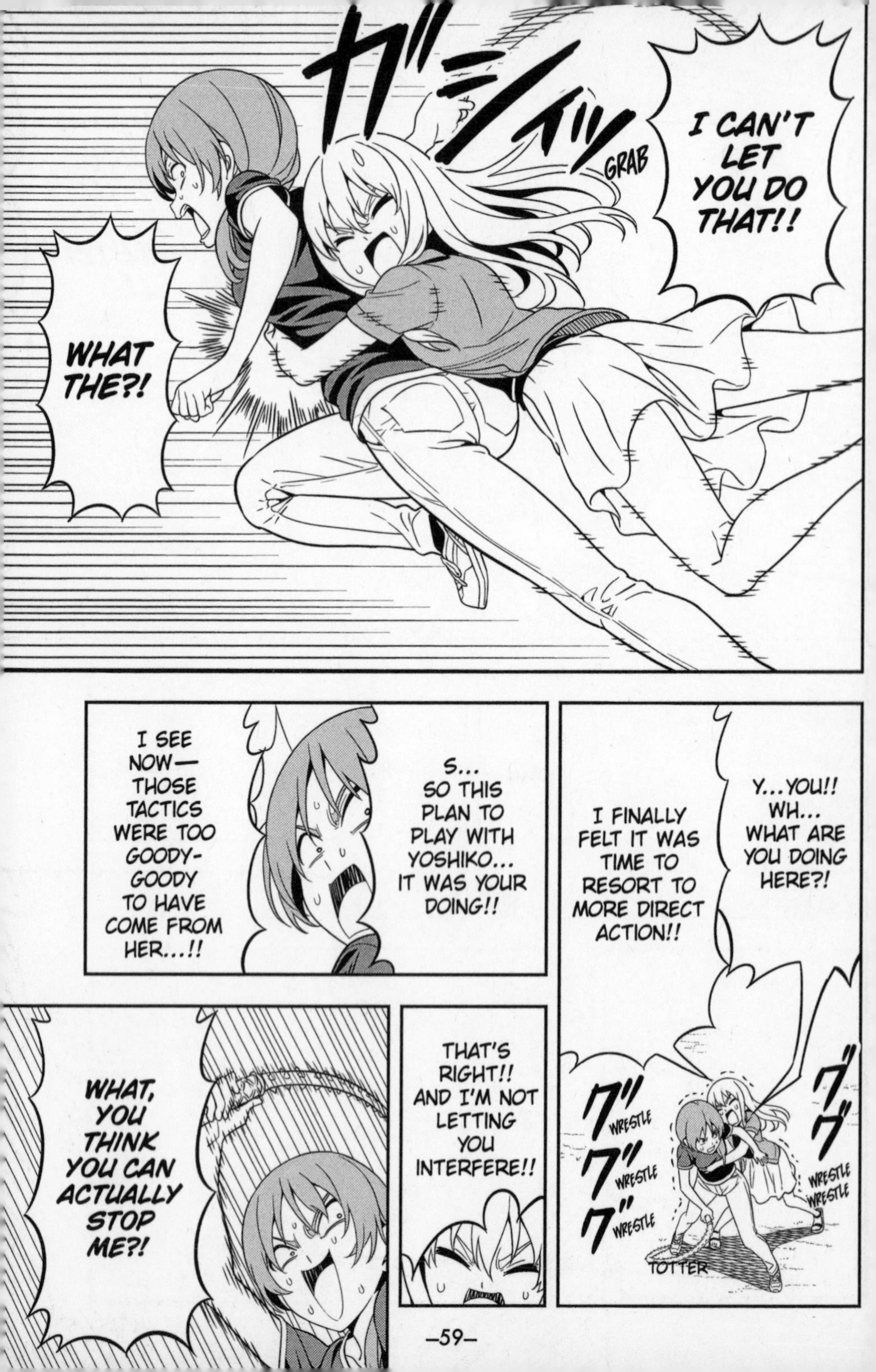
GRAB
I CAN'T LET YOU DO THAT!!
WHAT THE?!
Y...YOU!! WH... WHAT ARE YOU DOING HERE?!
I FINALLY FELT IT WAS TIME TO RESORT TO MORE DIRECT ACTION!!
WRESTLE WRESTLE
WRESTLE
WRESTLE
WRESTLE
TOTTER
S... SO THIS PLAN TO PLAY WITH YOSHIKO... IT WAS YOUR DOING!!
I SEE NOW— THOSE TACTICS WERE TOO GOODY-GOODY TO HAVE COME FROM HER...!!
THAT'S RIGHT!! AND I'M NOT LETTING YOU INTERFERE!!
WHAT, YOU THINK YOU CAN ACTUALLY STOP ME?!

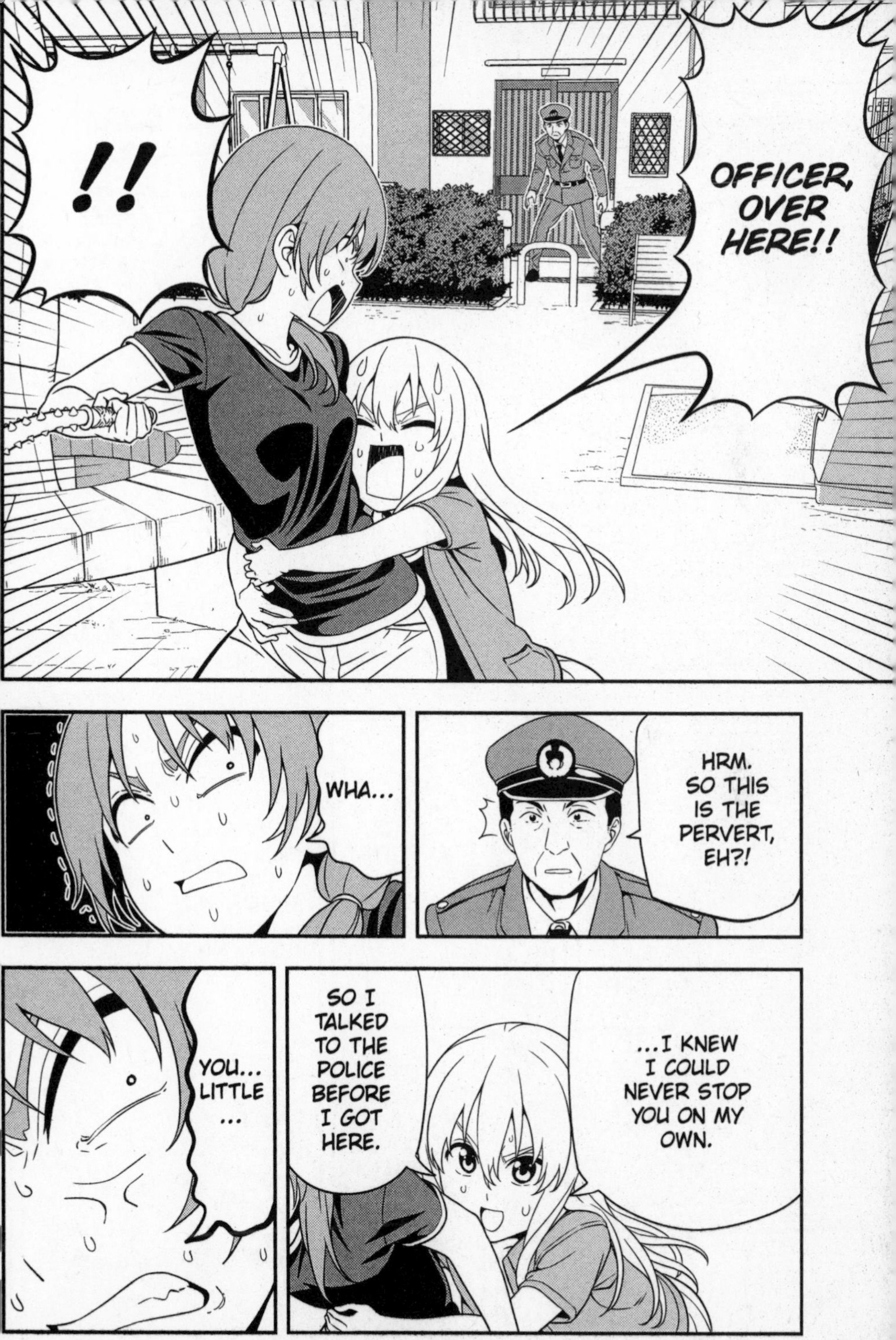
OFFICER, OVER HERE!!
!!
HRM. SO THIS IS THE PERVERT, EH?!
WHA...
...I KNEW I COULD NEVER STOP YOU ON MY OWN.
SO I TALKED TO THE POLICE BEFORE I GOT HERE.
YOU... LITTLE ...

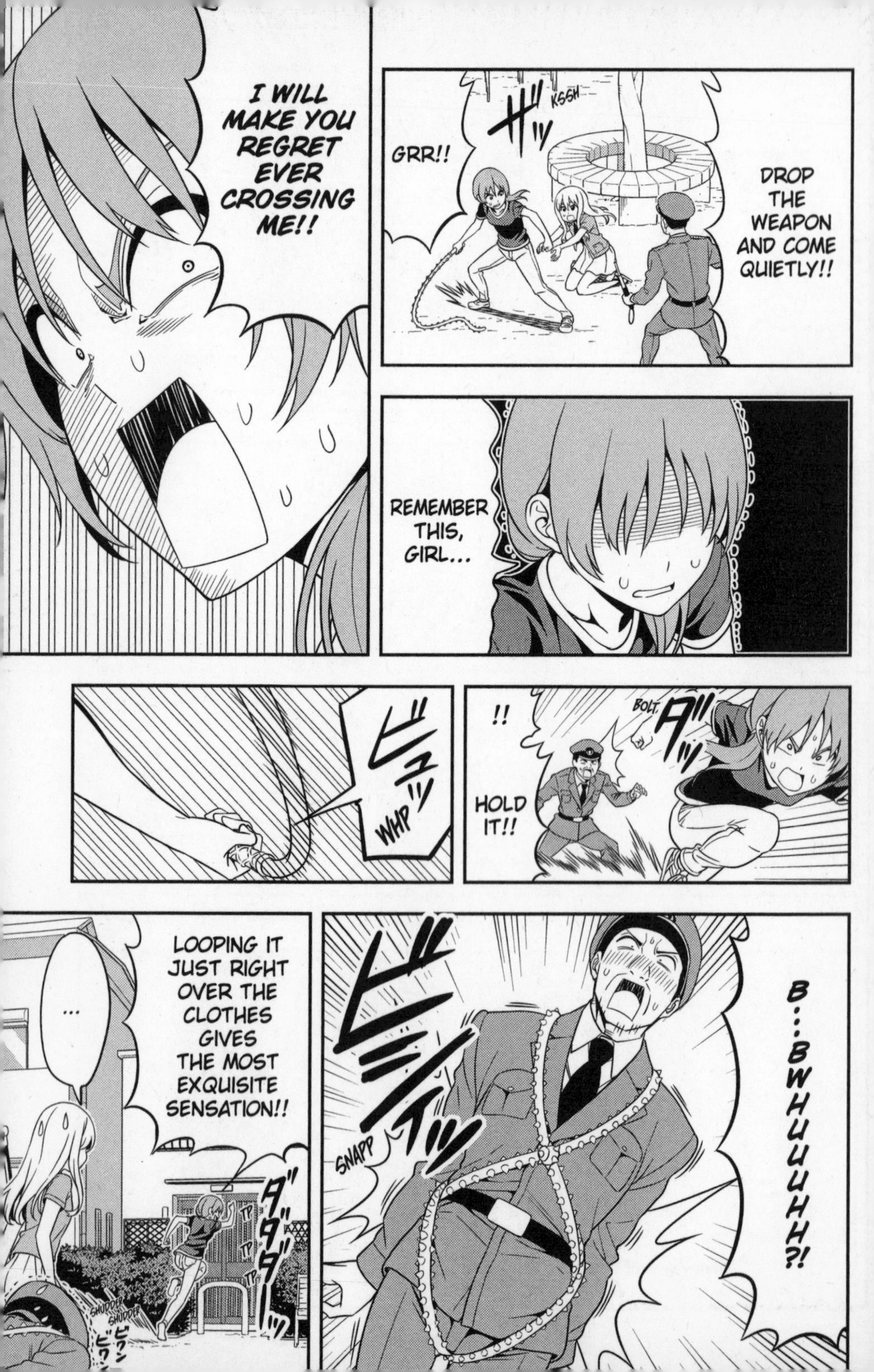

DROP THE WEAPON AND COME QUIETLY!!
KSSH
GRR!!
REMEMBER THIS, GIRL...
I WILL MAKE YOU REGRET EVER CROSSING ME!!
BOLT
!!
HOLD IT!!
WHP
B...BWHUUUUHH?!
SNAPP
LOOPING IT JUST RIGHT OVER THE CLOTHES GIVES THE MOST EXQUISITE SENSATION!!
...
TP TP TP
SHUDDER SHUDDER

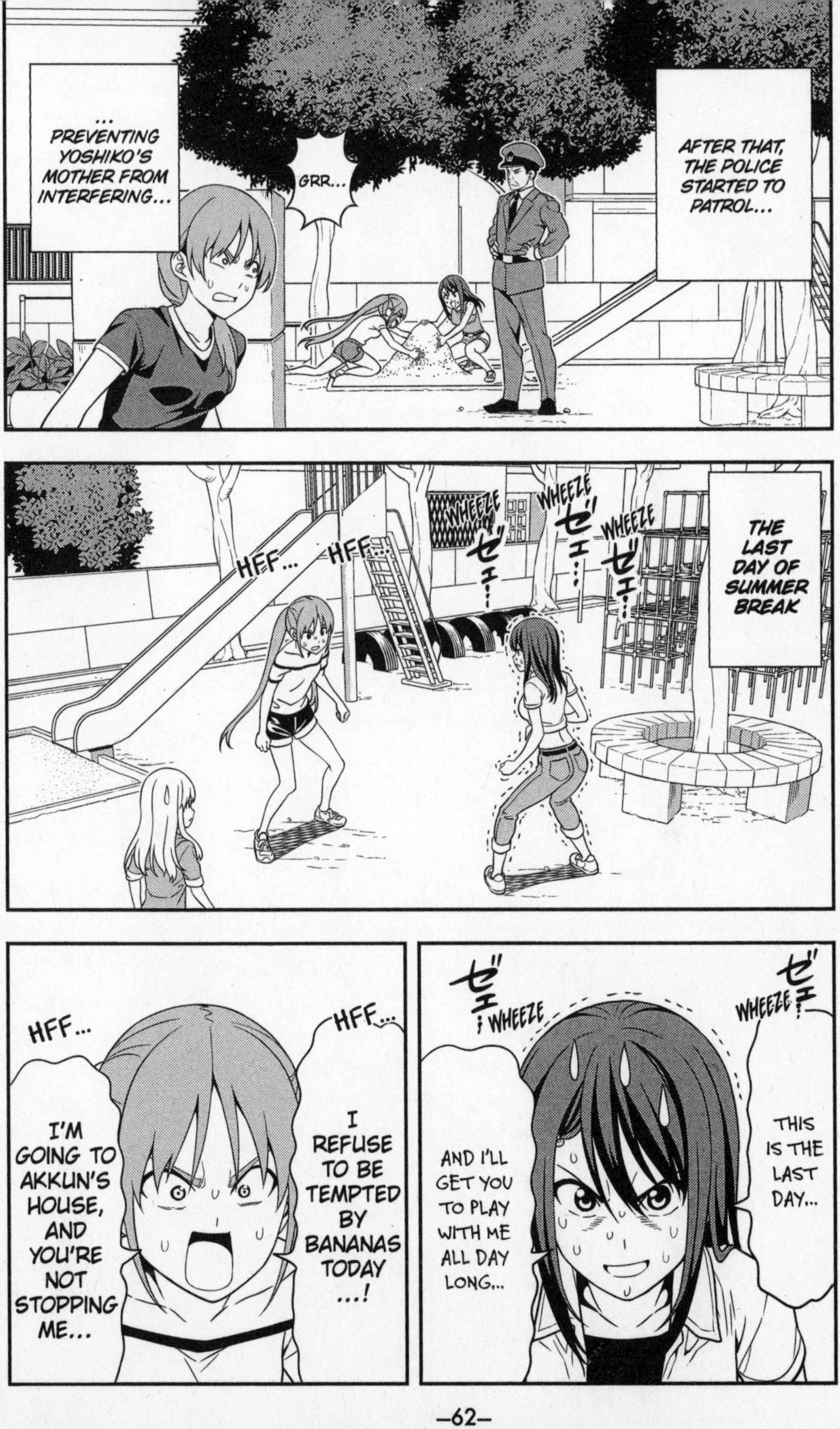
AFTER THAT, THE POLICE STARTED TO PATROL...
GRR...
...PREVENTING YOSHIKO'S MOTHER FROM INTERFERING...
THE LAST DAY OF SUMMER BREAK
WHEEZE ゼェ...
WHEEZE ゼェ...
WHEEZE ゼェ...
HFF... HFF...
HFF...
ゼェ WHEEZE
ゼェ WHEEZE
THIS IS THE LAST DAY...
AND I'LL GET YOU TO PLAY WITH ME ALL DAY LONG...
HFF...
HFF...
I REFUSE TO BE TEMPTED BY BANANAS TODAY ...!
I'M GOING TO AKKUN'S HOUSE, AND YOU'RE NOT STOPPING ME...

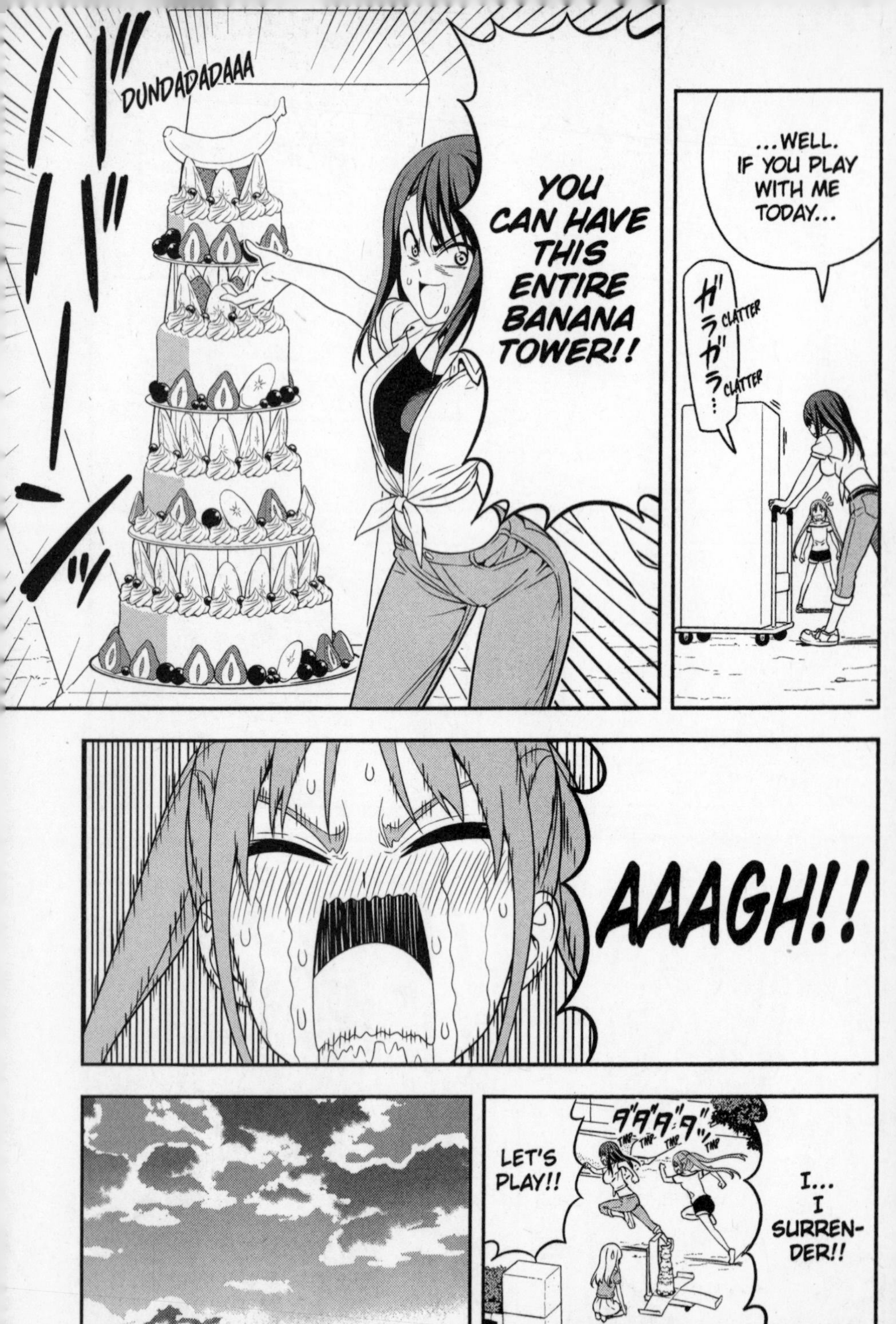
...WELL. IF YOU PLAY WITH ME TODAY...
ガラガラ… CLATTER CLATTER
YOU CAN HAVE THIS ENTIRE BANANA TOWER!!
DUNDADADAAA
AAAGH!!
ダダダダッ TMP TMP TMP TMP
I... I SURREN-DER!!
LET'S PLAY!!

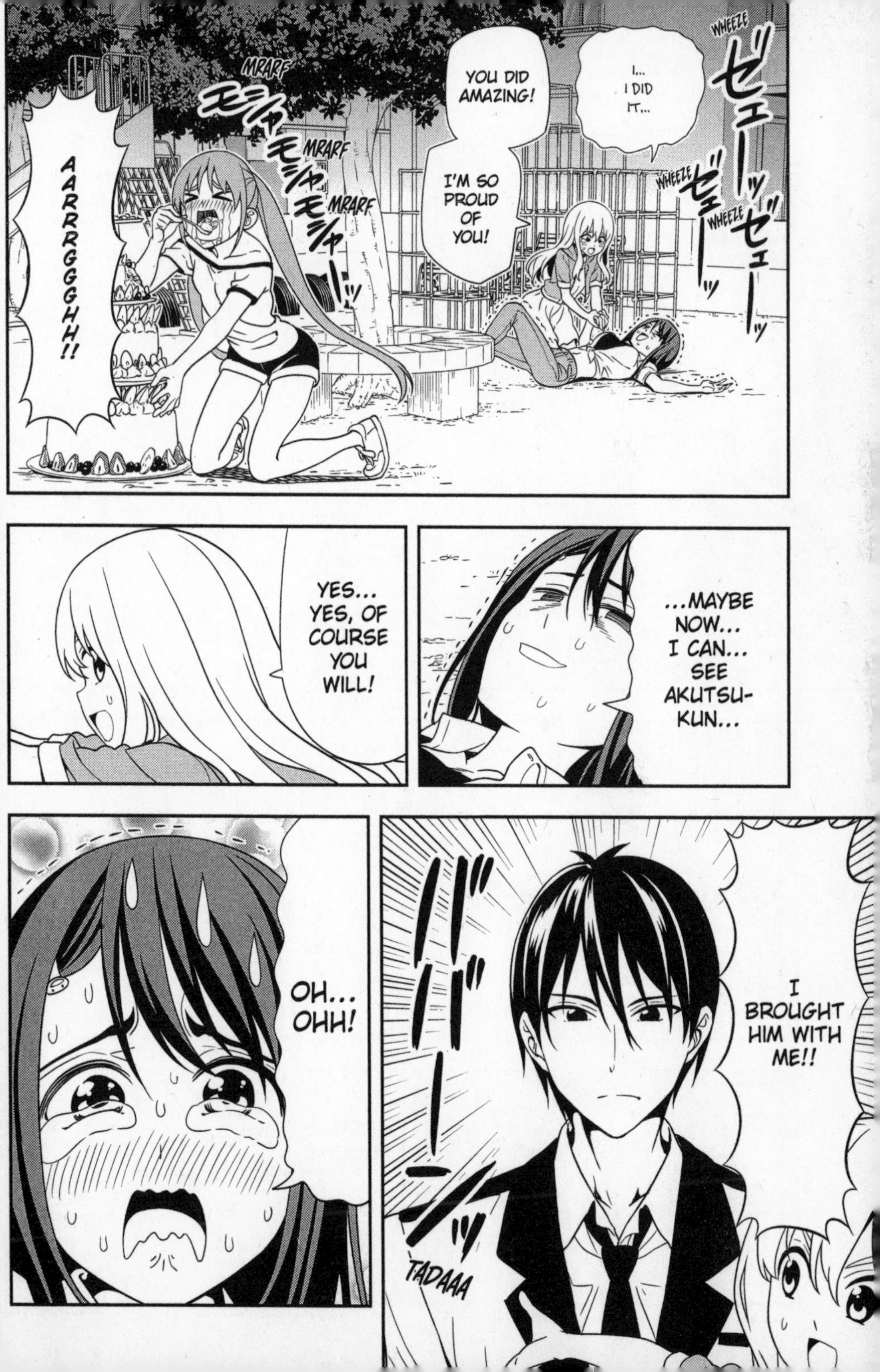
WHEEZE
WHEEZE
WHEEZE
I... I DID IT...
YOU DID AMAZING!
I'M SO PROUD OF YOU!
MRARF
MRARF
MRARF
AARRRGGGHH!!
...MAYBE NOW... I CAN... SEE AKUTSU-KUN...
YES... YES, OF COURSE YOU WILL!
I BROUGHT HIM WITH ME!!
TADAAA
OH... OHH!

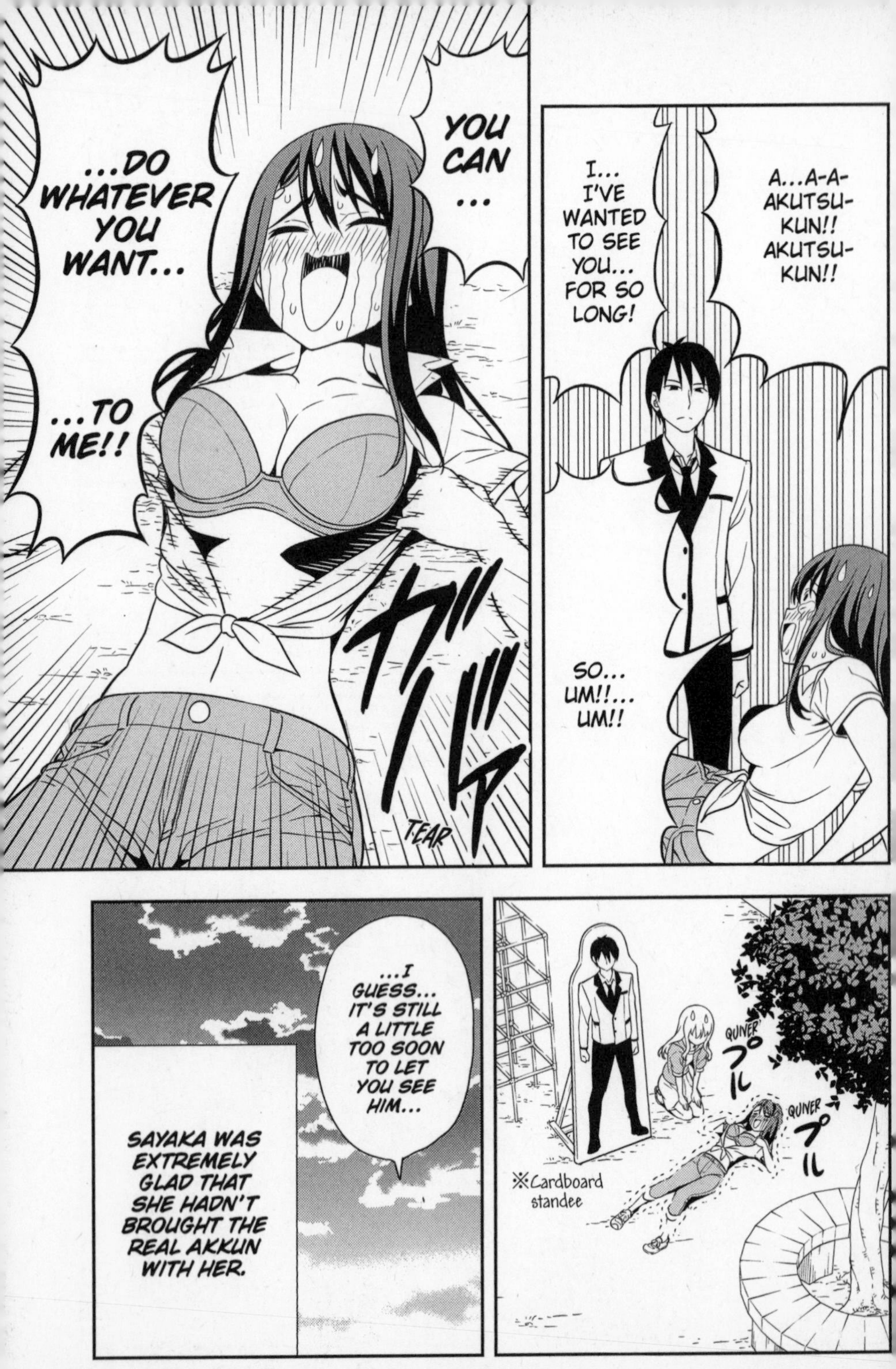
A...A-A-AKUTSU-KUN!! AKUTSU-KUN!!
I... I'VE WANTED TO SEE YOU... FOR SO LONG!
SO... UM!!... UM!!
YOU CAN ...
...DO WHATEVER YOU WANT...
...TO ME!!
TEAR
QUIVER
プル
QUIVER
プル
※Cardboard standee
...I GUESS... IT'S STILL A LITTLE TOO SOON TO LET YOU SEE HIM...
SAYAKA WAS EXTREMELY GLAD THAT SHE HADN'T BROUGHT THE REAL AKKUN WITH HER.

Good Work Takes Dedication

TAKE THE PIC-TURE.
パシャ
CHAK
?
EDIT.
ORDER.
I'D LIKE A LIFE-SIZE CARD-BOARD STANDEE ...
YES... YES...
¥10,000 FOR DELIVERY IN FIVE DAYS...
...ALL RIGHT, THEN...

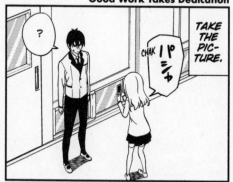

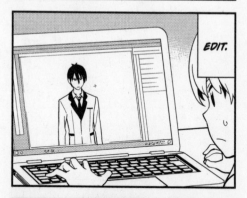

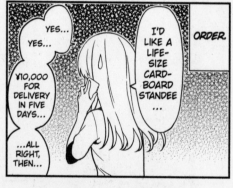

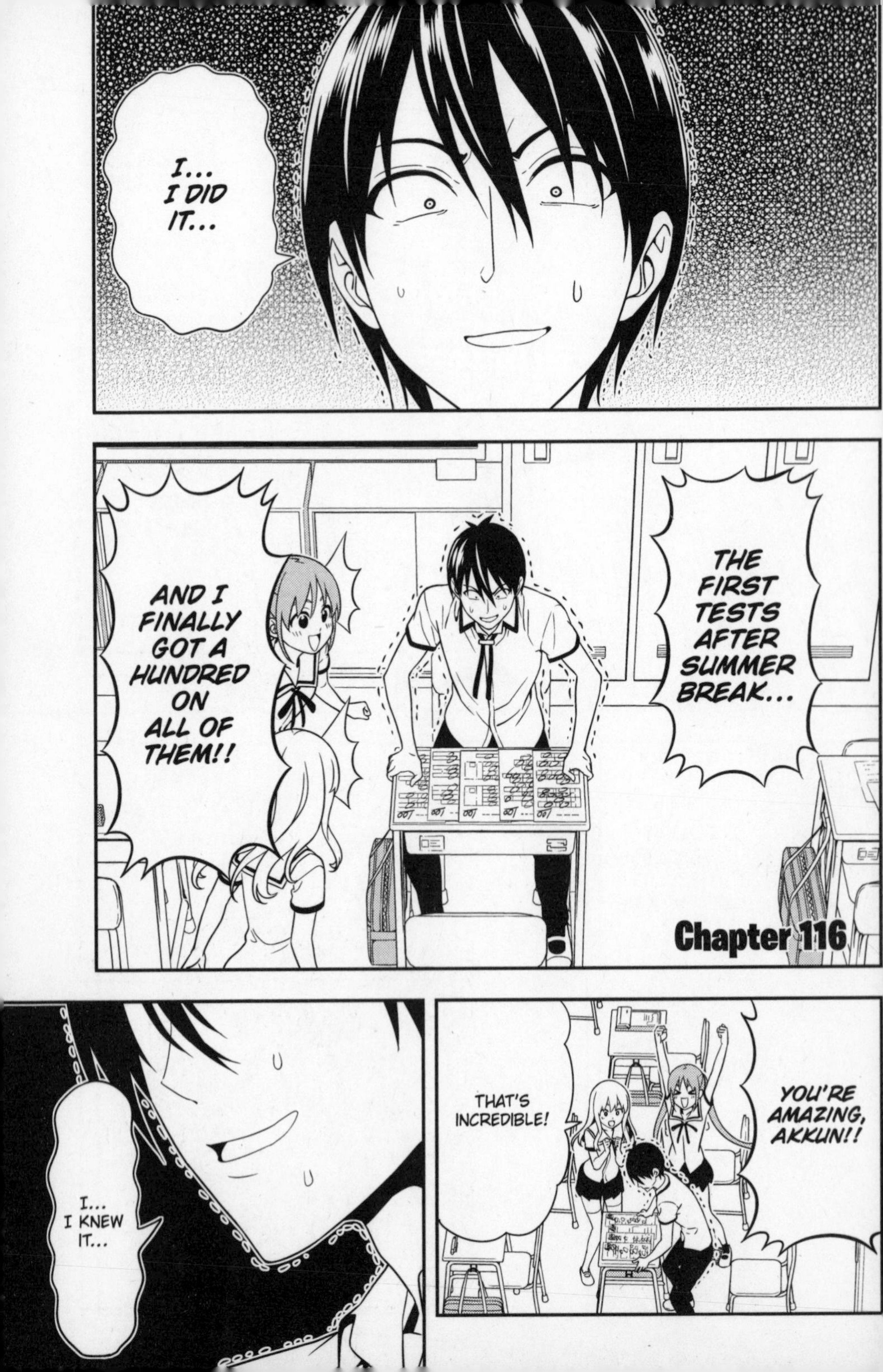
I... I DID IT...
THE FIRST TESTS AFTER SUMMER BREAK...
AND I FINALLY GOT A HUNDRED ON ALL OF THEM!!
Chapter 116
YOU'RE AMAZING, AKKUN!!
THAT'S INCREDIBLE!
I... I KNEW IT...

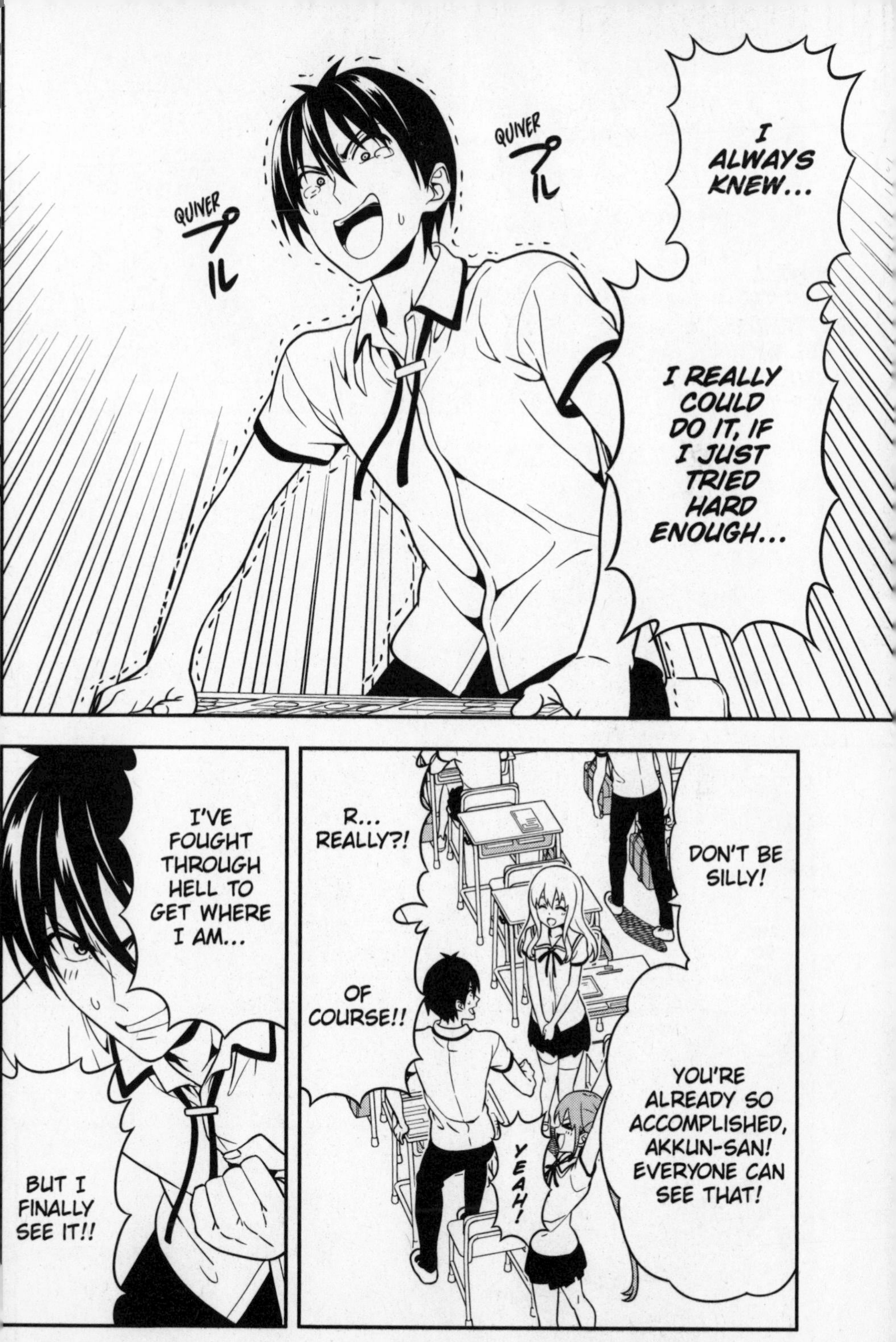
I ALWAYS KNEW...
I REALLY COULD DO IT, IF I JUST TRIED HARD ENOUGH...
QUIVER
QUIVER
DON'T BE SILLY!
R... REALLY?!
YOU'RE ALREADY SO ACCOMPLISHED, AKKUN-SAN! EVERYONE CAN SEE THAT!
OF COURSE!!
YEAH!
I'VE FOUGHT THROUGH HELL TO GET WHERE I AM...
BUT I FINALLY SEE IT!!

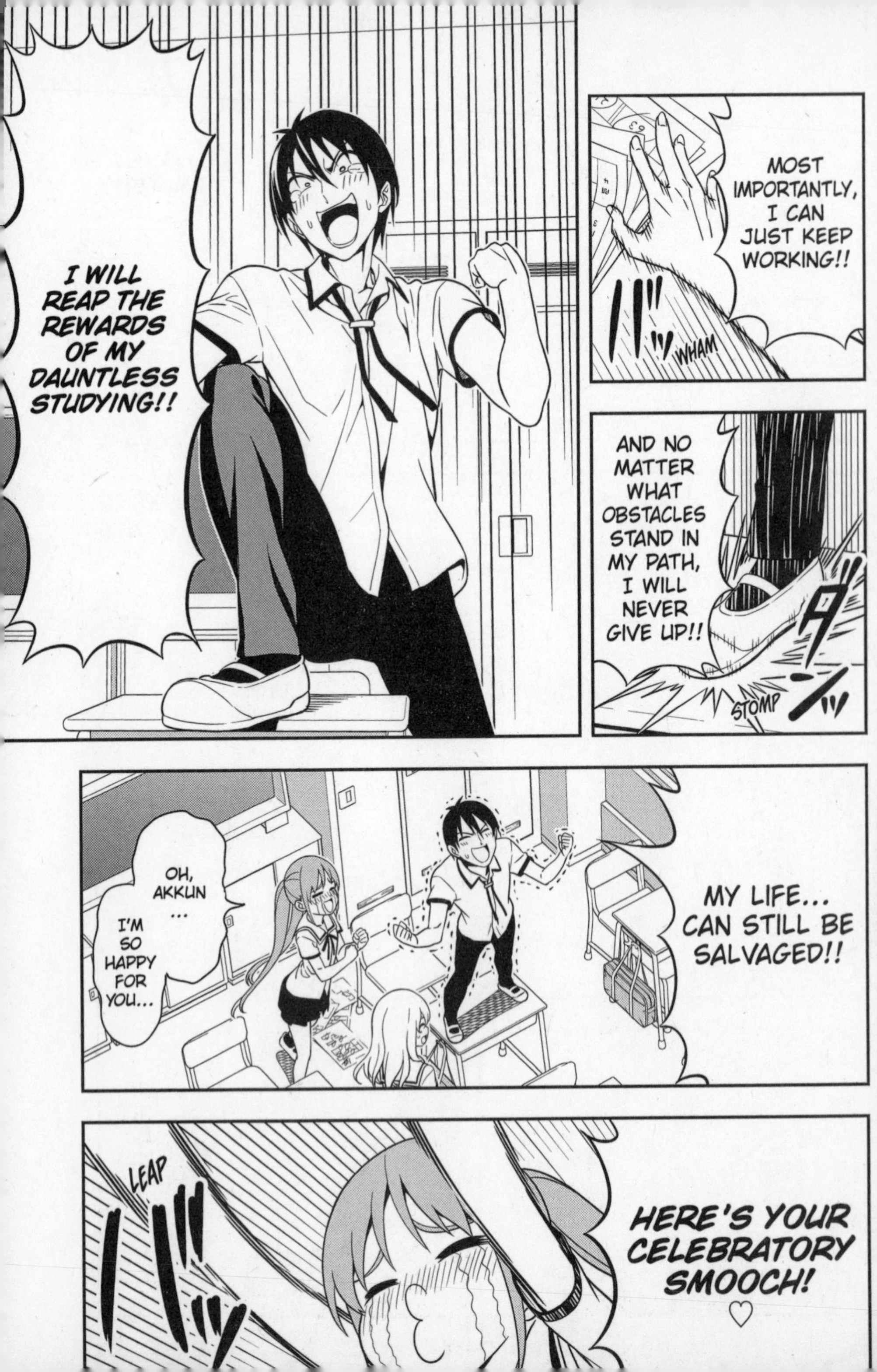
MOST IMPORTANTLY, I CAN JUST KEEP WORKING!!
WHAM
AND NO MATTER WHAT OBSTACLES STAND IN MY PATH, I WILL NEVER GIVE UP!!
STOMP
I WILL REAP THE REWARDS OF MY DAUNTLESS STUDYING!!
MY LIFE... CAN STILL BE SALVAGED!!
OH, AKKUN ... I'M SO HAPPY FOR YOU...
HERE'S YOUR CELEBRATORY SMOOCH! ♡
LEAP

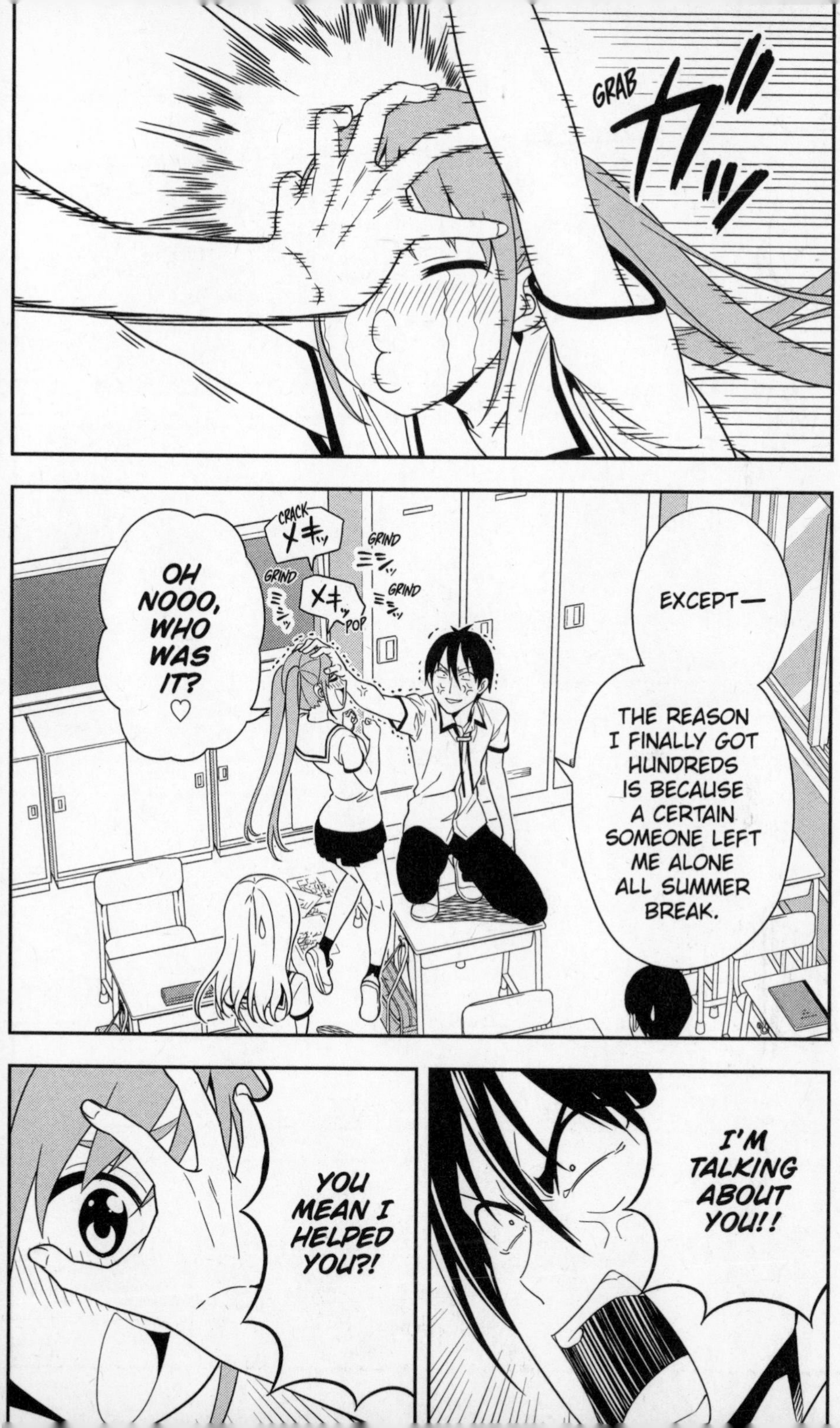
GRAB
ガッ
EXCEPT—
THE REASON I FINALLY GOT HUNDREDS IS BECAUSE A CERTAIN SOMEONE LEFT ME ALONE ALL SUMMER BREAK.
GRIND ミシッ
GRIND ミシッ
CRACK メキッ
POP メキッ
GRIND ミシッ
OH NOOO, WHO WAS IT? ♡
I'M TALKING ABOUT YOU!!
YOU MEAN I HELPED YOU?!

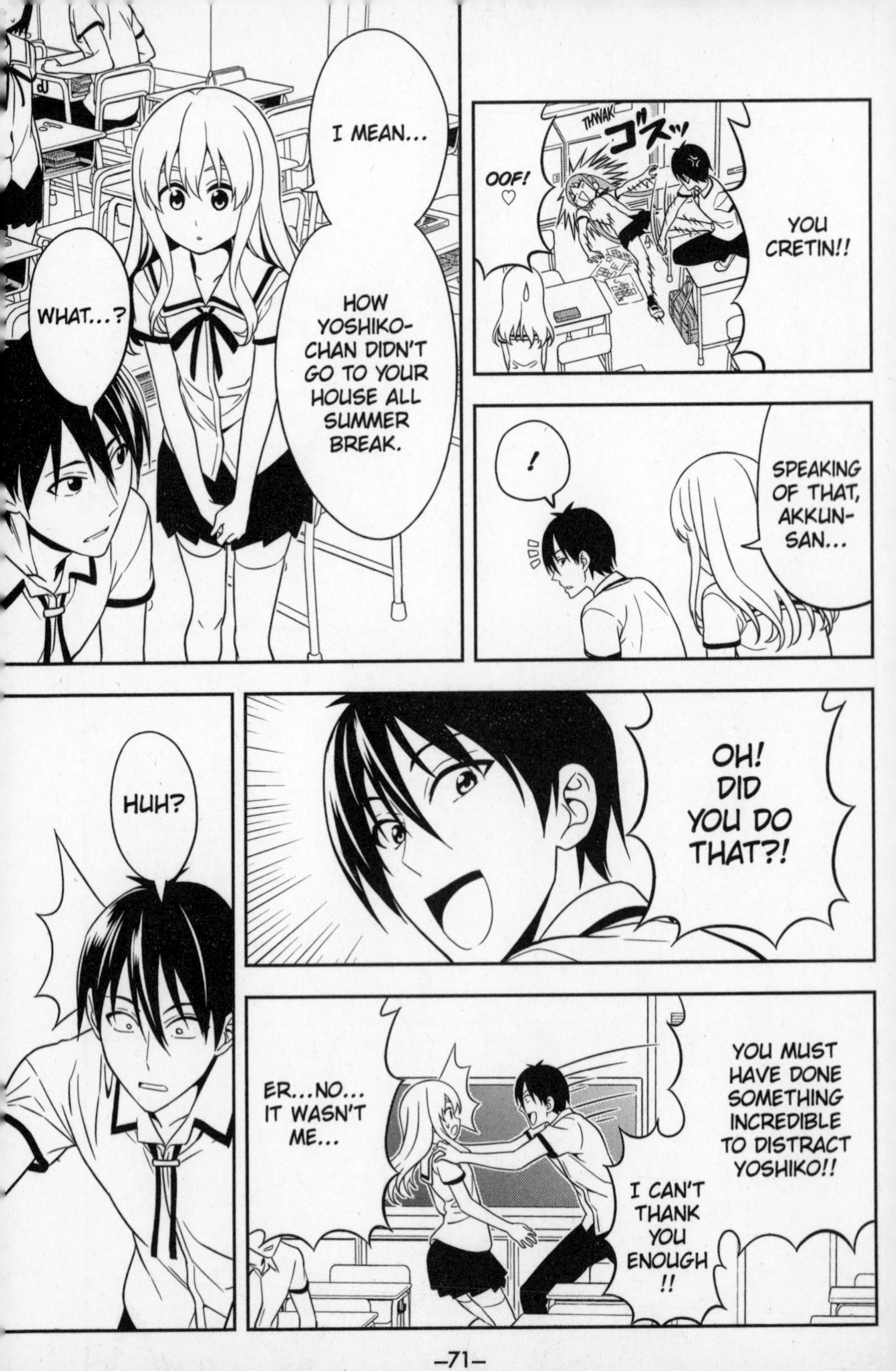

YOU CRETIN!!
THWAK ゴズッ
OOF! ♡
SPEAKING OF THAT, AKKUN-SAN...
!
I MEAN...
HOW YOSHIKO-CHAN DIDN'T GO TO YOUR HOUSE ALL SUMMER BREAK.
WHAT...?
OH! DID YOU DO THAT?!
YOU MUST HAVE DONE SOMETHING INCREDIBLE TO DISTRACT YOSHIKO!!
I CAN'T THANK YOU ENOUGH!!
ER...NO... IT WASN'T ME...
HUH?

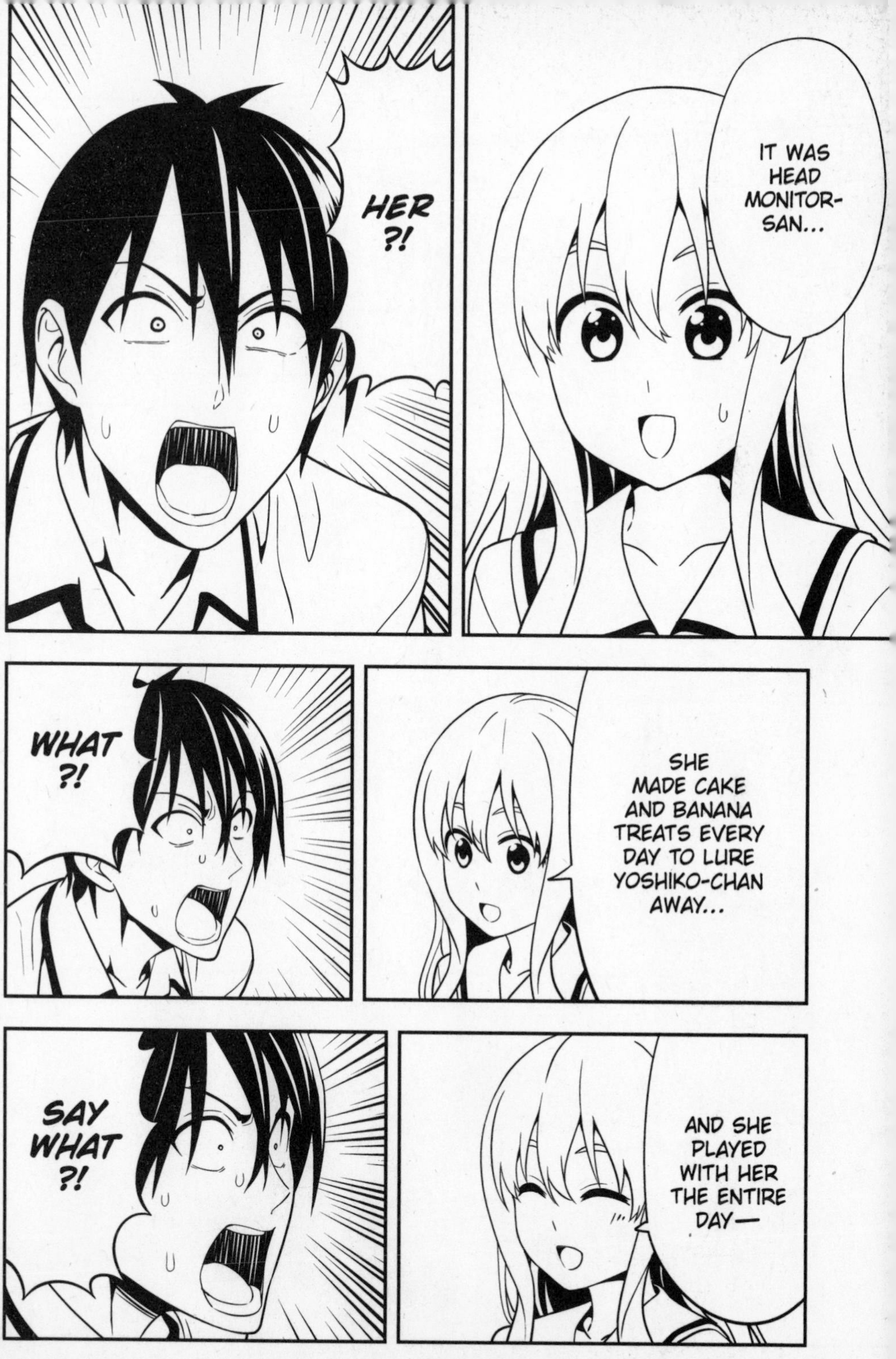
IT WAS HEAD MONITOR-SAN...
HER ?!
SHE MADE CAKE AND BANANA TREATS EVERY DAY TO LURE YOSHIKO-CHAN AWAY...
WHAT ?!
AND SHE PLAYED WITH HER THE ENTIRE DAY—
SAY WHAT ?!

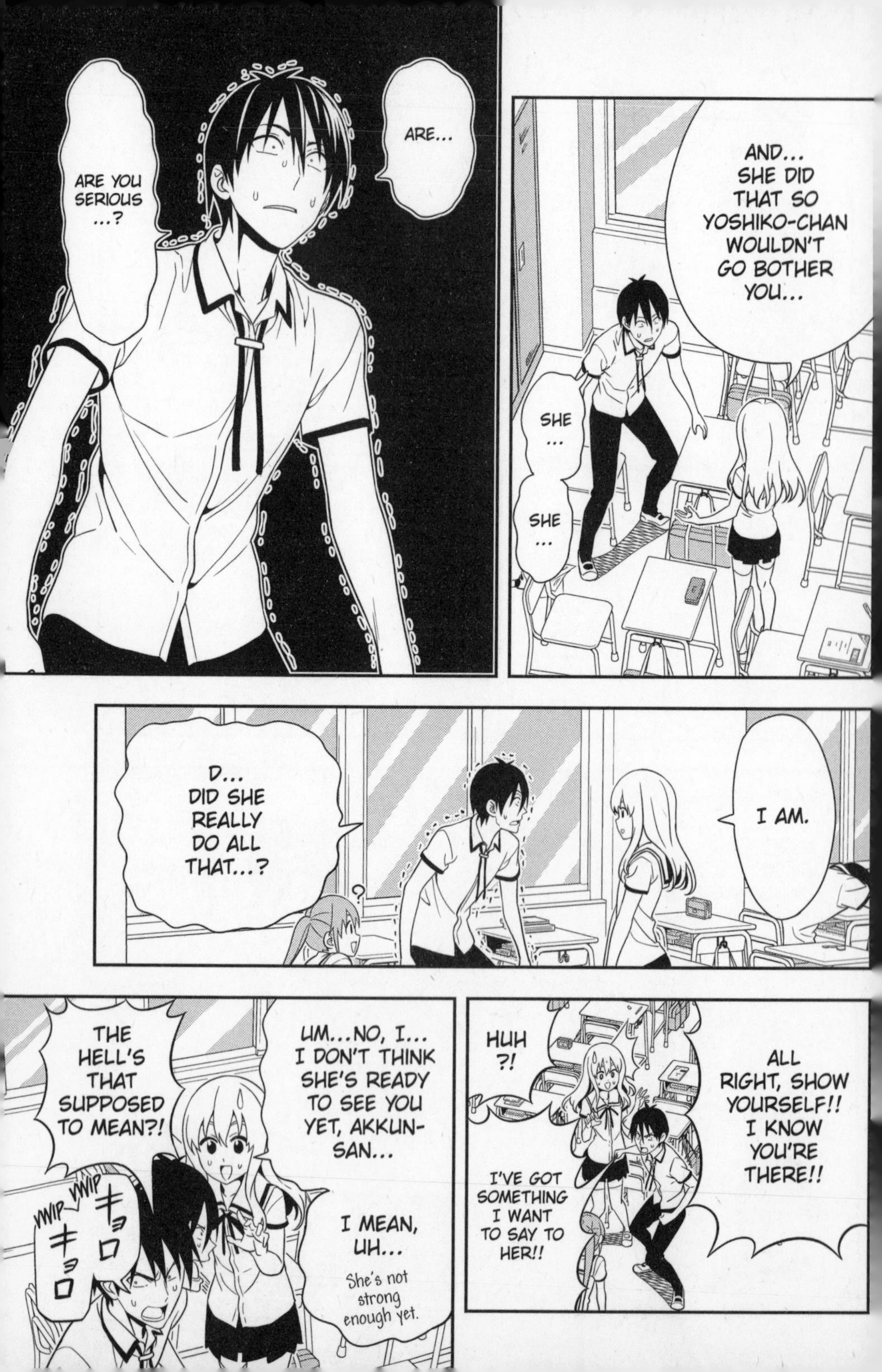
AND... SHE DID THAT SO YOSHIKO-CHAN WOULDN'T GO BOTHER YOU...
SHE ...
SHE ...
ARE...
ARE YOU SERIOUS ...?
I AM.
D... DID SHE REALLY DO ALL THAT...?
ALL RIGHT, SHOW YOURSELF!! I KNOW YOU'RE THERE!!
HUH ?!
I'VE GOT SOMETHING I WANT TO SAY TO HER!!
UM...NO, I... I DON'T THINK SHE'S READY TO SEE YOU YET, AKKUN-SAN...
THE HELL'S THAT SUPPOSED TO MEAN?!
I MEAN, UH...
She's not strong enough yet.
WHIP WHIP
キョロ キョロ

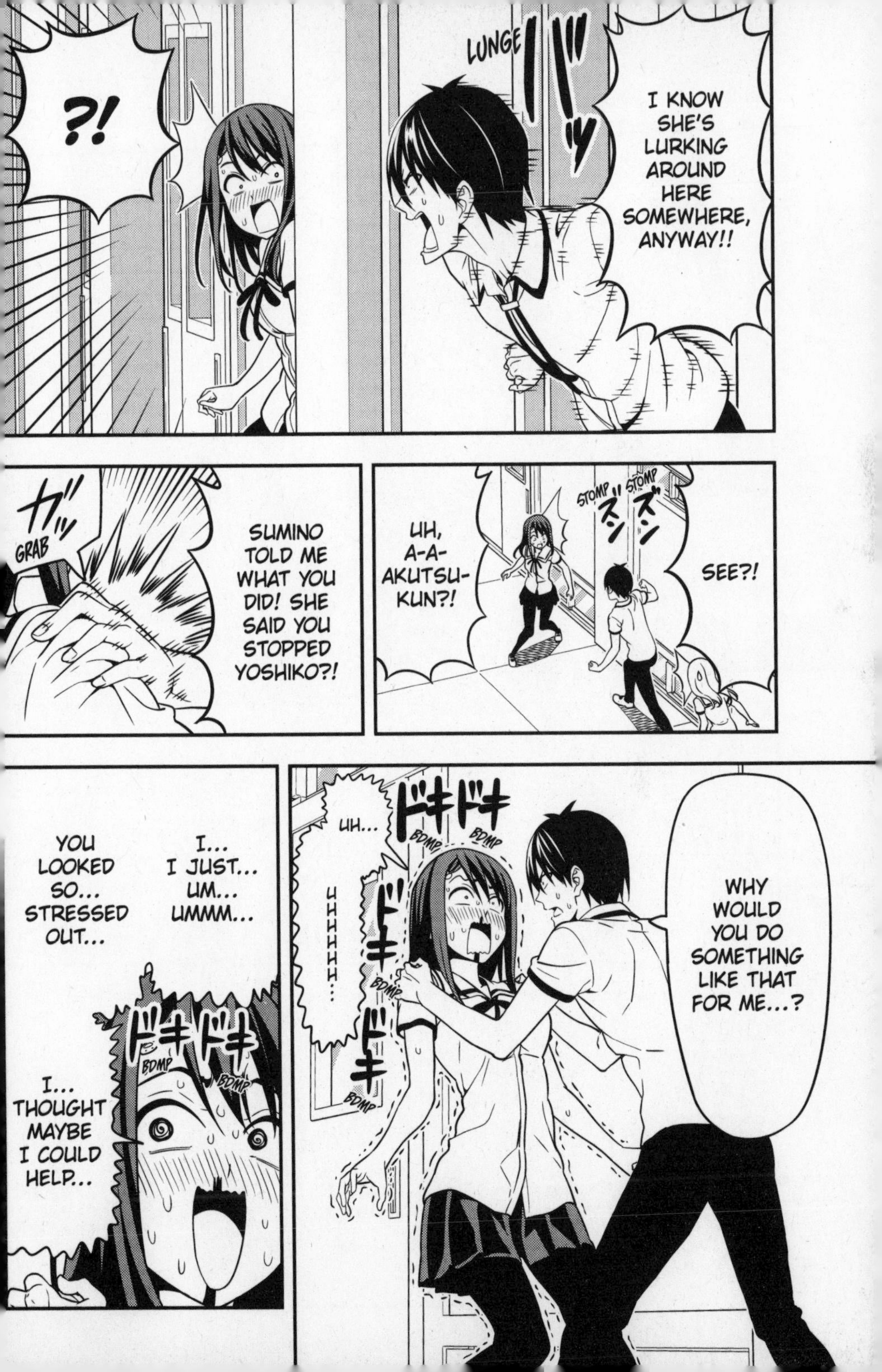
LUNGE
I KNOW SHE'S LURKING AROUND HERE SOMEWHERE, ANYWAY!!
?!
STOMP STOMP
ズン ズン
SEE?!
UH, A-A-AKUTSU-KUN?!
ガッ
GRAB
SUMINO TOLD ME WHAT YOU DID! SHE SAID YOU STOPPED YOSHIKO?!
WHY WOULD YOU DO SOMETHING LIKE THAT FOR ME...?
ドキドキ
BDMP BDMP
UH...
UHHHHHH...
ドキ BDMP
ドキ BDMP
I... I JUST... UM... UMMM...
YOU LOOKED SO... STRESSED OUT...
ドキドキ
BDMP BDMP
I... THOUGHT MAYBE I COULD HELP...

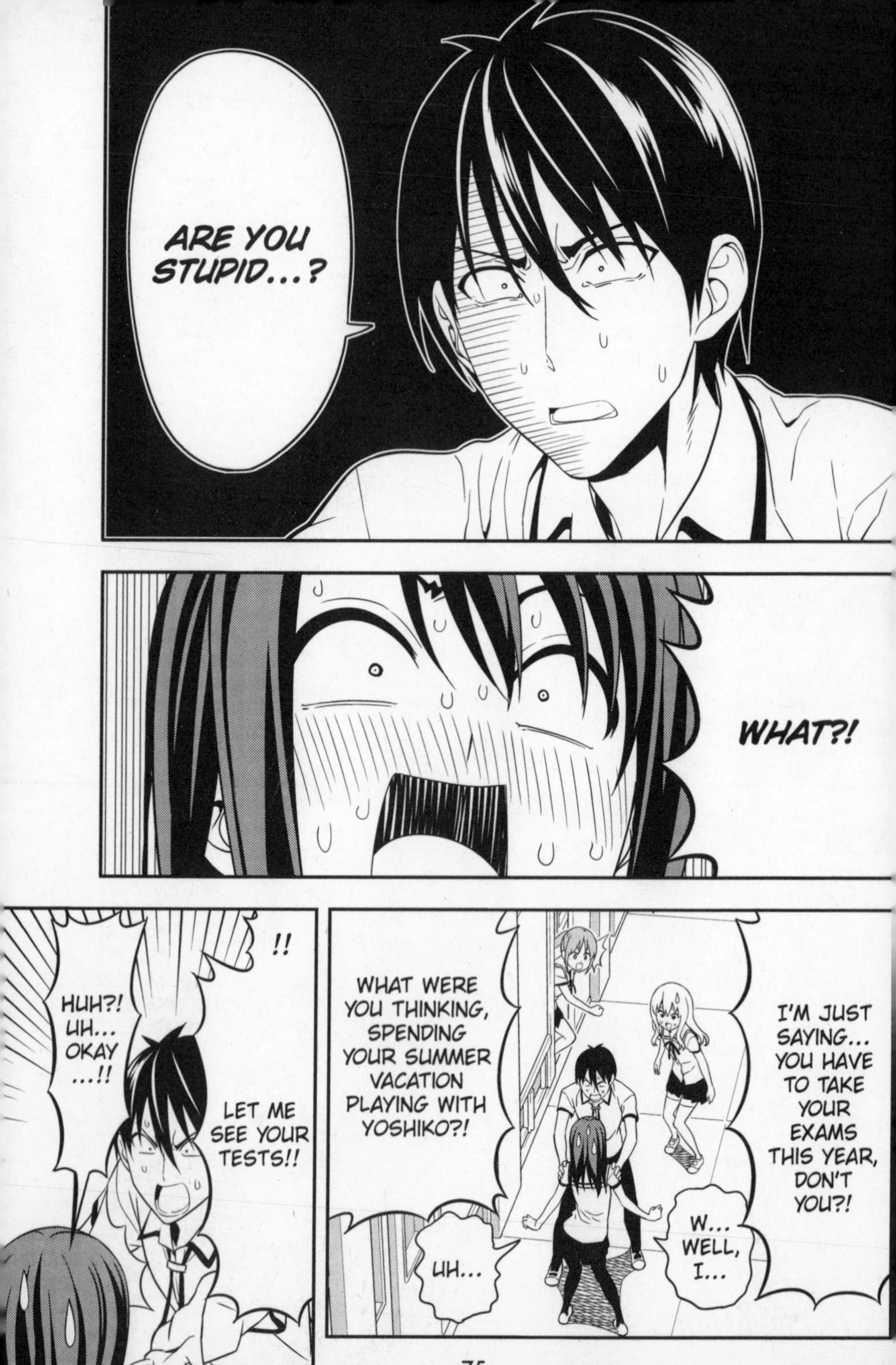
ARE YOU STUPID...?
WHAT?!
I'M JUST SAYING... YOU HAVE TO TAKE YOUR EXAMS THIS YEAR, DON'T YOU?!
W... WELL, I...
WHAT WERE YOU THINKING, SPENDING YOUR SUMMER VACATION PLAYING WITH YOSHIKO?!
UH...
!!
LET ME SEE YOUR TESTS!!
HUH?! UH... OKAY ...!!

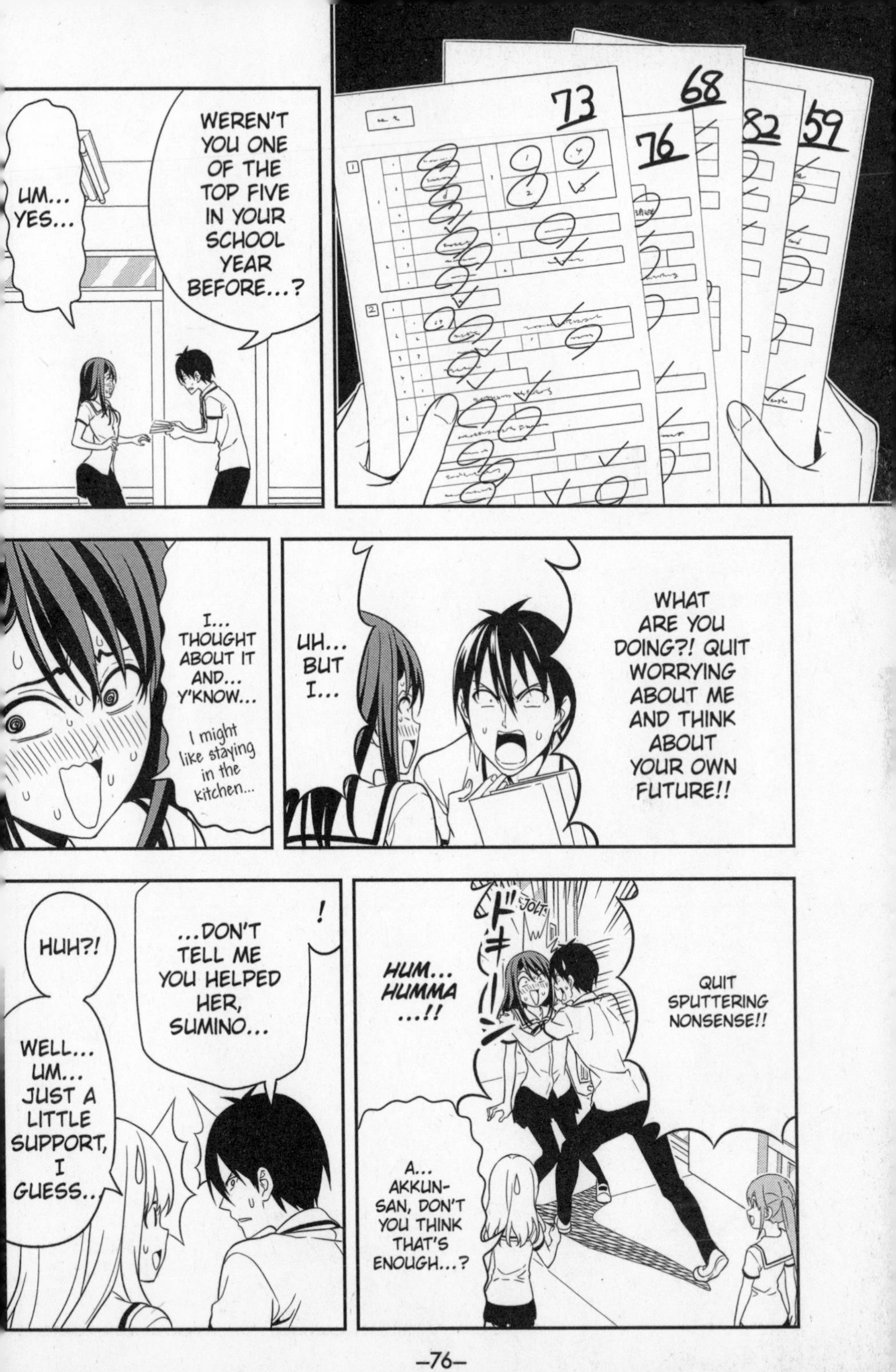
73
68
76
82
59
WEREN'T YOU ONE OF THE TOP FIVE IN YOUR SCHOOL YEAR BEFORE...?
UM... YES...
WHAT ARE YOU DOING?! QUIT WORRYING ABOUT ME AND THINK ABOUT YOUR OWN FUTURE!!
UH... BUT I...
I... THOUGHT ABOUT IT AND... Y'KNOW...
I might like staying in the kitchen...
JOLT
QUIT SPUTTERING NONSENSE!!
HUM... HUMMA ...!!
A... AKKUN-SAN, DON'T YOU THINK THAT'S ENOUGH...?
!
...DON'T TELL ME YOU HELPED HER, SUMINO...
HUH?!
WELL... UM... JUST A LITTLE SUPPORT, I GUESS...

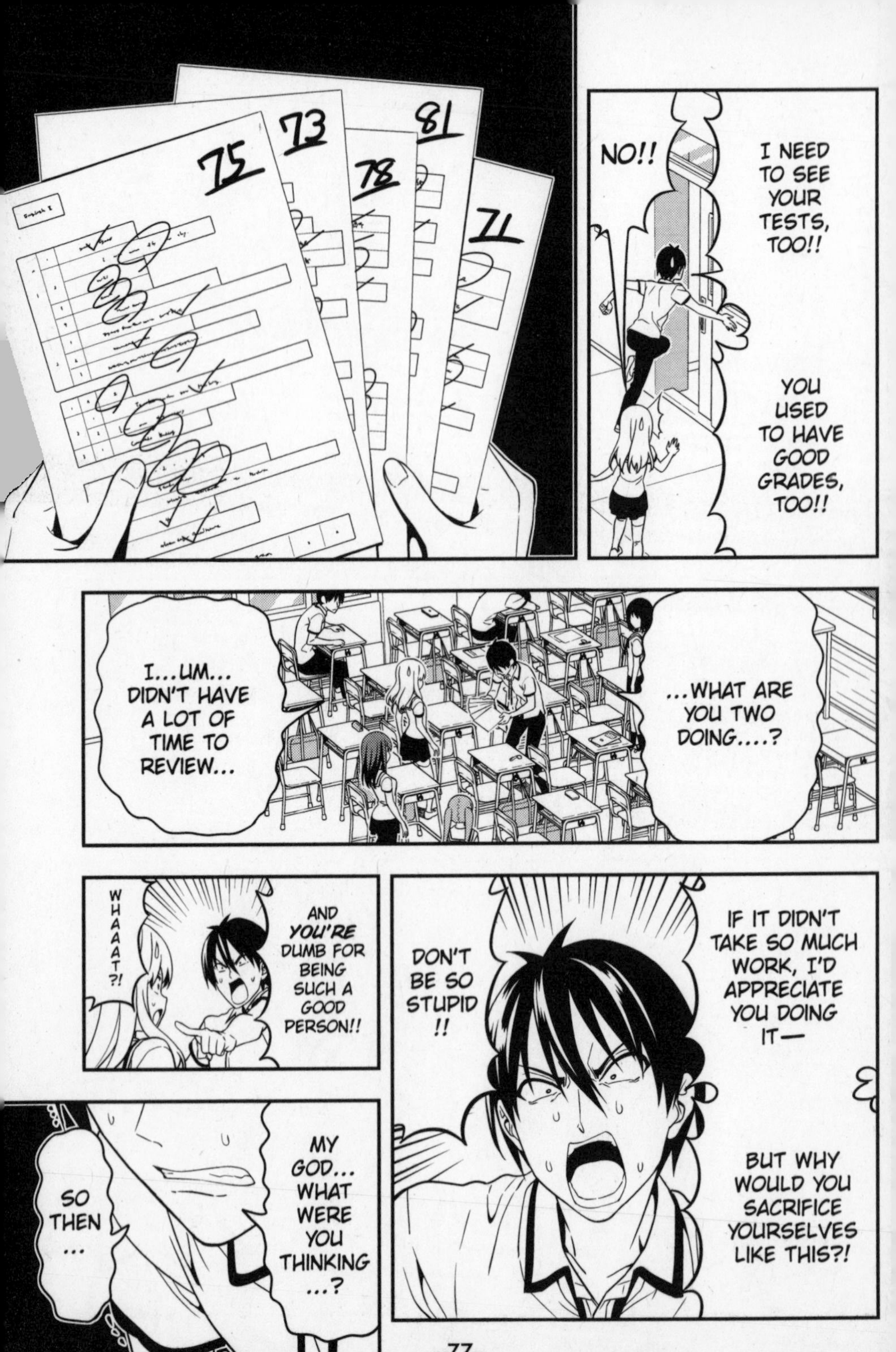
NO!!
I NEED TO SEE YOUR TESTS, TOO!!
YOU USED TO HAVE GOOD GRADES, TOO!!
75
73
78
81
71
...WHAT ARE YOU TWO DOING....?
I...UM... DIDN'T HAVE A LOT OF TIME TO REVIEW...
IF IT DIDN'T TAKE SO MUCH WORK, I'D APPRECIATE YOU DOING IT—
DON'T BE SO STUPID!!
BUT WHY WOULD YOU SACRIFICE YOURSELVES LIKE THIS?!
AND *YOU'RE* DUMB FOR BEING SUCH A GOOD PERSON!!
WHAAAAT?!
MY GOD... WHAT WERE YOU THINKING...?
SO THEN...

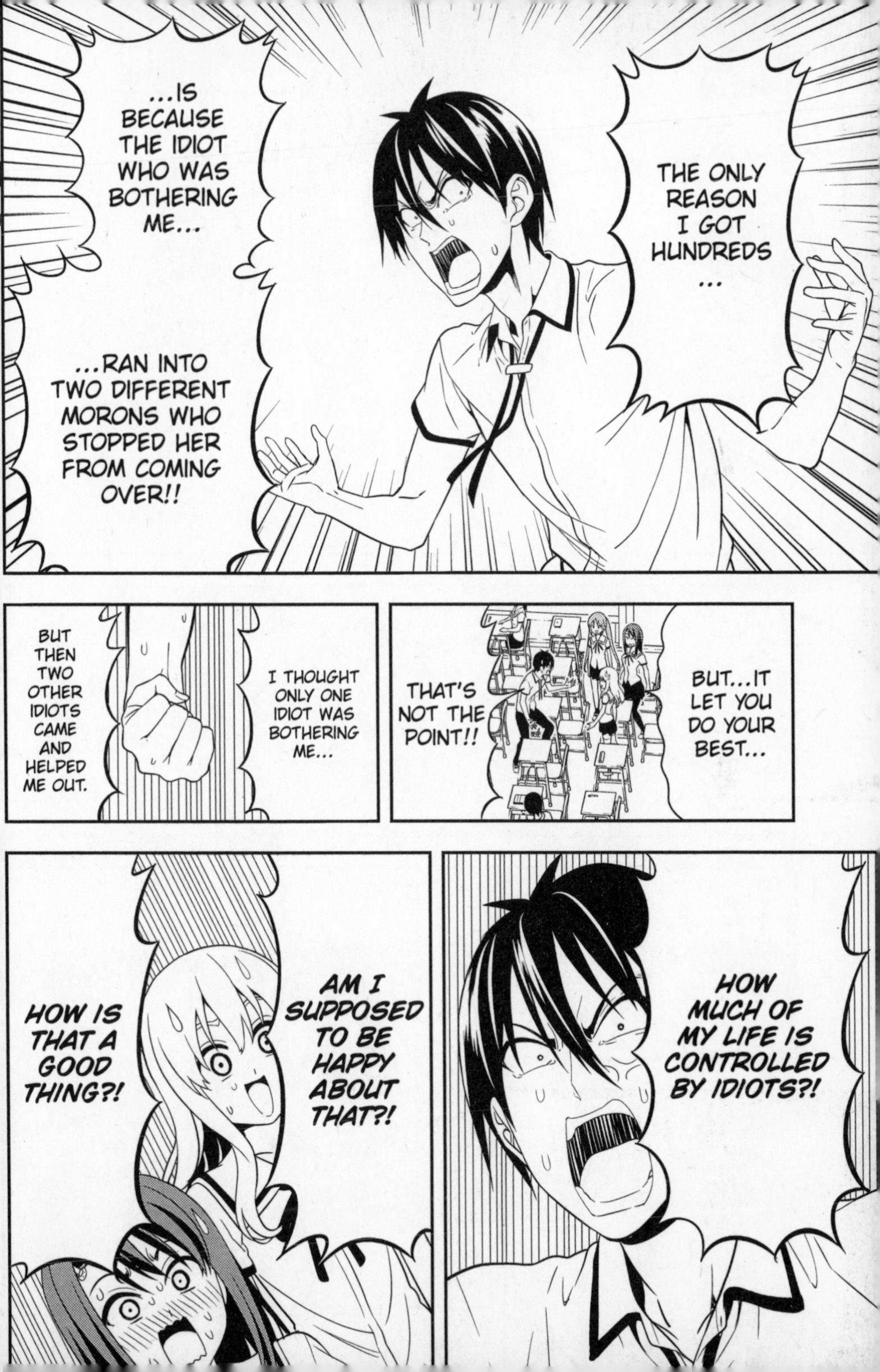
THE ONLY REASON I GOT HUNDREDS ...
...IS BECAUSE THE IDIOT WHO WAS BOTHERING ME...
...RAN INTO TWO DIFFERENT MORONS WHO STOPPED HER FROM COMING OVER!!
BUT...IT LET YOU DO YOUR BEST...
THAT'S NOT THE POINT!!
I THOUGHT ONLY ONE IDIOT WAS BOTHERING ME...
BUT THEN TWO OTHER IDIOTS CAME AND HELPED ME OUT.
HOW MUCH OF MY LIFE IS CONTROLLED BY IDIOTS?!
AM I SUPPOSED TO BE HAPPY ABOUT THAT?!
HOW IS THAT A GOOD THING?!

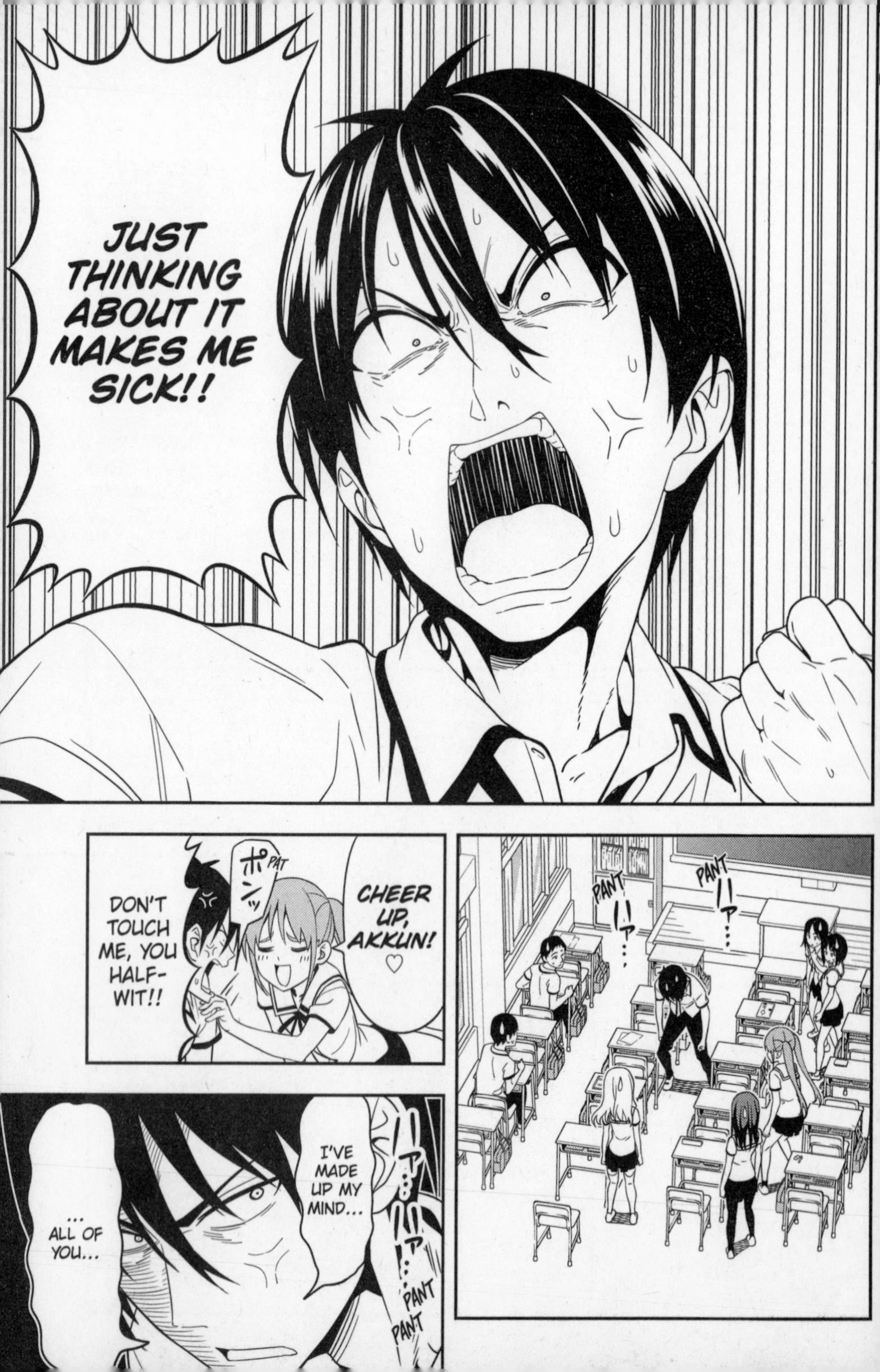
JUST THINKING ABOUT IT MAKES ME SICK!!
PANT
ハァ…
PANT
ハァ…
CHEER UP, AKKUN! ♡
ポンッ
PAT
DON'T TOUCH ME, YOU HALF-WIT!!
I'VE MADE UP MY MIND...
ハァ… ハァ…
PANT
PANT
... ALL OF YOU...

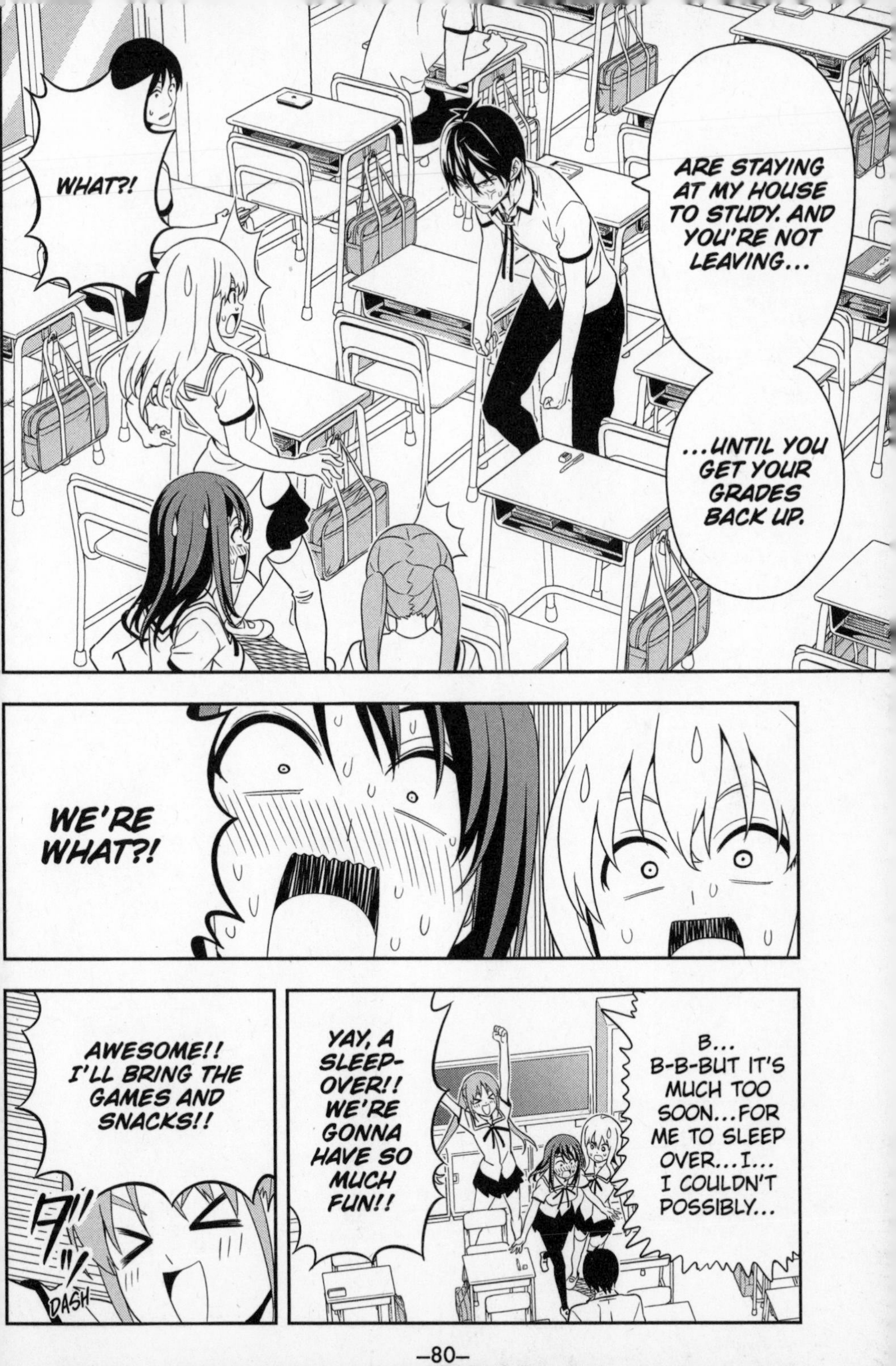
ARE STAYING AT MY HOUSE TO STUDY. AND YOU'RE NOT LEAVING...
...UNTIL YOU GET YOUR GRADES BACK UP.
WHAT?!
WE'RE WHAT?!
B... B-B-BUT IT'S MUCH TOO SOON...FOR ME TO SLEEP OVER...I... I COULDN'T POSSIBLY...
YAY, A SLEEP-OVER!! WE'RE GONNA HAVE SO MUCH FUN!!
AWESOME!! I'LL BRING THE GAMES AND SNACKS!!
DASH

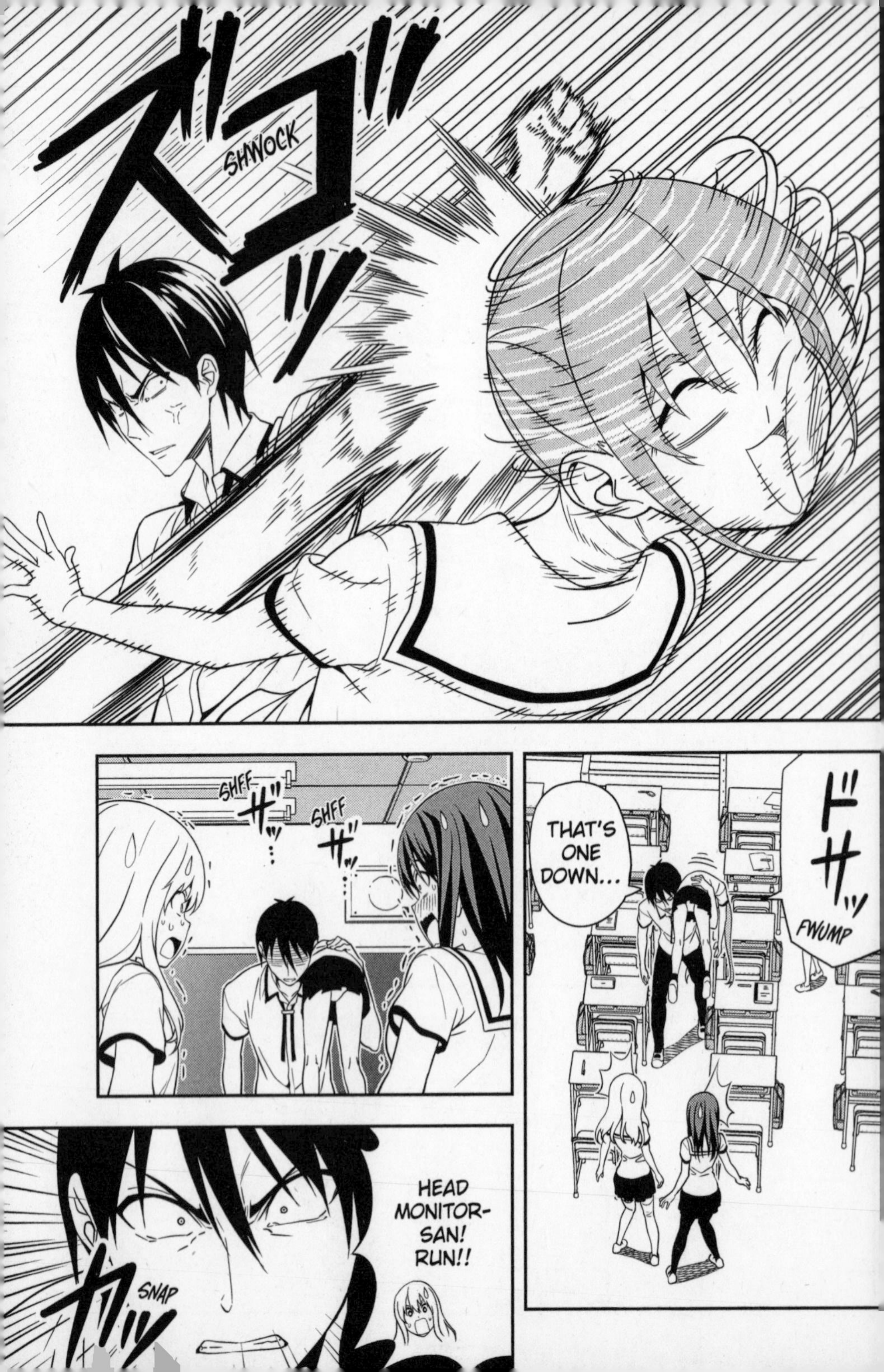
ズゴッ
SHWOCK
ドサッ
FWUMP
THAT'S ONE DOWN...
ザッ
SHFF
ザッ
SHFF
HEAD MONITOR-SAN! RUN!!
カッ
SNAP

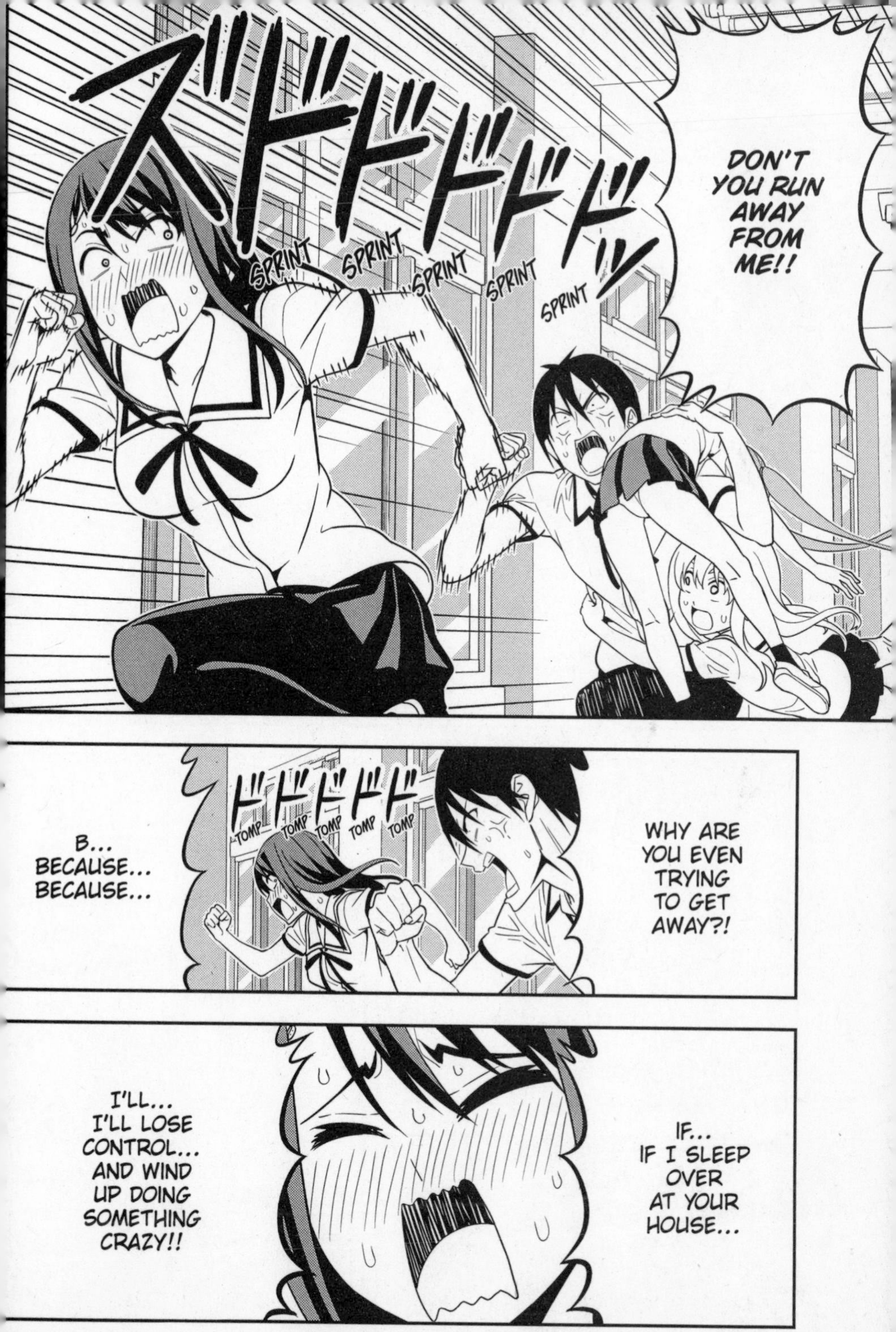
DON'T YOU RUN AWAY FROM ME!!
ズドドドドドッ
SPRINT SPRINT SPRINT SPRINT SPRINT
WHY ARE YOU EVEN TRYING TO GET AWAY?!
ドドドドド
TOMP TOMP TOMP TOMP TOMP
B... BECAUSE... BECAUSE...
IF... IF I SLEEP OVER AT YOUR HOUSE...
I'LL... I'LL LOSE CONTROL... AND WIND UP DOING SOMETHING CRAZY!!

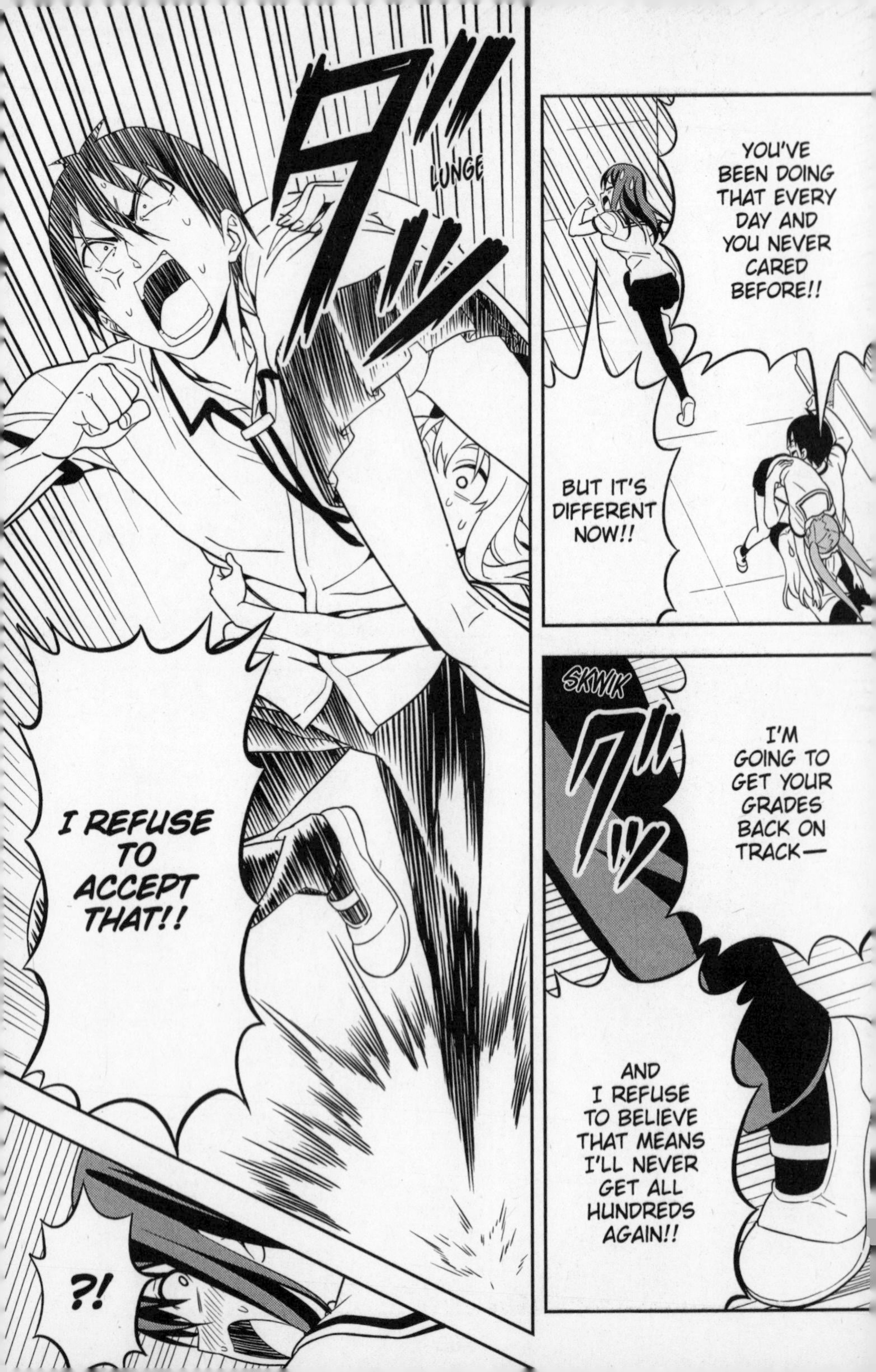
YOU'VE BEEN DOING THAT EVERY DAY AND YOU NEVER CARED BEFORE!!
BUT IT'S DIFFERENT NOW!!
SKWIK
I'M GOING TO GET YOUR GRADES BACK ON TRACK—
AND I REFUSE TO BELIEVE THAT MEANS I'LL NEVER GET ALL HUNDREDS AGAIN!!
LUNGE
I REFUSE TO ACCEPT THAT!!
?!

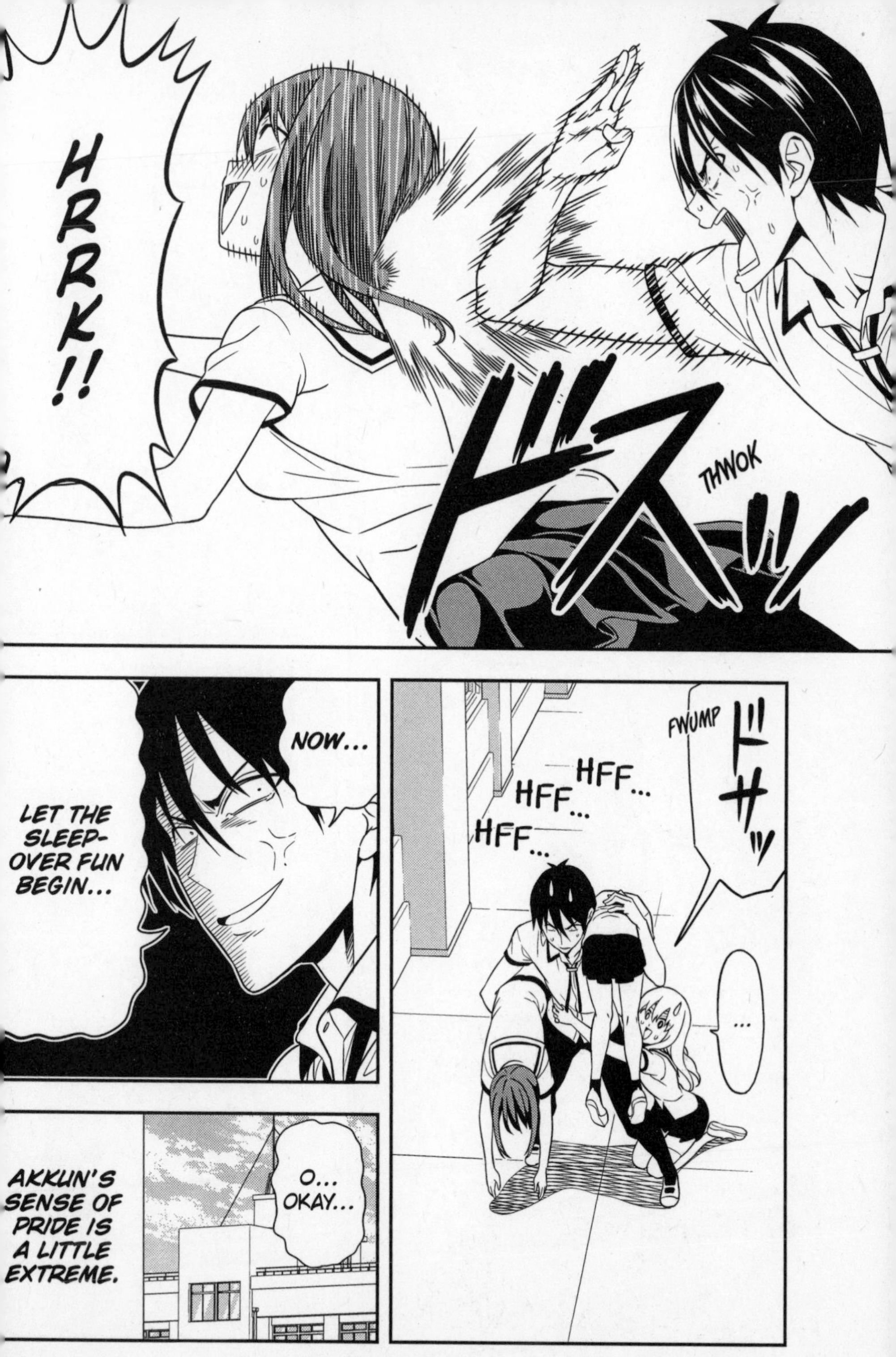
HRRK!!
ドスッ
THWOK
FWUMP
ドサッ
HFF...
HFF...
HFF...
...
NOW...
LET THE SLEEPOVER FUN BEGIN...
O... OKAY...
AKKUN'S SENSE OF PRIDE IS A LITTLE EXTREME.

Tired Already

HFF ...
HFF ...
...SHE'S... SO HEAVY...
GOTTA BE HER BOOBS ...

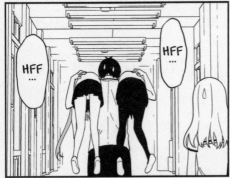

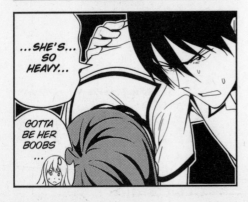

(Who Benefits, Who Loses Out?)

Aho-Girl

\'ahô͵gərl\ *Japanese, noun*.

A clueless girl.

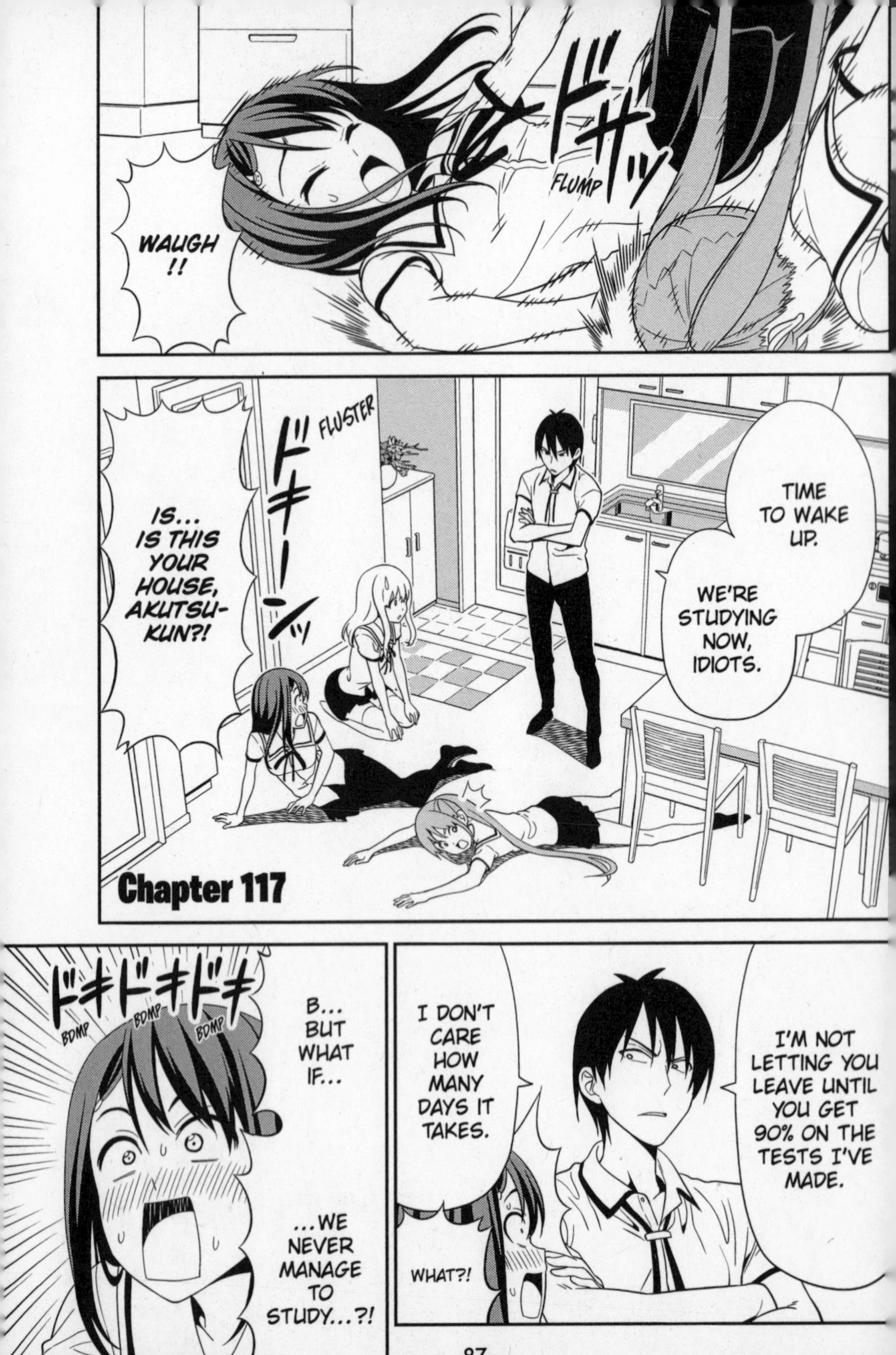
ドサッ
FLUMP
WAUGH!!
TIME TO WAKE UP.
WE'RE STUDYING NOW, IDIOTS.
ドキーンッ
FLUSTER
IS... IS THIS YOUR HOUSE, AKUTSU-KUN?!
Chapter 117
I'M NOT LETTING YOU LEAVE UNTIL YOU GET 90% ON THE TESTS I'VE MADE.
I DON'T CARE HOW MANY DAYS IT TAKES.
WHAT?!
ドキドキドキ
BDMP BDMP BDMP
B... BUT WHAT IF...
...WE NEVER MANAGE TO STUDY...?!

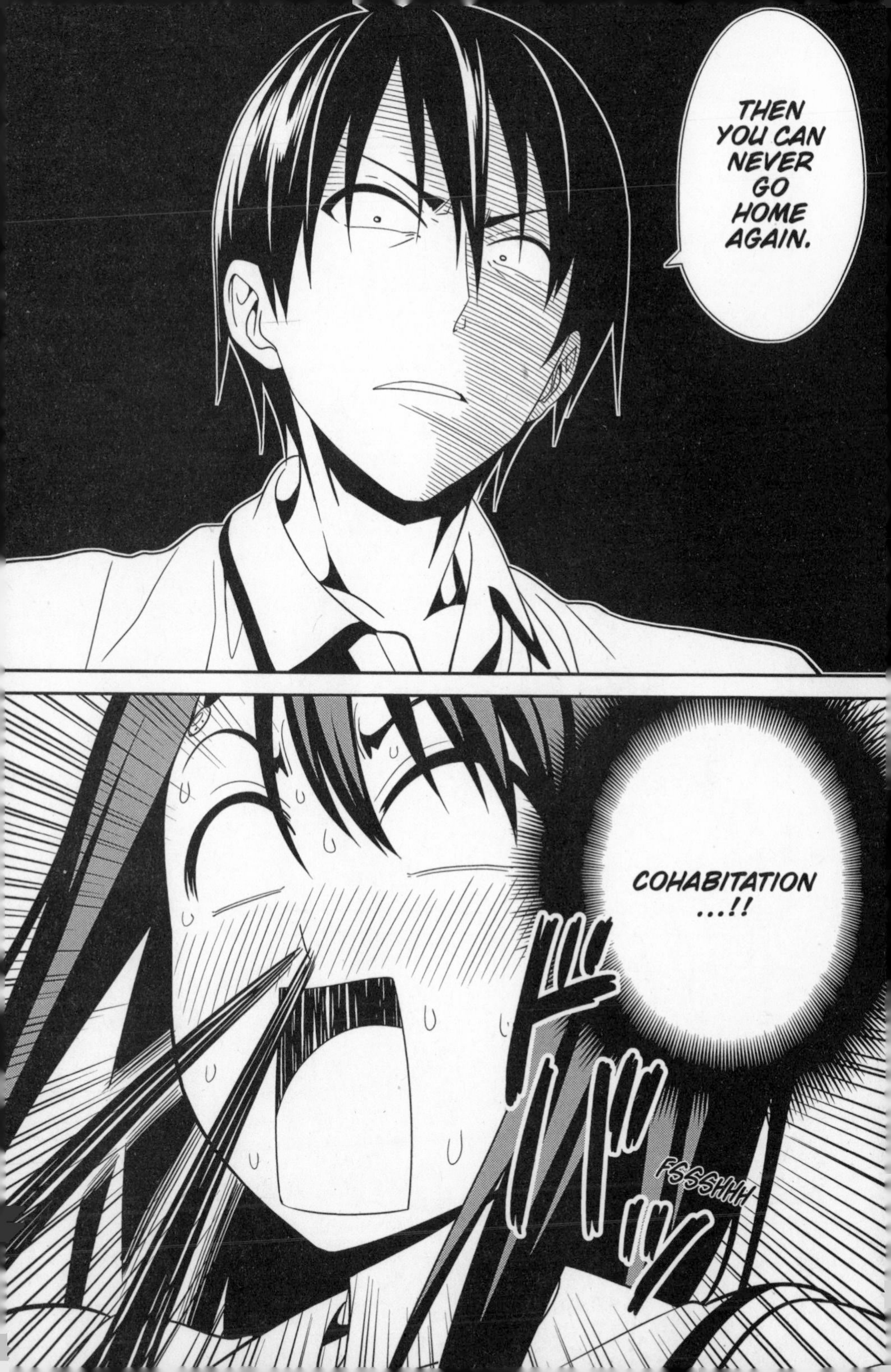
THEN YOU CAN NEVER GO HOME AGAIN.
COHABITATION ...!!
FSSSHHH

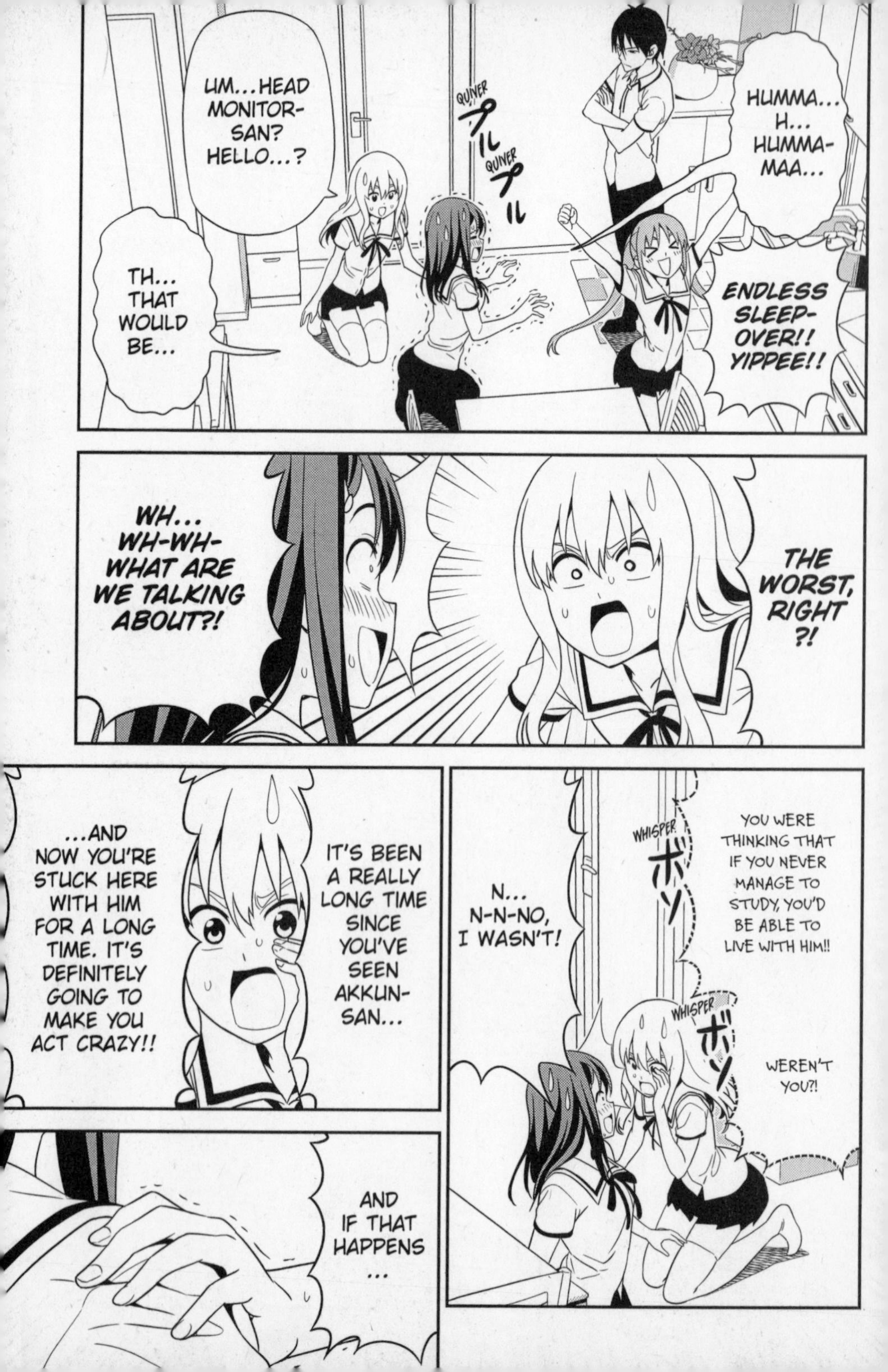

HUMMA... H... HUMMA-MAA...
ENDLESS SLEEP-OVER!! YIPPEE!!
QUIVER プル
QUIVER プル
UM...HEAD MONITOR-SAN? HELLO...?
TH... THAT WOULD BE...
THE WORST, RIGHT?!
WH... WH-WH-WHAT ARE WE TALKING ABOUT?!
YOU WERE THINKING THAT IF YOU NEVER MANAGE TO STUDY, YOU'D BE ABLE TO LIVE WITH HIM!!
WHISPER ボソ
N... N-N-NO, I WASN'T!
WHISPER ボソ
WEREN'T YOU?!
IT'S BEEN A REALLY LONG TIME SINCE YOU'VE SEEN AKKUN-SAN...
...AND NOW YOU'RE STUCK HERE WITH HIM FOR A LONG TIME. IT'S DEFINITELY GOING TO MAKE YOU ACT CRAZY!!
AND IF THAT HAPPENS...

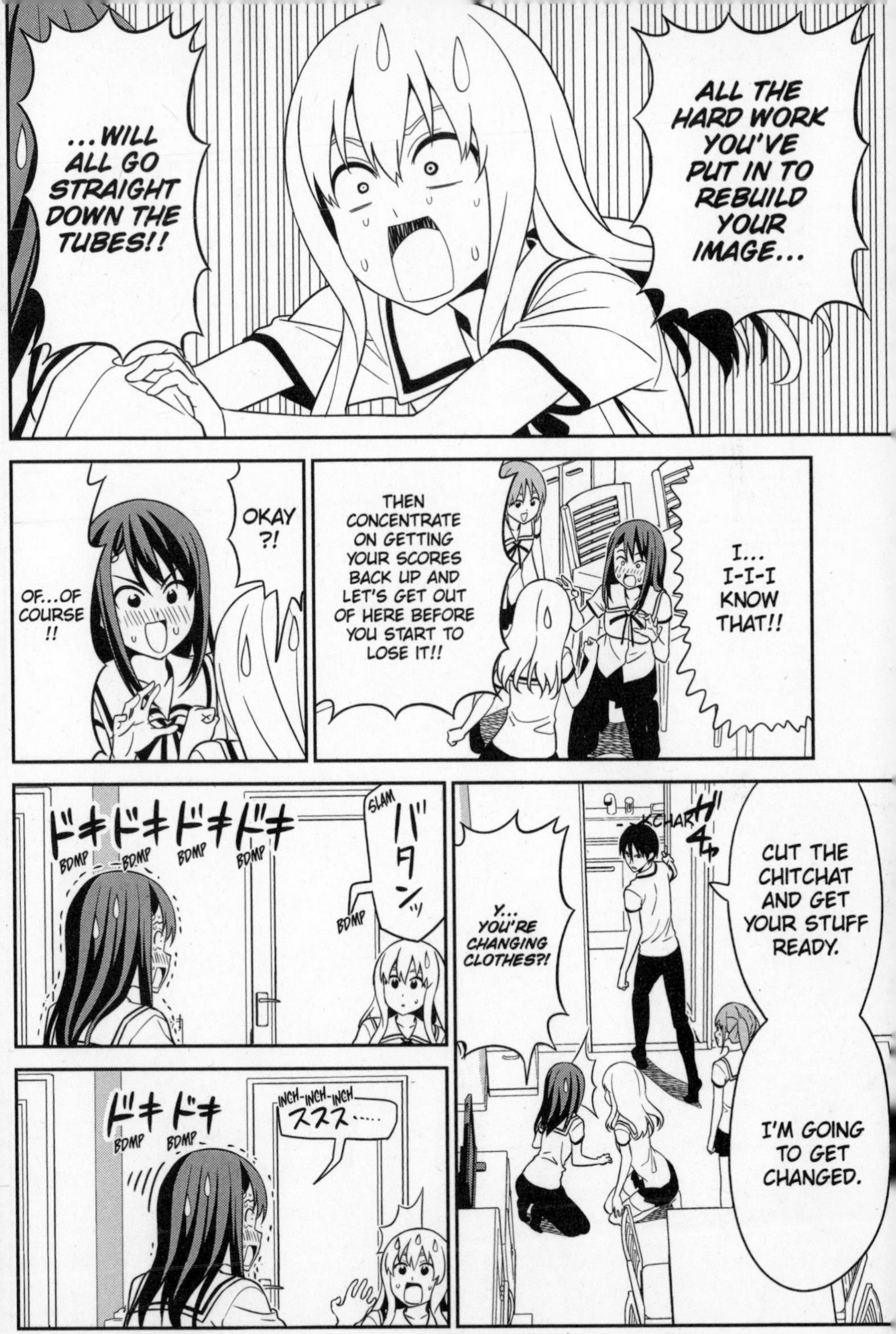

ALL THE HARD WORK YOU'VE PUT IN TO REBUILD YOUR IMAGE...
...WILL ALL GO STRAIGHT DOWN THE TUBES!!
I... I-I-I KNOW THAT!!
THEN CONCENTRATE ON GETTING YOUR SCORES BACK UP AND LET'S GET OUT OF HERE BEFORE YOU START TO LOSE IT!!
OKAY ?!
OF...OF COURSE !!
ガチャ
KCHAK
CUT THE CHITCHAT AND GET YOUR STUFF READY.
I'M GOING TO GET CHANGED.
Y... YOU'RE CHANGING CLOTHES?!
バタンッ
SLAM
BDMP
ドキドキドキドキ
BDMP BDMP BDMP BDMP
ススス.....
INCH-INCH-INCH
ドキドキ
BDMP BDMP

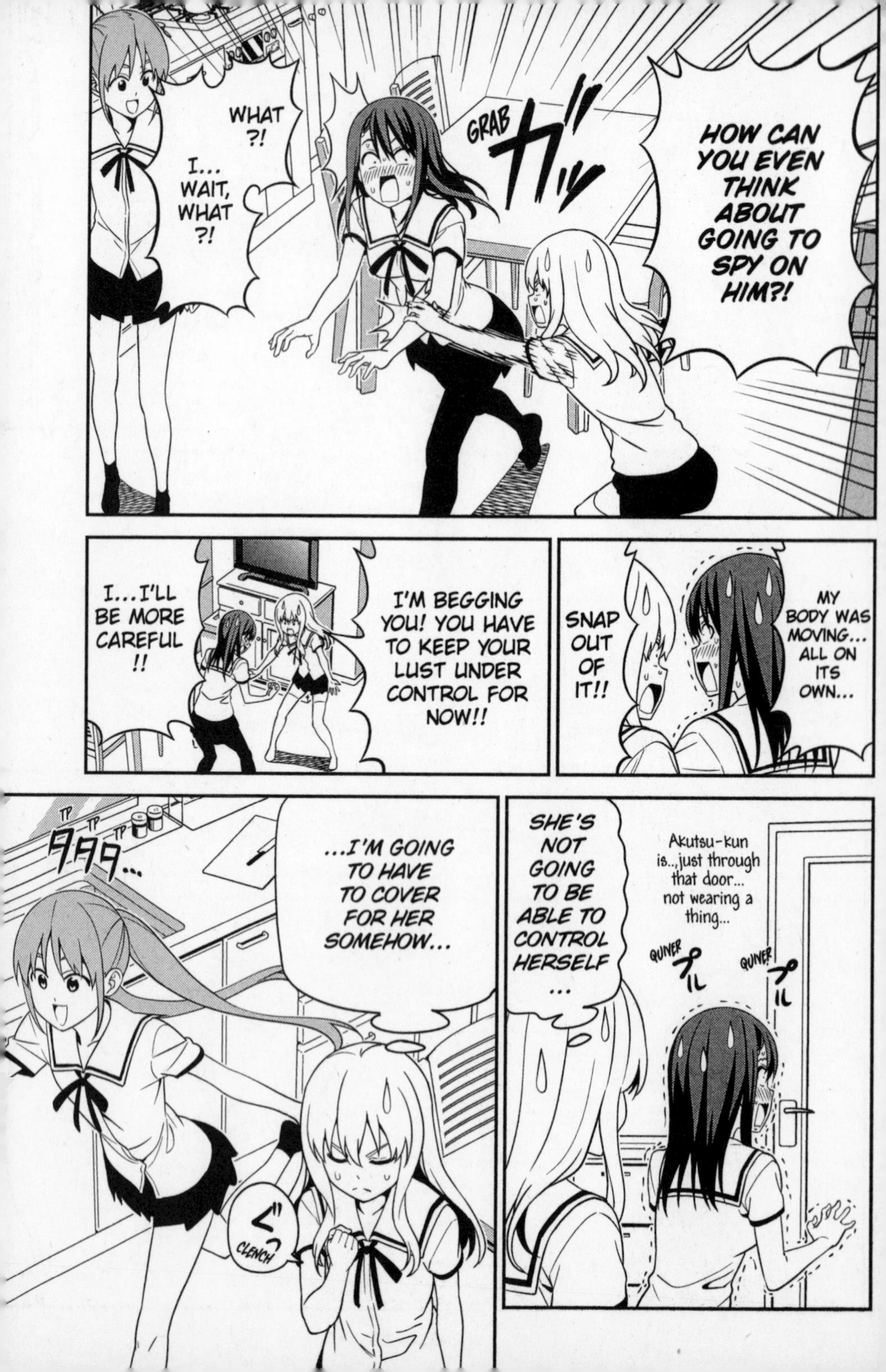
HOW CAN YOU EVEN THINK ABOUT GOING TO SPY ON HIM?!
GRAB
ガッ
WHAT ?!
I... WAIT, WHAT ?!
MY BODY WAS MOVING... ALL ON ITS OWN...
SNAP OUT OF IT!!
I'M BEGGING YOU! YOU HAVE TO KEEP YOUR LUST UNDER CONTROL FOR NOW!!
I... I'LL BE MORE CAREFUL !!
Akutsu-kun is... just through that door... not wearing a thing...
QUIVER
ぷル
QUIVER
ぷル
SHE'S NOT GOING TO BE ABLE TO CONTROL HERSELF ...
...I'M GOING TO HAVE TO COVER FOR HER SOMEHOW...
TP TP TP
タタタ...
ぐっ
CLENCH

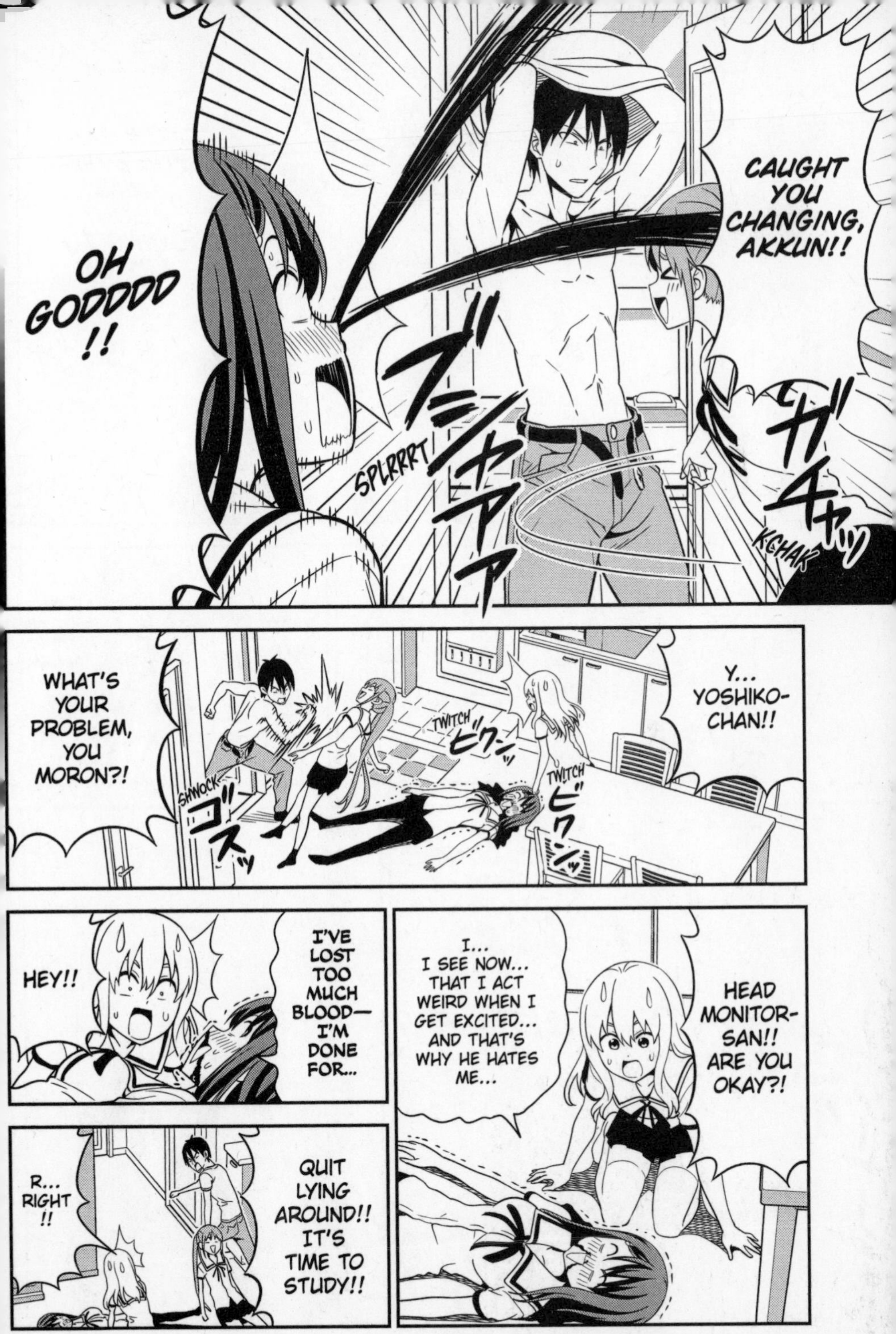
CAUGHT YOU CHANGING, AKKUN!!
KCHAK
SPLRRRT
OH GODDDDD !!
Y... YOSHIKO-CHAN!!
TWITCH
TWITCH
WHAT'S YOUR PROBLEM, YOU MORON?!
SHNOCK
HEAD MONITOR-SAN!! ARE YOU OKAY?!
I... I SEE NOW... THAT I ACT WEIRD WHEN I GET EXCITED... AND THAT'S WHY HE HATES ME...
I'VE LOST TOO MUCH BLOOD— I'M DONE FOR...
HEY!!
QUIT LYING AROUND!! IT'S TIME TO STUDY!!
R... RIGHT !!

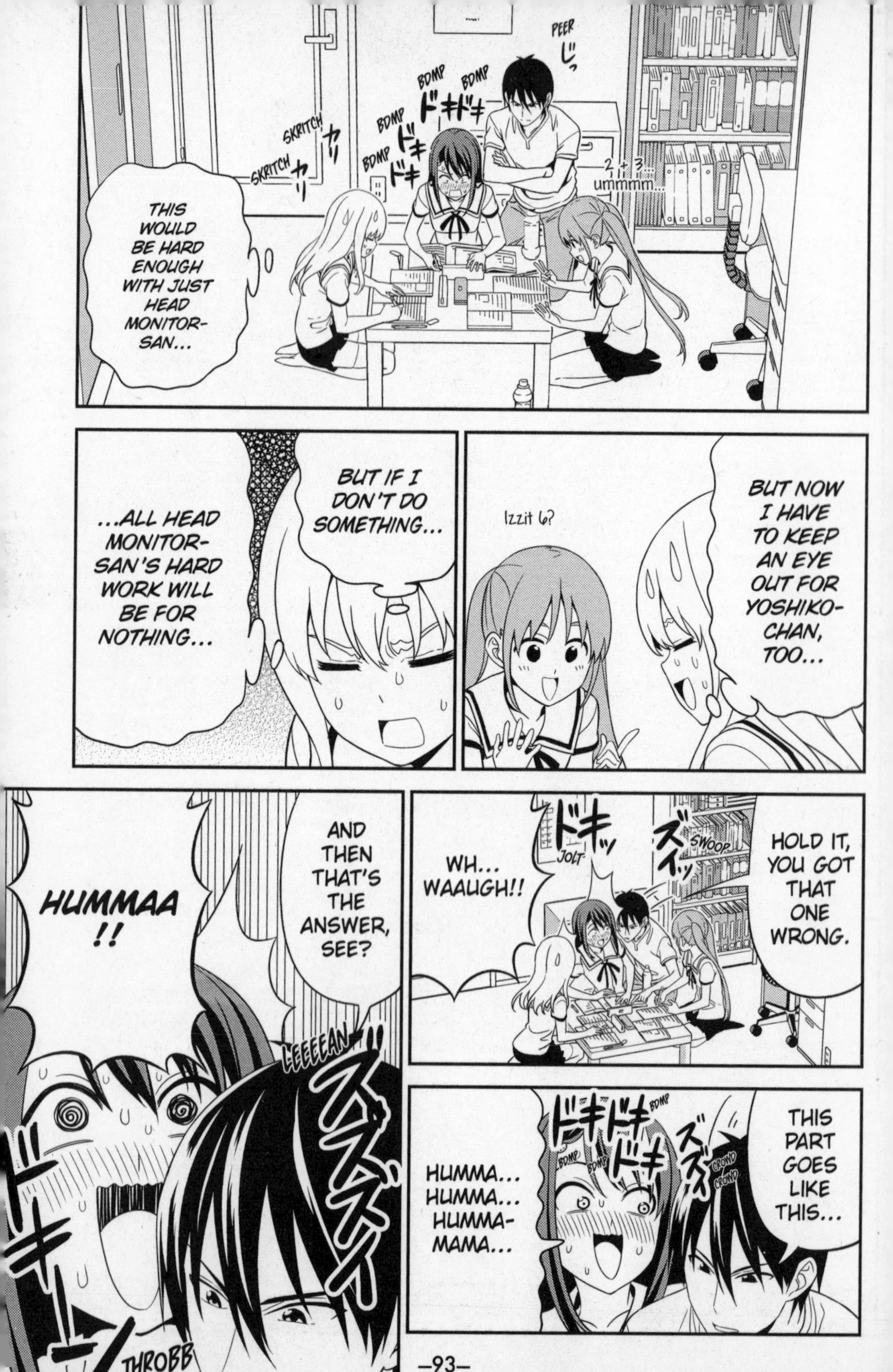
PEER
BDMP BDMP
BDMP BDMP
SKRITCH SKRITCH
2 + 3... ummmm...
THIS WOULD BE HARD ENOUGH WITH JUST HEAD MONITOR-SAN...
BUT NOW I HAVE TO KEEP AN EYE OUT FOR YOSHIKO-CHAN, TOO...
Izzit 6?
BUT IF I DON'T DO SOMETHING...
...ALL HEAD MONITOR-SAN'S HARD WORK WILL BE FOR NOTHING...
HOLD IT, YOU GOT THAT ONE WRONG.
SWOOP
JOLT
WH... WAAUGH!!
THIS PART GOES LIKE THIS...
CROWD CROWD
BDMP BDMP BDMP
HUMMA... HUMMA... HUMMA-MAMA...
AND THEN THAT'S THE ANSWER, SEE?
LEEEEAN
HUMMAA!!
THROBB

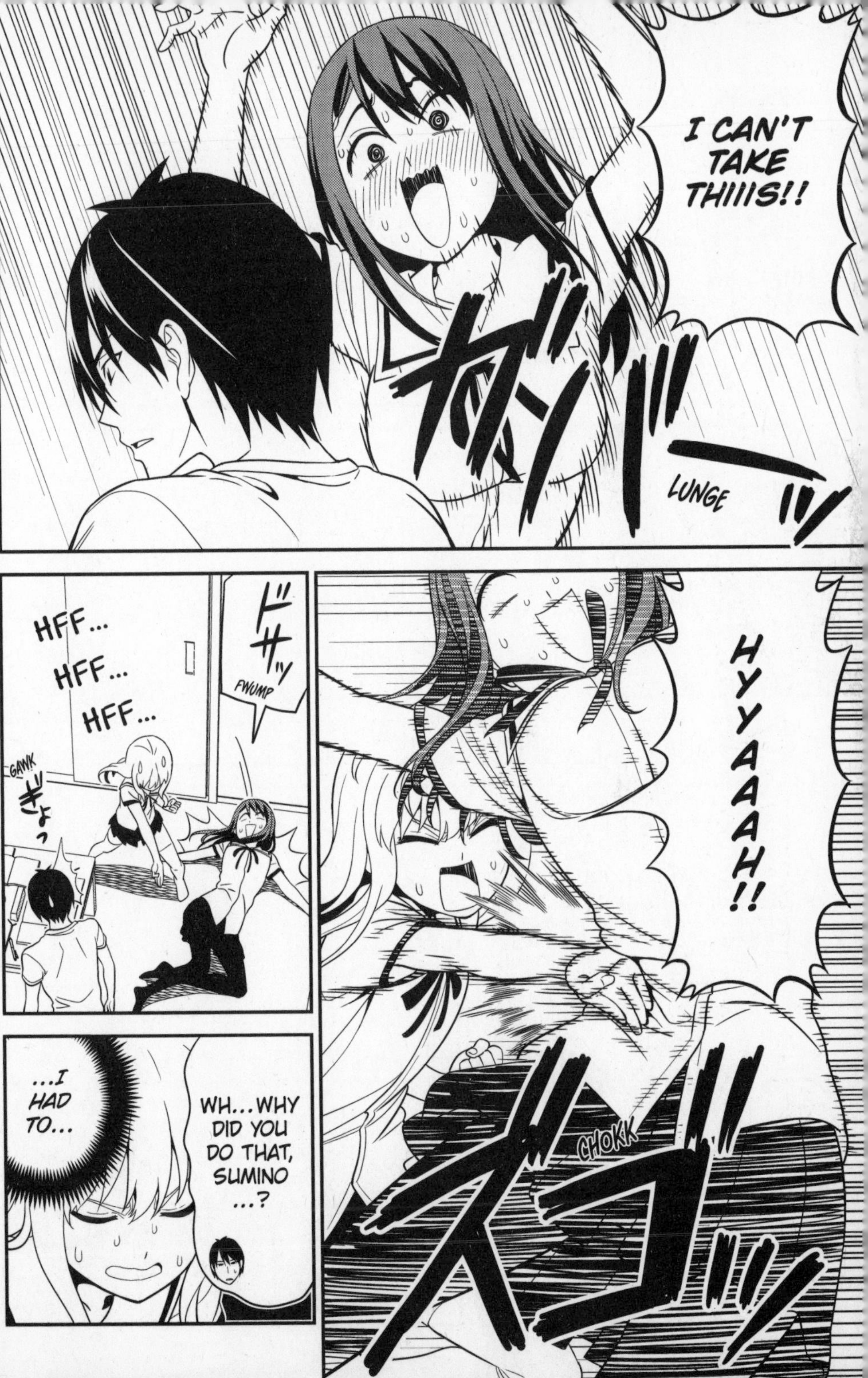
I CAN'T TAKE THIIIS!!
LUNGE
HYYAAAAH!!
CHOKK
ドサッ
FWUMP
HFF... HFF... HFF...
ぎょっ
GAWK
WH...WHY DID YOU DO THAT, SUMINO ...?
...I HAD TO...

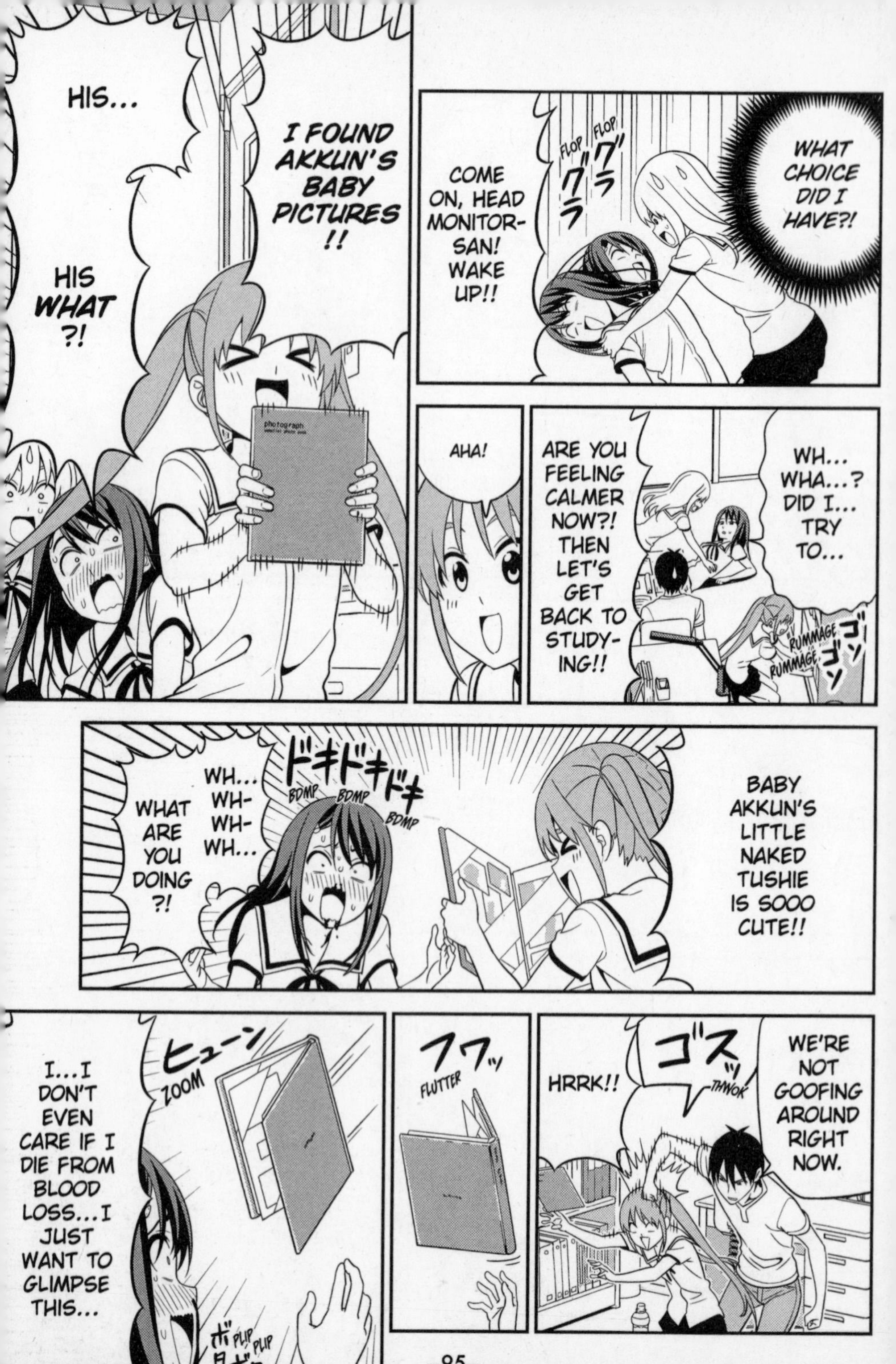
WHAT CHOICE DID I HAVE?!
COME ON, HEAD MONITOR-SAN! WAKE UP!!
グラグラ FLOP FLOP
WH... WHA...? DID I... TRY TO...
ARE YOU FEELING CALMER NOW?! THEN LET'S GET BACK TO STUDY-ING!!
ゴソゴソ RUMMAGE RUMMAGE
AHA!
I FOUND AKKUN'S BABY PICTURES!!
HIS...
HIS WHAT?!
BABY AKKUN'S LITTLE NAKED TUSHIE IS SOOO CUTE!!
ドキドキドキ BDMP BDMP BDMP
WH... WH-WH-WH...
WHAT ARE YOU DOING?!
WE'RE NOT GOOFING AROUND RIGHT NOW.
ゴスッ THWOK
HRRK!!
フワッ FLUTTER
ヒューン ZOOM
I...I DON'T EVEN CARE IF I DIE FROM BLOOD LOSS...I JUST WANT TO GLIMPSE THIS...
ボタボタ PLIP PLIP

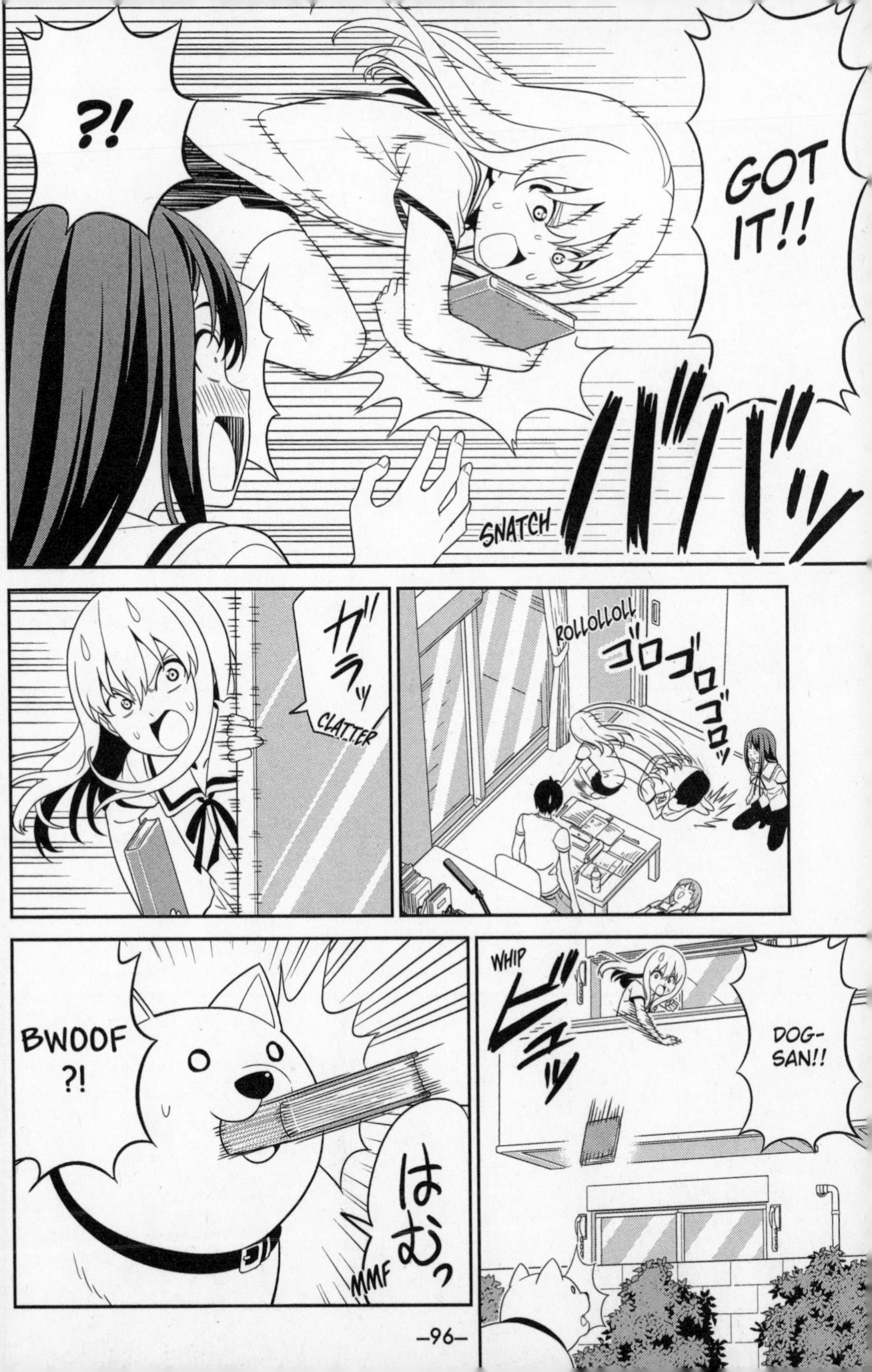
GOT IT!!
?!
SNATCH
バッ
ROLLOLLOLL
ゴロゴロゴロッ
ガラッ
CLATTER
DOG-SAN!!
WHIP
ビュッ
BWOOF ?!
はむっ
MMF

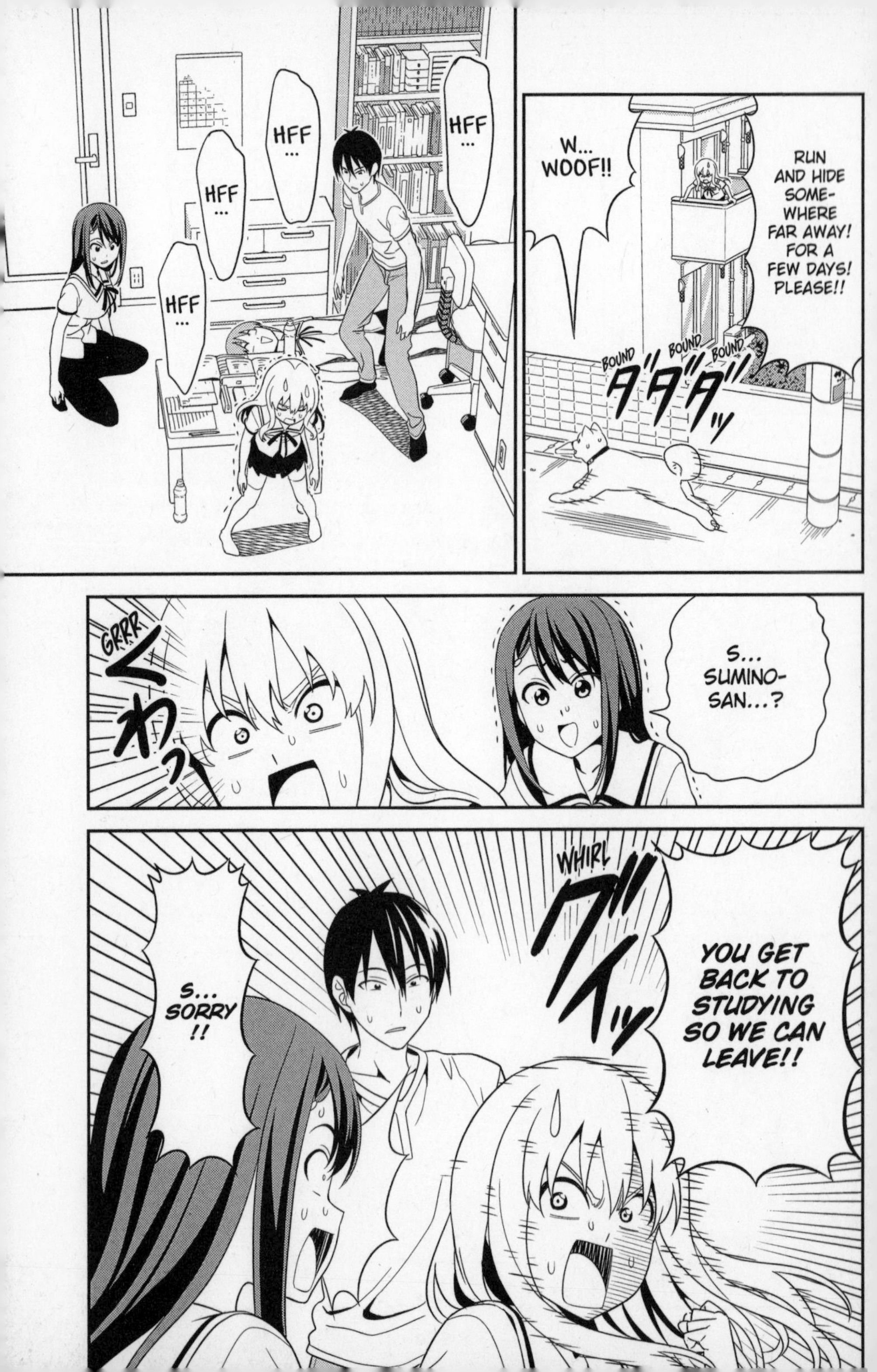

RUN AND HIDE SOMEWHERE FAR AWAY! FOR A FEW DAYS! PLEASE!!
W... WOOF!!
BOUND BOUND BOUND
HFF ...
HFF ...
HFF ...
HFF ...
S... SUMINO-SAN...?
GRRR
WHIRL
YOU GET BACK TO STUDYING SO WE CAN LEAVE!!
S... SORRY !!

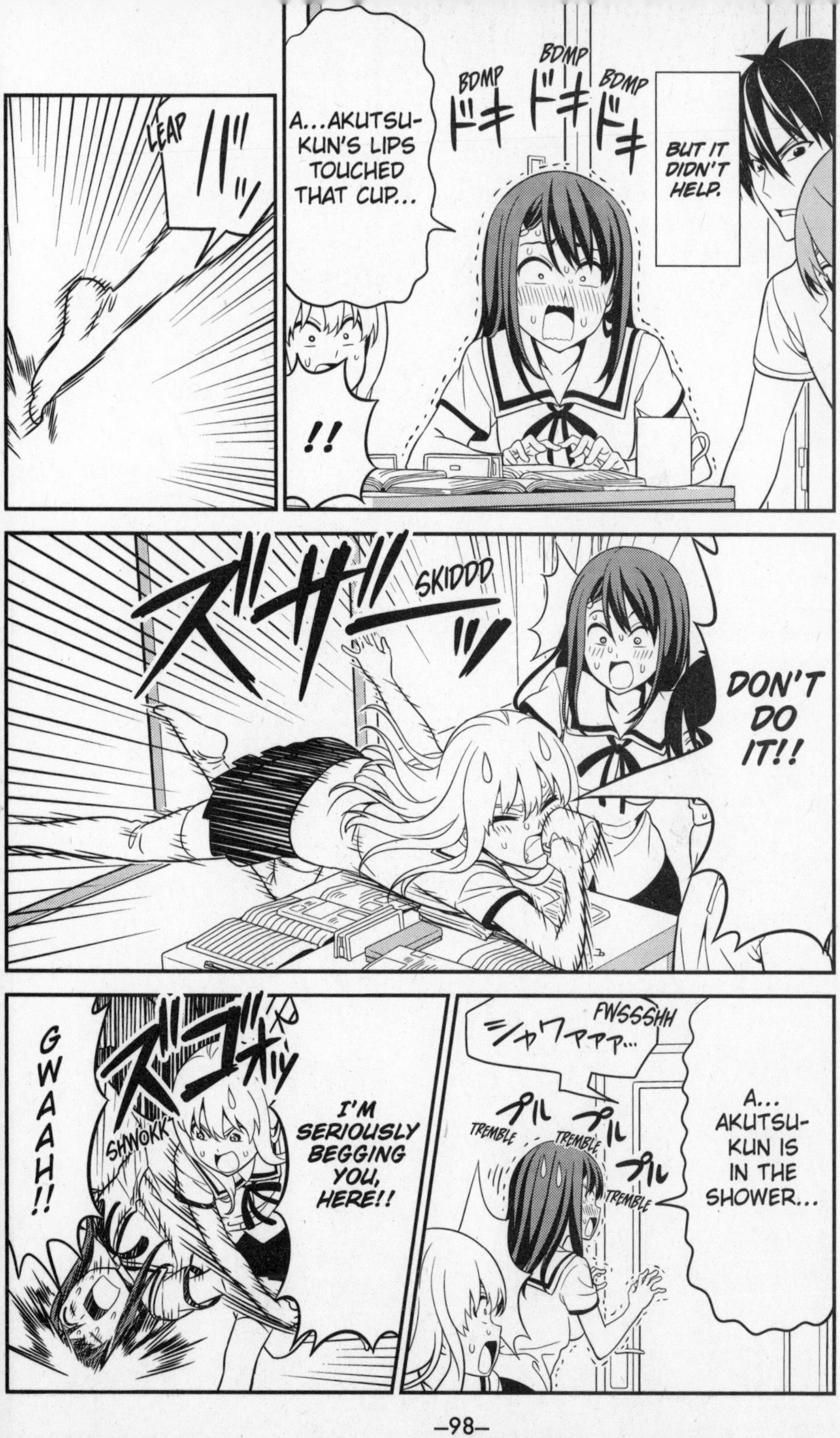
BUT IT DIDN'T HELP.
BDMP BDMP BDMP
ドキドキドキ
A...AKUTSU-KUN'S LIPS TOUCHED THAT CUP...
!!
LEAP
DON'T DO IT!!
SKIDDD
ズザーッ
A... AKUTSU-KUN IS IN THE SHOWER...
TREMBLE TREMBLE TREMBLE
プルプルプル
FWSSSHH
シャワァァァ...
I'M SERIOUSLY BEGGING YOU, HERE!!
SHWOKK
GWAAAH!!

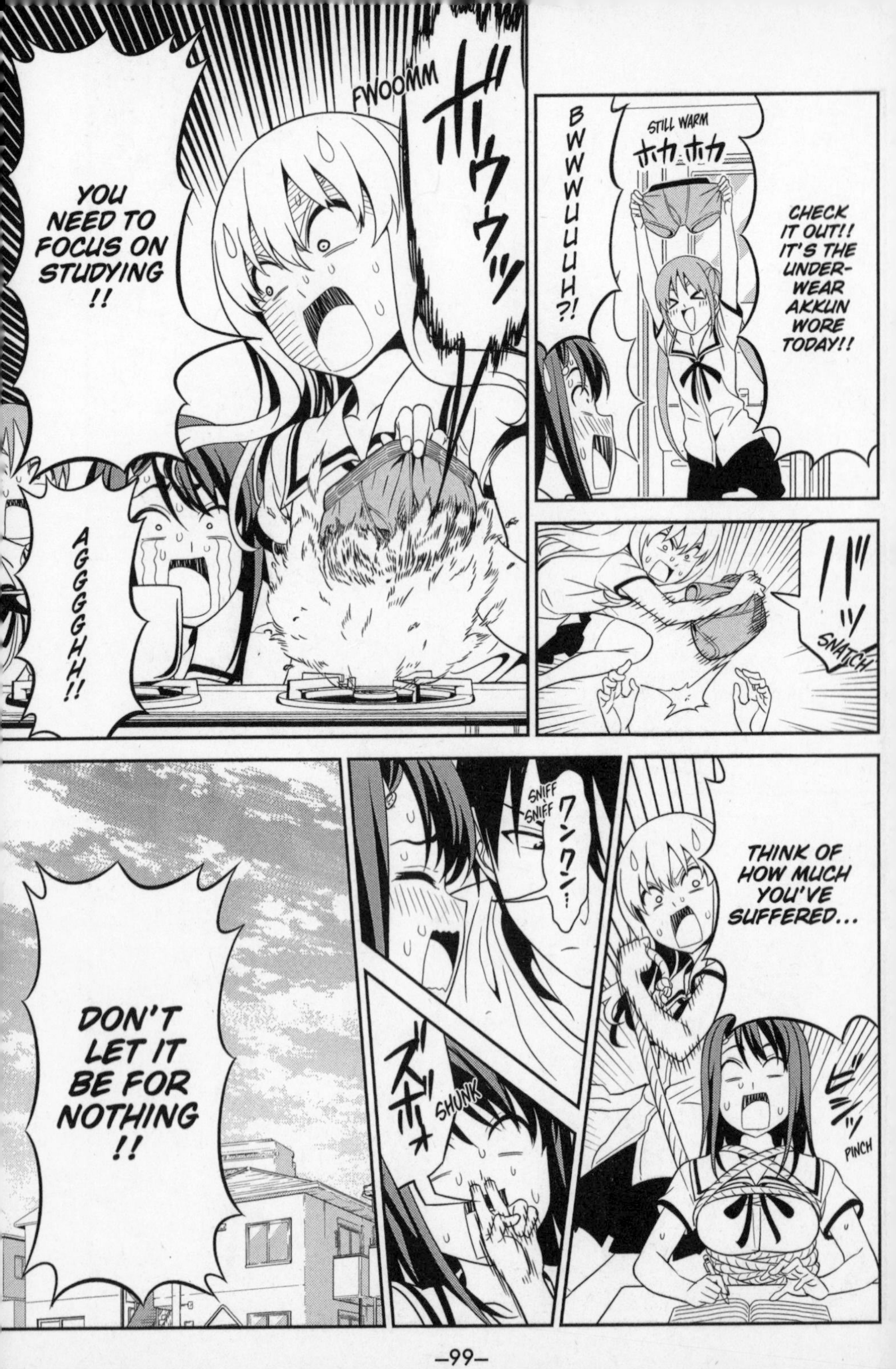
CHECK IT OUT!! IT'S THE UNDER-WEAR AKKUN WORE TODAY!!
ホカホカ
STILL WARM
BWWWUUUUH?!
バッ
SNATCH
ボウウッ
FWOOMM
YOU NEED TO FOCUS ON STUDYING!!
AGGGGHH!!
THINK OF HOW MUCH YOU'VE SUFFERED...
PINCH
クンクン…
SNIFF SNIFF
ズボォ
SHUNK
DON'T LET IT BE FOR NOTHING!!

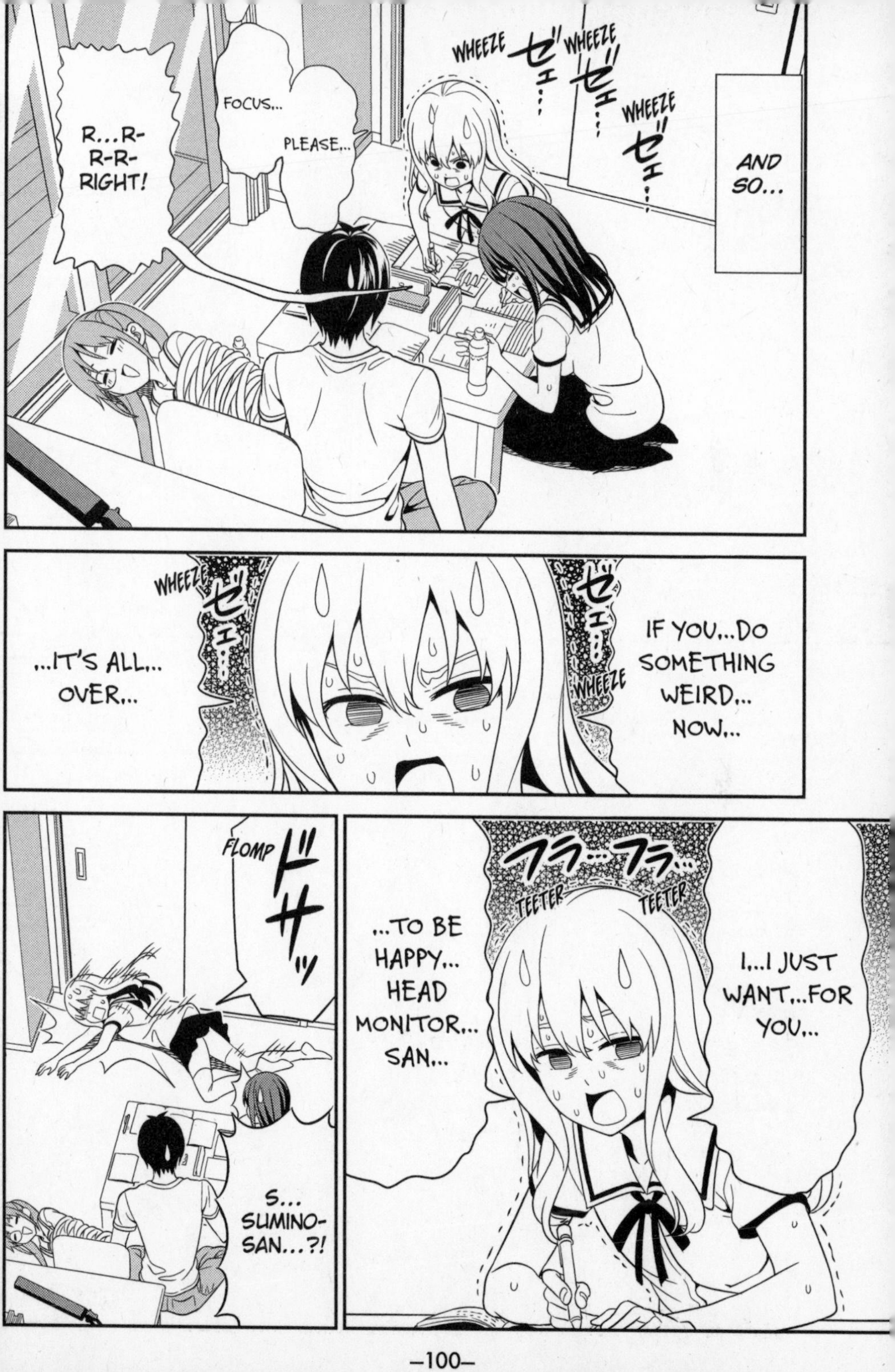
AND SO...
WHEEZE ゼェ…
WHEEZE ゼェ…
WHEEZE ゼェ…
FOCUS...
PLEASE...
R...R-R-R-RIGHT!
IF YOU...DO SOMETHING WEIRD... NOW...
ゼェ… WHEEZE
WHEEZE ゼェ…
...IT'S ALL... OVER...
I...I JUST WANT...FOR YOU...
フラ… フラ…
TEETER TEETER
...TO BE HAPPY... HEAD MONITOR... SAN...
FLOMP ドサッ
S... SUMINO-SAN...?!

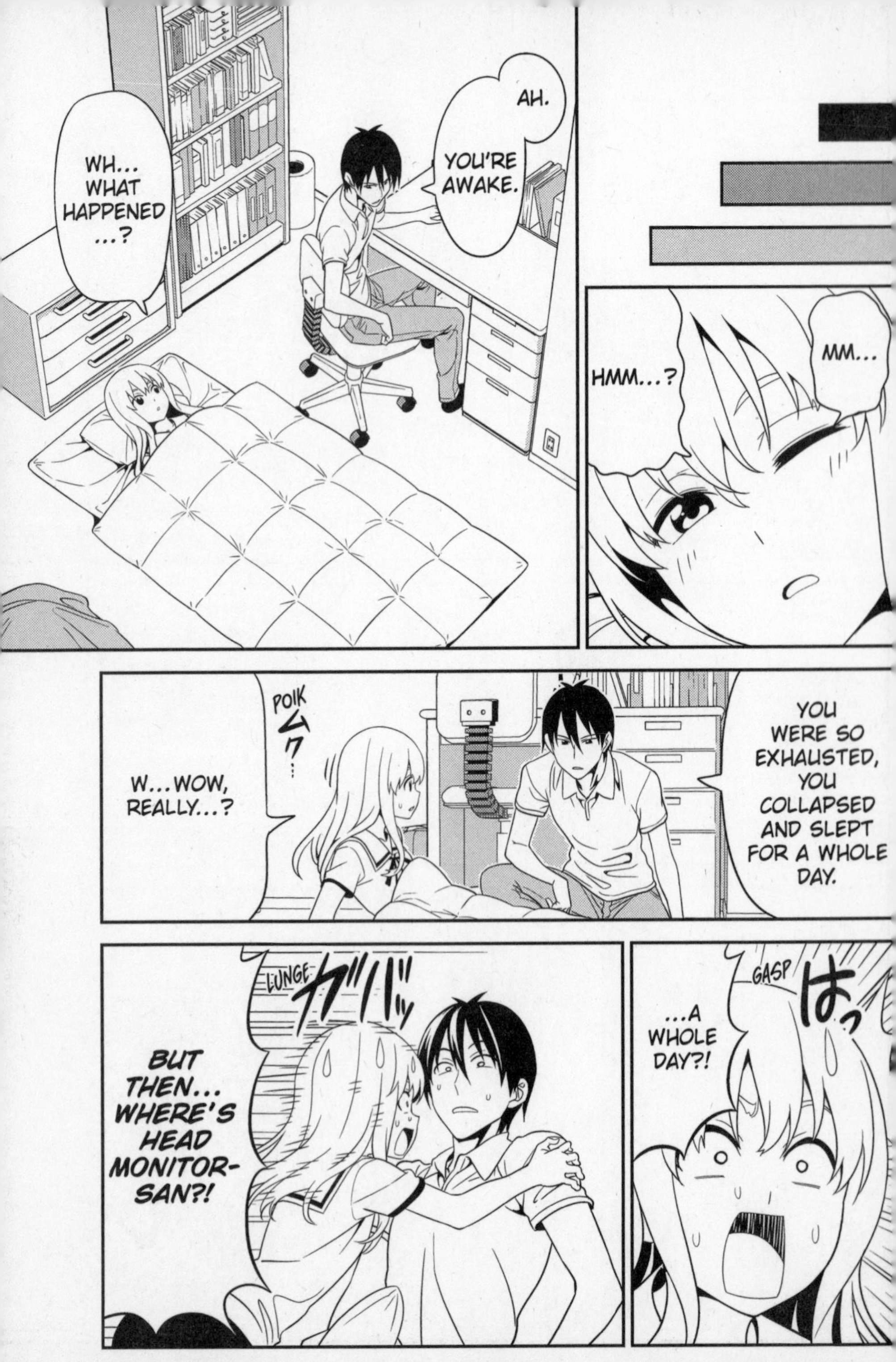
MM...
HMM...?
AH.
YOU'RE AWAKE.
WH... WHAT HAPPENED ...?
YOU WERE SO EXHAUSTED, YOU COLLAPSED AND SLEPT FOR A WHOLE DAY.
POIK
ムク
W...WOW, REALLY...?
GASP
はっ
...A WHOLE DAY?!
LUNGE
ガバッ
BUT THEN... WHERE'S HEAD MONITOR-SAN?!

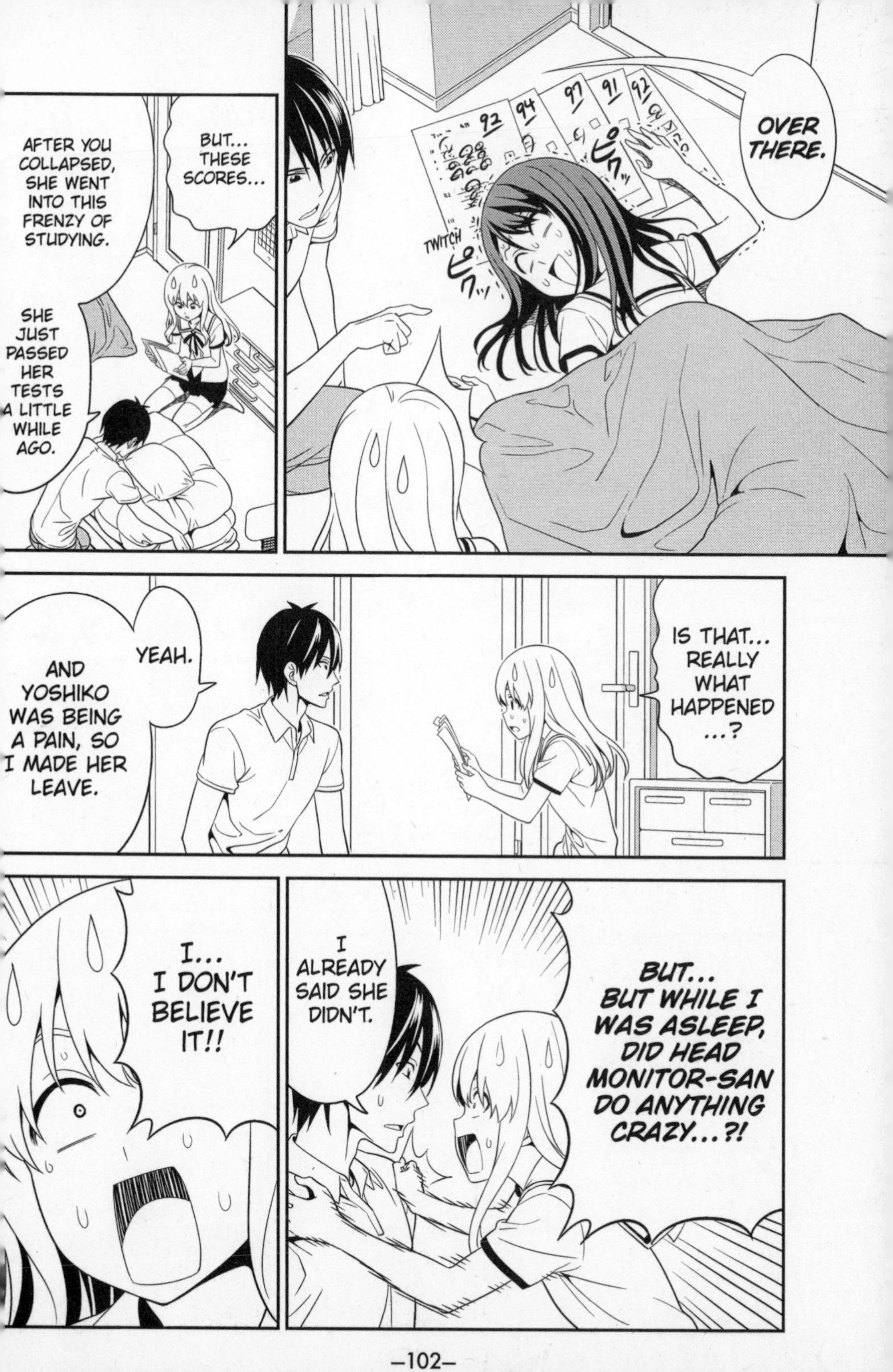
OVER THERE.
TWITCH
BUT... THESE SCORES...
AFTER YOU COLLAPSED, SHE WENT INTO THIS FRENZY OF STUDYING.
SHE JUST PASSED HER TESTS A LITTLE WHILE AGO.
IS THAT... REALLY WHAT HAPPENED ...?
YEAH.
AND YOSHIKO WAS BEING A PAIN, SO I MADE HER LEAVE.
BUT... BUT WHILE I WAS ASLEEP, DID HEAD MONITOR-SAN DO ANYTHING CRAZY...?!
I ALREADY SAID SHE DIDN'T.
I... I DON'T BELIEVE IT!!

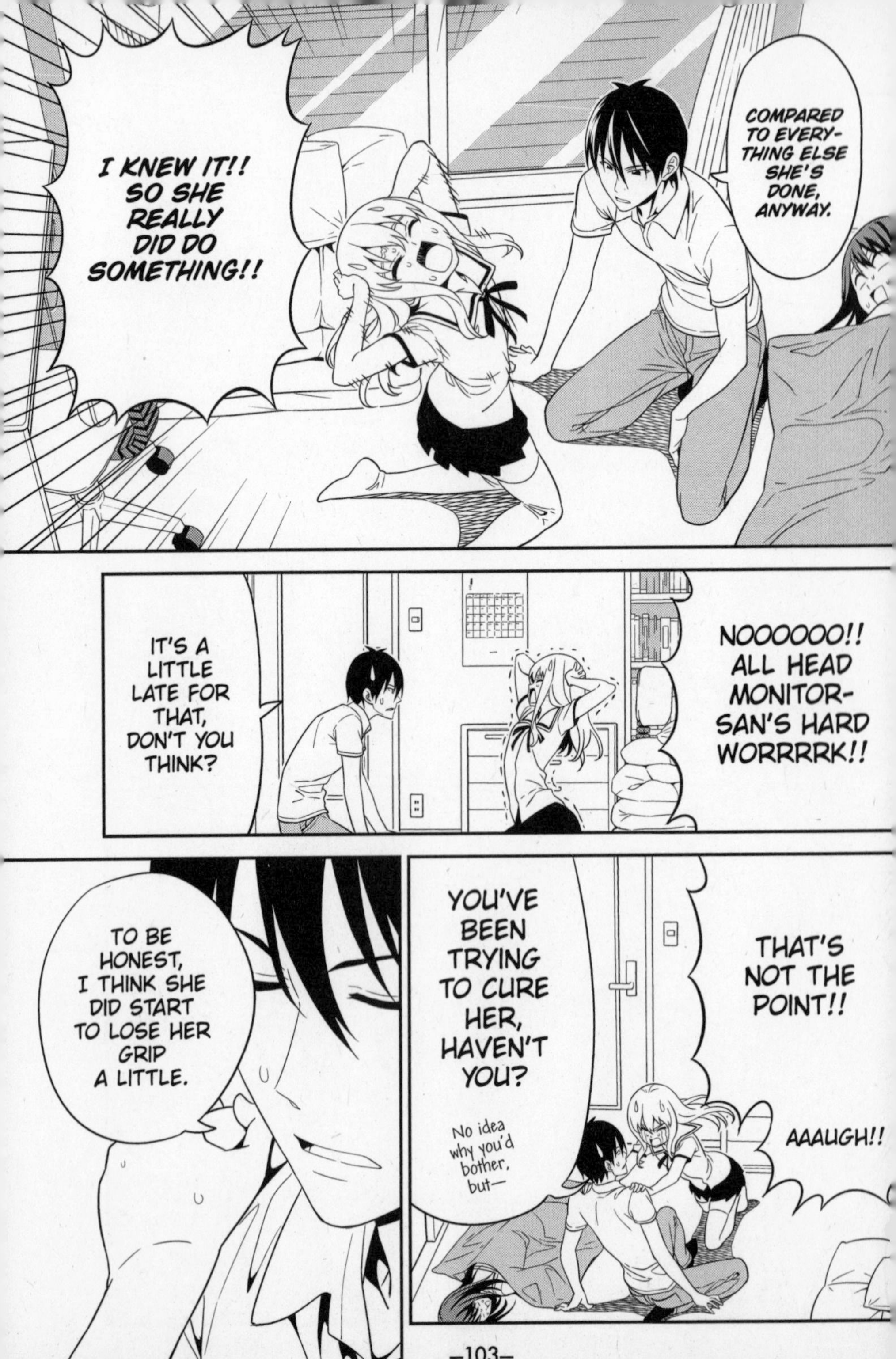
COMPARED TO EVERY-THING ELSE SHE'S DONE, ANYWAY.
I KNEW IT!! SO SHE REALLY DID DO SOMETHING!!
NOOOOOO!! ALL HEAD MONITOR-SAN'S HARD WORRRRK!!
IT'S A LITTLE LATE FOR THAT, DON'T YOU THINK?
THAT'S NOT THE POINT!!
AAAUGH!!
YOU'VE BEEN TRYING TO CURE HER, HAVEN'T YOU?
No idea why you'd bother, but—
TO BE HONEST, I THINK SHE DID START TO LOSE HER GRIP A LITTLE.

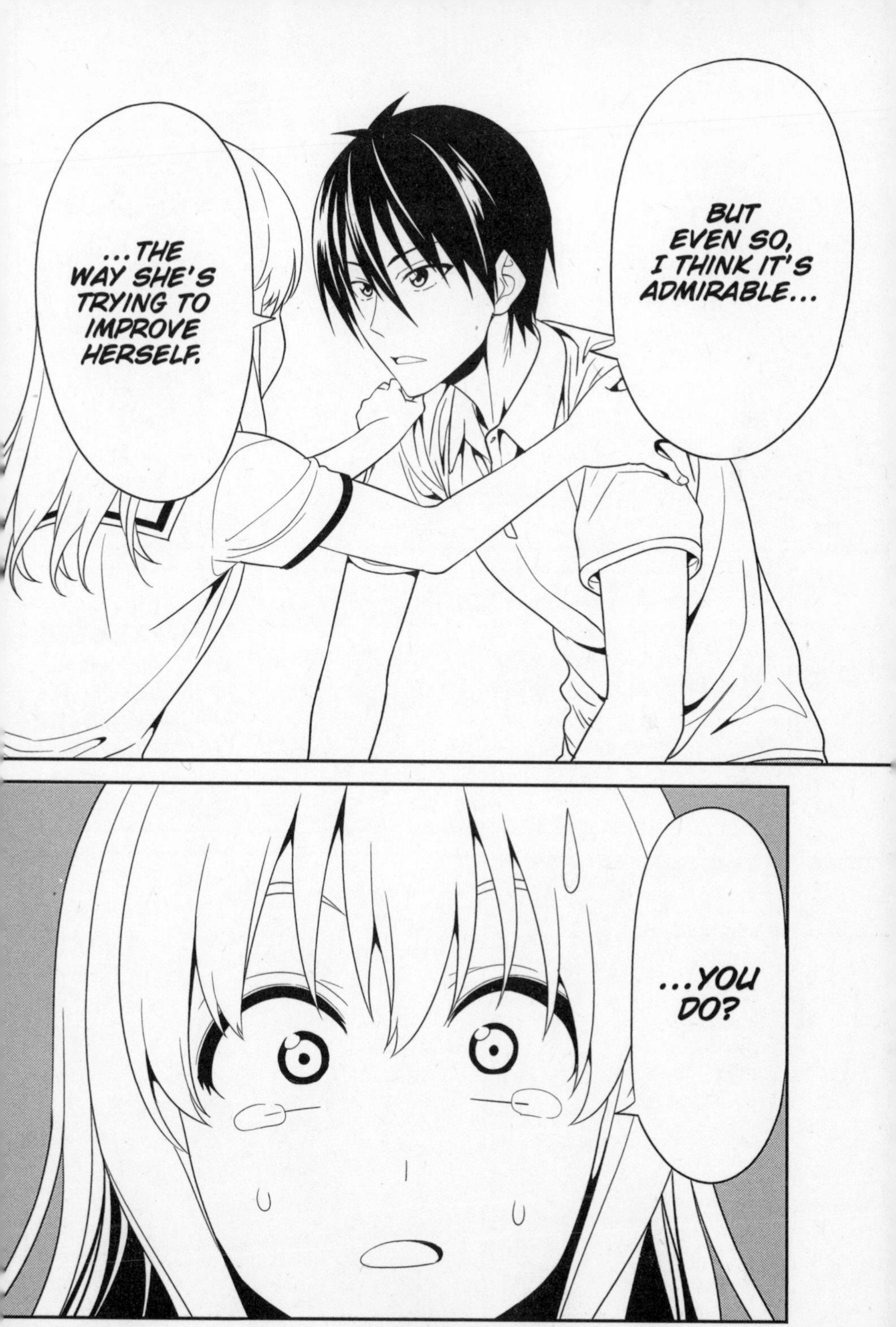
BUT EVEN SO, I THINK IT'S ADMIRABLE...
...THE WAY SHE'S TRYING TO IMPROVE HERSELF.
...YOU DO?

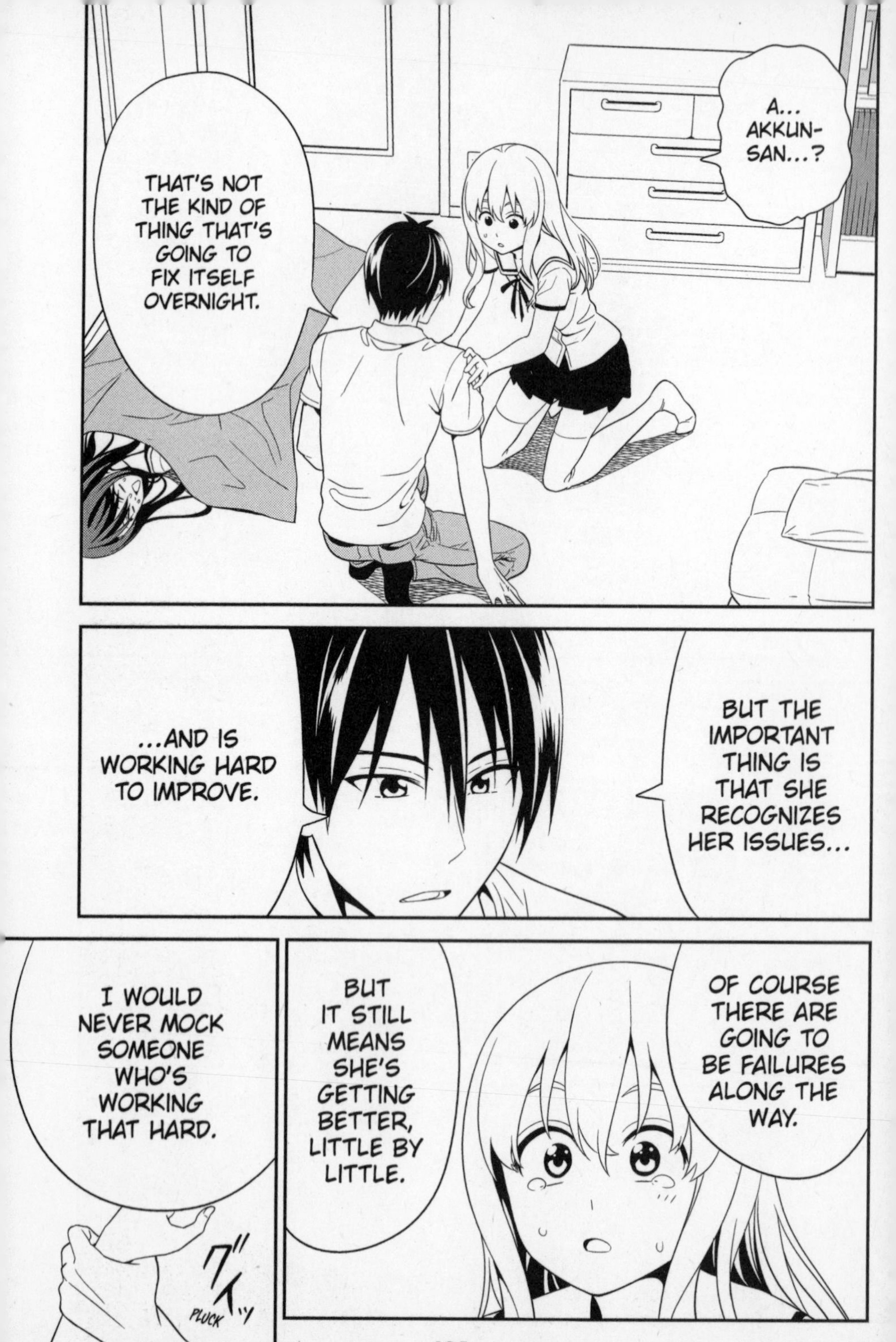
A... AKKUN-SAN...?
THAT'S NOT THE KIND OF THING THAT'S GOING TO FIX ITSELF OVERNIGHT.
BUT THE IMPORTANT THING IS THAT SHE RECOGNIZES HER ISSUES...
...AND IS WORKING HARD TO IMPROVE.
OF COURSE THERE ARE GOING TO BE FAILURES ALONG THE WAY.
BUT IT STILL MEANS SHE'S GETTING BETTER, LITTLE BY LITTLE.
I WOULD NEVER MOCK SOMEONE WHO'S WORKING THAT HARD.
PLUCK

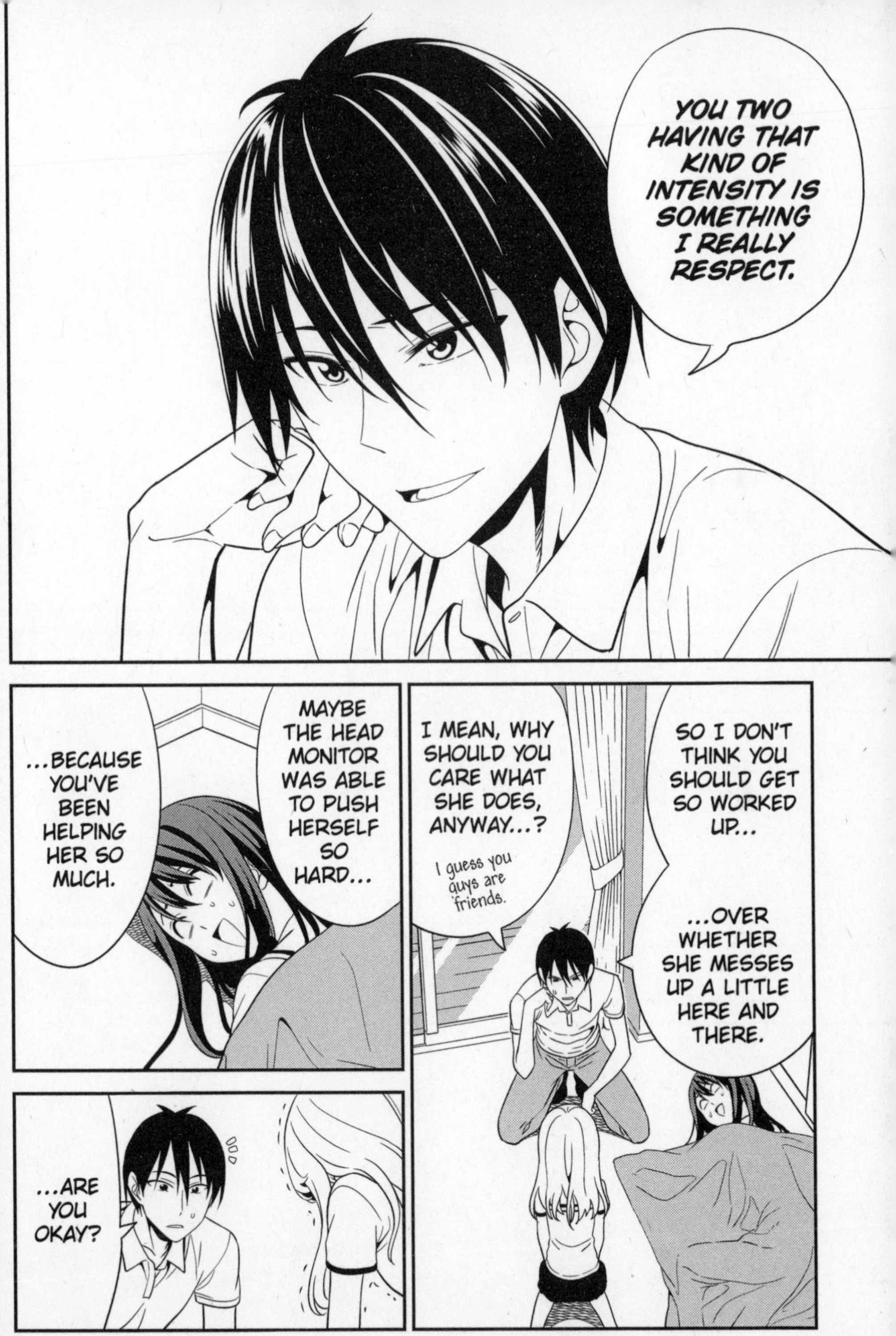
YOU TWO HAVING THAT KIND OF INTENSITY IS SOMETHING I REALLY RESPECT.
SO I DON'T THINK YOU SHOULD GET SO WORKED UP...
...OVER WHETHER SHE MESSES UP A LITTLE HERE AND THERE.
I MEAN, WHY SHOULD YOU CARE WHAT SHE DOES, ANYWAY...?
I guess you guys are friends.
MAYBE THE HEAD MONITOR WAS ABLE TO PUSH HERSELF SO HARD...
...BECAUSE YOU'VE BEEN HELPING HER SO MUCH.
...ARE YOU OKAY?

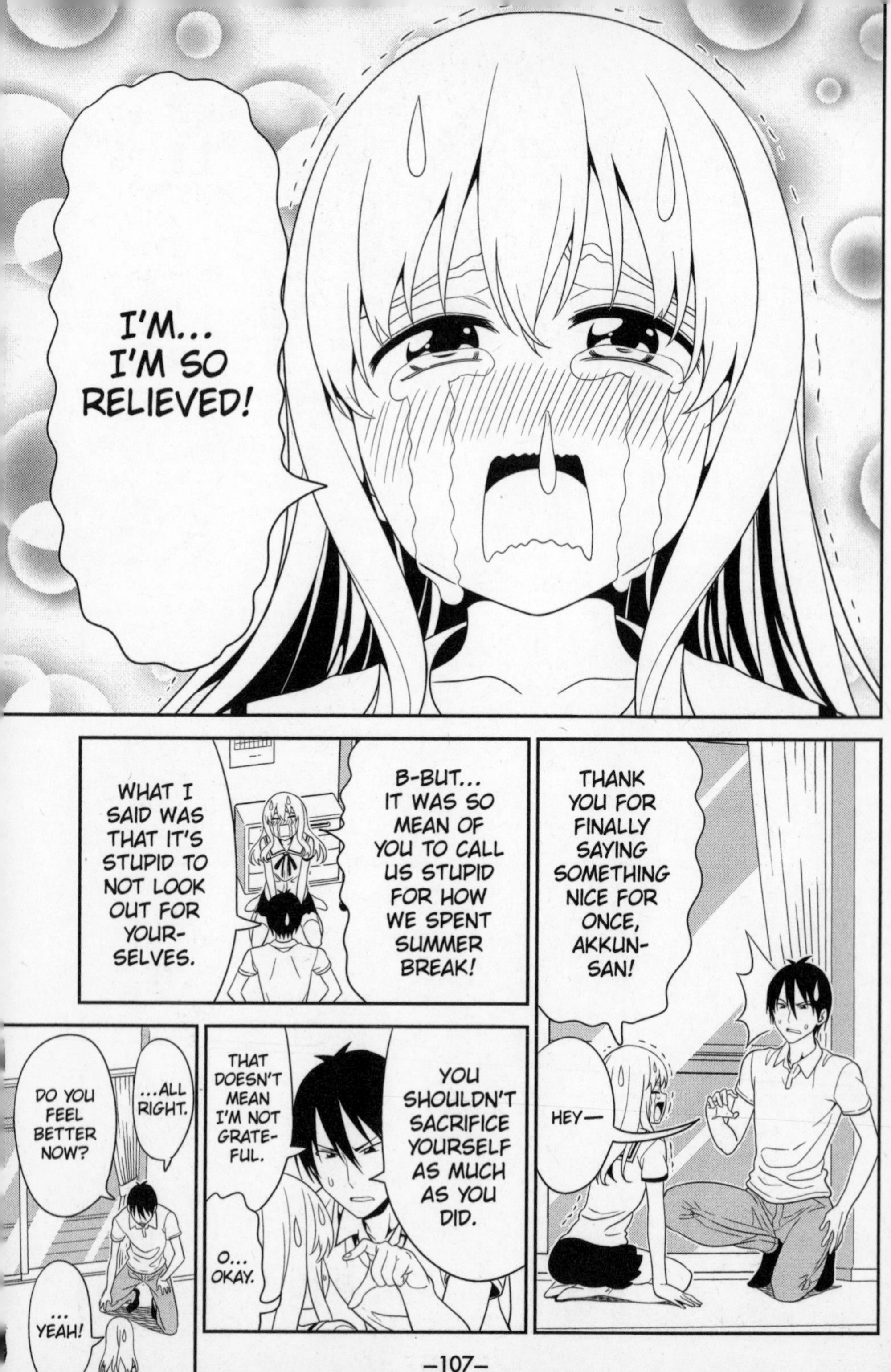
I'M... I'M SO RELIEVED!
THANK YOU FOR FINALLY SAYING SOMETHING NICE FOR ONCE, AKKUN-SAN!
HEY—
B-BUT... IT WAS SO MEAN OF YOU TO CALL US STUPID FOR HOW WE SPENT SUMMER BREAK!
WHAT I SAID WAS THAT IT'S STUPID TO NOT LOOK OUT FOR YOUR-SELVES.
YOU SHOULDN'T SACRIFICE YOURSELF AS MUCH AS YOU DID.
THAT DOESN'T MEAN I'M NOT GRATE-FUL.
O... OKAY.
...ALL RIGHT.
DO YOU FEEL BETTER NOW?
... YEAH!

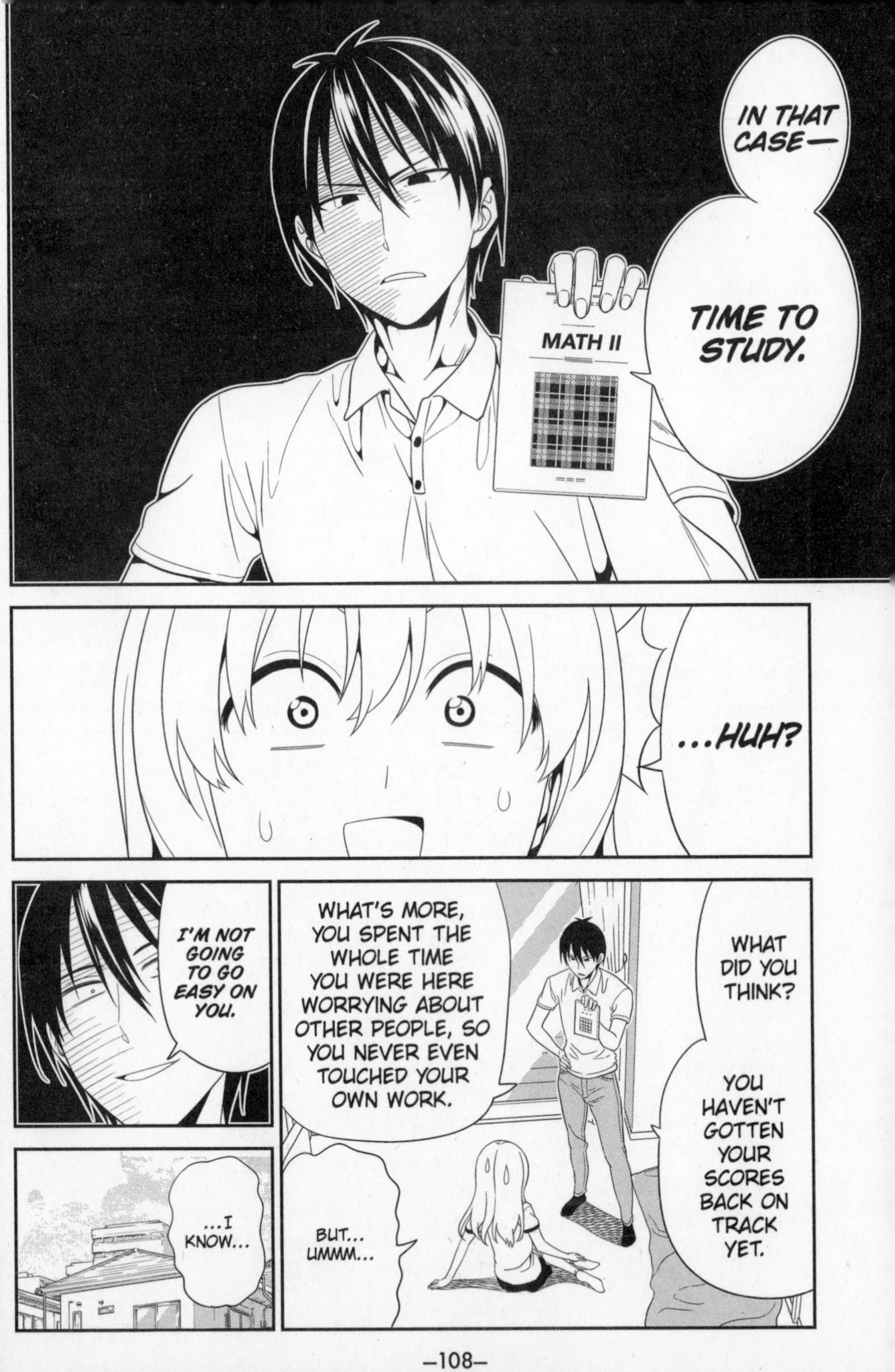
IN THAT CASE—
TIME TO STUDY.
MATH II
...HUH?
WHAT DID YOU THINK?
YOU HAVEN'T GOTTEN YOUR SCORES BACK ON TRACK YET.
WHAT'S MORE, YOU SPENT THE WHOLE TIME YOU WERE HERE WORRYING ABOUT OTHER PEOPLE, SO YOU NEVER EVEN TOUCHED YOUR OWN WORK.
BUT... UMMM...
I'M NOT GOING TO GO EASY ON YOU.
...I KNOW...

Merciless

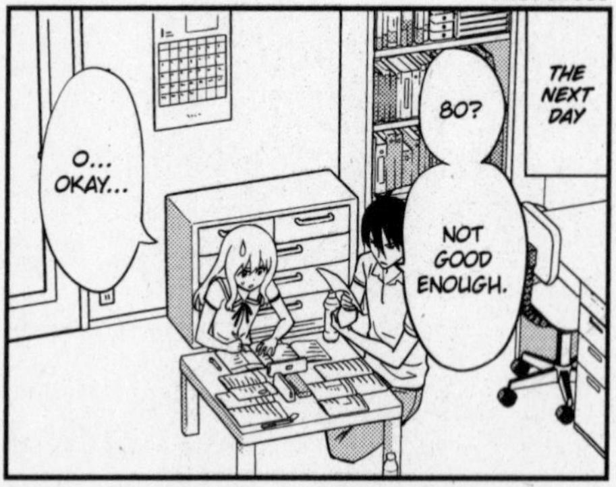
THE NEXT DAY
80?
NOT GOOD ENOUGH.
O... OKAY...

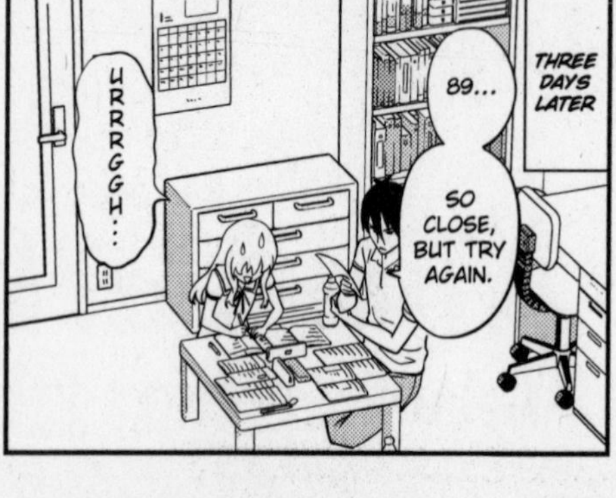
THREE DAYS LATER
89...
SO CLOSE, BUT TRY AGAIN.
URRRGGH...

Aho-Girl

\\'ahô͵gərl\\ *Japanese, noun.*
A clueless girl.

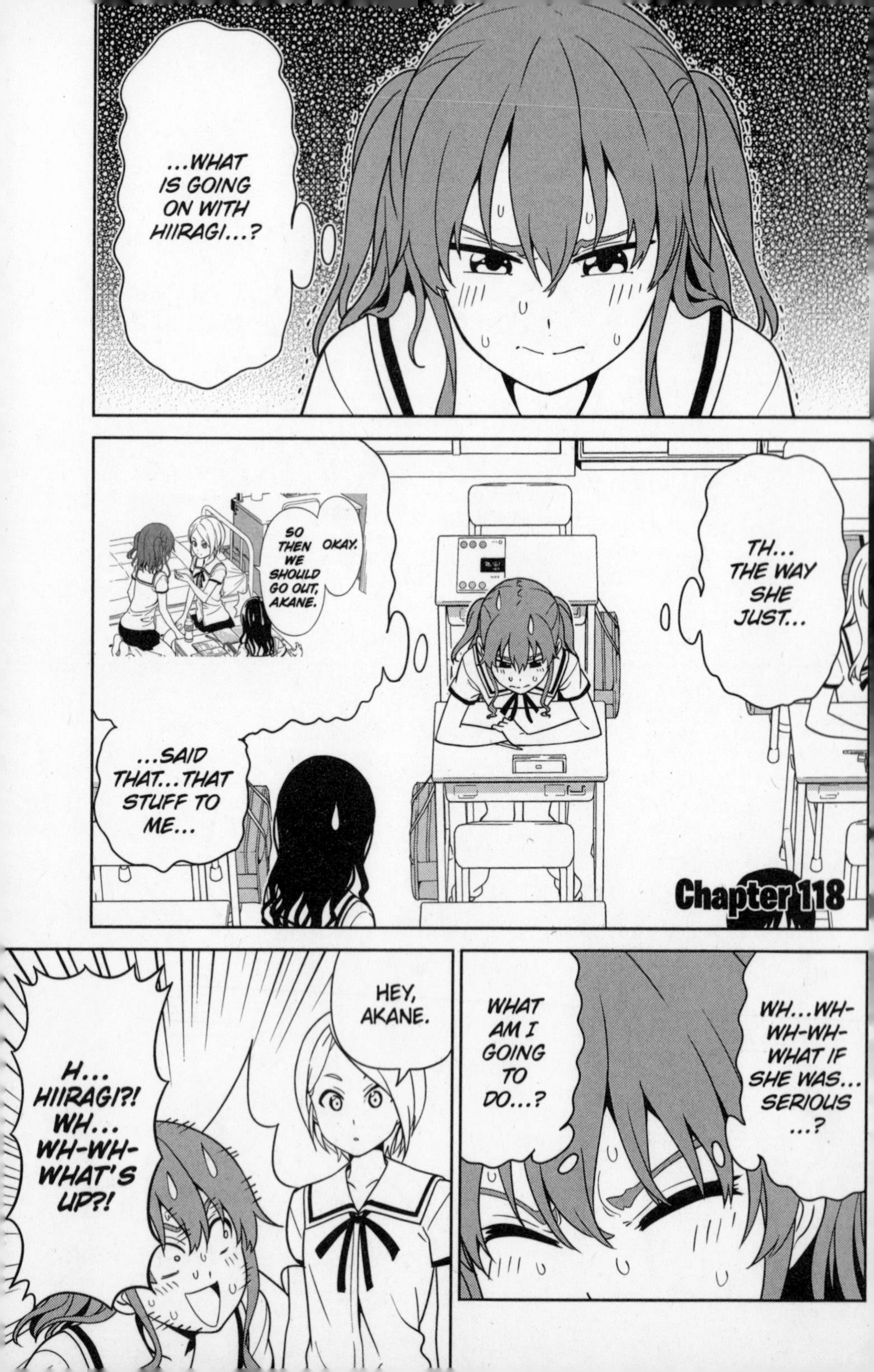
...WHAT IS GOING ON WITH HIIRAGI...?
TH... THE WAY SHE JUST...
OKAY.
SO THEN WE SHOULD GO OUT, AKANE.
...SAID THAT...THAT STUFF TO ME...
Chapter 118
WH...WH-WH-WH-WHAT IF SHE WAS... SERIOUS ...?
WHAT AM I GOING TO DO...?
HEY, AKANE.
H... HIIRAGI?! WH... WH-WH-WHAT'S UP?!

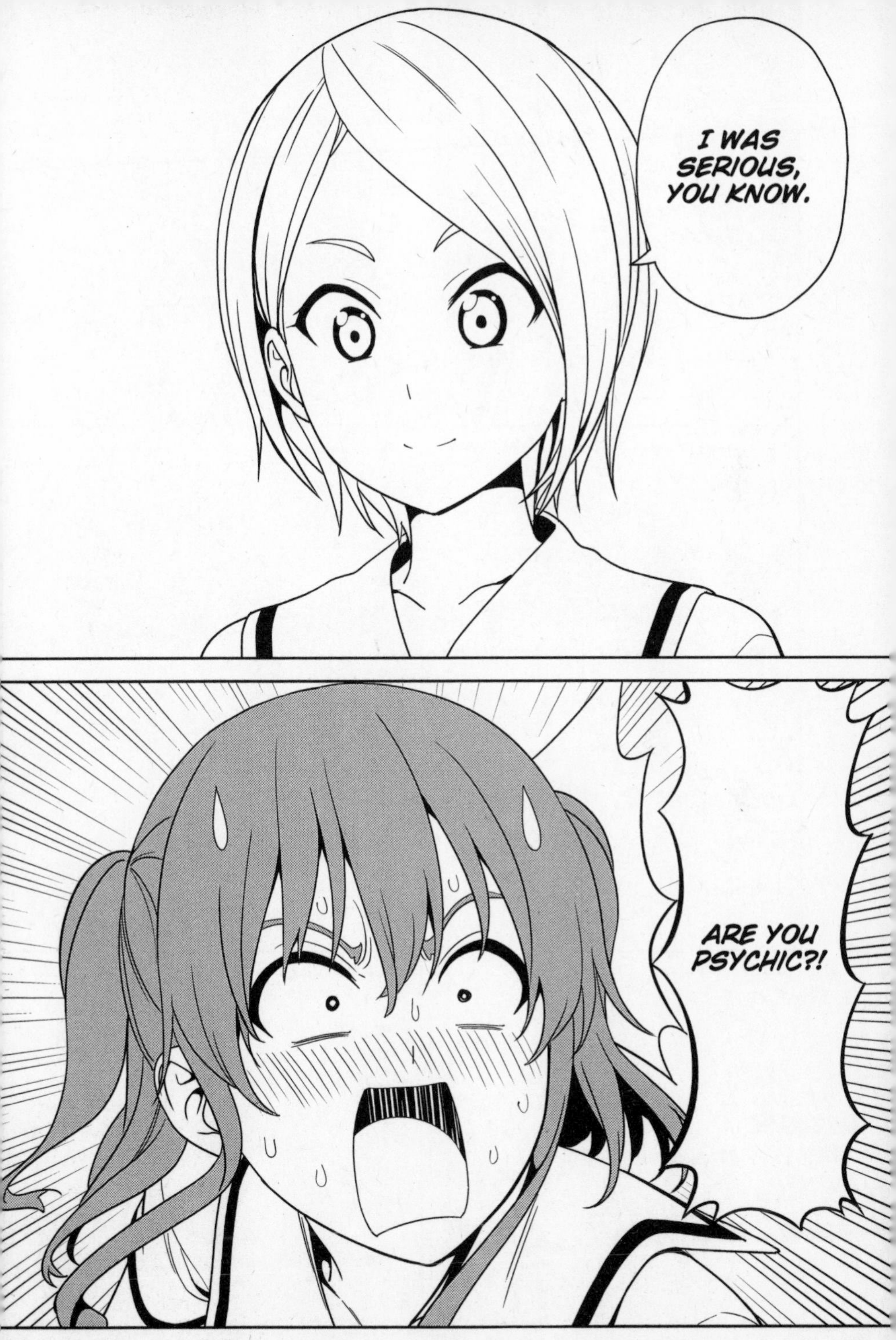
I WAS SERIOUS, YOU KNOW.
ARE YOU PSYCHIC?!

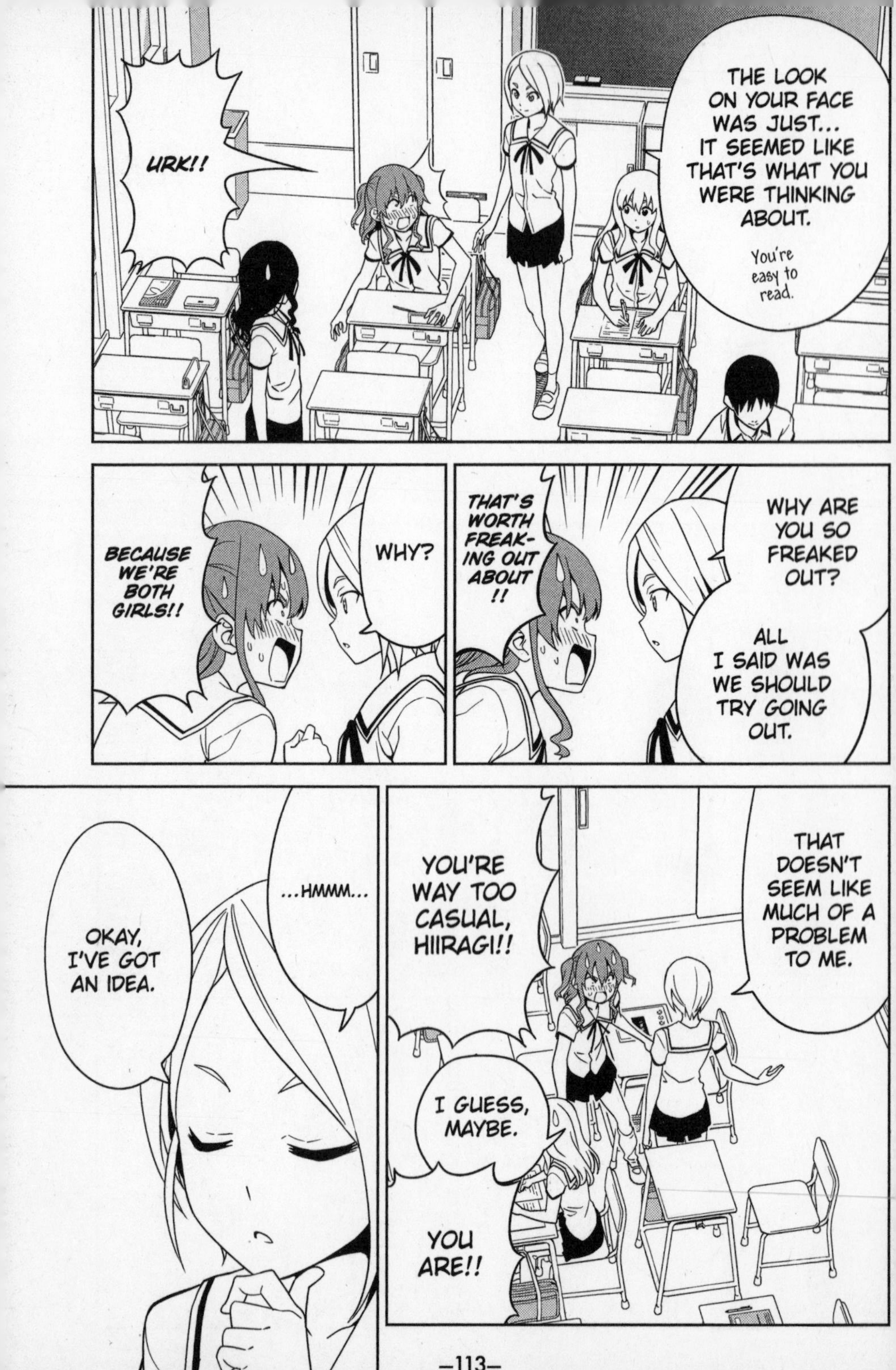
THE LOOK ON YOUR FACE WAS JUST... IT SEEMED LIKE THAT'S WHAT YOU WERE THINKING ABOUT.
You're easy to read.
URK!!
WHY ARE YOU SO FREAKED OUT?
ALL I SAID WAS WE SHOULD TRY GOING OUT.
THAT'S WORTH FREAK-ING OUT ABOUT!!
WHY?
BECAUSE WE'RE BOTH GIRLS!!
THAT DOESN'T SEEM LIKE MUCH OF A PROBLEM TO ME.
YOU'RE WAY TOO CASUAL, HIIRAGI!!
I GUESS, MAYBE.
YOU ARE!!
...HMMM...
OKAY, I'VE GOT AN IDEA.

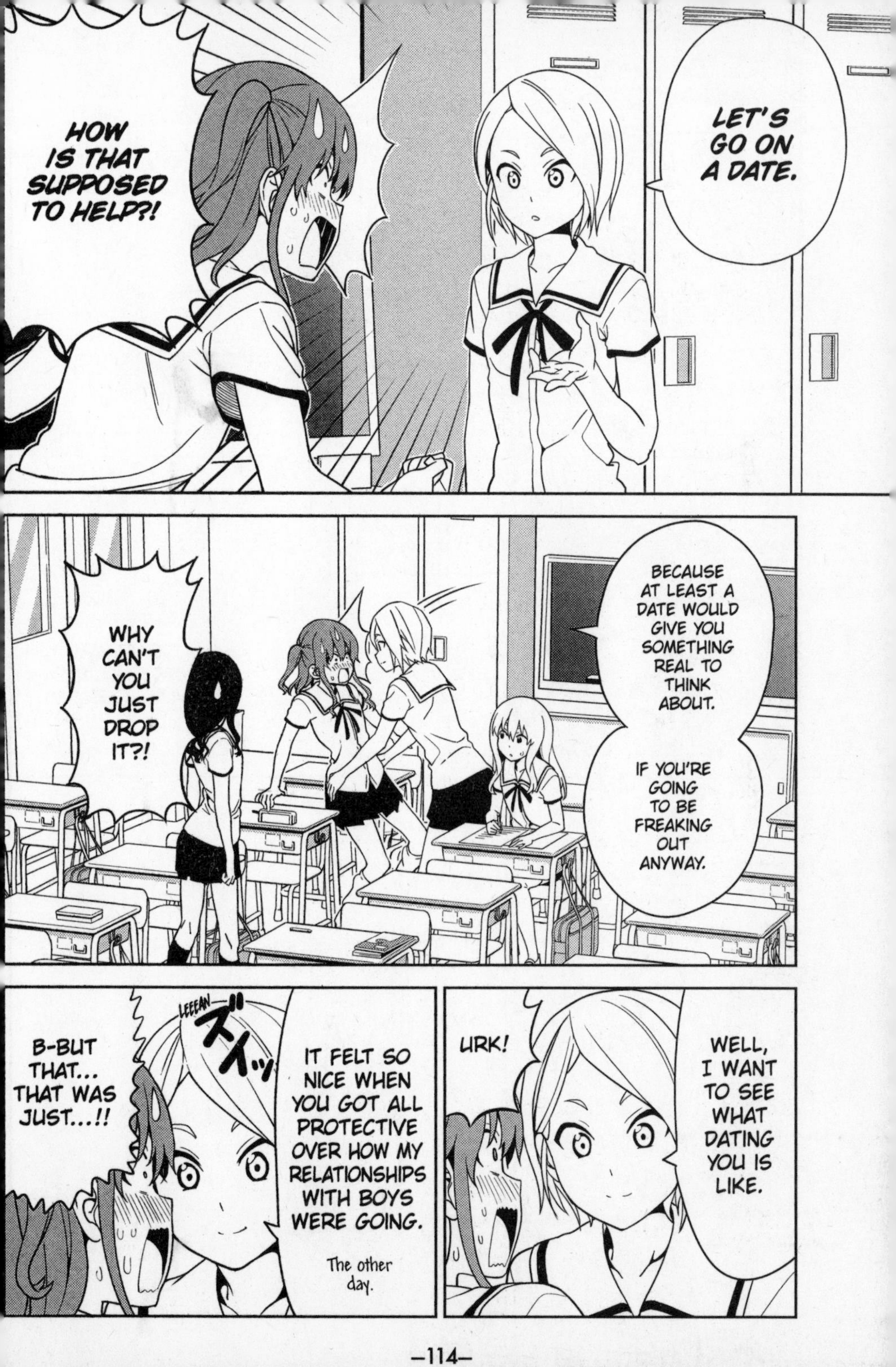

LET'S GO ON A DATE.
HOW IS THAT SUPPOSED TO HELP?!
BECAUSE AT LEAST A DATE WOULD GIVE YOU SOMETHING REAL TO THINK ABOUT.
IF YOU'RE GOING TO BE FREAKING OUT ANYWAY.
WHY CAN'T YOU JUST DROP IT?!
WELL, I WANT TO SEE WHAT DATING YOU IS LIKE.
URK!
IT FELT SO NICE WHEN YOU GOT ALL PROTECTIVE OVER HOW MY RELATIONSHIPS WITH BOYS WERE GOING.
The other day.
LEEEAN
ズイッ
B-BUT THAT... THAT WAS JUST...!!

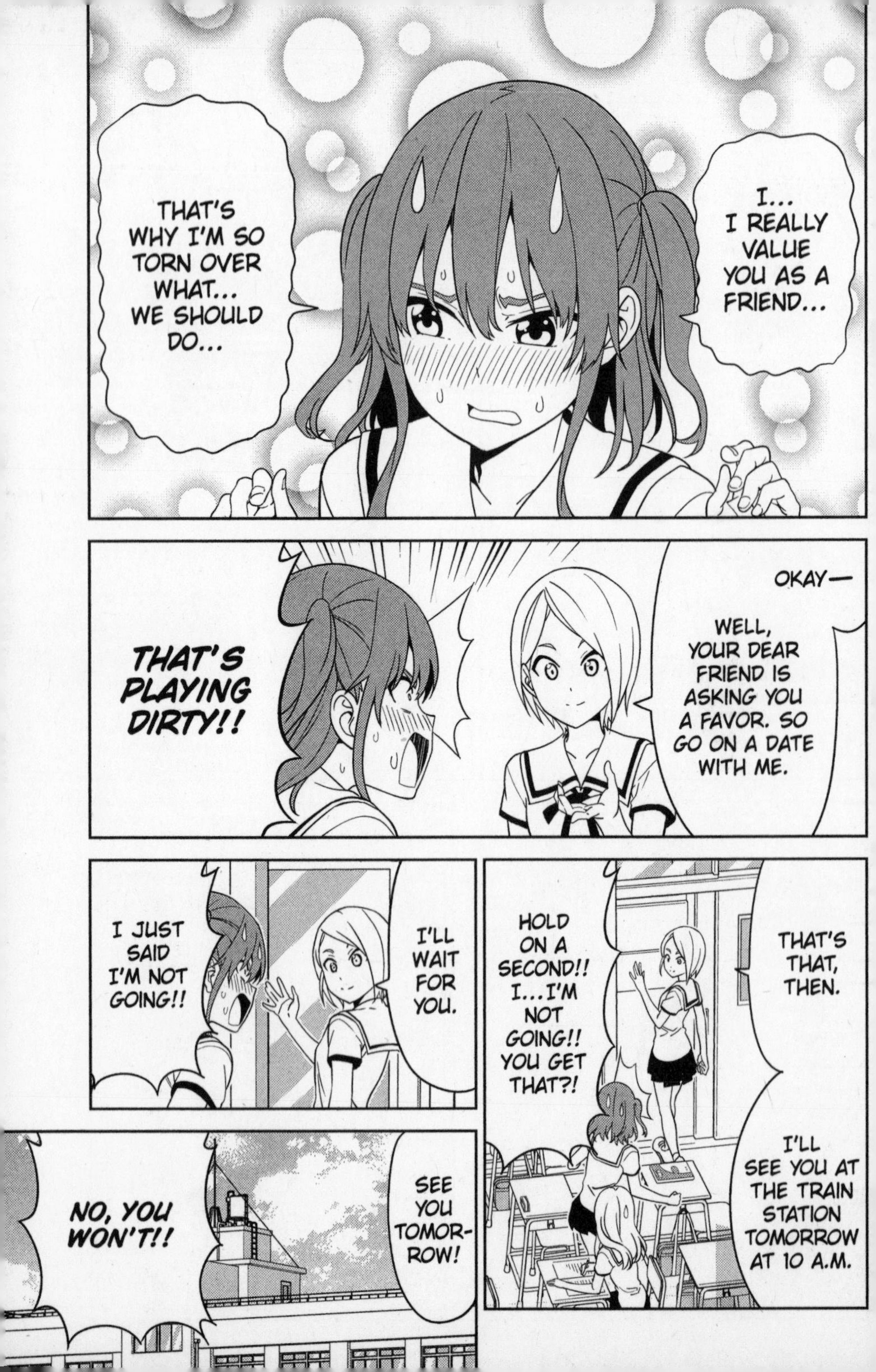

I... I REALLY VALUE YOU AS A FRIEND...
THAT'S WHY I'M SO TORN OVER WHAT... WE SHOULD DO...
OKAY—
WELL, YOUR DEAR FRIEND IS ASKING YOU A FAVOR. SO GO ON A DATE WITH ME.
THAT'S PLAYING DIRTY!!
THAT'S THAT, THEN.
HOLD ON A SECOND!! I...I'M NOT GOING!! YOU GET THAT?!
I'LL SEE YOU AT THE TRAIN STATION TOMORROW AT 10 A.M.
I'LL WAIT FOR YOU.
I JUST SAID I'M NOT GOING!!
SEE YOU TOMOR-ROW!
NO, YOU WON'T!!

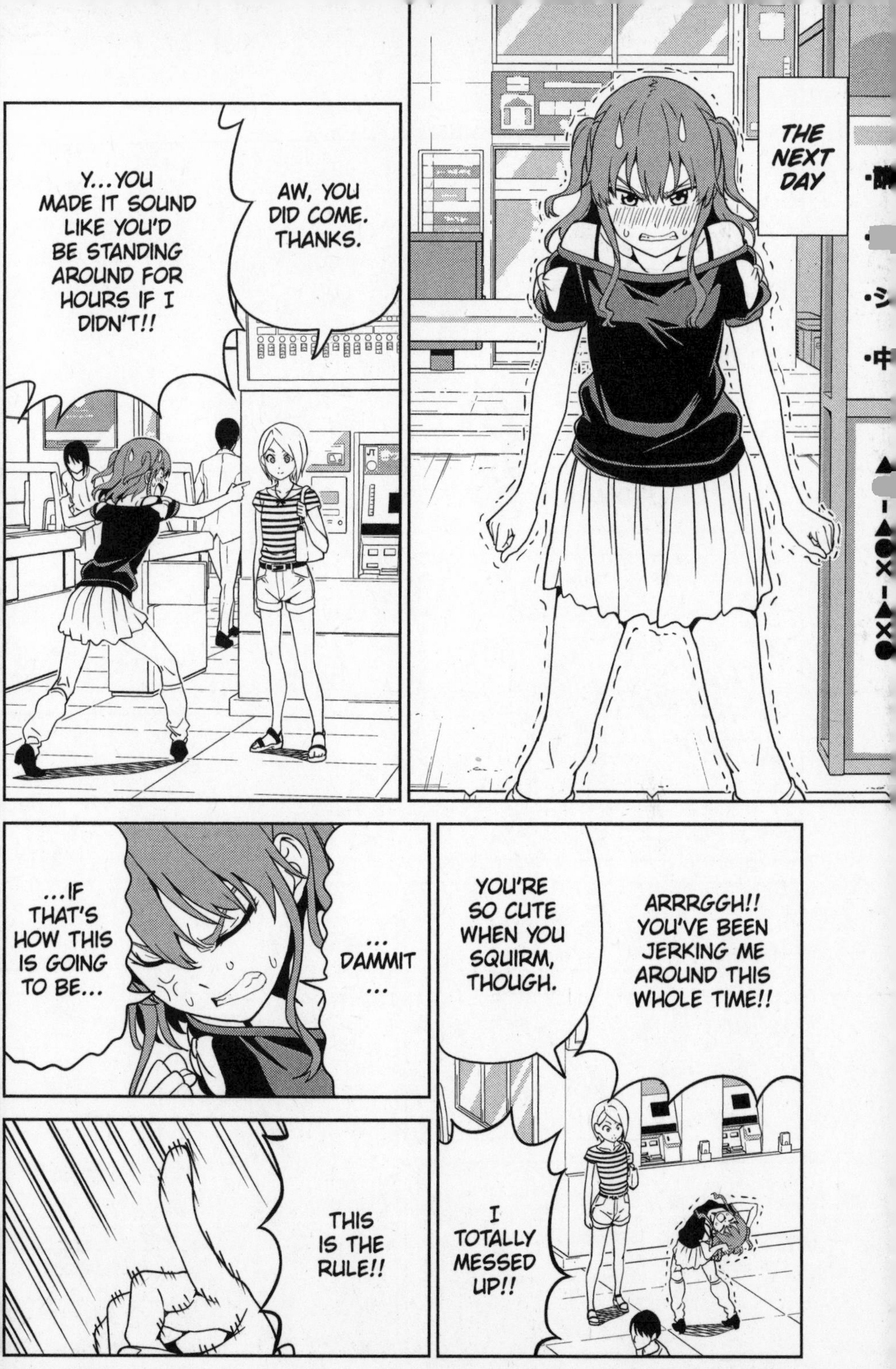
THE NEXT DAY
AW, YOU DID COME. THANKS.
Y...YOU MADE IT SOUND LIKE YOU'D BE STANDING AROUND FOR HOURS IF I DIDN'T!!
ARRRGGH!! YOU'VE BEEN JERKING ME AROUND THIS WHOLE TIME!!
YOU'RE SO CUTE WHEN YOU SQUIRM, THOUGH.
I TOTALLY MESSED UP!!
... DAMMIT ...
...IF THAT'S HOW THIS IS GOING TO BE...
THIS IS THE RULE!!

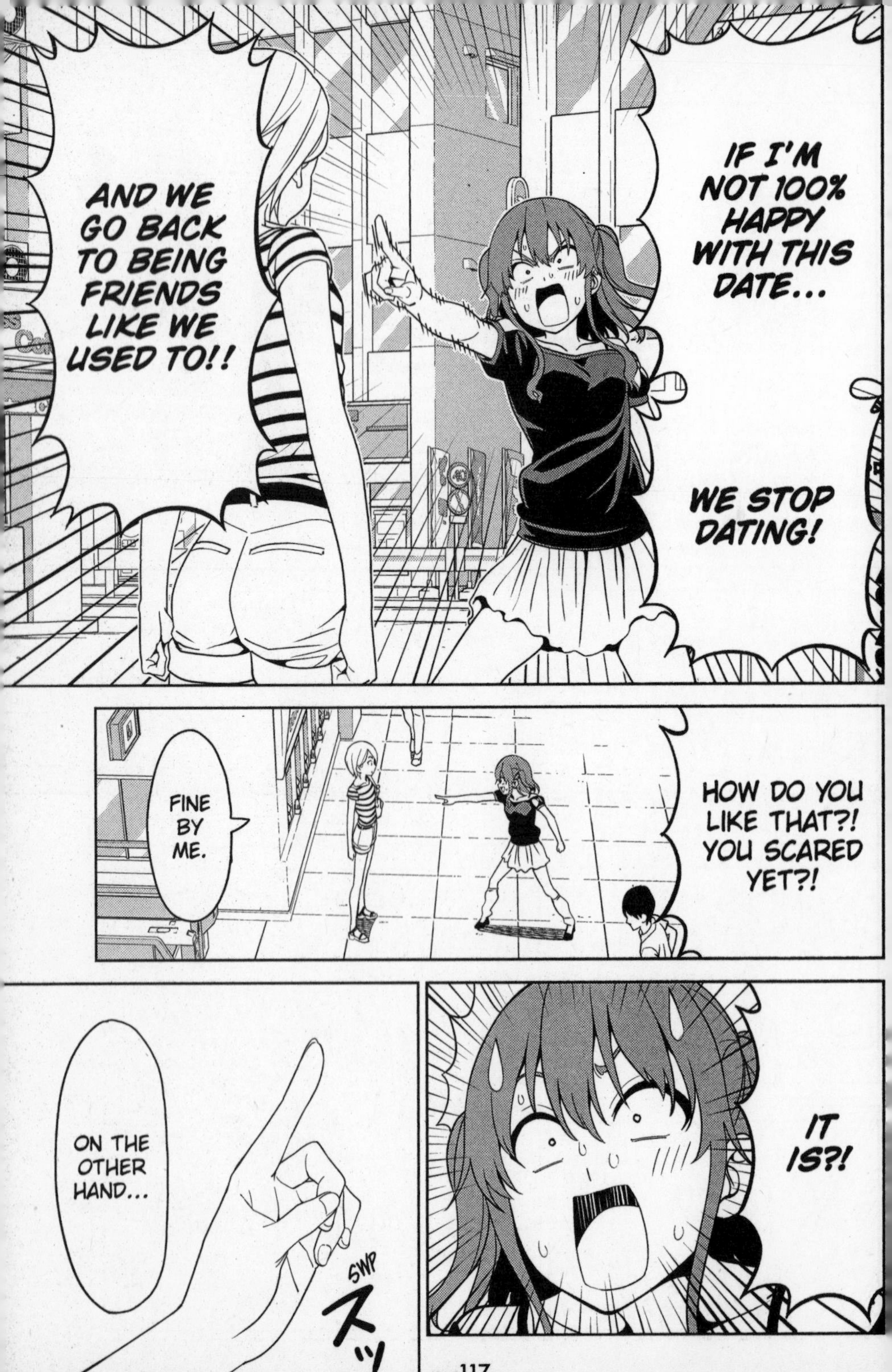
IF I'M NOT 100% HAPPY WITH THIS DATE...
WE STOP DATING!
AND WE GO BACK TO BEING FRIENDS LIKE WE USED TO!!
HOW DO YOU LIKE THAT?! YOU SCARED YET?!
FINE BY ME.
IT IS?!
ON THE OTHER HAND...
SWP
スッ

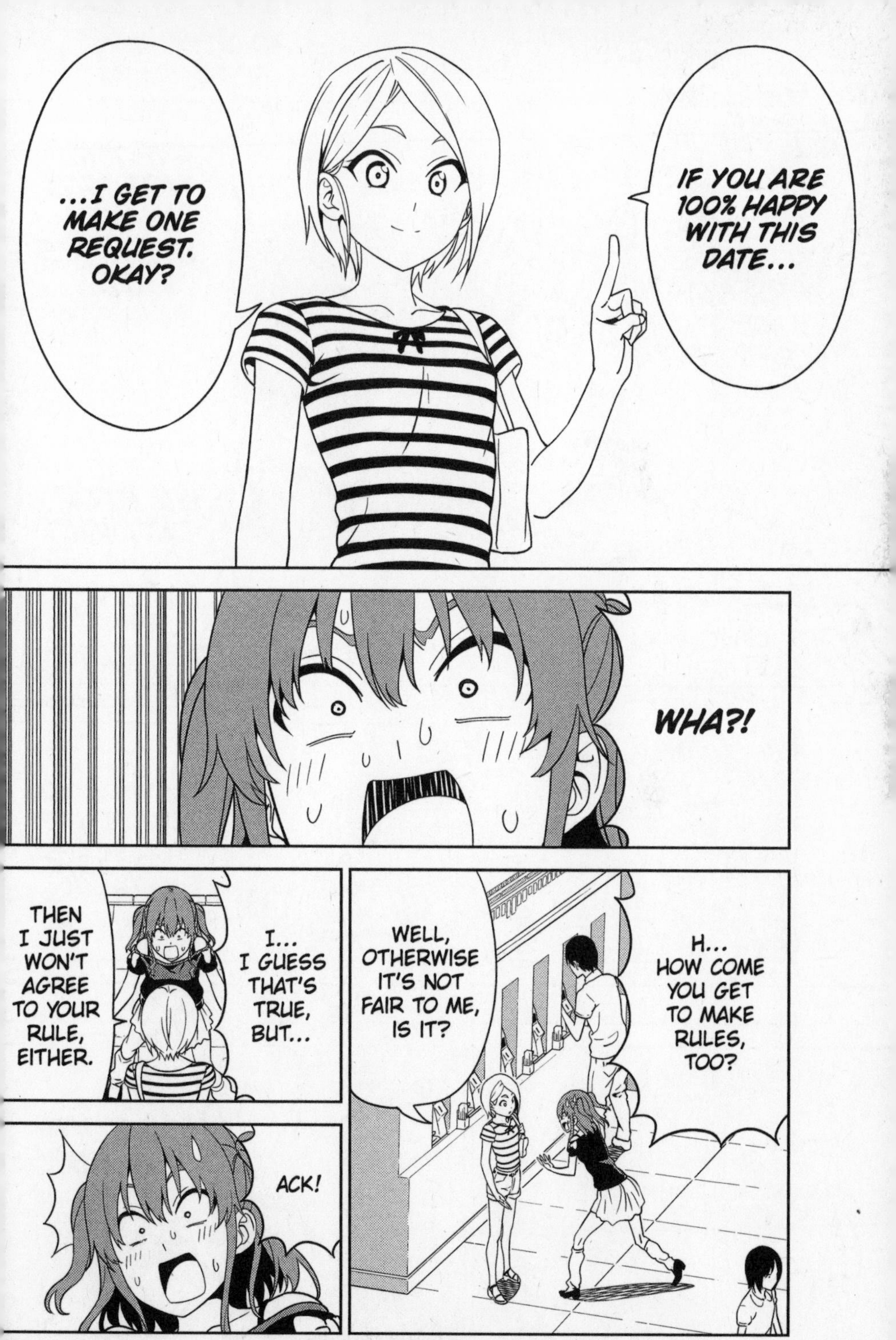
IF YOU ARE 100% HAPPY WITH THIS DATE...
...I GET TO MAKE ONE REQUEST. OKAY?
WHA?!
H... HOW COME YOU GET TO MAKE RULES, TOO?
WELL, OTHERWISE IT'S NOT FAIR TO ME, IS IT?
I... I GUESS THAT'S TRUE, BUT...
THEN I JUST WON'T AGREE TO YOUR RULE, EITHER.
ACK!

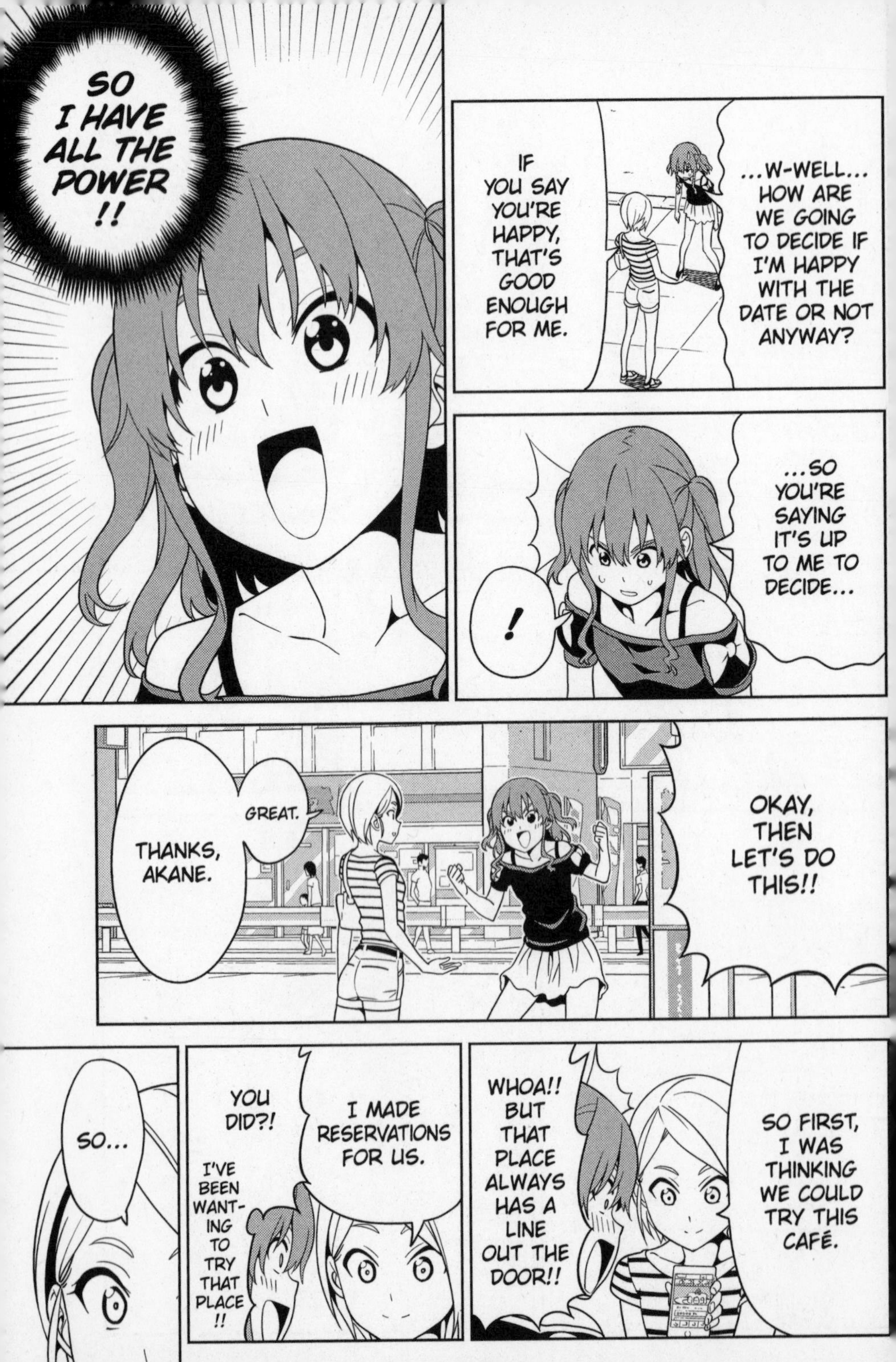
...W-WELL... HOW ARE WE GOING TO DECIDE IF I'M HAPPY WITH THE DATE OR NOT ANYWAY?
IF YOU SAY YOU'RE HAPPY, THAT'S GOOD ENOUGH FOR ME.
...SO YOU'RE SAYING IT'S UP TO ME TO DECIDE...
!
SO I HAVE ALL THE POWER!!
OKAY, THEN LET'S DO THIS!!
GREAT.
THANKS, AKANE.
SO FIRST, I WAS THINKING WE COULD TRY THIS CAFÉ.
WHOA!! BUT THAT PLACE ALWAYS HAS A LINE OUT THE DOOR!!
I MADE RESERVATIONS FOR US.
YOU DID?!
I'VE BEEN WANTING TO TRY THAT PLACE!!
SO...

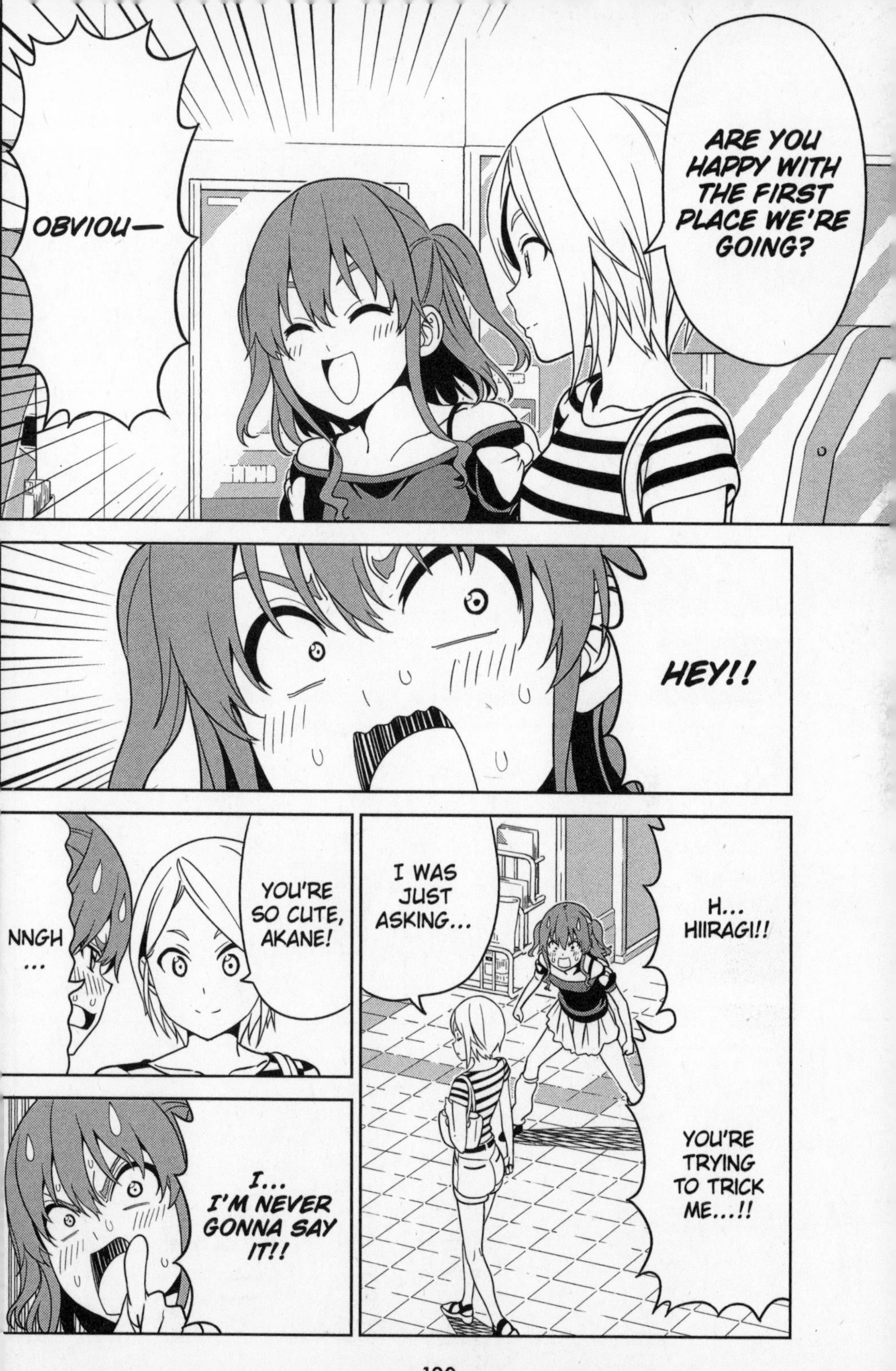
ARE YOU HAPPY WITH THE FIRST PLACE WE'RE GOING?
OBVIOU—
HEY!!
H... HIIRAGI!!
YOU'RE TRYING TO TRICK ME...!!
I WAS JUST ASKING...
YOU'RE SO CUTE, AKANE!
NNGH ...
I... I'M NEVER GONNA SAY IT!!

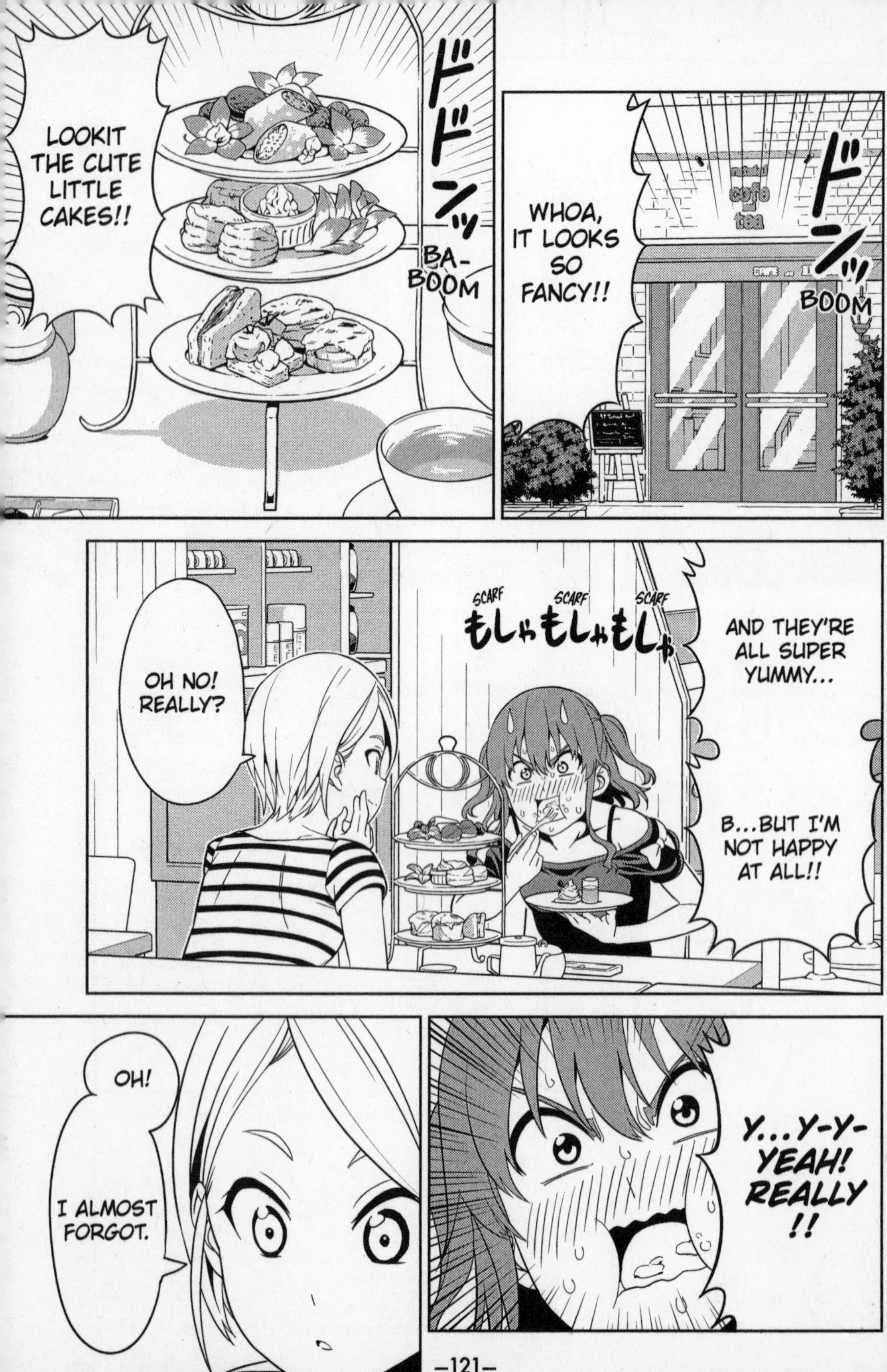
ドドンッ
BOOM
WHOA, IT LOOKS SO FANCY!!
ドドンッ
BA-BOOM
LOOKIT THE CUTE LITTLE CAKES!!
AND THEY'RE ALL SUPER YUMMY...
B...BUT I'M NOT HAPPY AT ALL!!
もしゃもしゃもしゃ
SCARF SCARF SCARF
OH NO! REALLY?
Y...Y-Y-YEAH! REALLY!!
OH!
I ALMOST FORGOT.

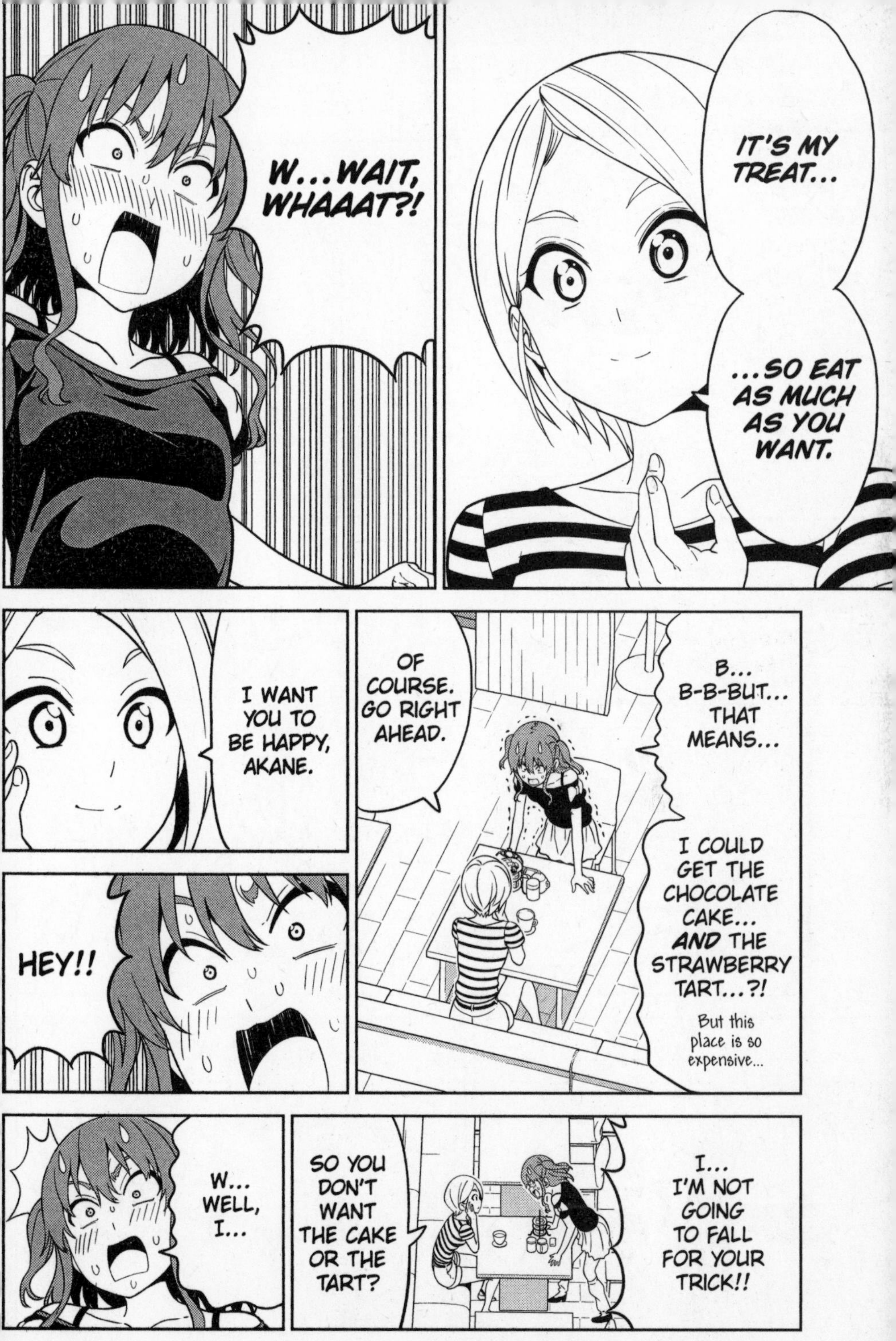
IT'S MY TREAT...
...SO EAT AS MUCH AS YOU WANT.
W...WAIT, WHAAAT?!
B... B-B-BUT... THAT MEANS...
I COULD GET THE CHOCOLATE CAKE... AND THE STRAWBERRY TART...?!
But this place is so expensive...
OF COURSE. GO RIGHT AHEAD.
I WANT YOU TO BE HAPPY, AKANE.
HEY!!
I... I'M NOT GOING TO FALL FOR YOUR TRICK!!
SO YOU DON'T WANT THE CAKE OR THE TART?
W... WELL, I...

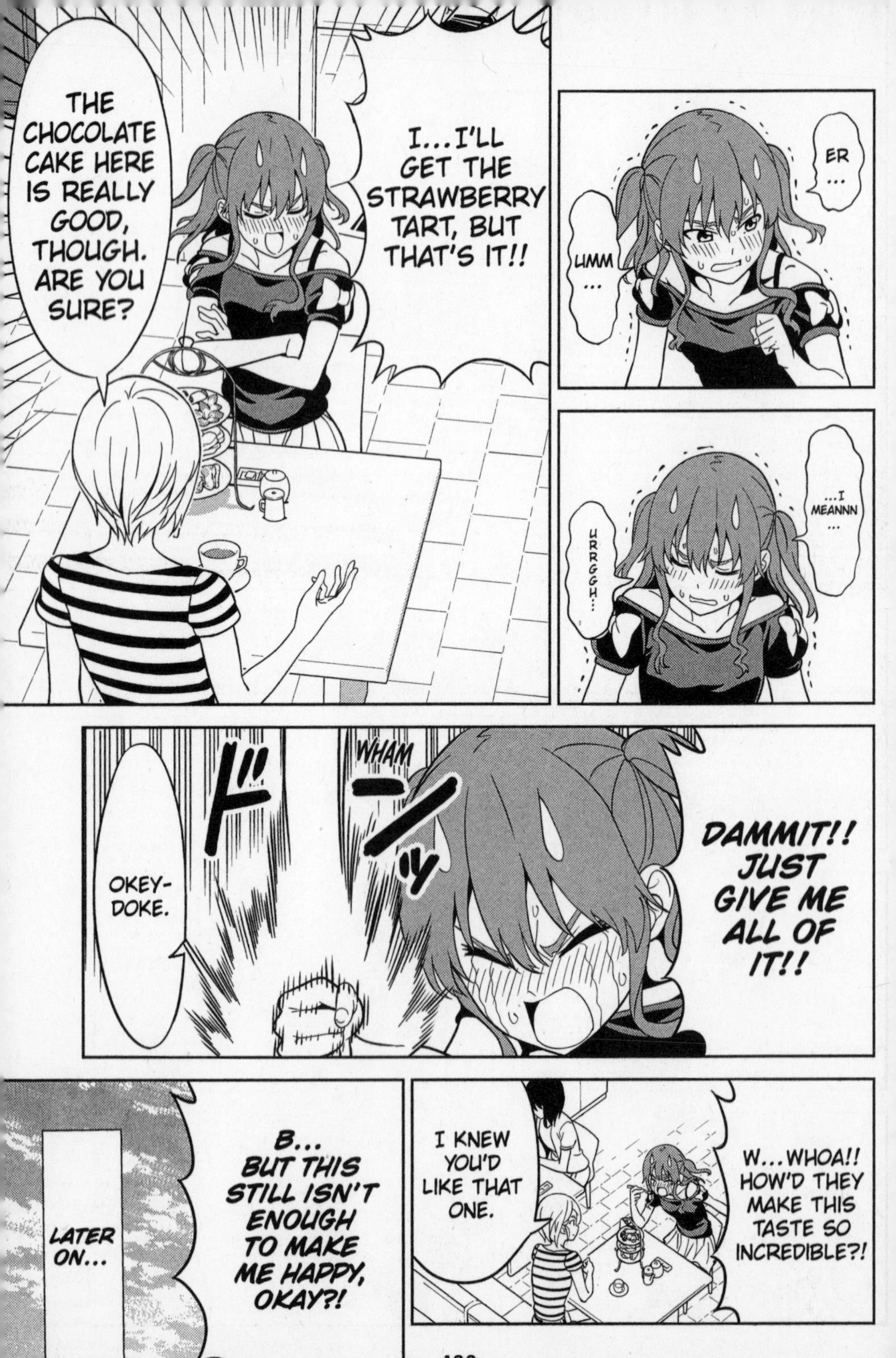

I...I'LL GET THE STRAWBERRY TART, BUT THAT'S IT!!
THE CHOCOLATE CAKE HERE IS REALLY GOOD, THOUGH. ARE YOU SURE?
ER ...
UMM ...
...I MEANNN ...
URRGGH...
WHAM
DAMMIT!! JUST GIVE ME ALL OF IT!!
OKEY-DOKE.
LATER ON...
B... BUT THIS STILL ISN'T ENOUGH TO MAKE ME HAPPY, OKAY?!
W...WHOA!! HOW'D THEY MAKE THIS TASTE SO INCREDIBLE?!
I KNEW YOU'D LIKE THAT ONE.

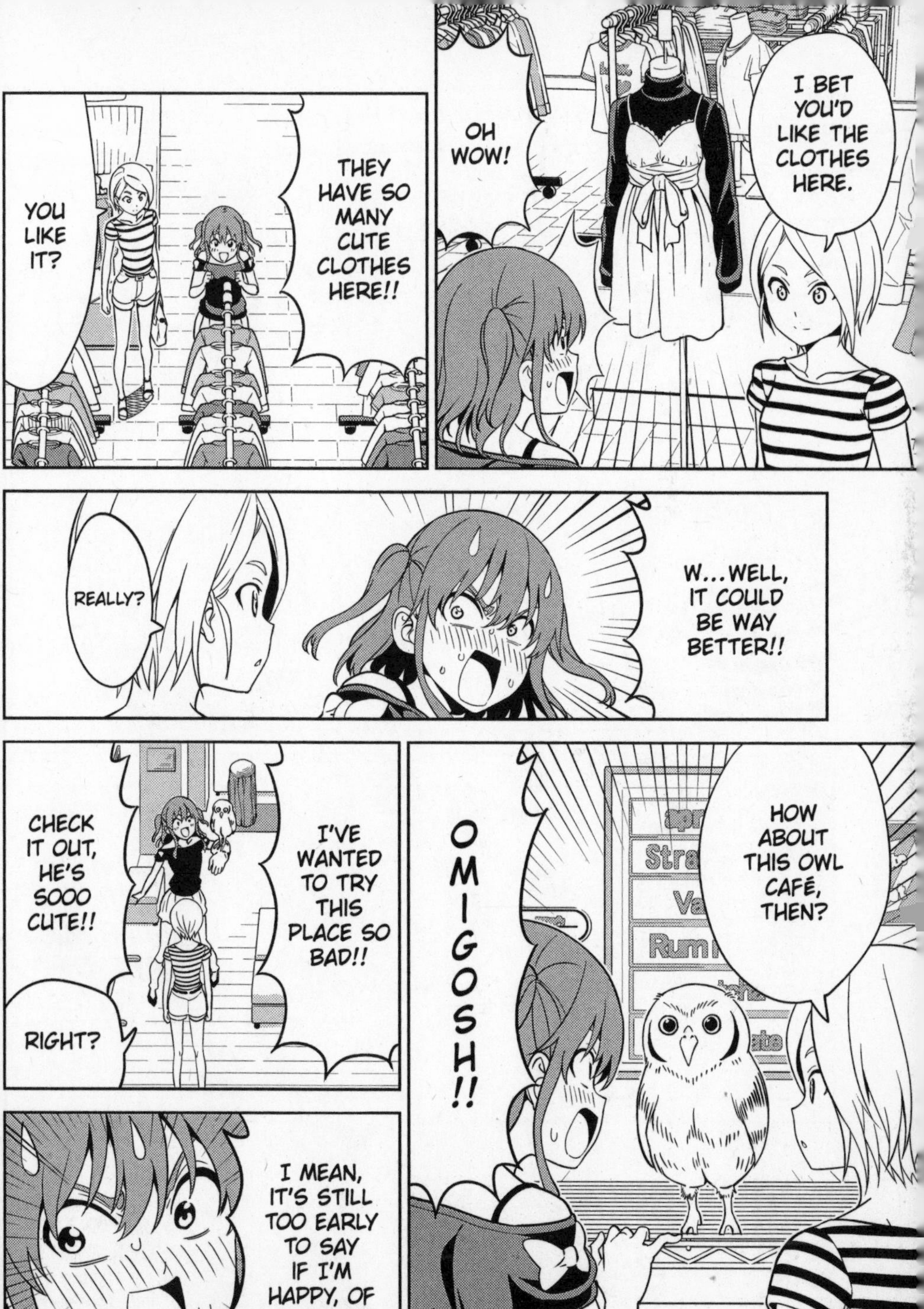
I BET YOU'D LIKE THE CLOTHES HERE.
OH WOW!
THEY HAVE SO MANY CUTE CLOTHES HERE!!
YOU LIKE IT?
W...WELL, IT COULD BE WAY BETTER!!
REALLY?
HOW ABOUT THIS OWL CAFÉ, THEN?
OMIGOSH!!
I'VE WANTED TO TRY THIS PLACE SO BAD!!
CHECK IT OUT, HE'S SOOO CUTE!!
RIGHT?
I MEAN, IT'S STILL TOO EARLY TO SAY IF I'M HAPPY, OF COURSE!!

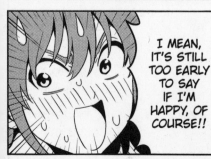

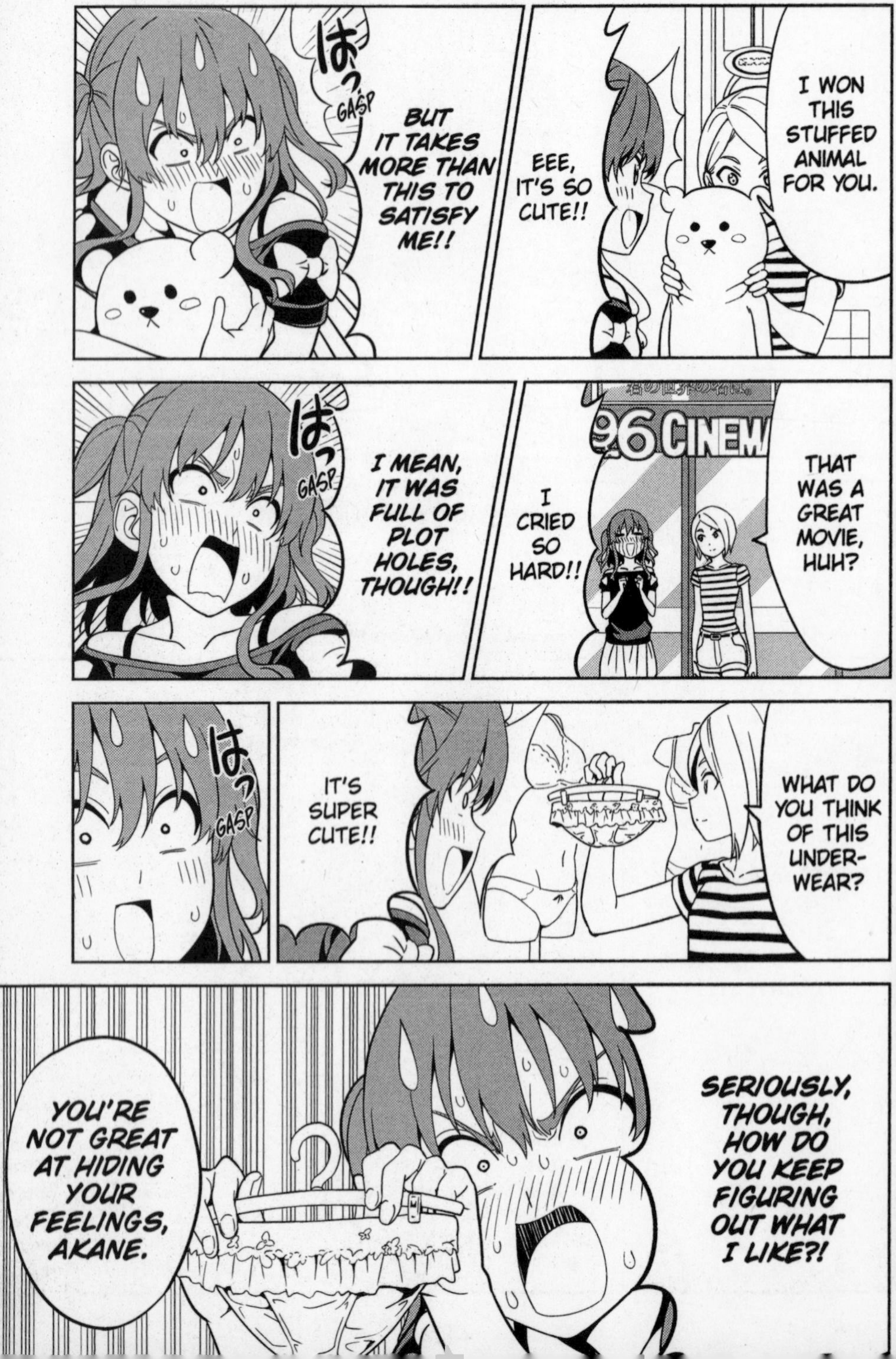
I WON THIS STUFFED ANIMAL FOR YOU.
EEE, IT'S SO CUTE!!
はっ
GASP
BUT IT TAKES MORE THAN THIS TO SATISFY ME!!
96 CINEM
THAT WAS A GREAT MOVIE, HUH?
I CRIED SO HARD!!
はっ
GASP
I MEAN, IT WAS FULL OF PLOT HOLES, THOUGH!!
WHAT DO YOU THINK OF THIS UNDERWEAR?
IT'S SUPER CUTE!!
はっ
GASP
SERIOUSLY, THOUGH, HOW DO YOU KEEP FIGURING OUT WHAT I LIKE?!
YOU'RE NOT GREAT AT HIDING YOUR FEELINGS, AKANE.

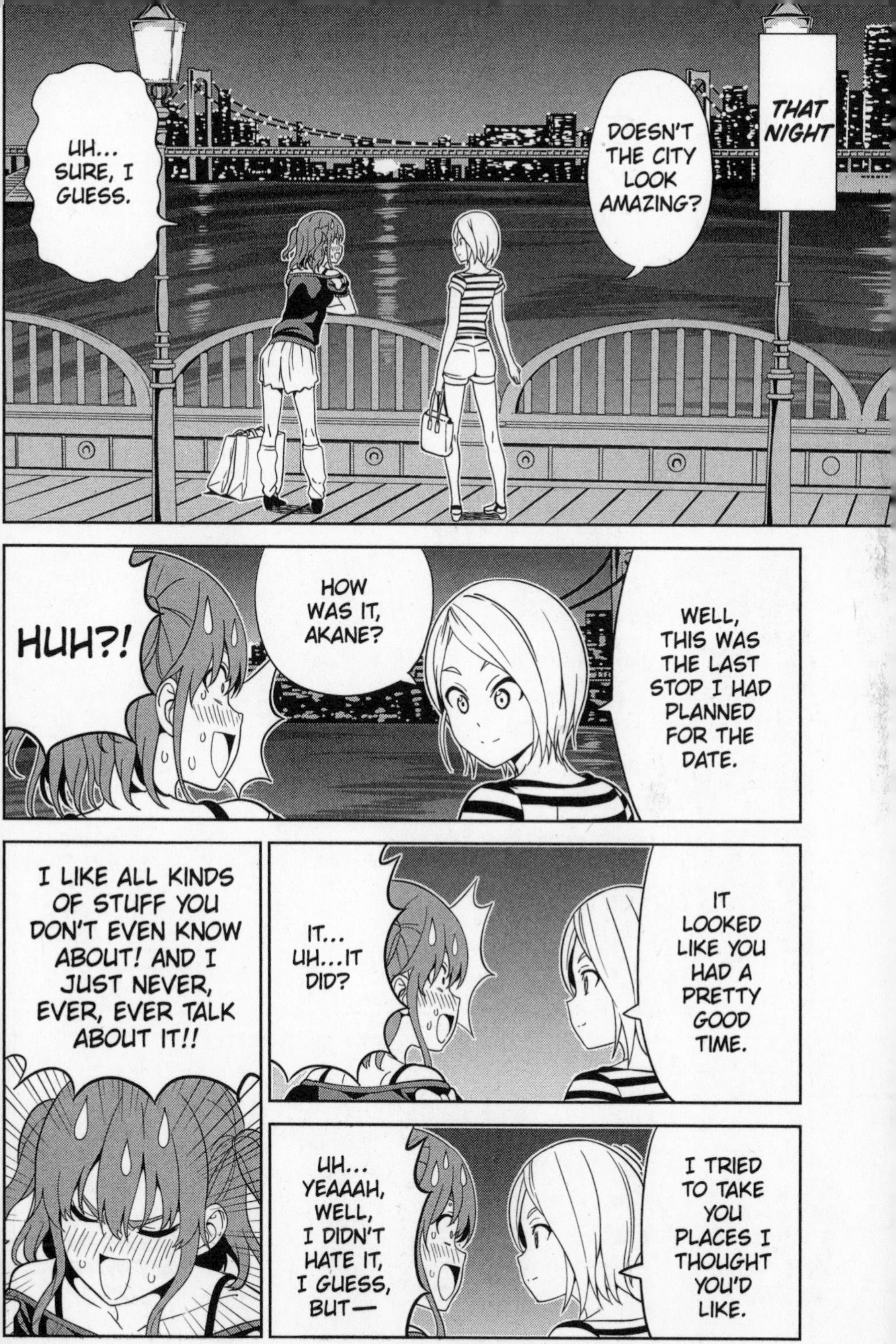
THAT NIGHT
DOESN'T THE CITY LOOK AMAZING?
UH... SURE, I GUESS.
WELL, THIS WAS THE LAST STOP I HAD PLANNED FOR THE DATE.
HOW WAS IT, AKANE?
HUH?!
IT LOOKED LIKE YOU HAD A PRETTY GOOD TIME.
IT... UH...IT DID?
I TRIED TO TAKE YOU PLACES I THOUGHT YOU'D LIKE.
UH... YEAAAH, WELL, I DIDN'T HATE IT, I GUESS, BUT—
I LIKE ALL KINDS OF STUFF YOU DON'T EVEN KNOW ABOUT! AND I JUST NEVER, EVER, EVER TALK ABOUT IT!!

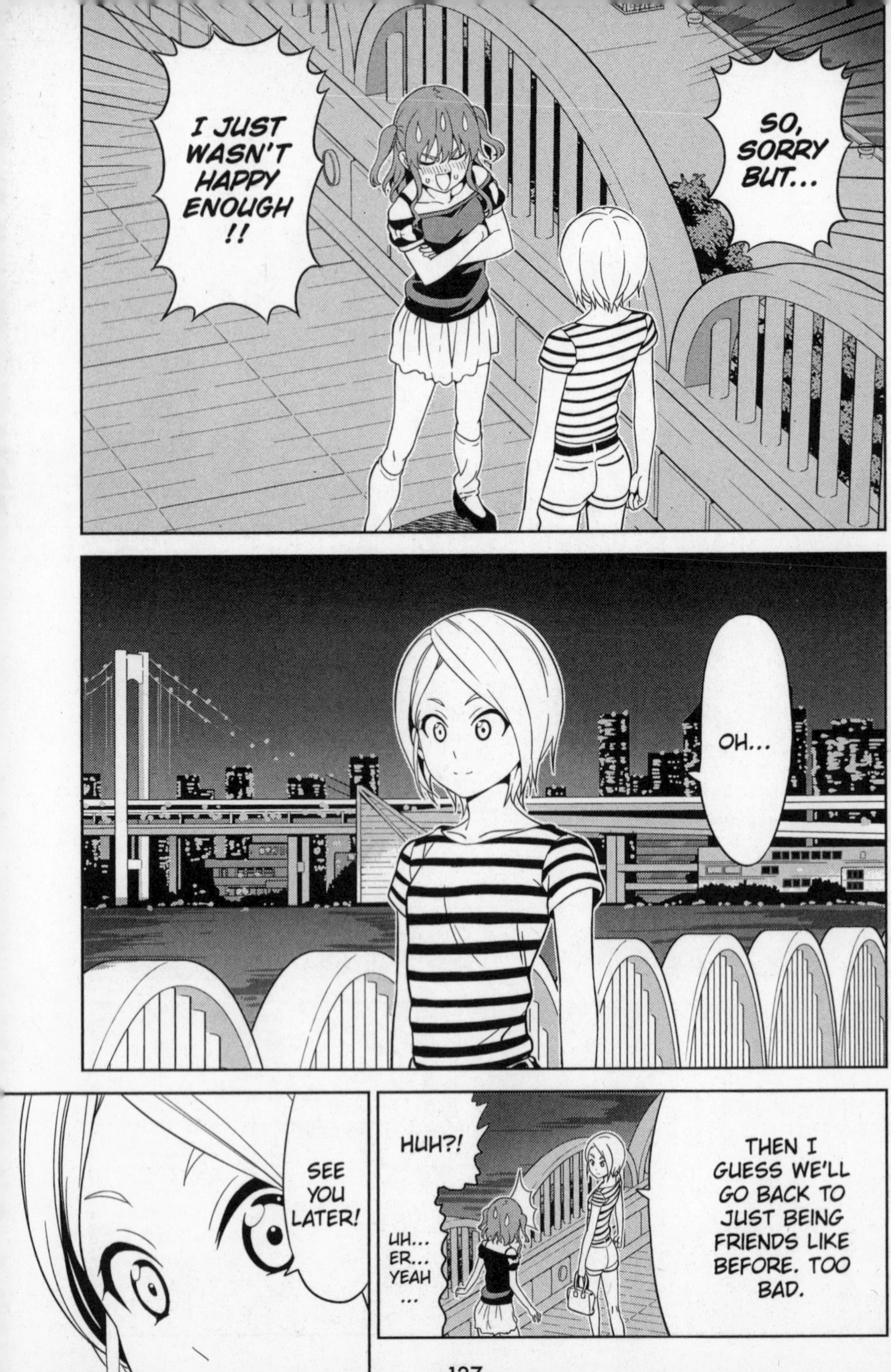
SO, SORRY BUT...
I JUST WASN'T HAPPY ENOUGH !!
OH...
THEN I GUESS WE'LL GO BACK TO JUST BEING FRIENDS LIKE BEFORE. TOO BAD.
HUH?!
UH... ER... YEAH ...
SEE YOU LATER!

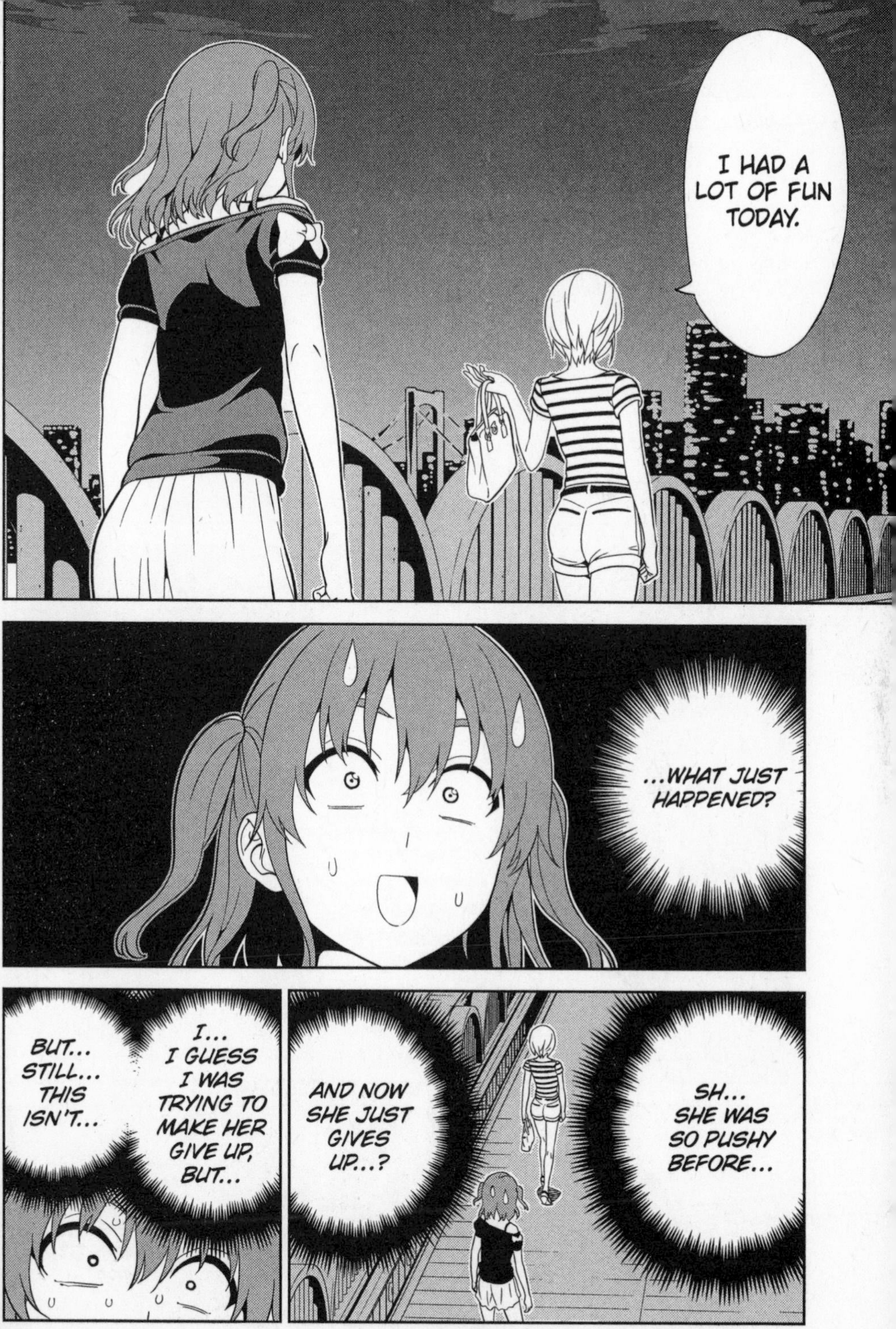
I HAD A LOT OF FUN TODAY.
...WHAT JUST HAPPENED?
SH... SHE WAS SO PUSHY BEFORE...
AND NOW SHE JUST GIVES UP...?
I... I GUESS I WAS TRYING TO MAKE HER GIVE UP, BUT...
BUT... STILL... THIS ISN'T...

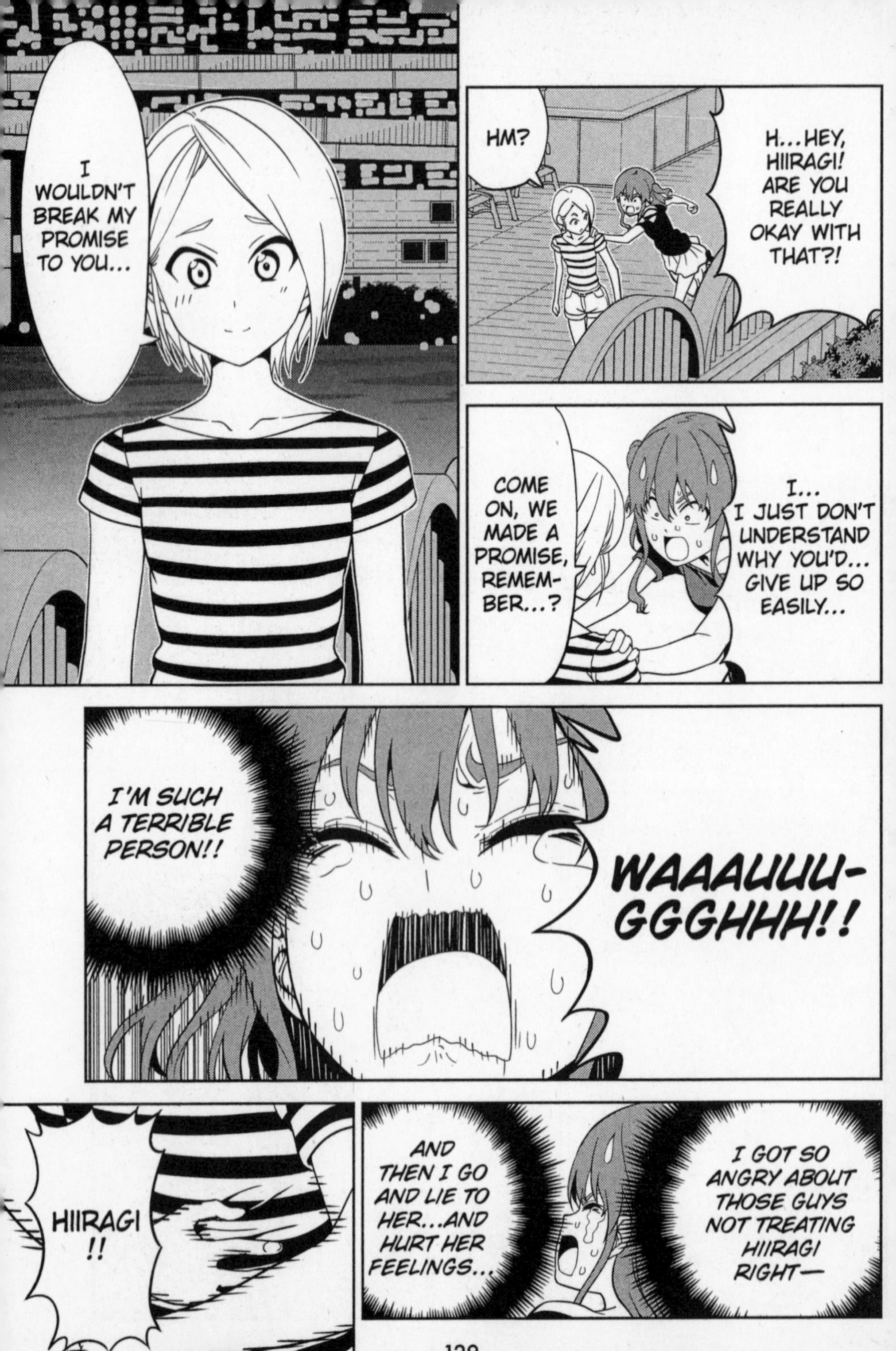
H...HEY, HIIRAGI! ARE YOU REALLY OKAY WITH THAT?!
HM?
I... I JUST DON'T UNDERSTAND WHY YOU'D... GIVE UP SO EASILY...
COME ON, WE MADE A PROMISE, REMEMBER...?
I WOULDN'T BREAK MY PROMISE TO YOU...
WAAAUUU-GGGHHH!!
I'M SUCH A TERRIBLE PERSON!!
I GOT SO ANGRY ABOUT THOSE GUYS NOT TREATING HIIRAGI RIGHT—
AND THEN I GO AND LIE TO HER...AND HURT HER FEELINGS...
HIIRAGI!!

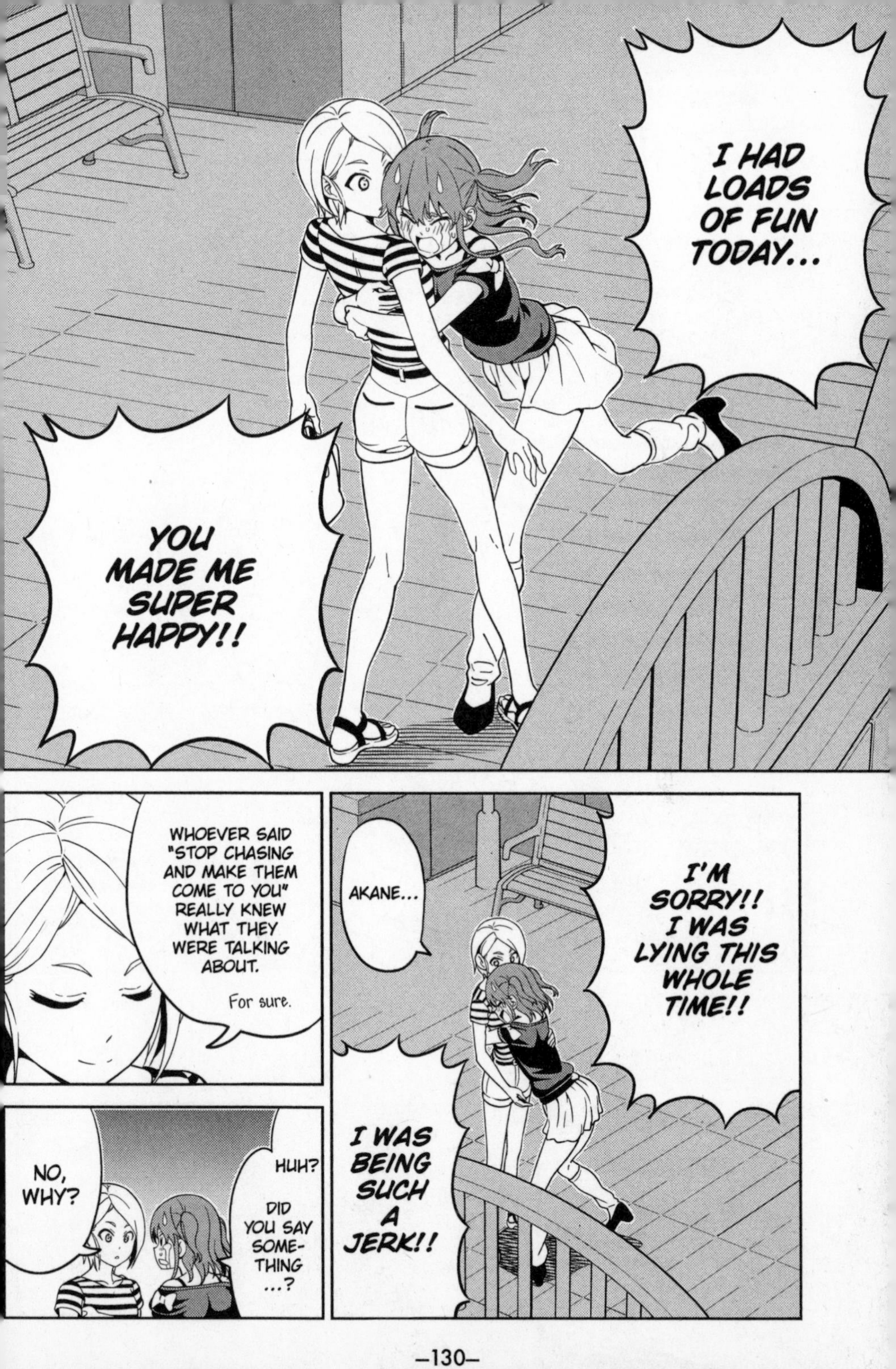
I HAD LOADS OF FUN TODAY...
YOU MADE ME SUPER HAPPY!!
I'M SORRY!! I WAS LYING THIS WHOLE TIME!!
AKANE...
I WAS BEING SUCH A JERK!!
WHOEVER SAID "STOP CHASING AND MAKE THEM COME TO YOU" REALLY KNEW WHAT THEY WERE TALKING ABOUT.
For sure.
HUH?
DID YOU SAY SOME-THING ...?
NO, WHY?

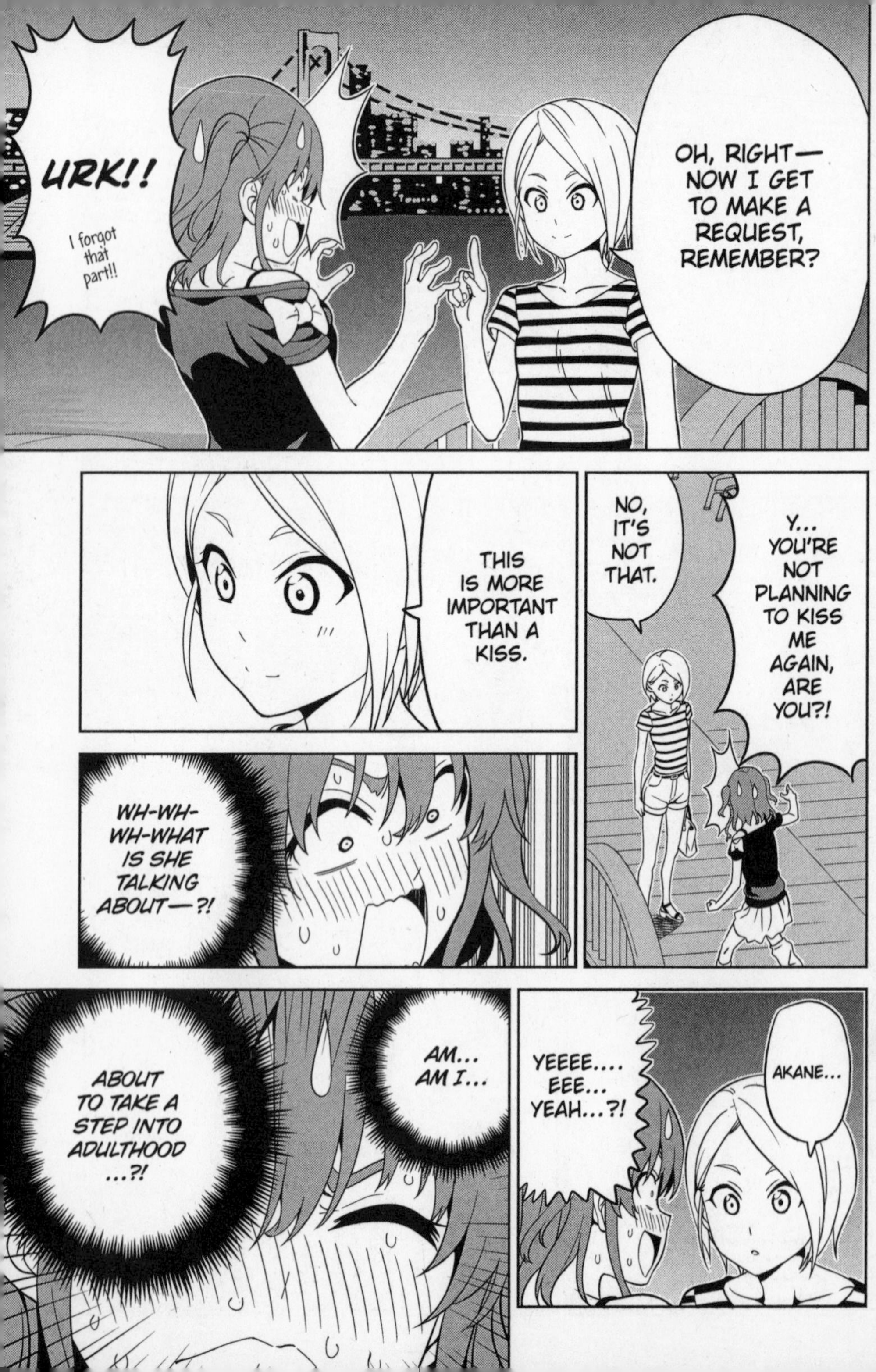
OH, RIGHT— NOW I GET TO MAKE A REQUEST, REMEMBER?
URK!!
I forgot that part!!
Y... YOU'RE NOT PLANNING TO KISS ME AGAIN, ARE YOU?!
NO, IT'S NOT THAT.
THIS IS MORE IMPORTANT THAN A KISS.
WH-WH-WH-WHAT IS SHE TALKING ABOUT—?!
AKANE...
YEEEE.... EEE... YEAH...?!
AM... AM I...
ABOUT TO TAKE A STEP INTO ADULTHOOD ...?!

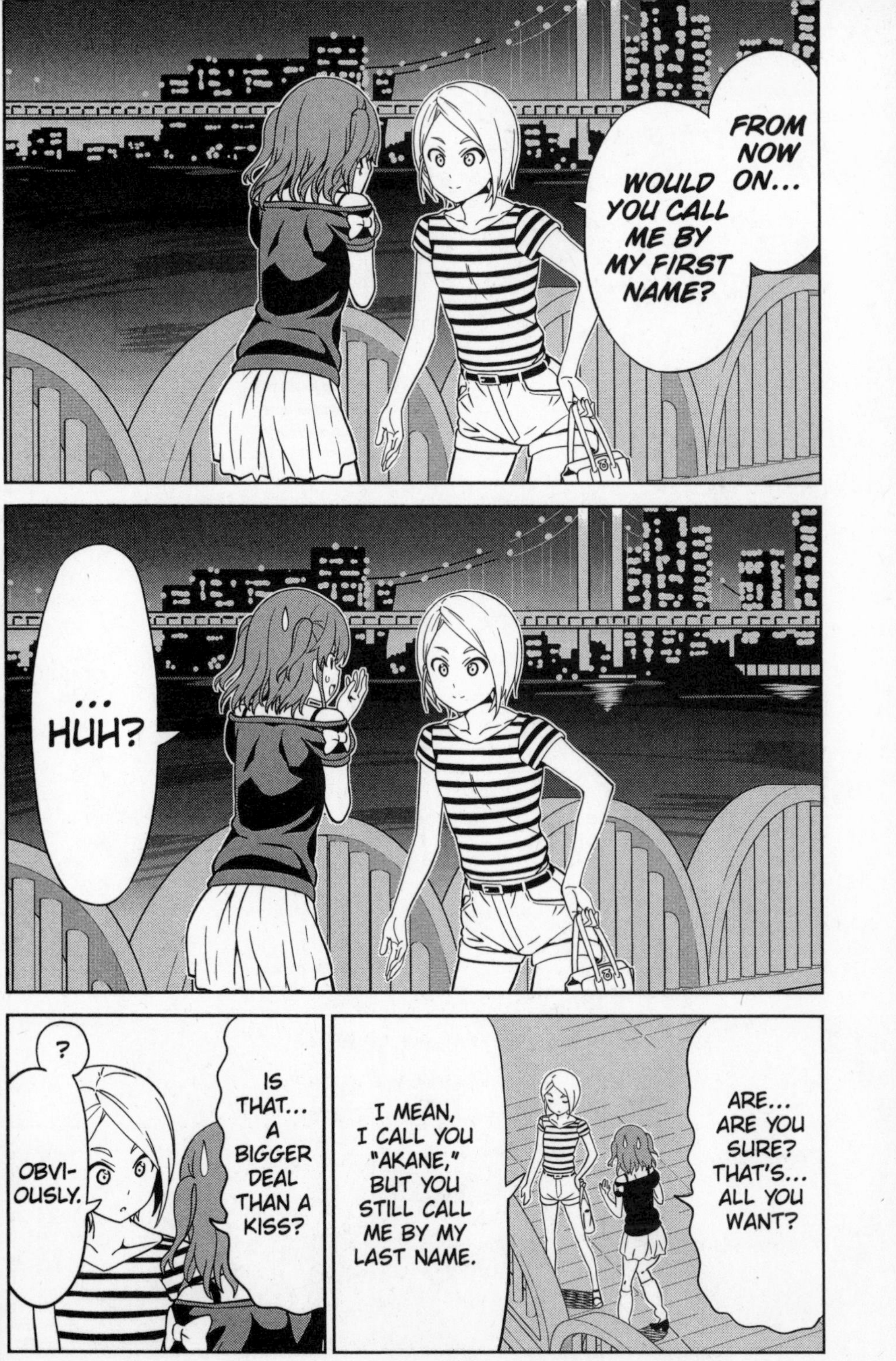

FROM NOW ON... WOULD YOU CALL ME BY MY FIRST NAME?
... HUH?
ARE... ARE YOU SURE? THAT'S... ALL YOU WANT?
I MEAN, I CALL YOU "AKANE," BUT YOU STILL CALL ME BY MY LAST NAME.
IS THAT... A BIGGER DEAL THAN A KISS?
?
OBVI-OUSLY.

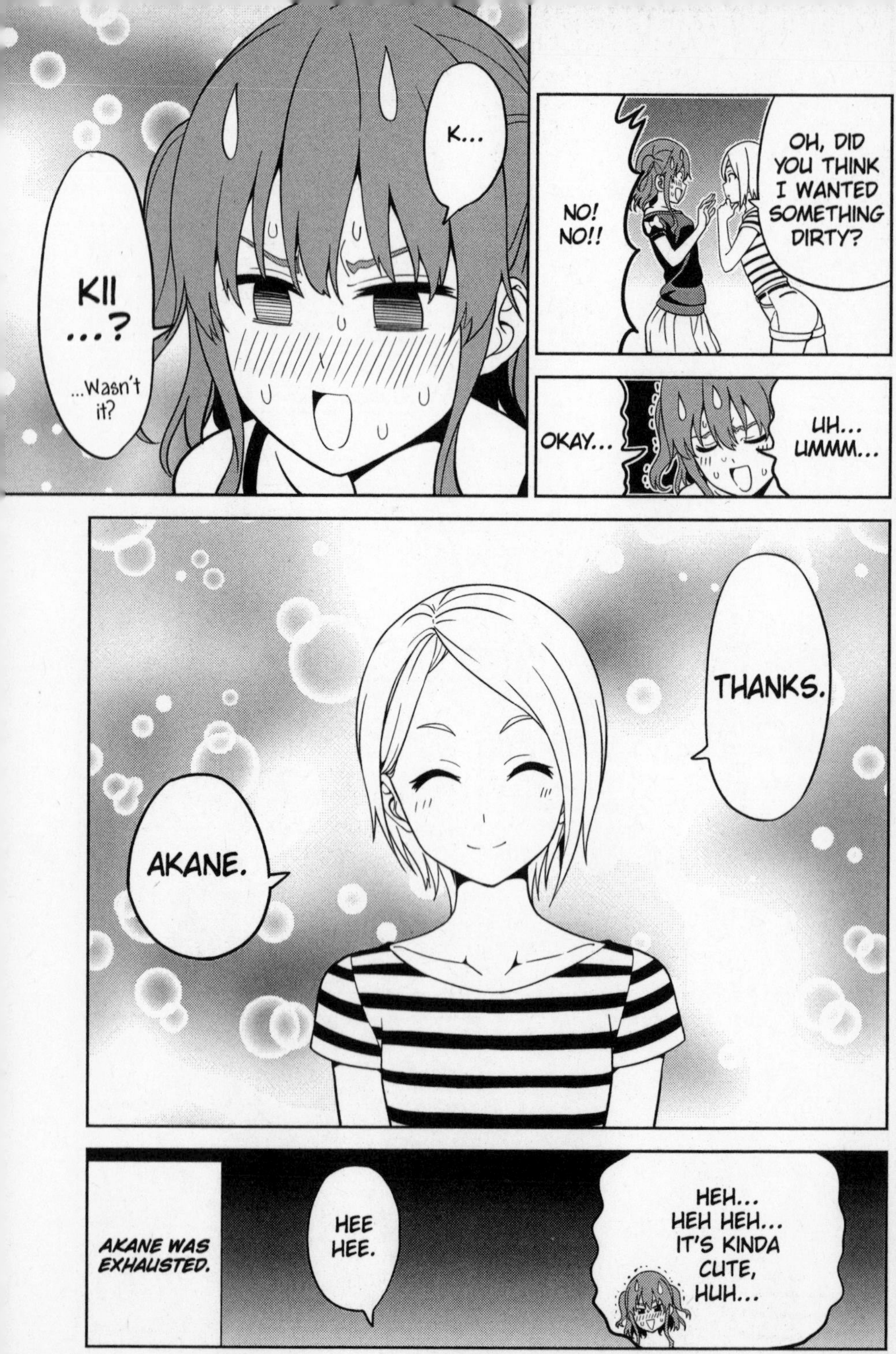
OH, DID YOU THINK I WANTED SOMETHING DIRTY?
NO! NO!!
UH... UMMM...
OKAY...
K...
KII ...?
...Wasn't it?
THANKS.
AKANE.
HEH... HEH HEH... IT'S KINDA CUTE, HUH...
HEE HEE.
AKANE WAS EXHAUSTED.

How Do You Even Talk About It?

THE NEXT DAY
SO... UHH... HOW'D... YESTERDAY GO...?
UH... WELLLL...
HA... HAHAHA...
WHAT DOES THAT MEAN?!

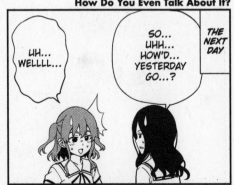

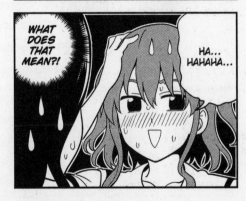

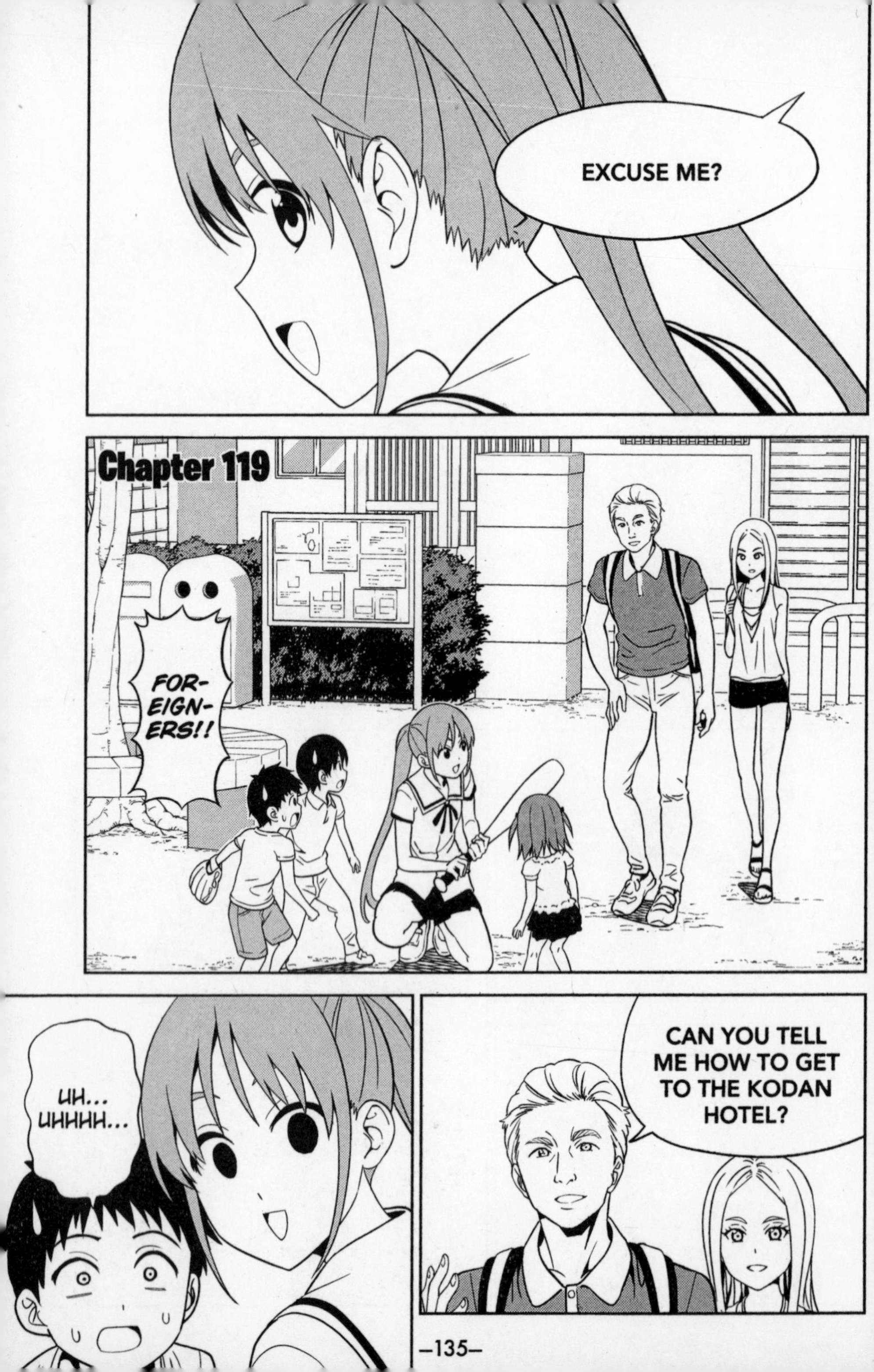
EXCUSE ME?
Chapter 119
FOR-EIGN-ERS!!
CAN YOU TELL ME HOW TO GET TO THE KODAN HOTEL?
UH... UHHHH...

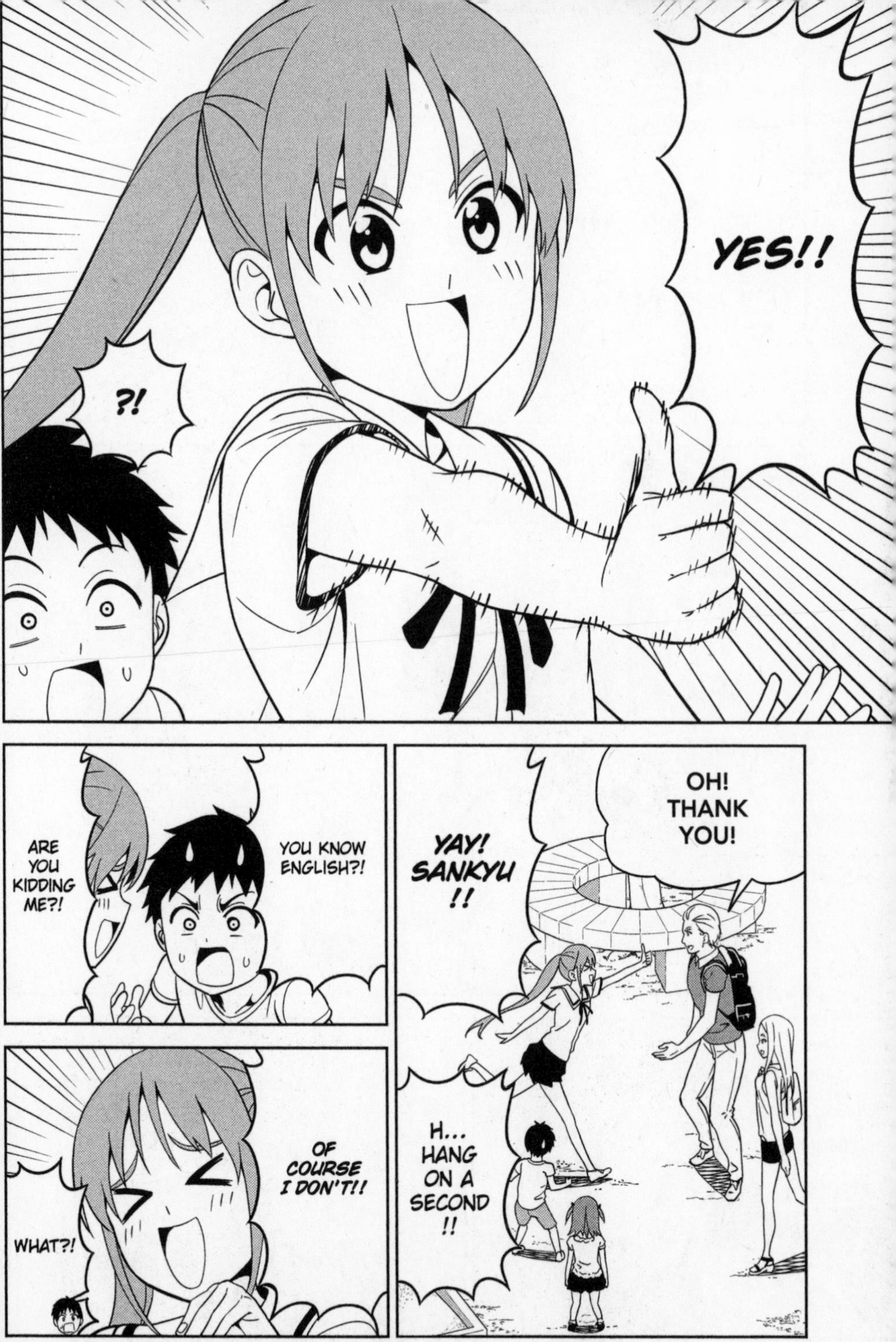
YES!!
?!
OH! THANK YOU!
YAY! SANKYU!!
H... HANG ON A SECOND!!
YOU KNOW ENGLISH?!
ARE YOU KIDDING ME?!
OF COURSE I DON'T!!
WHAT?!

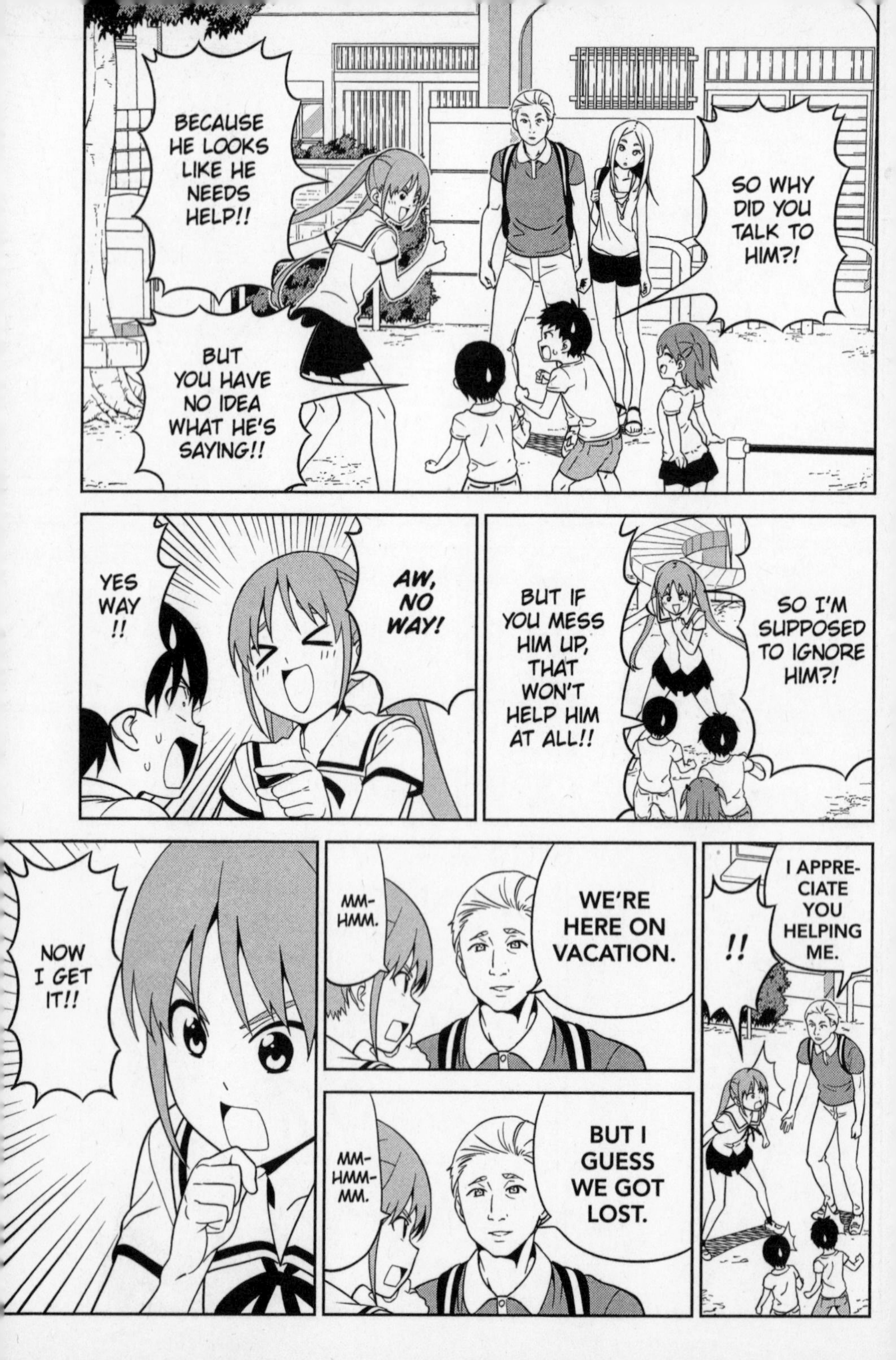
SO WHY DID YOU TALK TO HIM?!
BECAUSE HE LOOKS LIKE HE NEEDS HELP!!
BUT YOU HAVE NO IDEA WHAT HE'S SAYING!!
SO I'M SUPPOSED TO IGNORE HIM?!
BUT IF YOU MESS HIM UP, THAT WON'T HELP HIM AT ALL!!
AW, NO WAY!
YES WAY!!
I APPRE-CIATE YOU HELPING ME.
!!
WE'RE HERE ON VACATION.
MM-HMM.
BUT I GUESS WE GOT LOST.
MM-HMM-MM.
NOW I GET IT!!

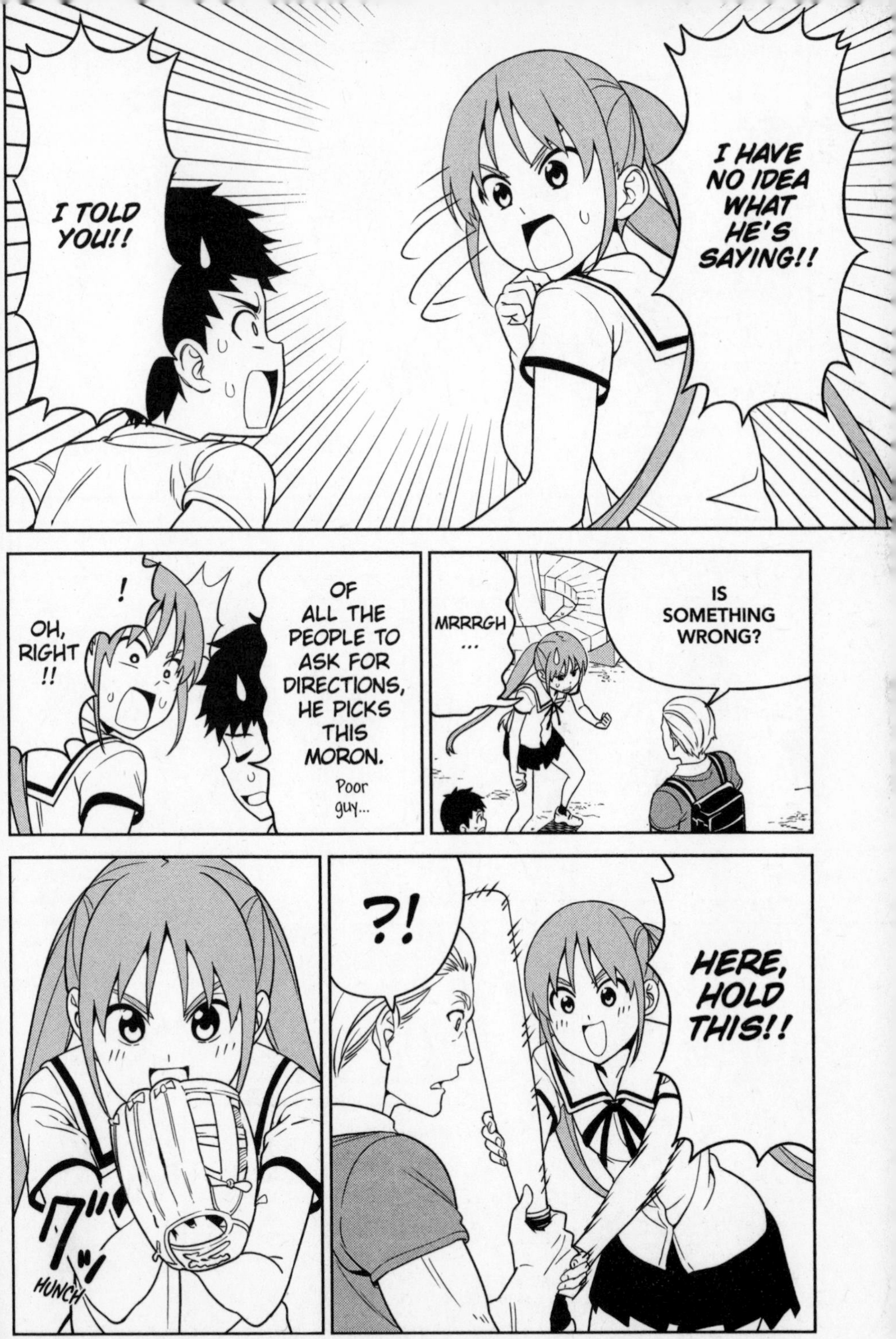
I HAVE NO IDEA WHAT HE'S SAYING!!
I TOLD YOU!!
IS SOMETHING WRONG?
MRRRGH ...
OF ALL THE PEOPLE TO ASK FOR DIRECTIONS, HE PICKS THIS MORON.
Poor guy...
!
OH, RIGHT !!
HERE, HOLD THIS!!
?!
HUNCH

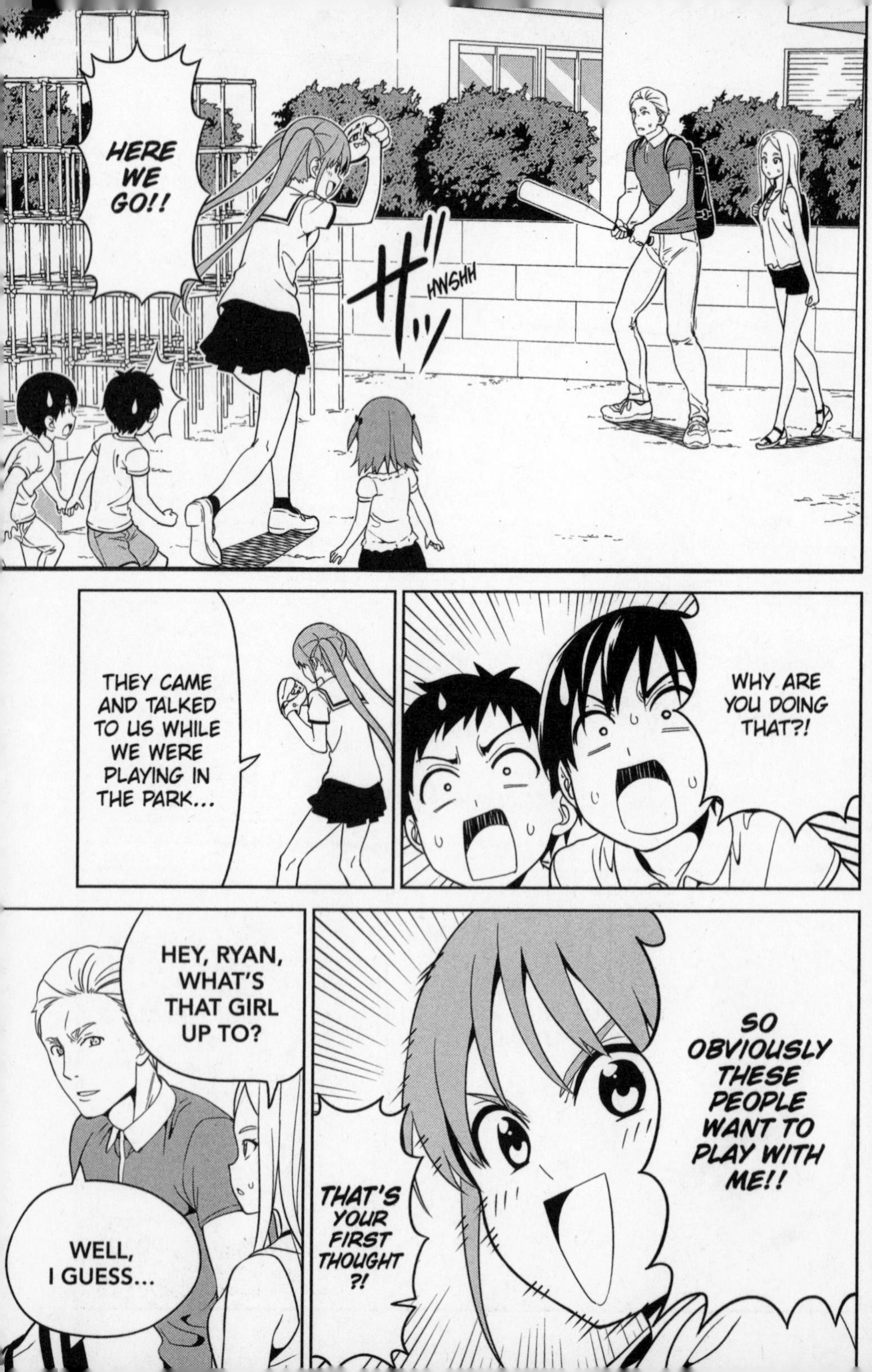
HERE WE GO!!
HWSHH
WHY ARE YOU DOING THAT?!
THEY CAME AND TALKED TO US WHILE WE WERE PLAYING IN THE PARK...
SO OBVIOUSLY THESE PEOPLE WANT TO PLAY WITH ME!!
THAT'S YOUR FIRST THOUGHT?!
HEY, RYAN, WHAT'S THAT GIRL UP TO?
WELL, I GUESS...

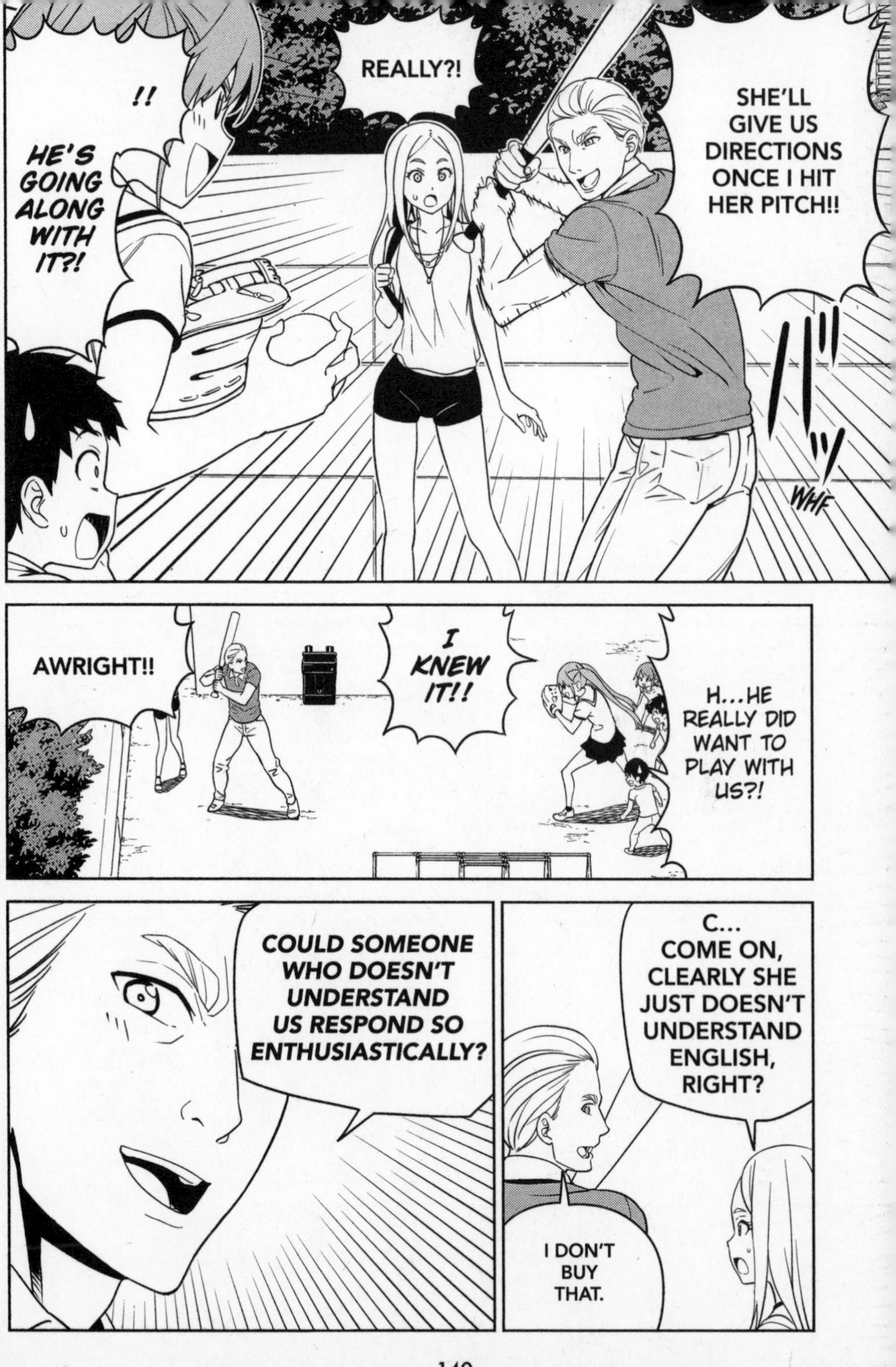
SHE'LL GIVE US DIRECTIONS ONCE I HIT HER PITCH!!
WHF
REALLY?!
!!
HE'S GOING ALONG WITH IT?!
H...HE REALLY DID WANT TO PLAY WITH US?!
I KNEW IT!!
AWRIGHT!!
C... COME ON, CLEARLY SHE JUST DOESN'T UNDERSTAND ENGLISH, RIGHT?
I DON'T BUY THAT.
COULD SOMEONE WHO DOESN'T UNDERSTAND US RESPOND SO ENTHUSIASTICALLY?

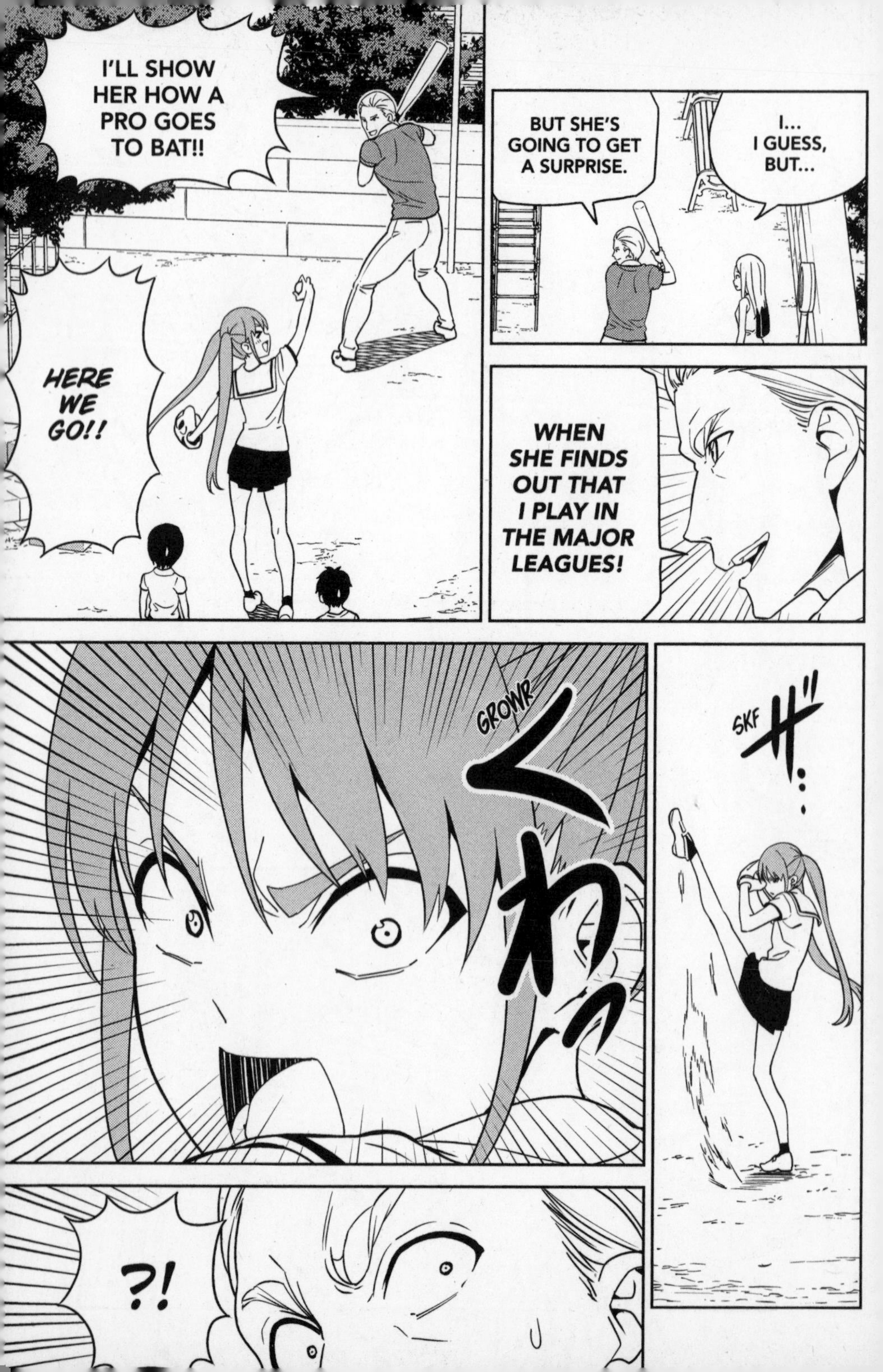
I... I GUESS, BUT...
BUT SHE'S GOING TO GET A SURPRISE.
WHEN SHE FINDS OUT THAT I PLAY IN THE MAJOR LEAGUES!
I'LL SHOW HER HOW A PRO GOES TO BAT!!
HERE WE GO!!
SKF
ザ…
GROWR
くわっ
?!

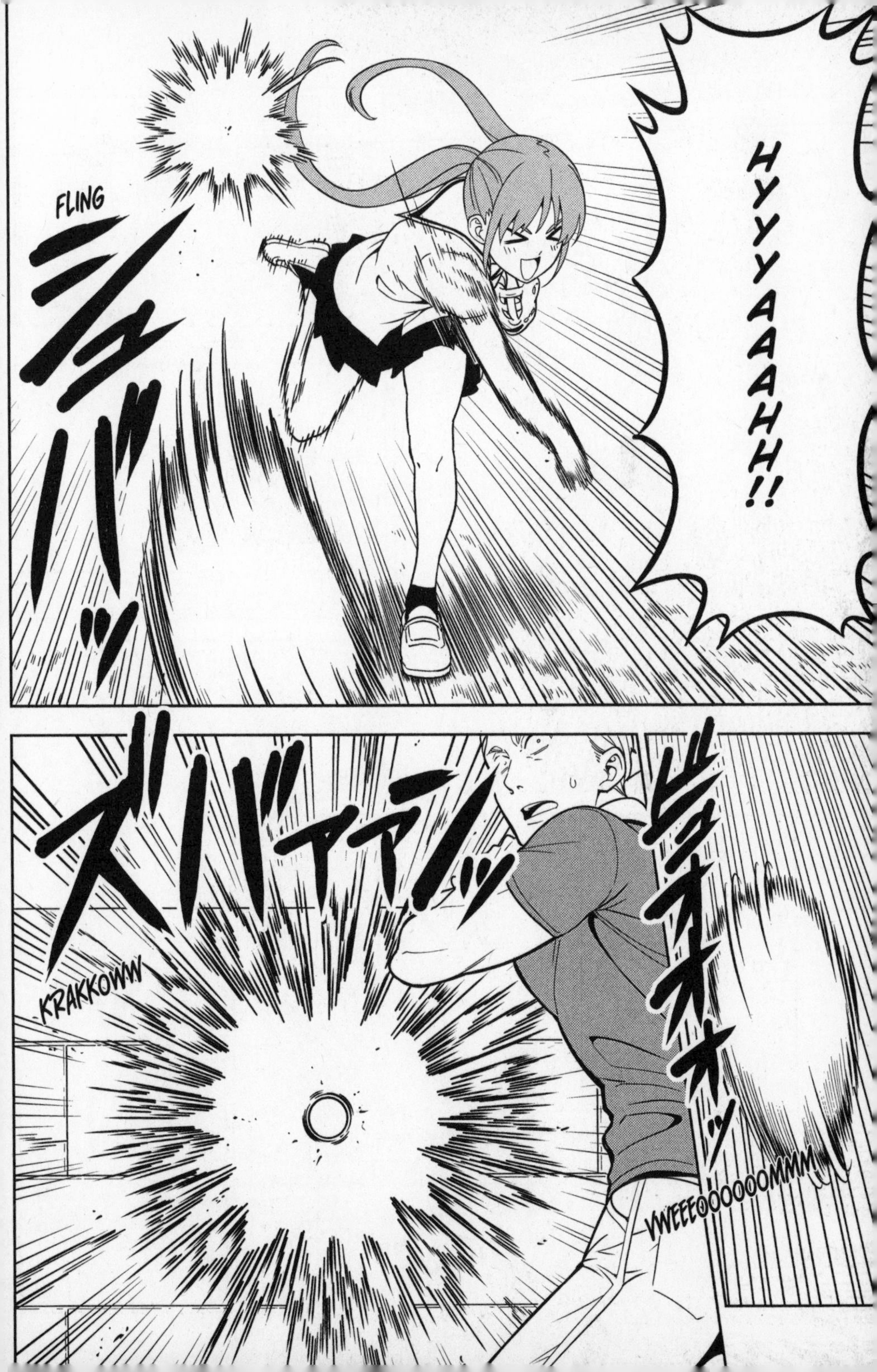
HYYYAAAAHH!!
FLING
VWEEEOOOOOOMMMM
KRAKKOWW

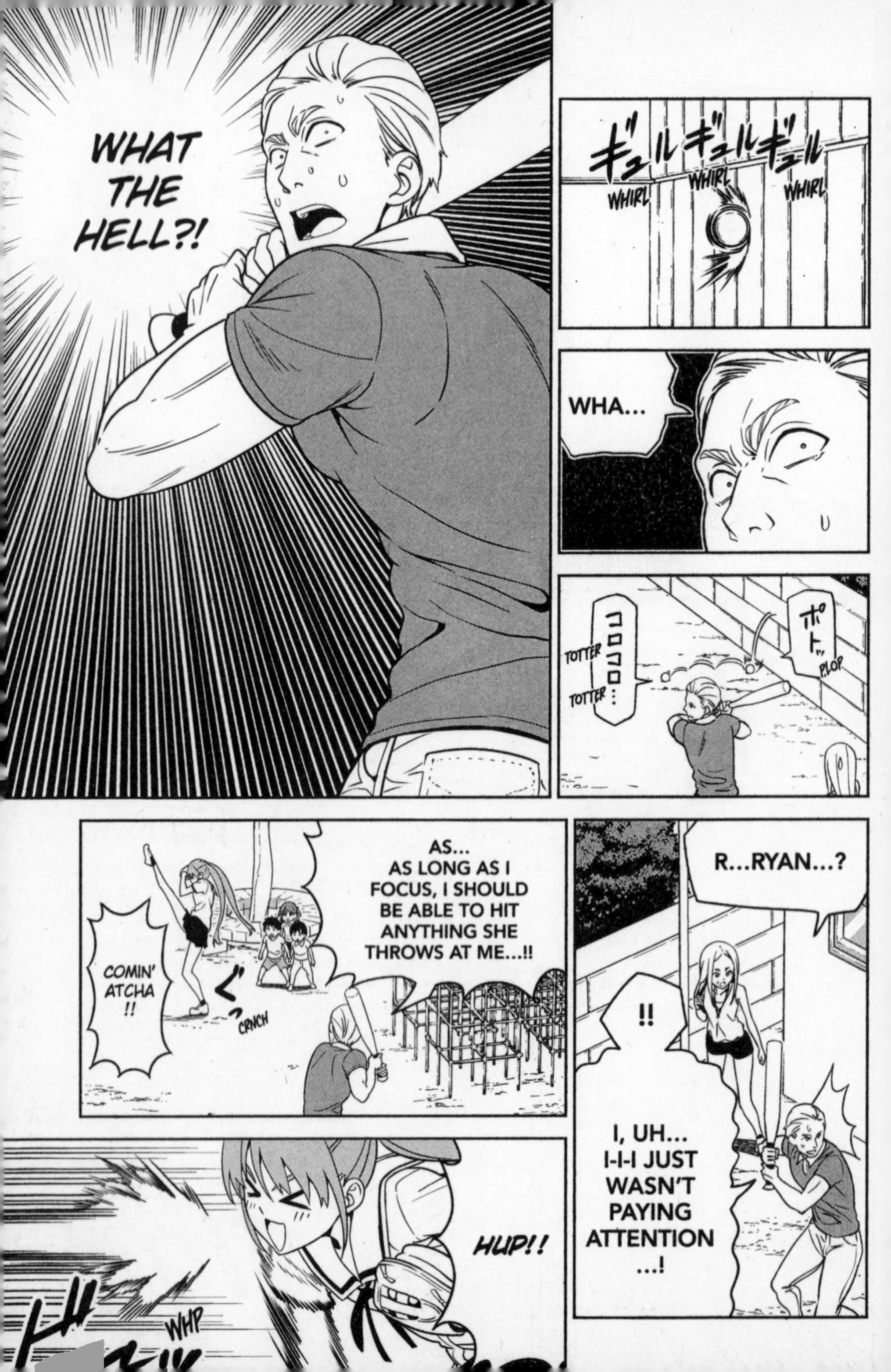

ギュルギュルギュル
WHIRL
WHIRL
WHIRL
WHA...
ポトッ
PLOP
コロコロ...
TOTTER
TOTTER
WHAT THE HELL?!
R...RYAN...?
!!
I, UH... I-I-I JUST WASN'T PAYING ATTENTION ...!
AS... AS LONG AS I FOCUS, I SHOULD BE ABLE TO HIT ANYTHING SHE THROWS AT ME...!!
COMIN' ATCHA !!
ぐっ
CRNCH
HUP!!
WHP

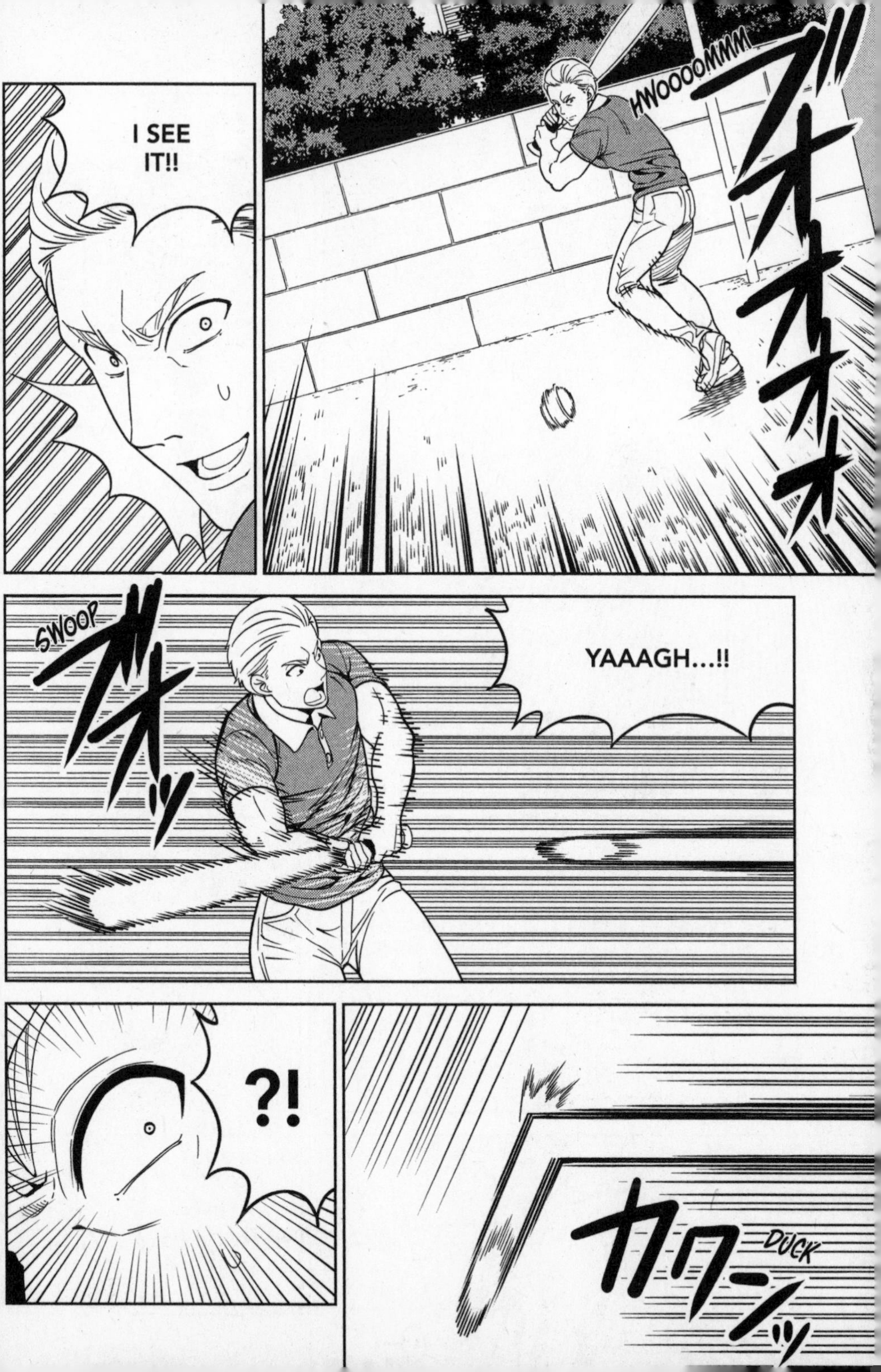
HWOOOOMMM
ブオオオオ
I SEE IT!!
YAAAGH...!!
SWOOP
ザオッ
DUCK
カワーンッ
?!

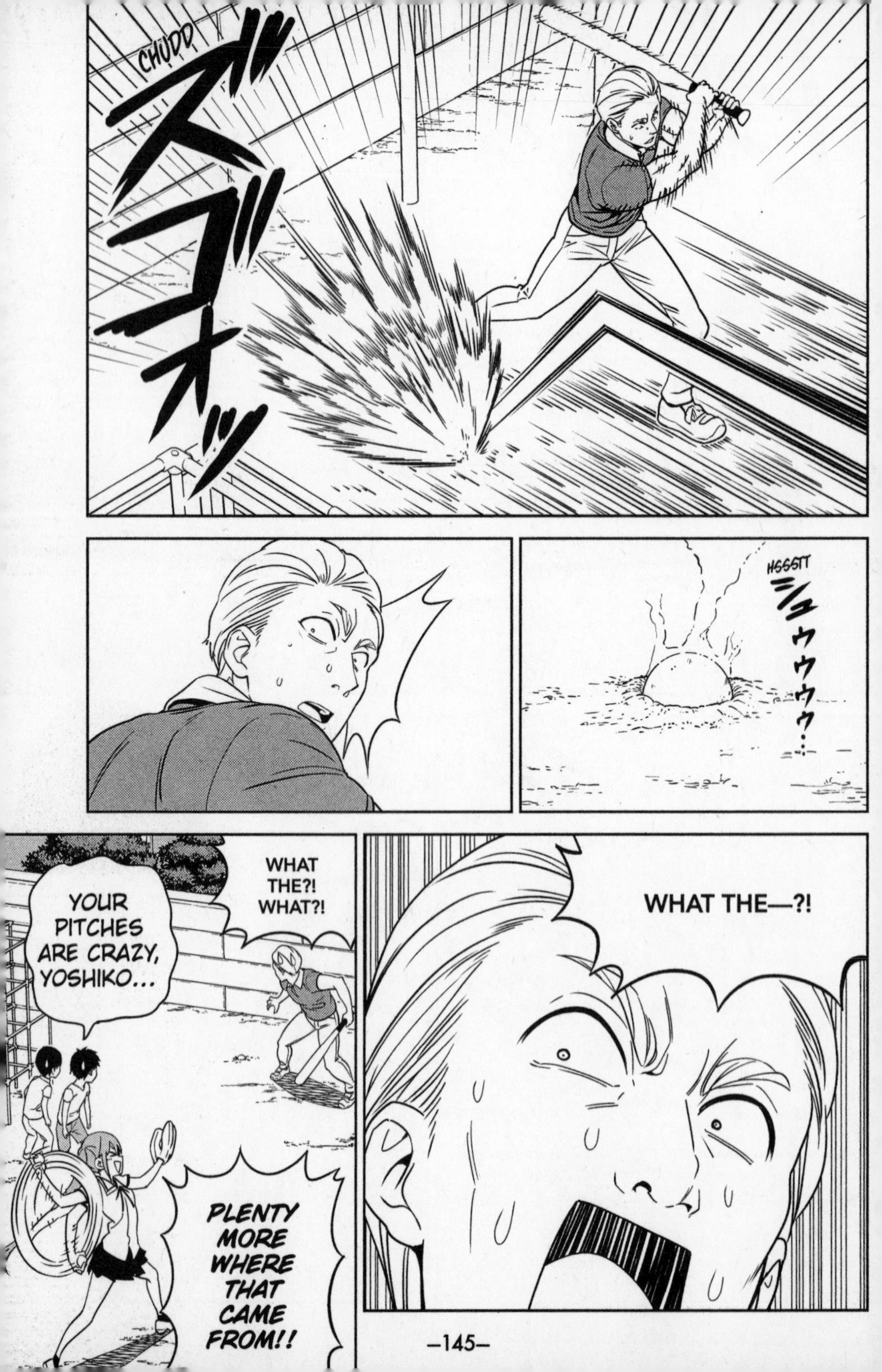
CHUDD
ズゴオッ
HSSSTT
シュウウウウ…
WHAT THE—?!
WHAT THE?! WHAT?!
YOUR PITCHES ARE CRAZY, YOSHIKO…
PLENTY MORE WHERE THAT CAME FROM!!

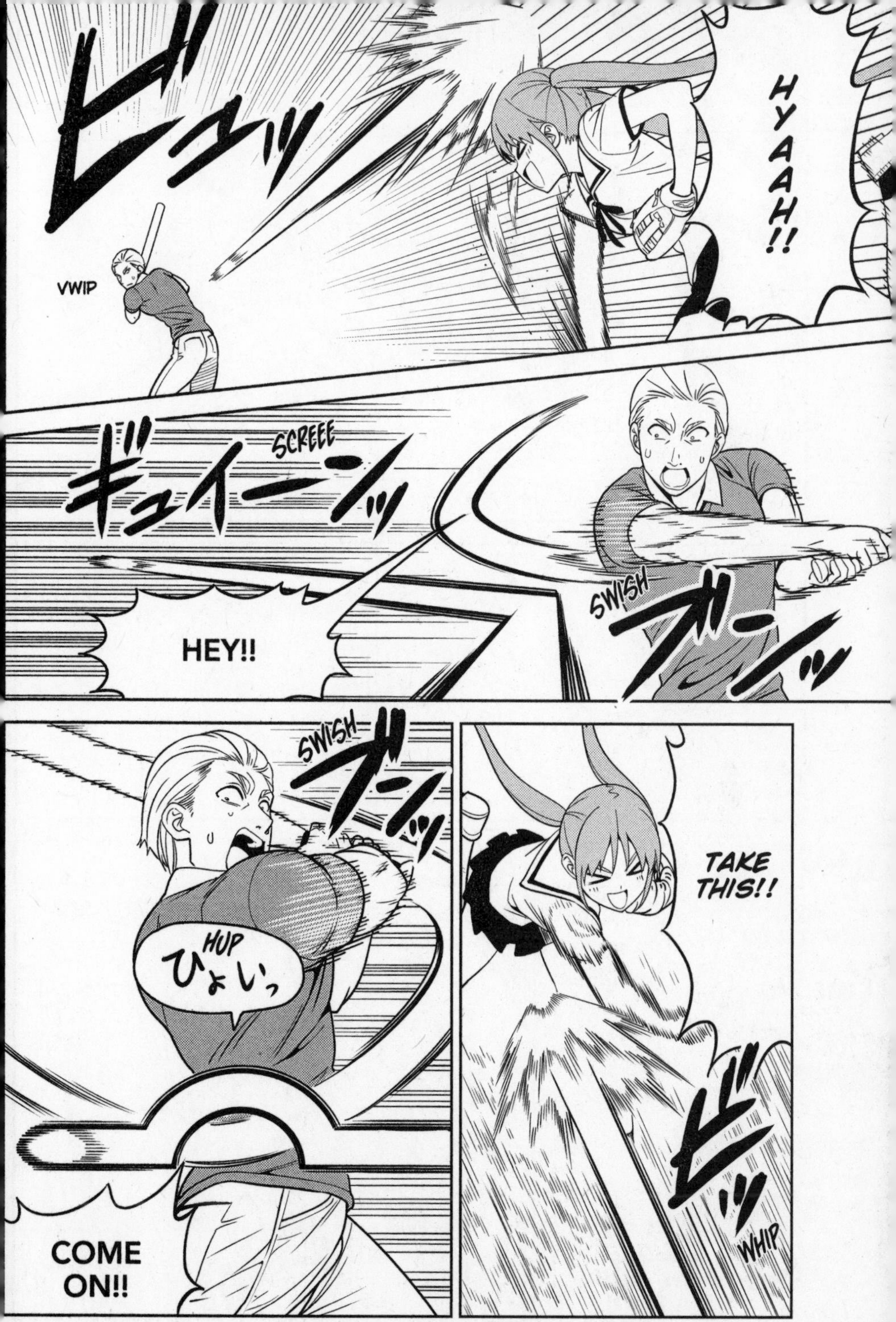
HYAAAH!!
ビュッ
VWIP
SCREEE
ギュイーンッ
SWISH
ブーンッ
HEY!!
TAKE THIS!!
ビッ
WHIP
SWISH
ブンッ
HUP
ひょいっ
COME ON!!

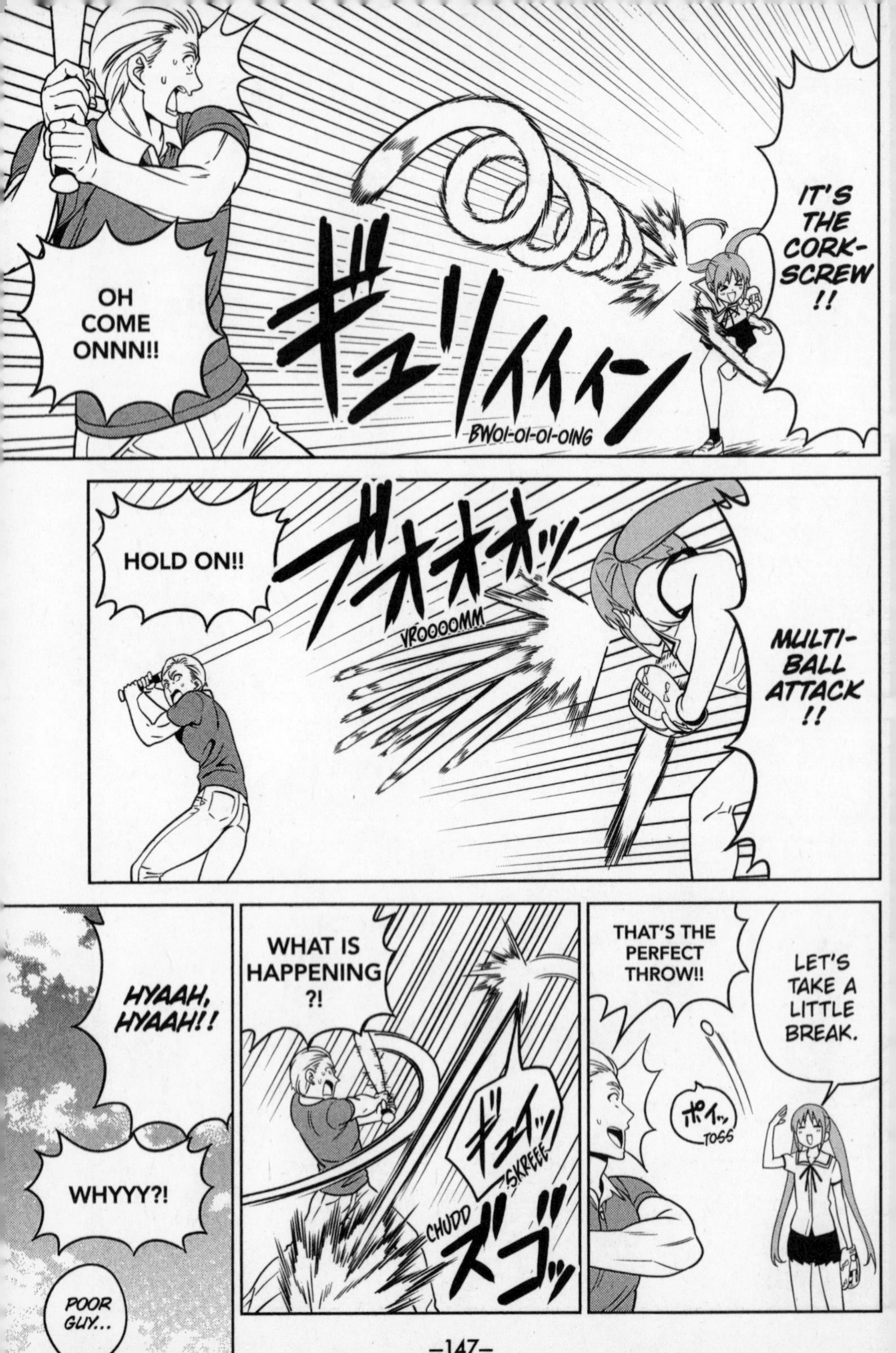
IT'S THE CORK-SCREW!!
ギュリイイイン
BWOI-OI-OI-OING
OH COME ONNN!!
MULTI-BALL ATTACK!!
ブオオオッ
VROOOOMM
HOLD ON!!
LET'S TAKE A LITTLE BREAK.
THAT'S THE PERFECT THROW!!
ポイッ
TOSS
WHAT IS HAPPENING ?!
ギュイッ
SKREEE
ズゴッ
CHUDD
HYAAH, HYAAH!!
WHYYY?!
POOR GUY...

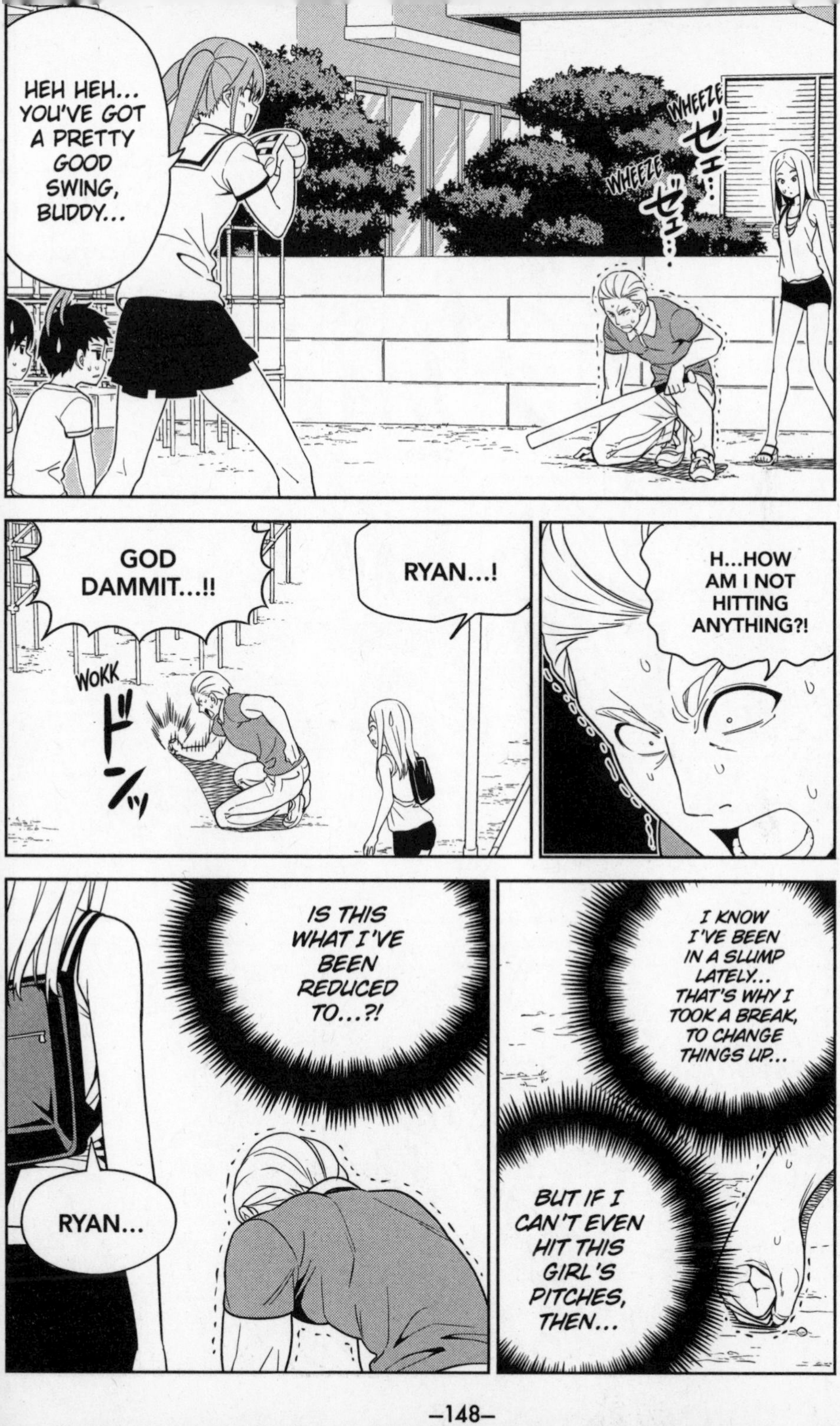
WHEEZE
ゼェ…
WHEEZE
ゼェ…
HEH HEH... YOU'VE GOT A PRETTY GOOD SWING, BUDDY...
H...HOW AM I NOT HITTING ANYTHING?!
RYAN...!
GOD DAMMIT...!!
WOKK
ドーンッ
I KNOW I'VE BEEN IN A SLUMP LATELY... THAT'S WHY I TOOK A BREAK, TO CHANGE THINGS UP...
BUT IF I CAN'T EVEN HIT THIS GIRL'S PITCHES, THEN...
IS THIS WHAT I'VE BEEN REDUCED TO...?!
RYAN...

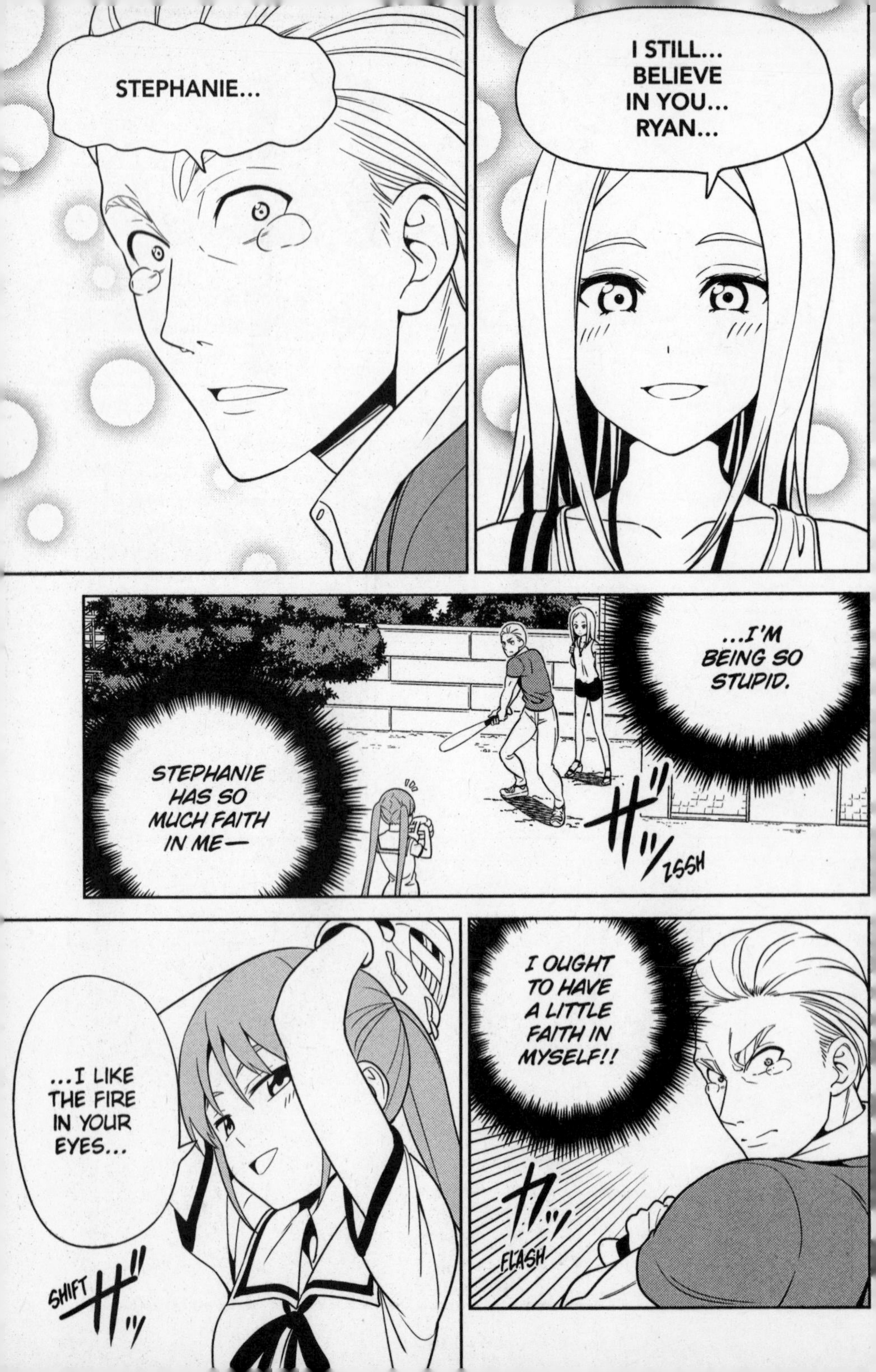
I STILL... BELIEVE IN YOU... RYAN...
STEPHANIE...
...I'M BEING SO STUPID.
ZSSH
STEPHANIE HAS SO MUCH FAITH IN ME—
I OUGHT TO HAVE A LITTLE FAITH IN MYSELF!!
FLASH
...I LIKE THE FIRE IN YOUR EYES...
SHIFT

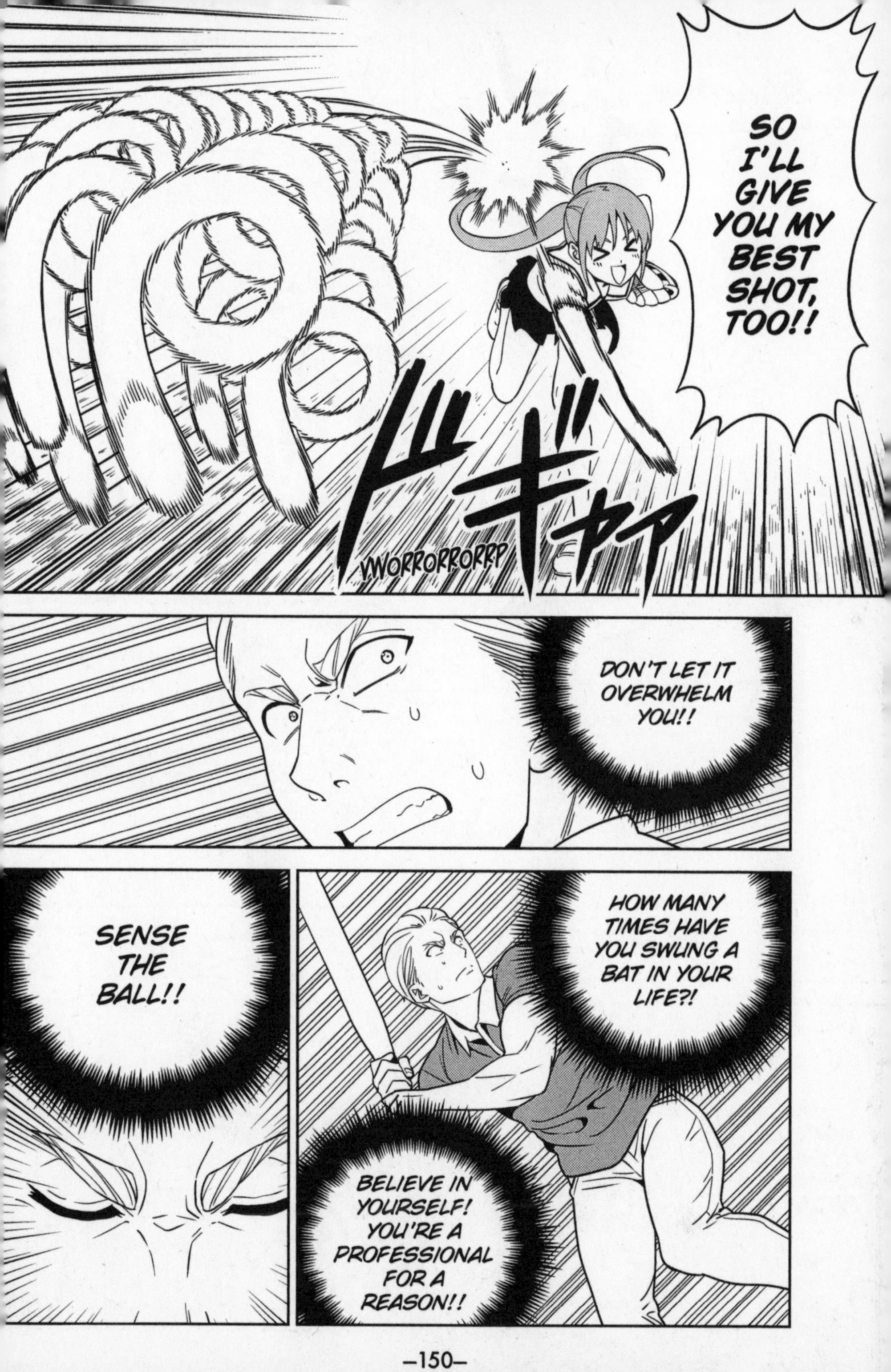
SO I'LL GIVE YOU MY BEST SHOT, TOO!!
VWORRORRORRP
DON'T LET IT OVERWHELM YOU!!
HOW MANY TIMES HAVE YOU SWUNG A BAT IN YOUR LIFE?!
BELIEVE IN YOURSELF! YOU'RE A PROFESSIONAL FOR A REASON!!
SENSE THE BALL!!

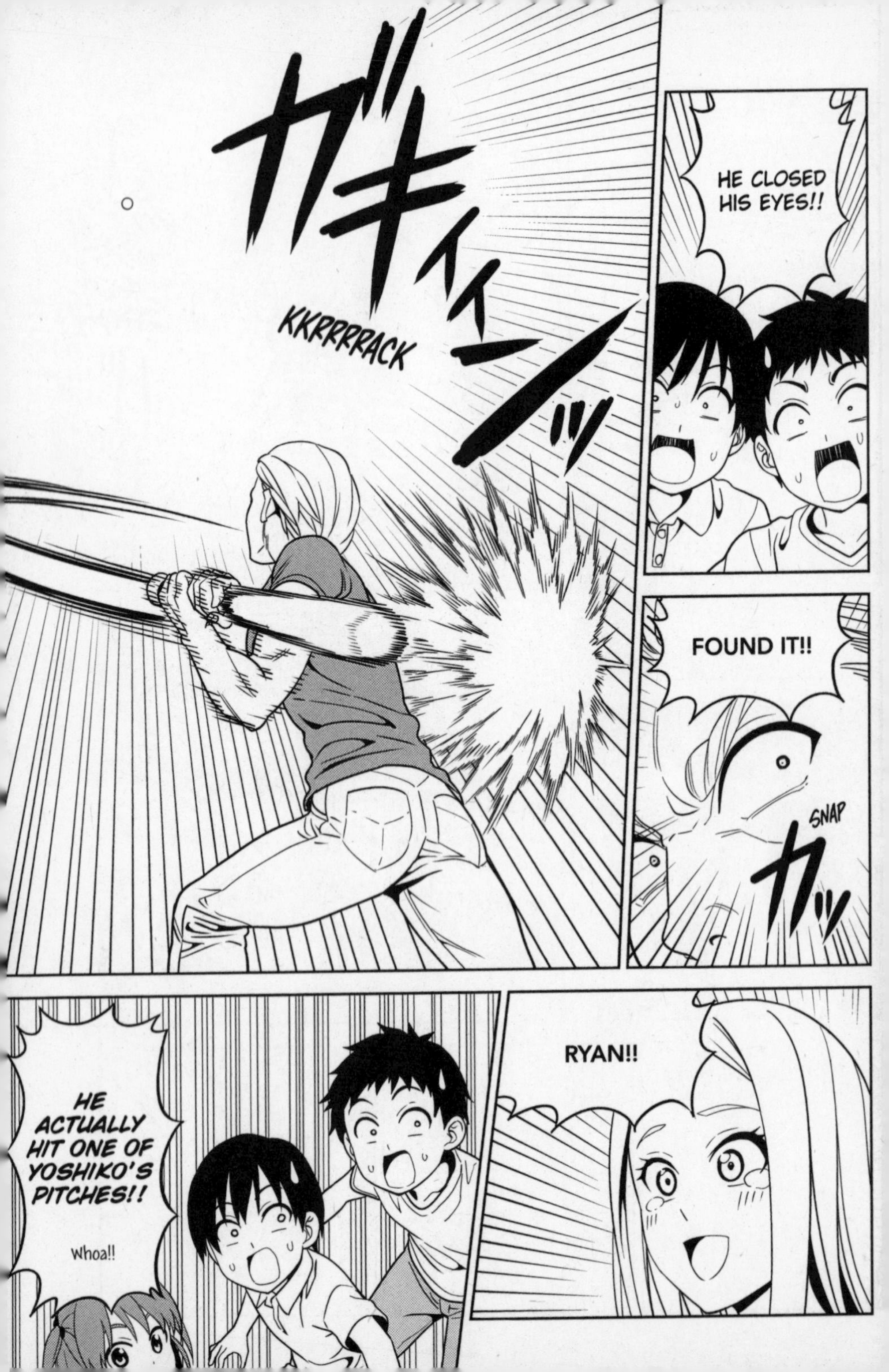
HE CLOSED HIS EYES!!
FOUND IT!!
SNAP
カッ
ガキィィンッ
KKRRRRACK
RYAN!!
HE ACTUALLY HIT ONE OF YOSHIKO'S PITCHES!!
Whoa!!

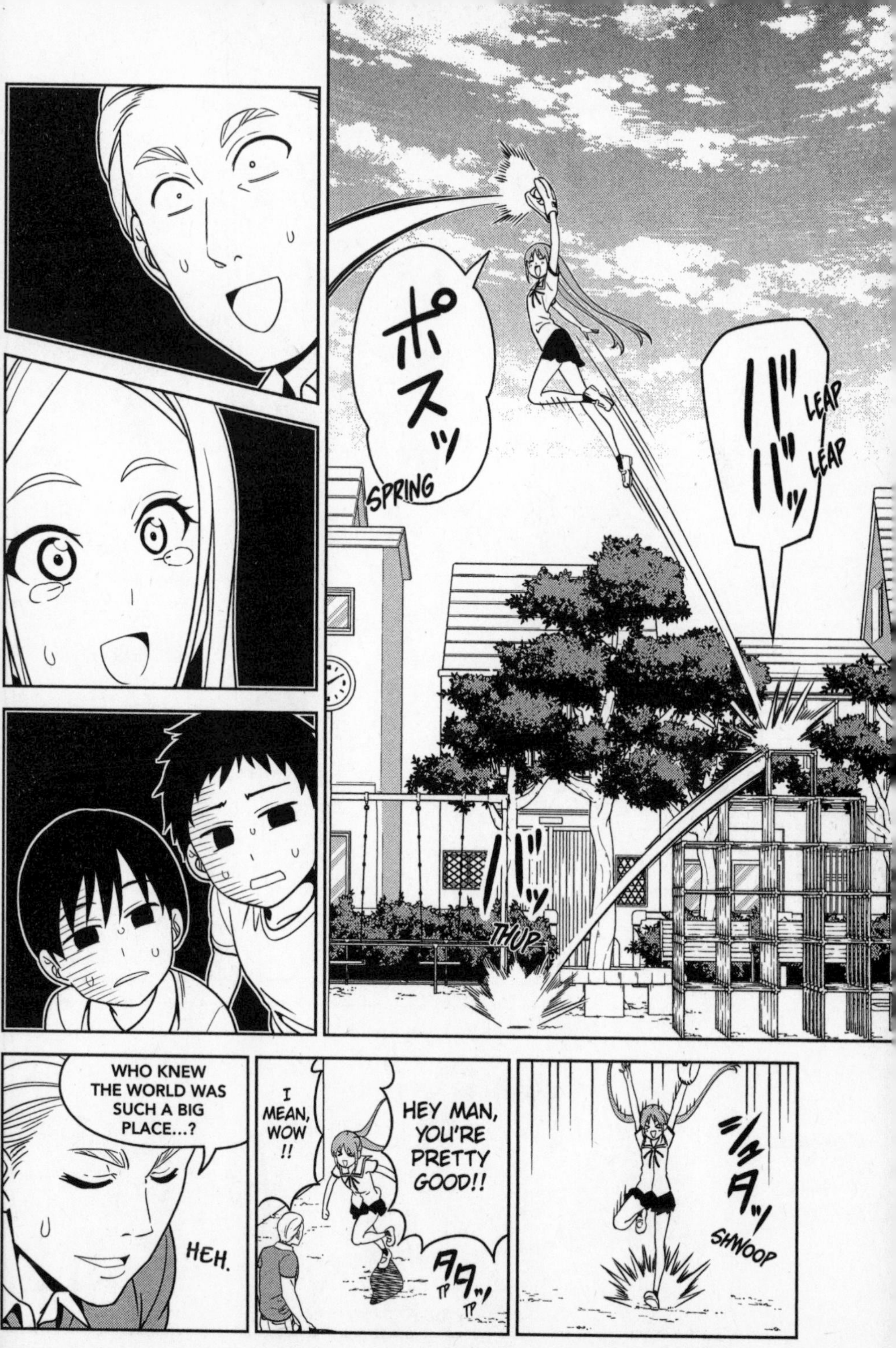
ババッ
LEAP LEAP
ポスッ
SPRING
バッ
THUP
シュタッ
SHWOOP
HEY MAN, YOU'RE PRETTY GOOD!!
I MEAN, WOW !!
タタッ
TP TP
WHO KNEW THE WORLD WAS SUCH A BIG PLACE...?
HEH.

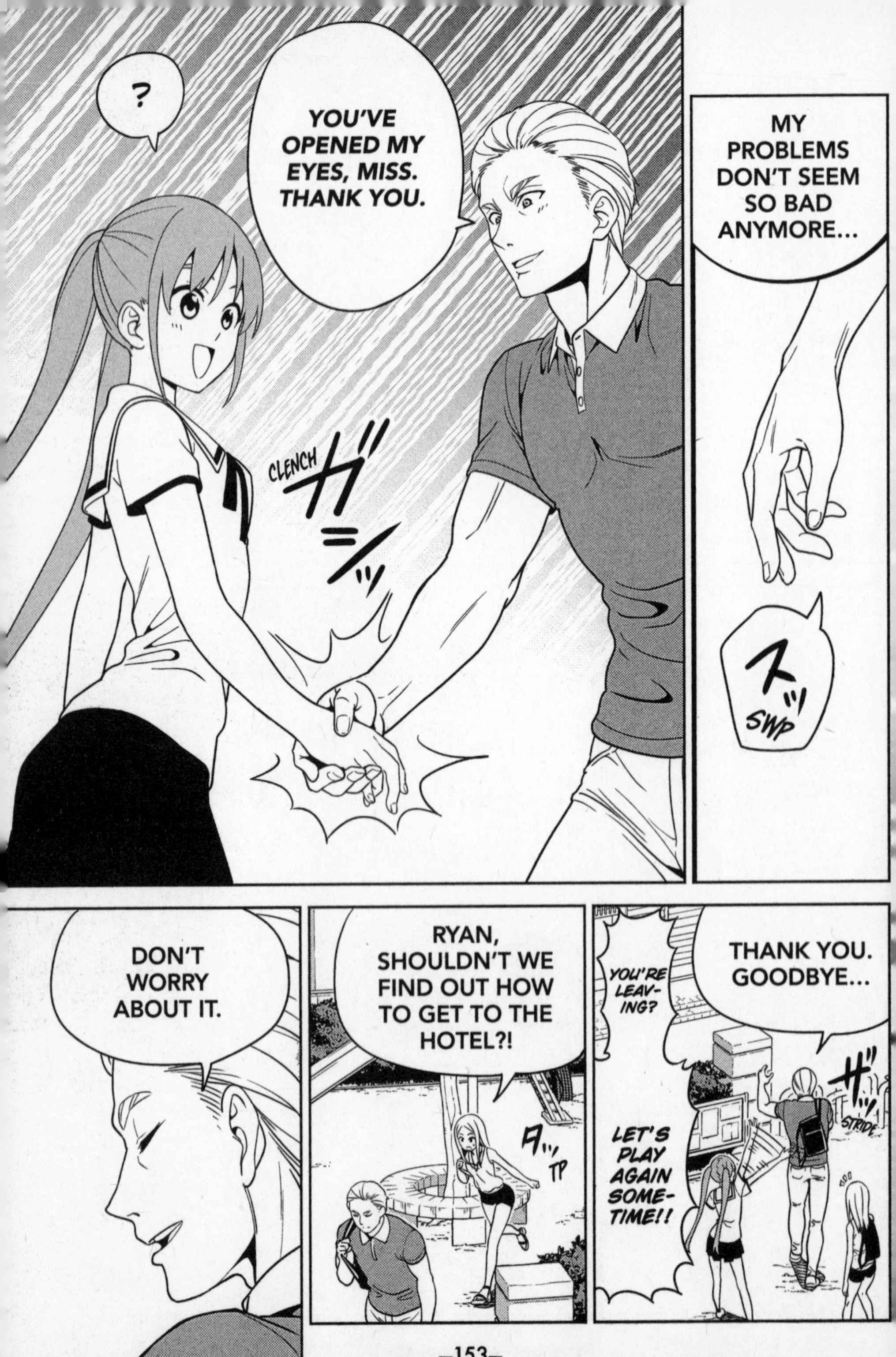

MY PROBLEMS DON'T SEEM SO BAD ANYMORE...
SWP
YOU'VE OPENED MY EYES, MISS. THANK YOU.
?
CLENCH
THANK YOU. GOODBYE...
YOU'RE LEAV-ING?
STRIDE
LET'S PLAY AGAIN SOME-TIME!!
RYAN, SHOULDN'T WE FIND OUT HOW TO GET TO THE HOTEL?!
TP
DON'T WORRY ABOUT IT.

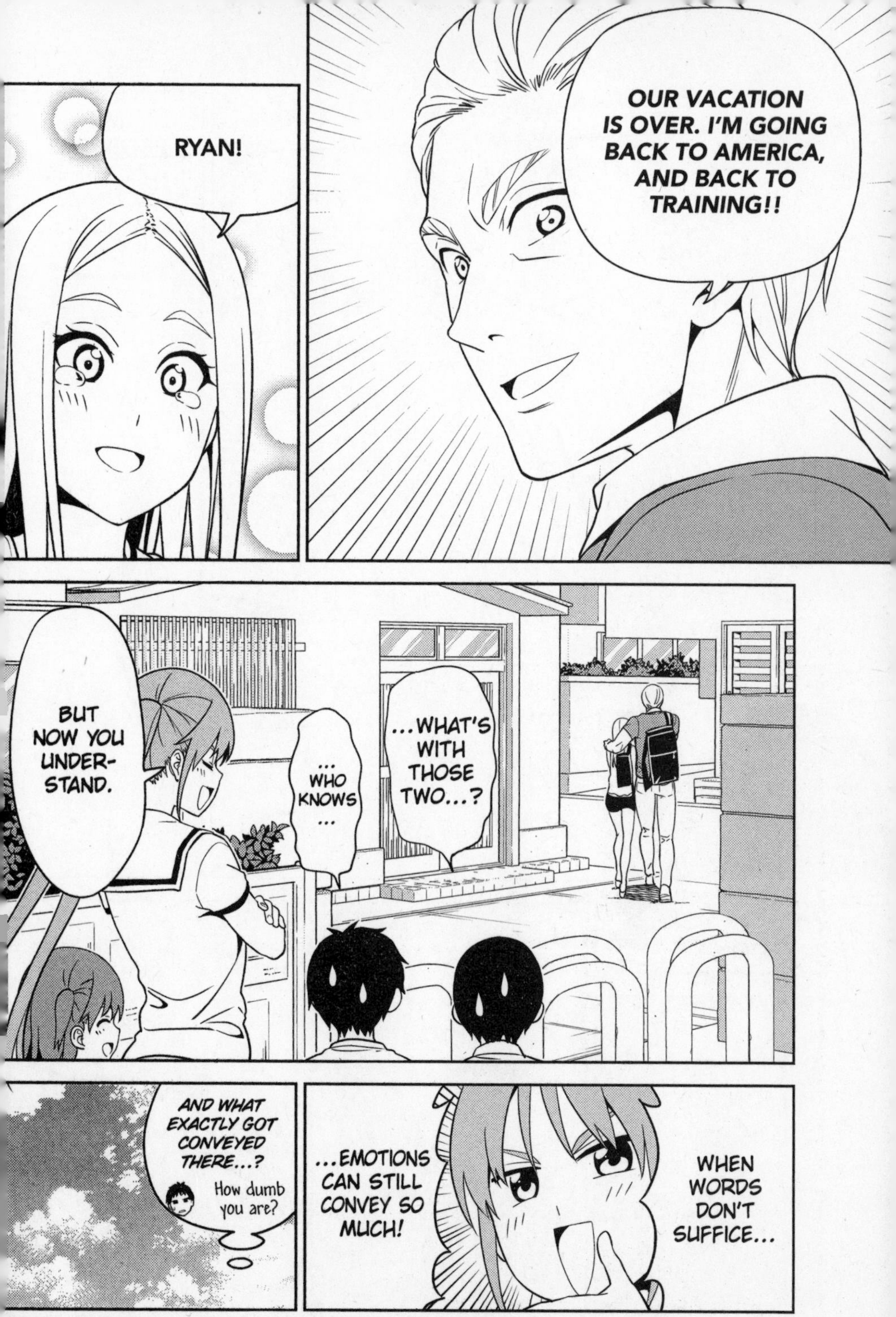
OUR VACATION IS OVER. I'M GOING BACK TO AMERICA, AND BACK TO TRAINING!!
RYAN!
...WHAT'S WITH THOSE TWO...?
...WHO KNOWS...
BUT NOW YOU UNDER-STAND.
WHEN WORDS DON'T SUFFICE...
...EMOTIONS CAN STILL CONVEY SO MUCH!
AND WHAT EXACTLY GOT CONVEYED THERE...?
How dumb you are?

Continued in volume 10!

My Boy's All Grown Up

RYAN IS IN PERFECT FORM LATELY, WITH A BATTING AVERAGE OF .388!!

WHAT A FINE PLAYER YOU'VE BECOME...

(Seriously, it's going to be an anime!)

Aho-Girl

\'ahô,gərl\ *Japanese, noun*.
A clueless girl.

The Drama of How Hiroyuki Became a Manga-Ka 8

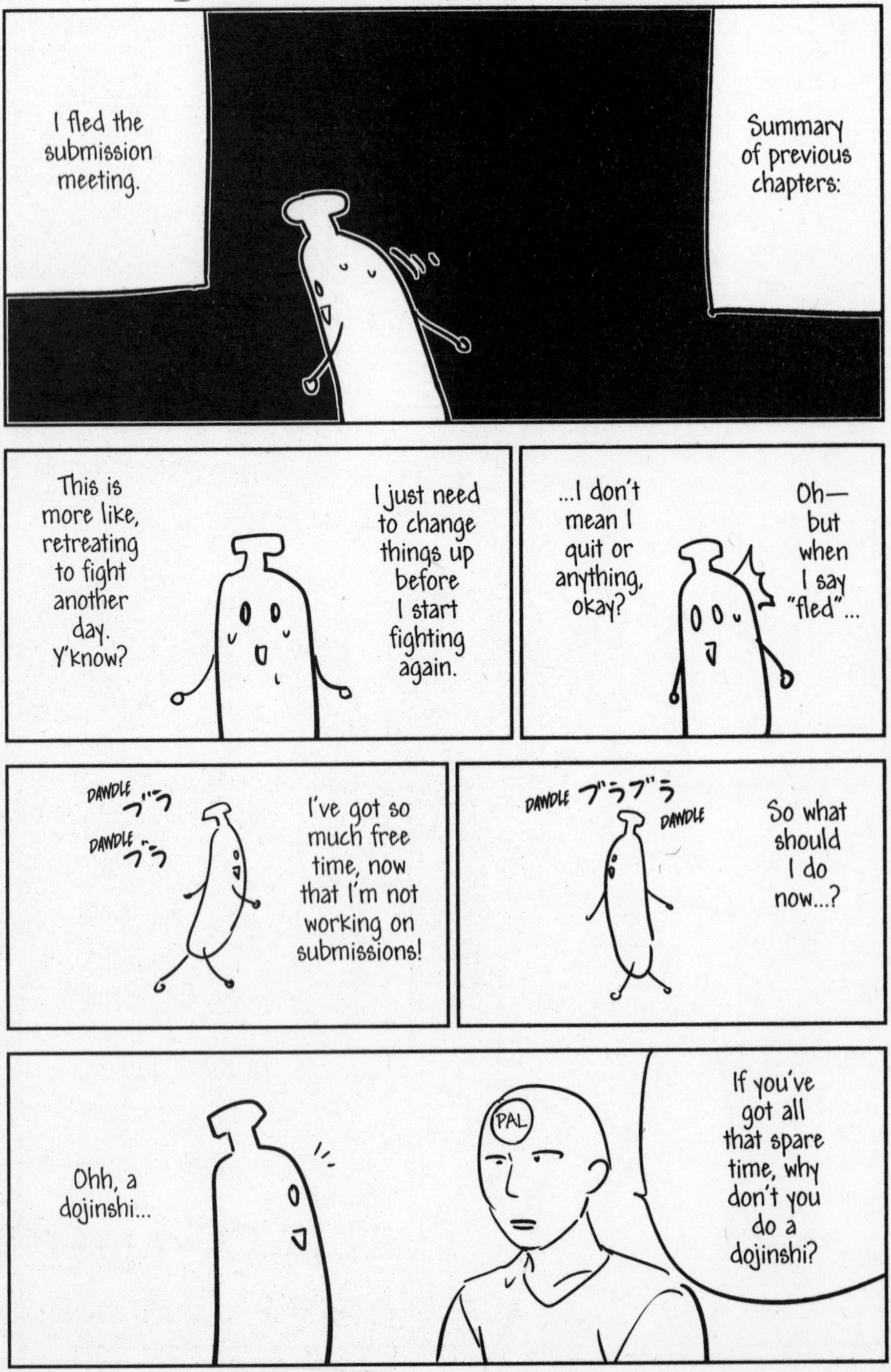
Summary of previous chapters:
I fled the submission meeting.
Oh— but when I say "fled"...
...I don't mean I quit or anything, okay?
I just need to change things up before I start fighting again.
This is more like, retreating to fight another day. Y'know?
DAWDLE ブラブラ DAWDLE
So what should I do now...?
DAWDLE ブラ
DAWDLE ブラ
I've got so much free time, now that I'm not working on submissions!
If you've got all that spare time, why don't you do a dojinshi?
PAL
Ohh, a dojinshi...

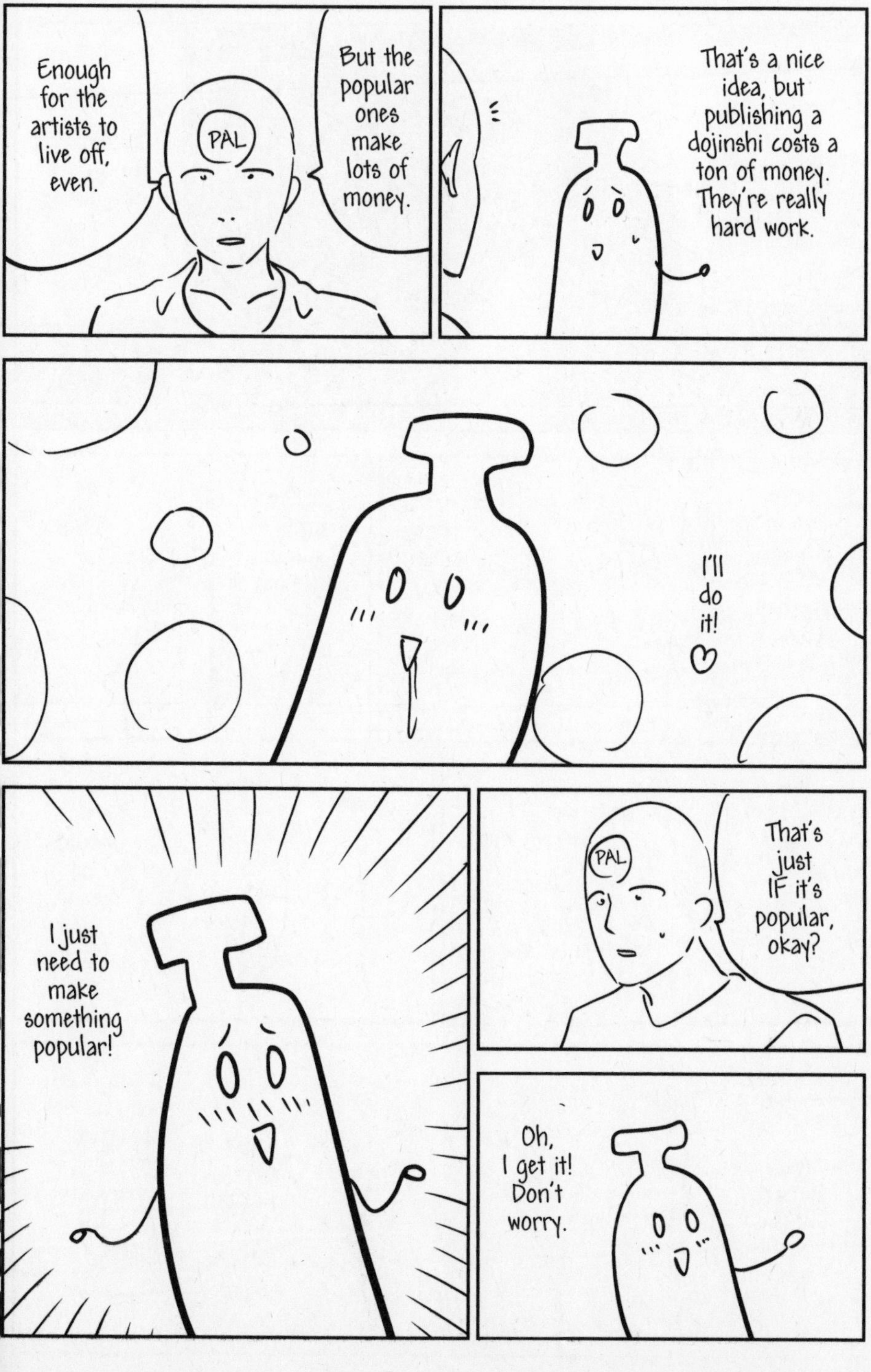
That's a nice idea, but publishing a dojinshi costs a ton of money. They're really hard work.
But the popular ones make lots of money.
Enough for the artists to live off, even.
I'll do it!
That's just IF it's popular, okay?
Oh, I get it! Don't worry.
I just need to make something popular!

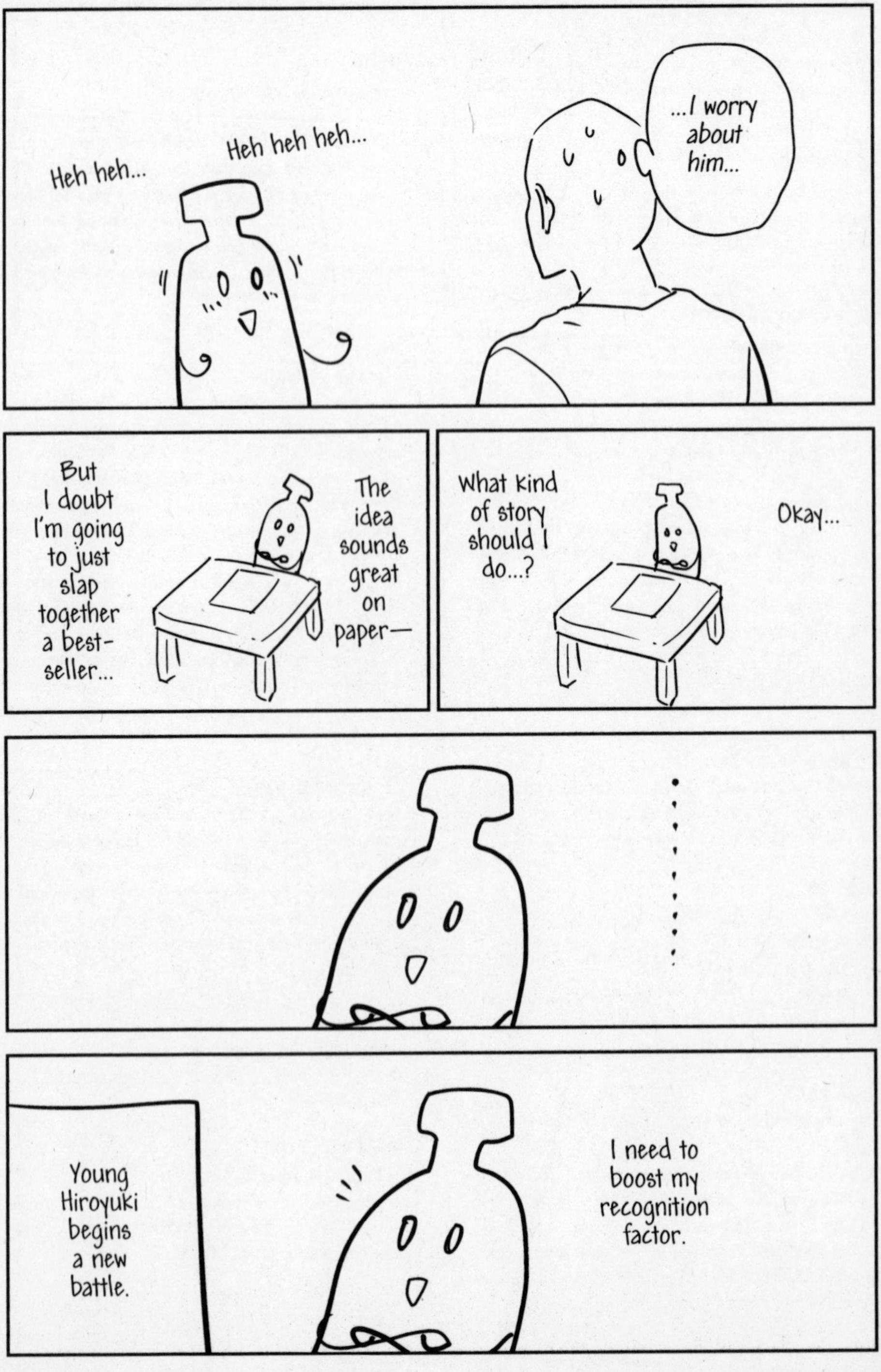
...I worry about him...
Heh heh heh...
Heh heh...
Okay...
What kind of story should I do...?
The idea sounds great on paper—
But I doubt I'm going to just slap together a best-seller...
....
I need to boost my recognition factor.
Young Hiroyuki begins a new battle.

Translation Notes

Page 2

"Aggravated straight man"

This is an explanatory gloss of the Japanese term "tsukkomi." The *tsukkomi* and *boke* duo are a common trope in *manzai*-style stand-up comedy routines. The boke, like Yoshiko, draws over-the-top and just plain stupid conclusions to the *tsukkomi*'s set-ups. The *tsukkomi* tries to remain calm and reasonable during the act, but is invariably pushed into extreme and sometimes violent reactions out of his frustration.

Page 3

"Gang of Gals"

The term "gal" (Japanese *gyaru*) refers to a broad segment of popular youth culture in Japan that began in the mid-1990s. The term encompasses many distinct subcultures with different stereotyped behaviors (such as extreme tanning, bleached-white hair, or casual dating in exchange for spending money) that are considered contrary to prevailing Japanese morality. In general, though, most people who are labeled by the term "gal" merely subscribe to a particular fashion aesthetic characterized by loose socks (the familiar slouchy socks that hang loose around the ankles), lightly bleached hair, extensive nail art or cell phone bangles, and school uniform skirts that are rolled up at the waist to be scandalously short.

"Head Monitor"

The head monitor's title in Japanese includes the word *fuuki*, which roughly translates to "moral order" or "discipline." She would not be merely checking for hall passes the way a hall monitor in a Western school might, and would be more broadly responsible for reporting anything in violation of the moral standards of the institution.

"G Cup"

Going by Japanese bra sizing conventions, the head monitor's "G cup" would be roughly equivalent to an American DDD.

Page 7

"I found a Twodo!"

The Japanese name *Tootoo* is a parody of a Pokémon named *Doodoo*, a two-headed bird, which has been localized for the US as "Doduo."

Page 9

"Oniichan"/"Oneechan"

Literally "older brother" and "older sister," respectively, these terms are also used to address teenage to early 30s-aged men and women not related to the speaker.

Page 14

"OXMORD"

The book Ruri is reading is the "Kojihen," a parody on the gold-standard Japanese dictionary *Kojien*, replacing the last syllable with the word "hen," meaning "weird."

Page 20

"POLKAMON GO"

The various original puns on "Pokomon" include "Bokomon" (where *boko* evokes the idea of "hollow" or "lumpy"), "Pokkomon" (where *pokko* evokes "crumple, collapse"), and "Pompokomon" (where *pompoko* alludes to the sound *tanuki* tricksters/shapeshifters make).

Page 26

"How far will you walk? How far, how far?"

This appears to be a slight misquote of a *Pokémon* song. A very similar lyric is found in the song "Kaze to Issho ni" ("Together with the Wind"), which is the end theme for the first Pokémon movie, *Mewtwo Strikes Back*.

Page 45

"It's almost summer break!! There's only eight months before we graduate!!"

The school year in Japan begins in April, with the first term running from April to mid-July, the second term running from early September to late December, and the third term running from January to late March.

Page 50

"¥1000"

Equivalent to about $9 in US dollars.

Page 66

"¥10,000"

Equivalent to about $90 in US dollars.

Page 75

"You have to take your exams this year, don't you?!"

In Japan, nationally administered standardized tests are used to evaluate all students hoping to enter college in the coming year. These subject-specific tests are given once a year, over the course of two days in January. Because summer break has just ended, the head monitor has about four months to get ready for college.

Page 134
"The next day"
Although the system varies widely between school districts, and has changed several times in the last twenty years, the Japanese school schedule may still include classes on Saturdays. In some cases, classes are held only every other Saturday, or the school is simply open to students for club activities. Whatever the case here, it would seem that our characters occasionally find themselves at school on Saturday. Hiiragi asked Akane out when they were at school on Saturday, the two went out on Sunday, and now they're back in school the day after for Shiina to check in on how the date went.

Page 136
"YES!!"
In the original Japanese text, Yoshiko is talking in *katakana*, the writing system primarily used for foreign loan words. This is somewhat analogous to meeting a French person and saying only "baguette, c'est la vie, s'il vous plait," and thinking that you're having a conversation.

Page 157
"Dojinshi"
This is the Japanese term for self-publishing. It can apply both to original works as well as to fan comics that riff on existing properties. Many manga artists have been discovered through their *dojinshi* work, such as Kiyohiko Azuma (the creator of *Azumanga Daioh*), Monkey Punch (the creator of *Lupin III*), Rumiko Takahashi, and CLAMP.

Page 76
Test results
In the Japanese style of marking up tests, circles are good, checks are bad, and every answer is marked (not just wrong answers).

"I might like staying in the kitchen"
The head monitor uses an outdated reference for marriage that translates literally to "eternal employment," i.e., working at home for the rest of her life as a housewife.

Page 86
"Who Benefits, Who Loses Out?"
This is a reference to the title of a TV show that has been broadcast on Nippon Television Network since 2013. The show originally discussed events in the news and examined how those events impacted various people. The show has since morphed slightly away from current events topics and more toward technological developments and products, and how those impact people's lives.

Page 110
"Walk through fire"
These are the opening words to the very first Japanese theme song of the Pokémon anime series, "Mezase Pokémon Master" ("Aim to Be a Pokémon Master"). The song continues "Walk through fire, dive through water, search the fields, search the forest, dig through dirt, soar through the clouds, check in that girl's skirt (yeeek!); everywhere, everywhere, everywhere, everywhere—" You never know where those Pokémon might be hiding!

Page 124
"How about this owl café, then?"
Japan has become somewhat known for the ongoing fad of animal cafés, where patrons can relax with normal café food and beverages while playing with various animals. Beginning in 2005 with cat cafés, the market has since expanded to include dogs, rabbits, goats, snakes—and yes, even owls.

Page 132
"Would you call me by my first name?"
Classmates generally call each other by last name, adding the suffix "san" for girls and "kun" for boys to convey some politeness. Dropping the suffix denotes some familiarity, but Akane is still holding Hiiragi at a little distance, addressing her as a nice classmate maybe, but not like a close friend.

Aho-Girl
\ˈahôˌgərl\ *Japanese, noun*.
A clueless girl.

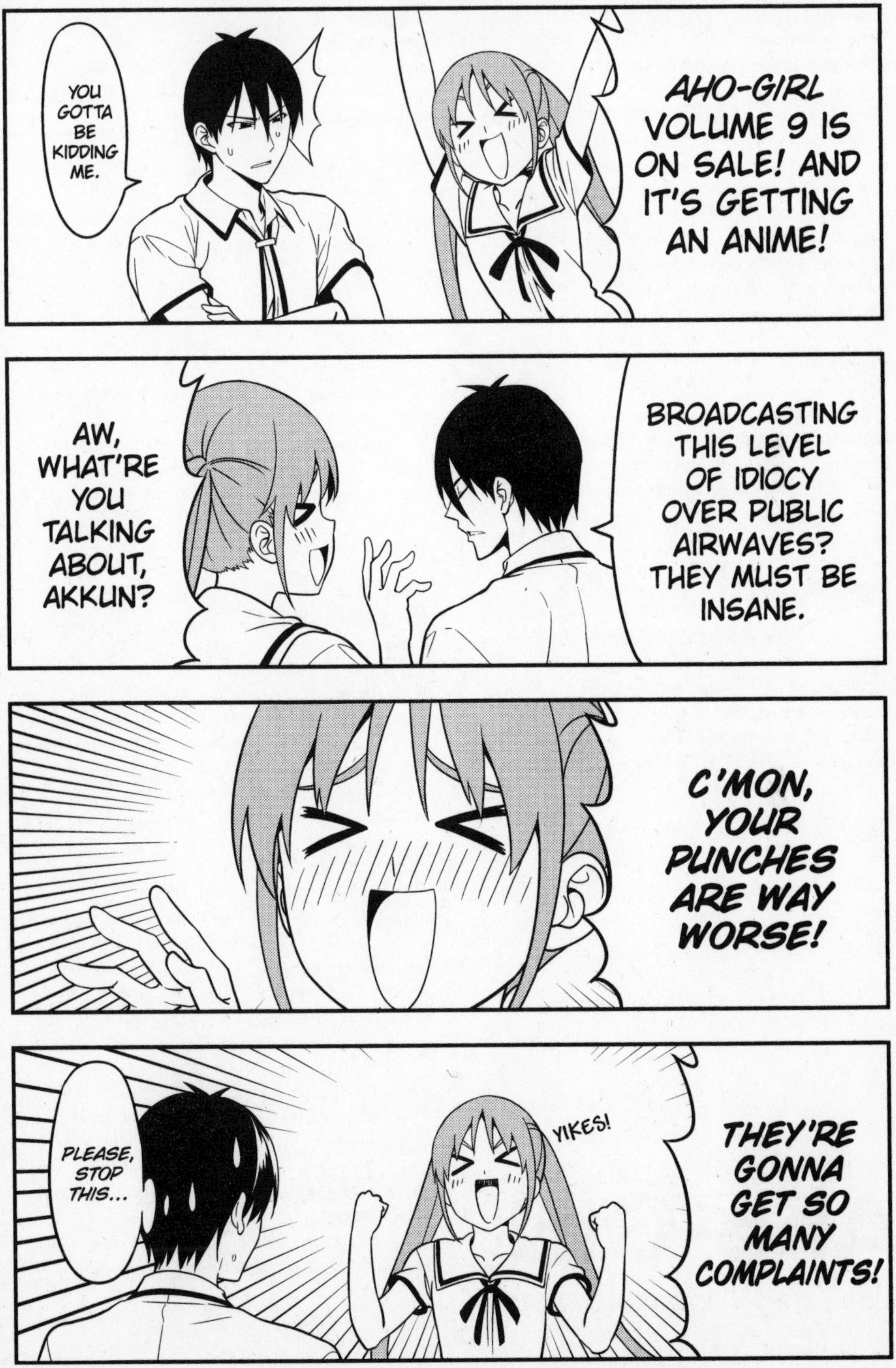
AHO-GIRL VOLUME 9 IS ON SALE! AND IT'S GETTING AN ANIME!
YOU GOTTA BE KIDDING ME.
BROADCASTING THIS LEVEL OF IDIOCY OVER PUBLIC AIRWAVES? THEY MUST BE INSANE.
AW, WHAT'RE YOU TALKING ABOUT, AKKUN?
C'MON, YOUR PUNCHES ARE WAY WORSE!
THEY'RE GONNA GET SO MANY COMPLAINTS!
YIKES!
PLEASE, STOP THIS...

MOVEMENT PRACTICE FOR WHEN SHE'S ANIMATED

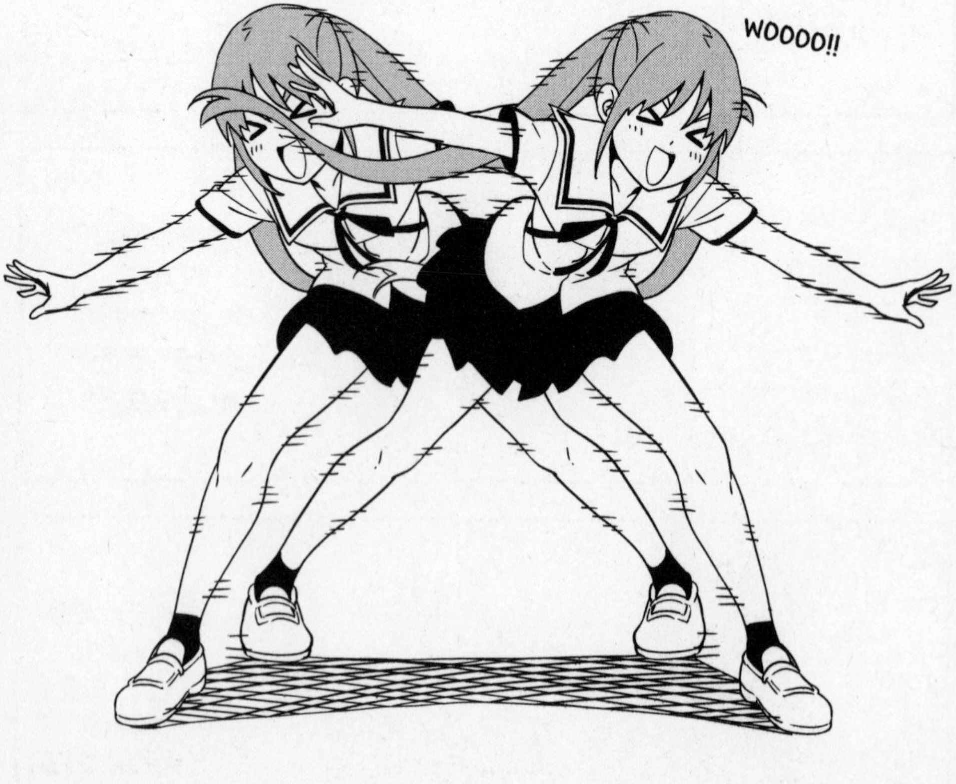
WOOOO!!

Aho-Girl

\'ahô͵gərl\ *Japanese, noun*.
A clueless girl.

In love, there are
no save points.

NOW AN
ANIME!

ヲ
タ
ク
に
恋
は
難
し
い

WOTAKOI:
LOVE IS HARD FOR OTAKU

by FUJITA

Narumi has had it rough: Every boyfriend she's had dumped her
once they found out she was an otaku, so she's gone to great
lengths to hide it. At her new job, she bumps into Hirotaka, her
childhood friend and fellow otaku. When Hirotaka almost gets
her secret outed at work, she comes up with a plan to keep him
quiet. But he comes up with a counter-proposal:
Why doesn't she just date him instead?

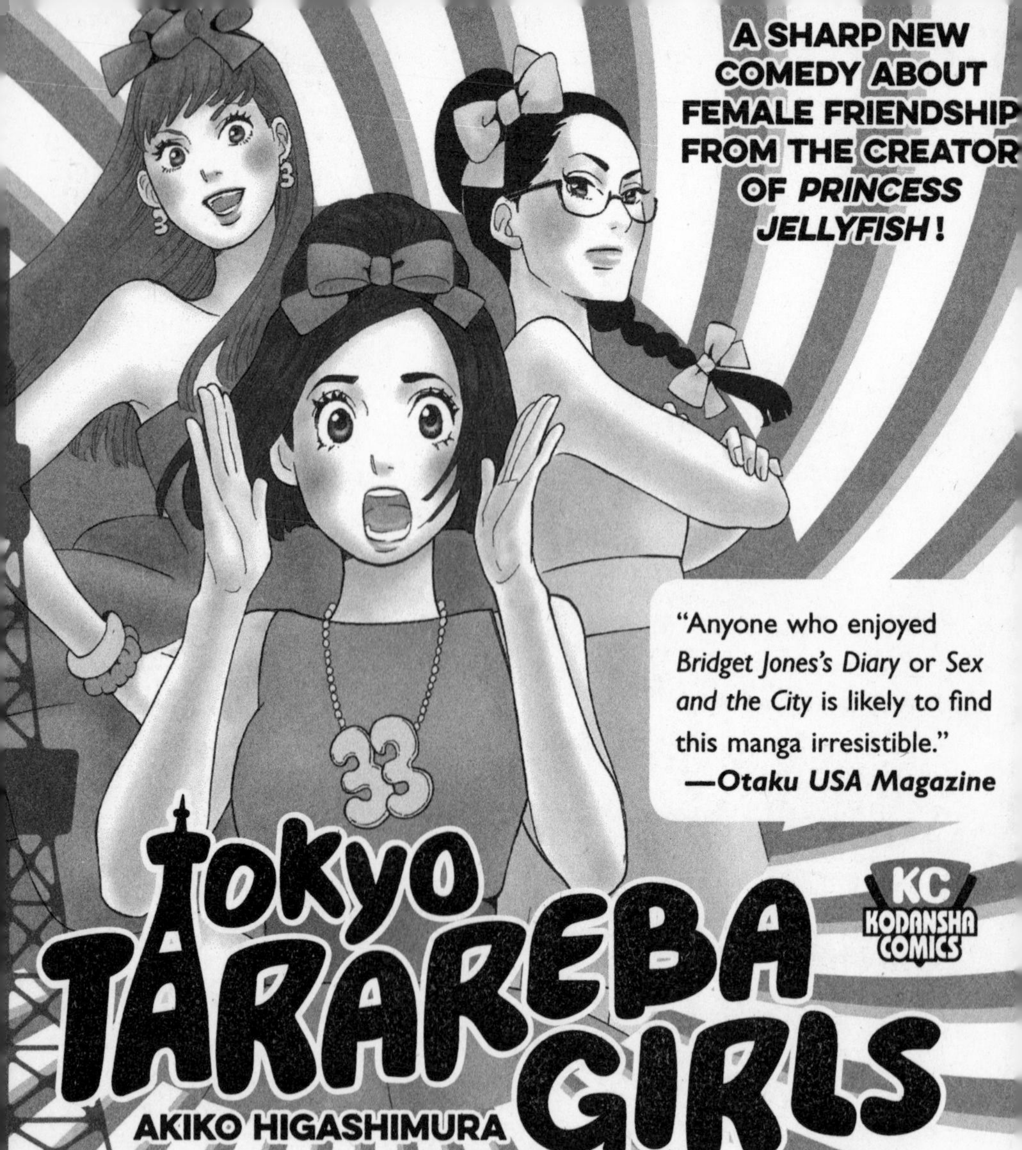
A SHARP NEW COMEDY ABOUT FEMALE FRIENDSHIP FROM THE CREATOR OF *PRINCESS JELLYFISH*!
"Anyone who enjoyed *Bridget Jones's Diary* or *Sex and the City* is likely to find this manga irresistible."
—*Otaku USA Magazine*
KC KODANSHA COMICS
TOKYO TARAREBA GIRLS
AKIKO HIGASHIMURA

"An emotional and artistic tour de force! We see incredible triumph, and crushing defeat... each panel [is] a thrill!"
—Anitay

"A journey that's instantly compelling."
—Anime News Network

WELCOME TO THE BALLROOM

By Tomo Takeuchi

Feckless high school student Tatara Fujita wants to be good at something—anything. Unfortunately, he's about as average as a slouchy teen can be. The local bullies know this, and make it a habit to hit him up for cash, but all that changes when the debonair Kaname Sengoku sends them packing. Sengoku's not the neighborhood watch, though. He's a professional ballroom dancer. And once Tatara Fujita gets pulled into the world of ballroom, his life will never be the same.

KC KODANSHA COMICS

The award-winning manga about what happens inside you!

"Far more entertaining than it ought to be... what kid doesn't want to think that every time they sneeze a torpedo shoots out their nose?"
—Anime News Network

Strep throat! Hay fever! Influenza! The world is a dangerous place for a red blood cell just trying to get her deliveries finished. Fortunately, she's not alone...she's got a whole human body's worth of cells ready to help out! The mysterious white blood cells, the buff and brash killer T cells, even the cute little platelets— everyone's got to come together if they want to keep you healthy!

Cells at Work!

By Akane Shimizu

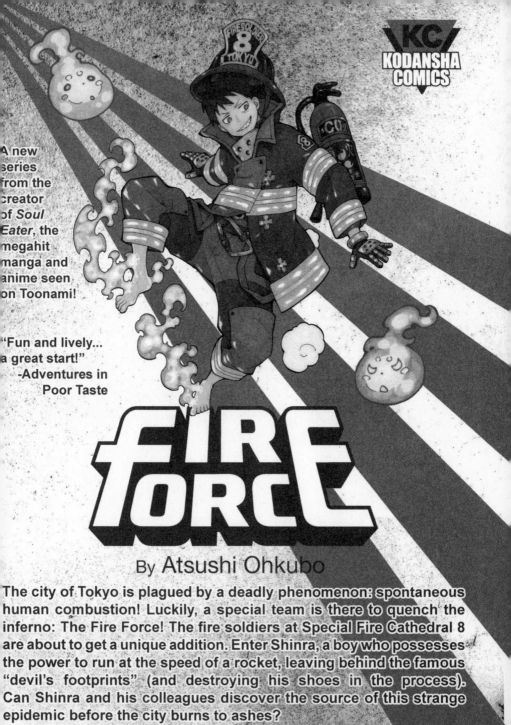

KC
KODANSHA
COMICS

A new series from the creator of *Soul Eater*, the megahit manga and anime seen on Toonami!

"Fun and lively... a great start!"
-Adventures in Poor Taste

FIRE FORCE

By Atsushi Ohkubo

The city of Tokyo is plagued by a deadly phenomenon: spontaneous human combustion! Luckily, a special team is there to quench the inferno: The Fire Force! The fire soldiers at Special Fire Cathedral 8 are about to get a unique addition. Enter Shinra, a boy who possesses the power to run at the speed of a rocket, leaving behind the famous "devil's footprints" (and destroying his shoes in the process). Can Shinra and his colleagues discover the source of this strange epidemic before the city burns to ashes?

The Black Museum: The Ghost and the Lady

By Kazuhiro Fujita

Deep in Scotland Yard in London sits an evidence room dedicated to the greatest mysteries of British history. In this "Black Museum" sits a misshapen hunk of lead—two bullets fused together—the key to a wartime encounter between Florence Nightingale, the mother of modern nursing, and a supernatural Man in Grey. This story is unknown to most scholars of history, but a special guest of the museum will tell the tale of The Ghost and the Lady...

Praise for Kazuhiro Fujita's *Ushio and Tora*

"A charming revival that combines a classic look with modern depth and pacing... **Essential viewing both for curmudgeons and new fans alike.**" — Anime News Network

"**GREAT!** The first episode of Ushio and Tora captures the essence of '90s anime." — IGN

KC

KODANSHA
COMICS

Japan's most powerful spirit medium delves into the ghost world's greatest mysteries!

Story by Kyo Shirodaira, famed author of mystery fiction and creator of *Spiral*, *Blast of Tempest*, and *The Record of a Fallen Vampire*.

Both touched by spirits called yôkai, Kotoko and Kurô have gained unique superhuman powers. But to gain her powers Kotoko has given up an eye and a leg, and Kurô's personal life is in shambles. So when Kotoko suggests they team up to deal with renegades from the spirit world, Kurô doesn't have many other choices, but Kotoko might just have a few ulterior motives...

IN/SPECTRE

STORY BY KYO SHIRODAIRA
ART BY CHASHIBA KATASE

HAPPINESS

——ハピネス——

By Shuzo Oshimi

From the creator of *The Flowers of Evil*

Nothing interesting is happening in Makoto Ozaki's first year of high school. His life is a series of quiet humiliations: low-grade bullies, unreliable friends, and the constant frustration of his adolescent lust. But one night, a pale, thin girl knocks him to the ground in an alley and offers him a choice. Now everything is different. Daylight is searingly bright. Food tastes awful. And worse than anything is the terrible, consuming thirst...

Praise for Shuzo Oshimi's *The Flowers of Evil*

"A shockingly readable story that vividly—one might even say queasily—evokes the fear and confusion of discovering one's own sexuality. Recommended." —The Manga Critic

"A page-turning tale of sordid middle school blackmail." —Otaku USA Magazine

"A stunning new horror manga." —Third Eye Comics

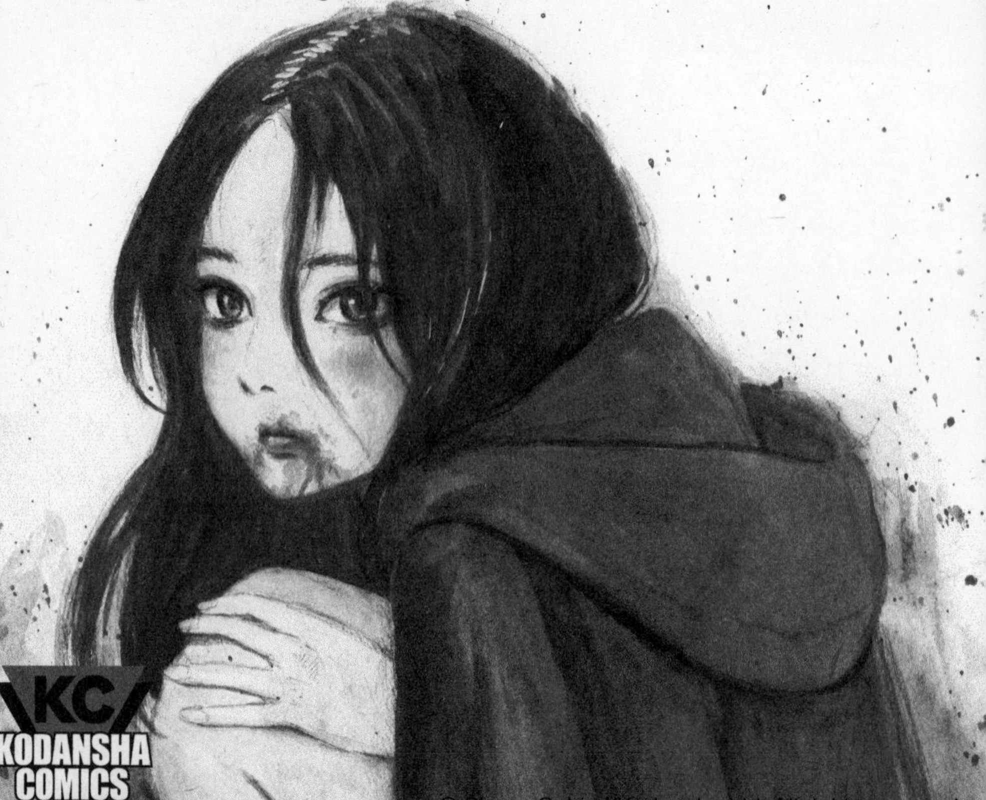

KODANSHA COMICS

Based on the critically acclaimed classic horror manga

The first new *Parasyte* manga in over 20 years!

NEO Parasyte f

BY ASUMIKO NAKAMURA, EMA TOYAMA, MIKI RINNO, LALAKO KOJIMA, KAORI YUKI, BANKO KUZE, YUUKI OBATA, KASHIO, YUI KUROE, ASIA WATANABE, MIKIMAKI, HIKARU SURUGA, HAJIME SHINJO, RENJURO KINDAICHI, AND YURI NARUSHIMA

A collection of chilling new *Parasyte* stories from Japan's top shojo artists!

Parasites: shape-shifting aliens whose only purpose is to assimilate with and consume the human race... but do these monsters have a different side? A parasite becomes a prince to save his romance-obsessed female host from a dangerous stalker. Another hosts a cooking show, in which the real monsters are revealed. These and 13 more stories, from some of the greatest shojo manga artists alive today, together make up a chilling, funny, and entertaining tribute to one of manga's horror classics!

KC KODANSHA COMICS

KC
KODANSHA
COMICS

New action series from Hiroyuki Takei, creator of the classic shonen franchise Shaman King!

In medieval Japan, a bell hanging on the collar is a sign that a ca has a master. Norachiyo's bell hangs from his katana sheath, but he nonetheless a stray — a ronin. This one-eyed cat samurai travels across dishonest world, cutting through pretense and deception with his blade

By
Hiroyuki Takei

Aho-Girl volume 9 is a work of fiction. Names, characters, places, and incidents are the products of the author's imagination or are used fictitiously. Any resemblance to actual events, locales, or persons, living or dead, is entirely coincidental.

A Kodansha Comics Trade Paperback Original.

Published in the United States by Kodansha Comics, an imprint of Kodansha USA Publishing, LLC, New York.

Publication rights for this English edition arranged through Kodansha Ltd., Tokyo.

First published in Japan in 2017 by Kodansha Ltd., Tokyo, as *Aho Gaaru* volume 9.

ISBN 978-1-63236-652-8

Printed in the United States of America.

www.kodanshacomics.com

9 8 7 6 5 4 3 2 1

Translator: Karen McGillicuddy
Lettering: S. Lee
Editing: Paul Starr
Kodansha Comics edition cover design by Phil Balsman